The history of

Rastrick and Hipperholme

With monorial notes on Coley, Lightcliffe, Northowram, Shelf, Fixby, Clifton and Kirklees

J. Horsfall Turner

Alpha Editions

This edition published in 2019

ISBN : 9789353601768

Design and Setting By
Alpha Editions
email - alphaedis@gmail.com

THE HISTORY

OF

Brighouse, Rastrick,

AND

Hipperholme;

WITH MANORIAL NOTES ON

Coley, Lightcliffe, Northowram, Shelf, Fixby, Clifton and Kirklees.

By J. HORSFALL TURNER, F.R.H.S.,

IDEL, BRADFORD.

———:———

ONE HUNDRED AND SEVENTY ILLUSTRATIONS.

———:———

INCORPORATION MEMORIAL.

———+———

PRINTED FOR THE AUTHOR, BY

THOMAS HARRISON AND SONS, BINGLEY, YORKS.

1893.

Morelei Wapentac.

In Morelei . vi . car̄ . In Erdeslau . v . car̄ 7 iii . bo . In Bestone . vi . car̄ .
In Rodouuelle 7 Cartenone Locthuse Torp 7 Mildentone . xxiii . car̄ .
In hunshelf . vi . c̄ . In Riston 7 Ermelai . vi . c̄ . In Bramelei . iiii . car̄ .
In Cauerlei 7 terselei . iii . c̄ . In podechelai . viii . c̄ . In Leuine . iii . c̄ .
In Breslingtone . iiii . c̄ . In Gomeshale 7 dualy bereuu . xxiii . car̄ .
In Bodeltone . iiii . c̄ . In Bradeford 7 vi . bereuu . xv . c̄ . In Botline iii . c̄ .
In Cleslau Torenton Alpeton Clatton 7 Wibetese . x . car̄ .
In Scipelei . iii . c̄ . In Birle . iiii . c̄ . In Wich . iiii . c̄ . In Treun . vi . c̄ .
In Cleftone . xii . c̄ . In Mirefeld . vi . c̄ . In Deusberie . iii . c̄ . In Bathelei . v . c̄ .
In Luuresech . iiii . c̄ . In hortesheuue . ii . c̄ . In Elone . iii . c̄ . In Ourefun . c̄ .
In husperun . ii . c̄ In Vfrun . ii . c̄ In Scelf . i . car̄ . In Stanlant . ii . c̄ .
In Linlei . Lun car̄ . In Sechesbi . i . car̄ . In Rastric . i . c̄ . In Egleshil . iii . c̄ .
In Ternelei . iii . c̄ . In Erdeslau . iiii . c̄ 7 o . bo . In Greland . dim car̄ .
In Treun . i . car̄ . Homo de Soca Wachefeld .

In Wachefeld cū . ix . bereuu . Sandala . Sorebi . Werla
feslei . Miclei . Wadesuurde . Griberonestun . Langesett .
Stanesfett . sunt ad gld . Lx . caruate qz . 7 iii . bouat .
7 iiii . parsuni bouat . Hanc q̄a post arare . xxv . caruc .
hoc maner̄ fuit regis Ed 7 in dnio . 7 in manu regis sut .
bi . iiii . uilli . 7 iii . puri . 7 ii . gede . 7 vii . sochem . 7 xvi . bord .
Simul hn̄t . vii . car̄ . Silua pasc . vi . leū lg . 7 iiii . leū lat .
Tou vi . leū lg . 7 vi . leū lat . T . R . E . Lx . lib . ualt . m . xv . lib .
bouet.

In holne Dunestan . ii . c̄ ad gld . tra ad . i . car̄ . hanc
trā alii dn̄t inland . alii soca in Wachefeld
In Linlere . Goduin dim car̄ ad gld .
In Rastric Goduin dim car̄ ad gld .

Introduction.

THERE is little need for a native, though more than half his lifetime up to the present has been spent outside the district, to apologise for the publication, however crudely the work may be done, of the history of the old haunts of childhood, especially as no such record has hitherto been attempted. True patriotism takes its rise from a love for the old homesteads, and from the touch of affinity engendered by a study of family alliances and human character. Heredity has much to do with religious bias also, and if the socialism of the future has to be true humanitarianism our sympathies and interests must be broadened, and selfishness curbed almost to eradication. There are in these pages, the writer believes, texts sufficient for those who will search for them, to convince both rich and poor that happiness and goodness are inseparable. My object has been to crowd as much information as possible into the available space, or many moral deductions might have been added. For instance, a footnote to the name of Alfieri, p. 252, ought to have been given, for no better sermon to young men can be preached than the warnings from the life of the great Italian dramatist,—a morbid, wasted life, as contrasted with Lord Ligonier's magnanimity.

Although the book has more pages than I intended, one-half the story remains to be told. The insertion of 170 illustrations, where only half that number was proposed, has robbed the space available for writing. Though this means extra cost to the author, it will be a gain to the reader. The ecclesiastical, and social chapters have had to be eliminated to do justice to the period that has been truly regarded as the "Dark Ages." But they were only the "Dark Ages" to us, because no local historian has hitherto unfolded our eyes. We have been in the dark as to their true condition: and however my local readers may look upon the long and wearisome records from the Manorial Rolls, the historical student will specially welcome them, for I know of no Yorkshire history that has so fully dwelt upon the Feudal period. The history of the people, in contradistinction to the chronology of kings, has yet to be written, and I may fairly claim that this Brighouse book is a local pioneer in supplying materials for the study, thus serving a more than local purpose. As to the diction, the punctuation, or the grammar, it must be remembered that the charter antiquary gathers notes, but the great historian generalizes from the labours of the antiquary. Be it remembered also that these notes have been gathered during thirty years of holiday time, and re-written and proofs read, and correspondence done at spare moments which ninety per cent. would have spent in self-ease. Sentences are often abrupt, and often purposely so to make room for more facts; a preposition or two might be changed with advantage; even a plural verb is once used instead of a singular one, but I leave these for the captious critic to detect like our Coley curate, Dr. Ogden, who

> " Placed in critics no reliance,
> So clothed his thoughts in Arabic,
> And bade them all defiance."

I don't find, on examination, any errata to acknowledge, except the *White* Swan, p. 259, ought to be a *Black* one. The Latin scholar will find faults, I know, with the fragmentary quotations, but I find fault with him that he has not set about the work himself. Wright's little history of Halifax called forth Watson's able and large one, which to-day is a most imperfect volume though fetching £5 at any sale. I am not conceited enough to think that the history of Brighouse before its incorporation is once and for ever written, for I hope to add another volume of omissions next year myself, and these will not satisfy the 20th century inhabitants. Most of my good neighbours thought till recently Brighouse had no history before 1750; I would remind them that a glance at the chapter on Wills shews that we are just at the beginning of some subjects. The Americans would go wild with enthusiasm had they a tithe of our information, and whilst our rule in printing this volume has been "Multum in parvo," they would have spun paragraphs into chapters. In Mr. Lister, Shibden Hall, we have a gentleman amongst us well able to edit the Wakefield Manorial Rolls for one of our learned Societies, and the Yorkshire Archæological Association could not devote its energies to better purpose than printing them. An idea of the writing of the Feudal times is conveyed by the facsimile deed on page 64, but sometimes faded and worn skins are not so easily decipherable. Saxon charters are more like the Doomsday facsimile on page *vi.* Over many of the place names in the latter are the letters "ilbt." This indicates Ilbert de Lacy as owner by grant from the King. Over Huperun (Hipper-holme,) is the word Rex, shewing that in 1087 the King had not conveyed our township to John, Earl of Warren, at that date. Car' or c' stands for carucate or as much land as a plough kept in cultivation; Hipperholme had two, Rastrick one. The places named in Morelei Wapentac are Morley, Ardsley, Bestone, Rothwell, Carlington, Locthouse, Thorp and Mildenton, Hunslet, Riston, Armley, Bramley, Calverley and Farsley. Pudsey, Tong, Breslington, Gomersall, Bolton, Bradford, Bolling, Celeslau (Chellow,) Thornton, Allerton, Clayton and Wibsey, Shipley, Bierley, Wyke, Heaton, Clifton, Mirfield, Dewsbury, Batley, Liversedge. In Hartshead, Ilbert had 2 car., in Elont (Elland,) Ilbert had 3 car., in Oure (Southowram,) Ilbert had 3 car., in Huperun (Hipperholme,) the King had 2 car., in Vfrun (Northowram,) 2 car., in Scelf, 1 car., in Stanland, 2 car., in Linlei, ½ car., in Fechesbi (Fixby; it may be noted that a man named Fech held Giggleswick at this time, though probably no relation of the Fech who gave his name to Fixby,) 1 car., in Rastric, 1 car., in Egleshil (Eccleshill.) 3 car., Farnley, Ardsley (East or West), Greland (? Greetland), Etun (?), in the Soke of Wakefield.

With Wachefeld were 9 berewicks, Sandal, Sowerby, Warley, Fesler or Seslei (this has been read as Feslei, and supposed to be Halifax-ley,) Midgley, Wadsworth, Crumbetonston, Langfeld, Stansfeld, (see p. 33). In Holme (Holmfirth valley), Dunstan held two carucates, in Linley, Godwin had a half-carucate, and another half in Rastric. Ilbert de Lacy also had Cornesbi (Quarmby,) 2 car., Gudlagesargo (Golcar,) ½ car., Lillai (Linley,) 2 car., Bradley, 2 car. Thus the great lords were recompensed for their help at Hastings in 1066, and sometimes the old tenants got a mere sop to quieten them. Godwin had estates in Rastrick, Linley, Bradley, Huddersfield. He and Gamel held lands in Quarmby. Gamel owned Elland and Southowram. Gerneber held Hartshead and Mirfield. He and Levenot held Liversedge. Escelf held Clifton. Swayne (Suuen,) had Crosland. Alric had Dalton. Levine had Golcar. From these old Anglians some of our first chief-tenants were descended.

As to our illustrations, the collecting of so many has been no slight work, but there are quite a hundred more available for a supplementary volume to be devoted to the absorbingly interesting accounts of Rastrick, Coley, Lightcliffe, and Brighouse Churches, with their curates; of George Fox's visits to Brighouse, and the dominion of Brighouse Monthly Meeting; of Moravian noblemen and worthies, and John Wesley's evangelistic labours; of the history of each denomination of Christians; of Hipperholme and Rastrick Grammar Schools; of Charities and Benefactors; of Town's books and Officers; of Folk-lore and Dialect; of Place and Surnames; of Pedigrees and Topography. For assistance and encouragement in the artistic embellishment of the present volume, I thankfully acknowledge my obligations to Messrs. H. J. Barber, J. C. Bottomley, J. W. Clay, T. T. Empsall, S. E. Hirst, R. Kershaw, F. Laxton, Henry Sugden, W. B. Woodhead, C. Jessop, J. B. Kershaw; Dr. Jessop, Dr. Farrer; Mrs. Brooke, Mrs. Kershaw, Mrs. Maile, Miss Ormerod, Miss G. A. Fryer; to Mr. Leach and Mr. Hepworth for several photographs, and to Mr. Hepworth especially for his father's portrait; to my friends, Mr. W. Andrews, Mr. W. Scruton, and Dr. Stuart for the loan of a block-illustration each; and to my eldest son, whose birthplace, at his grandmother's house on Rastrick Common, forms a subject for illustration, and whose name on the blocks indicates the extent of his artistic assistance.

I am proud of all this assistance, as also of the long list of subscribers, and hope the readers may appreciate this unity of good-will. As to the delay, the chief cause was the deplorable out-break of small pox in 1892, an event which Brighouse has cause to remember by financial losses as also by several deaths. I hoped also that the Incorporation Charter would arrive before issuing the volume, but there is no need to detain the publication on that account, as fuller justice can be done in another volume to the causes that have led to this result. One word as to the index and we must close. I find my time so limited that the whole work has to be done in snatches, but I have taken special care to compile a full index of every surname and place, in which one or two clerical errors in the text are corrected. It must be remembered that the same name may occur half-a-dozen times on a page, and the general spelling only is adopted. The utility of a complete index has stimulated me to do this laborious work myself, though entailing also extra cost in printing.

Idel, Bradford,   J. Horsfall Turner.
  August, 1893.

Contents.

ILLUSTRATIONS.

WHOLE PAGE PICTURES.

OTHER ILLUSTRATIONS.

George Hepworth

The History of
Brighouse, Rastrick and Hipperholme.

CELTIC FOOTPRINTS.—The valley of the Yorkshire Calder was originally occupied by a series of lakes, not temporary ones like those caused by the great flood of November 15th and 16th, 1866, when two inches depth of rain fell in twelve hours, but permanent ones which gradually became mere marshes owing to the heavy deposits of tidal waves, and the denuding of the boundary shores. Innumerable water-worn boulders, large and small, abound where digging occurs, and that to a great depth as shewn when the well at Mr. Burgess's dyeworks was sunk. Large sand deposits, on the ridge of Kirklees Park and other places, testify to the existence of these lakes, without going back to that remote period when our sandstone hills were formed. Igneous rock boulders have also been dug out at great depths near Brighouse, which were probably deposited by glacial influences. After long ages men penetrated these gulfs, and contended with wild beasts for peace and dominion; beasts that first reached this land when it was joined to the continent, and when elks and bears crossed where now the German Ocean rolls. Of these earliest

BRITISH BOAT.

B

men we have no traces in our locality for we have no high moorlands near us, where their footprints are usually found; nor of the next race who drove the older and weaker tribes to more desolate recesses.

The story of the Iberians and Celts,—Ancient Britons as we call them,—scarcely comes within our province, unless we could shew remains of their lake dwellings, their rock markings, stone circles and burial mounds more largely than we are able to do. Even the pits in Bradley Wood near Woodhouse, though very similar to those on Baildon and Rombalds Moors, are not likely to have been pit-dwellings. There has been no one to identify the piles for lake dwellings even if such have been discovered. On the higher ground near Fixby, and at Westercroft, near Coley, spear-heads have been found, and cinerary urns, relics of cremation, were exhumed at Castle Hill, Rastrick, and probably were British, but have generally been classed as Saxon remains, and as such we will refer to them again. On such meagre discoveries we will not venture to fill a chapter with fanciful descriptions of funeral pyres, druidical ceremonies, and so on. These old Britons, however, did leave us permanent records of their residence here in the names of our Calder, which means (according to some) in Celtic, narrow water, and therefore named after the subsidence of the lakes, or more probably woody or reedy water; though Mr. Leyland puts a Roman Collis before the British *der*, and gives hill-water as the result, and another writer finds Kaldur or cold water, (Danish,) the explanation. Der signifies water in various languages, and is found in numerous river-names shewing a very early origin, and the word " Calder " must have come down to the Britons from remote ancestors, as have the rest of the Yorkshire river-names. Even a few place-names, and names of hills, are of British origin as Cambodun, Scamonden, possibly also Rastrick, and Backbraid, a homestead in Rastrick, as Braidh, is Gaelic or British for the brow of a hill, a topping; Danish, bred, the edge; which description will answer for Bradford, being at the foot of a steep bank.

British coins have been found in Lightcliffe, and Canon Fawcett, of Low Moor, asserted that a British trackway struck through Lightcliffe towards Bradford. There is no reason to doubt this, for the Roman roads were necessarily based on British trackways, and one of the most favourable opportunities for crossing the Calder valley was found naturally at Brighouse. One writer in a newspaper was foolish enough to assert that Brighouse was called after the Celtic highland tribe, the Brigantes, or highland dwellers. This is the height of absurdity, equalled nearly by those who see remnants of Sun-worship in such words as *Light*cliffe and *B*ellee (Bailiffe) Bridge. One old word, along with other British words common to our English talk,— basket, clout, &c., has lingered in Brighouse down to our day in the expression:—' He'll make t' Shivin shake," where a mountain is meant, like the word Cevennes in France, and Chevin, the Otley hill.

The Romans.

As our object is to send forth a popular history, the mention of this people reminds us that there is a popular error as to the Romans, who are confounded with the Romish Church. In our account of the Romans we refer to the time when Britain and Palestine, and the lands between, were governed from Rome, without any reference to religion. In a similar manner as India is now ruled over by Britain, so Britain was then governed by Rome. About a hundred years after Christ's birth the powerful nation got hold of the main portion of our island, and as military rulers must do, they first attended to fortifying towns and outposts, and to making good roads to connect them. They did not come to colonize as we have done Australia, Canada, &c., but to subdue the aborigines as we have done with India. They seized the British villages that were worth seizing, and turned the old trackways into such solid streets that they are the marvel of the present day. Street and straight are words from the same Latin or Roman root, and as in the Scriptures we read of 'the street called Straight,' so in Britain if you look at a map of Yorkshire, you will find that the Great North Road and the main roads of to-day stretch along ten, twenty or thirty miles, as straight as the country surface would permit; and in many parts, outside towns, the name Street, as one in Lightcliffe last century, Tong Street, Adwick-le-Street, and so on, still remains to identify the course of these Roman roads. The Romans were indeed great road makers, and the inhabitants for fifteen centuries have been indebted to them on this account.

Their own safety and the marshy condition of the valleys necessitated the construction of these 'streets' along the ridges of hills, and the splendid remains yet seen on our moorlands testify to their excellent workmanship. They are generally slightly elevated, hence our word 'highways,' and connecting one with another were numerous subordinate or vicinal roads. In the days before bridges were generally constructed, the position of fordable parts of rivers had to be noted, and there we find the Romans secured the safety of the passage, by erecting a camp. There are many instances in Yorkshire, and the important ford at Snake Hill, crossing by the now-demolished Low Mill, would undoubtedly be thus protected. One of the main lines, distinctly traceable in many parts, and also mentioned and measured by early geographers, came from Chester and Manchester (Mancunium was their way of writing this name,) via Cambodunum (Slack near Outlane, the name probably surviving in the name of the township Scamonden) to Fixby Ridge, Rastrick Church (though, of course, there was no church then,) Gooder Lane, Snakehill ford, Clifton Common, Hartshead Highmoor Lane, Cleckheaton, &c., to York, then known as Eboracum, in which city the Roman Emperors sometimes resided. The importance of this *via* it would be impossible to exaggerate, and imagination may be safely left to re-people it with servile Britons, brave warriors, foreign traders, and gorgeous royalty;

to see the Eagle Standard fluttering in the breeze, and hear amidst the tramp of armies the old language spoken and mellower speeches uttered. As we follow the course of this road we are struck with the number of crosses that were erected along its borders, some of which remain to this day, whilst others have only left a name to be remembered by. Thus we have near Slack, Haigh Cross; in Rastrick churchyard, Rastrick cross; between Hartshead church and the Roman road, Walton cross; in Birstall churchyard, the base of another small cross, but as these are generally said to be of Saxon workmanship we pass them by at present. Three hills in Rastrick have been confused, and are likely to be, in the minds of visitors passing through, viz., Toothill, Roundhill, and Castlehill. Roundhill seems partially artificial, but an examination of its summit has shewn it to be natural, and it is out of the line of the Roman road, which passed close by Castle Hill, near Rastrick Church. This Castle Hill has also been generally regarded as Saxon, but it is quite likely that the Saxons, or Angles as we prefer to style them, utilized a Roman earthwork. As the surface has been molested, we cannot now compare it with such earthworks as that existing in Kirklees Park and other known Roman Camps, but an antiquary of Pontefract, Dr. Johnson, who sought out antiquities in this locality in 1669, records that the Castle Hill at Rastrick was trenched about and hollow in the middle, as if many stones had been got out of it. The circumference of it measured one hundred and eighty-eight yards within the trench, and on the top one hundred and seventeen, which shews the form of it. Mr. Watson added above a hundred years ago that it had "lately been destroyed for the sake of the stone which it contained, and it appeared upon examination that the top of it for a few yards perpendicular was cast-up earth, the rest a natural hill, the whole being hollow at the top, seemingly with design. Such a situation as this was very necessary in troublesome times, either for the neighbourhood to retire to upon alarms, or for way-faring men to make their nightly habitation; for being hollow at the top, it formed a kind of breastwork to protect the men in case of assault; there was also a considerable ascent to it on every side, and there was no rising ground about it, from whence it could be annoyed." This description answers for Round Hill but not for Castle Hill. Mr. Watson was also mistaken in saying that 'nothing sepulchral, nor indeed anything curious,' was found at Castle Hill. Just in his time there may not have been, but since then there has been a large sepulchral urn found. About 1820, my kinsman, Stephen Rushforth, was digging in his garden at Castle Hill, when he came upon one composed of dark-coloured earthenware, measuring about fourteen inches diameter by twenty inches in height, and containing a quantity of human bones. The urn and its contents adorned a window sill some time, but at Mrs. Rushforth's desire, out of a superstitious or reverential dread, it was again consigned to the earth, and so effectually that enquiries I have made from my oldest relatives, and diggings made by Mr. Fairless Barber, who owned the adjoining estate at Castle Hill, have failed to bring it to light again.

Mr. Leyland writing on this subject makes a mistake in stating that the site has been built upon. The croft where it was re-interred was afterwards quarried.

In 1797, about twenty urns are said to have been unearthed in Rastrick, containing ashes of burnt bodies, supposed then to have been Roman. Mr. Leyland records that Mr. Fryer, of Rastrick, about 1835, exhibited to the Halifax Philosophical Society several sepul chral urns of various sizes which had been found on Castle Hill, which were, like the former, returned to the earth near the place of their discovery. Mr. Leyland was of opinion they were Roman remains, and concludes that "the woods and moorlands of the district which surrounded this place of cremation and interment, were frequently illumined by the blaze of the funeral pyre." He has in his possession a copper coin of Gallienus in fine preservation, found by the road side at Castle Hill. He further argues in favour of the Roman origin of the earthwork from the discovery of querns or handmills in the neighbourhood. Three of these were discovered near Boothroyd, one of which was deposited by Mr. Charles Pitchforth, of Boothroyd, in the Halifax Philosophical Museum. Another was retained at Boothroyd, lately held by the Rev. Richard Judd, the owner of the estate in right of his wife. It is complete, having with it the lower stone on which it revolved, and which is usually wanting, as the handmills were frequently condemned by the lords of manors who claimed the privilege of grinding corn at the manorial mills. Around the base of the upper stone is a wrought moulding.

Mr. Fairless Barber recorded in the newspapers in Oct., 1867, that "some workmen digging for fence stuff in the Cote Close on the Woodhouse estate, discovered the upper stone of a quern. The stones surrounding it had been broken away so as more completely to encircle the deposit, and clearly showed that the remain had been placed there purposely for concealment. A fossil from the stone-beds had also been placed with it. All about, however, there were traces of fire upon the stones lying beneath the soil, which justify the presumption that we have in this find an indication of the occupation of the Close at a very early period. The quern had been a small one, and lay about $2\frac{1}{2}$ feet below the present surface at a point 34 yards from the corner of Round Wood and 30 yards from the west fence of the close." It may be remarked that the pits mentioned previously as supposed to be dwellings, though declared to be charcoal burners' pits, are in this locality, and the forest land has been largely 'stubbed' in recent times. Querns, to our mind, are not necessarily indications of days so remote as the Romans.

Mr. John Taylor, of Clough House, states that more than a century ago, Jonas Wilkinson, whilst reclaiming land from the waste in a field now known as Lower Hopper-take, near Slade Lane top, found his operations obstructed by a paved road which passed across the waste in the direction of Fixby Ridge. Similar difficulties were met with when the gas pipes were laid from Brighouse to Clifton, in Clifton

Common. The Roman method of road-making has been imitated in recent times. The stones, generally thin ones, were set on edge, and lime, cement, and even molten ironstone were poured upon it.

From Fixby Ridge, near the Western Park Lodge, the ancient Iter or Street leaves our locality, but such was the interest and assistance taken in and given by our esteemed townsman, the late Mr. Fairless Barber, in the excavations at Slack, which decided that place as identical with the ancient city of Cambodunum, that did space permit, we would record some of the chief discoveries then made. But ' Th'Aht Loin ' is out of our bounds.

Near Fixby Ridge, the Roman road from Doncaster, passing by Grimescar,—where Roman remains have been found, bearing, on tiles, &c., the stamp COH IIII BRE of the Cambodunum regiment or cohort, supposed to indicate a cohort gathered from a district in Germany,—crosses into Calderdale by Rastrick Lane Head, Old Earth, and passing the out-post at Greetland, where a Roman altar was found more than three centuries ago, to Ribchester, (Coccium.)

Rastrick had, three hundred years ago, a celebrated antiquary and genealogist in the person of Mr. John Hanson. Dodsworth's MSS., at Oxford, supply us with his account of the Grimescar discoveries :

"In the yeare of owre Lord 1590 certain Colyers working in Grymskar in Fekisbye in framynge a pitt to burne charcoles discoverid a certain worke in the earthe of most fyne bricke, yt resemblid a Roundewell a 4 yeards depe or not so much, cunynglye walled wth bricke and having upon the topp a very broad brickstone coveringe the same wth a round ledg wrought upon it wherein were written diverse Roman carrecterrs, as namelye these—COH. IIII. BRE. Next adjoyning to yt had bene a Archid Cave wherein great fyers had bene made and there was four condithes (conduits) going from the sd place in the lower pt of the grounde and comyng forth some 8 or 9 yeards of it, wherein had runyd sume kind of metall, for the stons was all congealed together. There was about it both redd, blewe and yelowe brick verye curyous and good, a kind of hard sinders in many places wth some traces of very thin earthin potts curiouslye wrought. What the work was is not clearlye knowne, but to be a Roman worke it is most likelye, and for the making of some kind of metall or glass. It was placid in the myddest of the wodd in a descending place neare unto a spring of water and not far from a cloughe of greater water. The name of the wodd is callid Grymeskarr but the old name is Springer. The Colyers had defaced manye of the letters and broken the stone before they perceavid what it was. The carrecters remaining be thus interpreted—Cohors quarta Brittannorum."

This conjecture is erroneous, Breuci being far more plausible than Britain. The Romans had more sense than to leave a British regiment here; such soldiers were sent to the Continent, whilst Continental regiments were drafted here, as is well known.

If anyone would learn the high state of Roman civilization they have but to see the carved gravestones, tesselated pavements, elaborate bathing rooms, coins, ornaments and the like stored at York, Aldboro', Ilkley, and other Roman towns.

That prince of antiquaries, Camden, travelling from Sir John Savile's house, at Bradley in Greetland, to Bradford, on August 5th, 1599, in company with our worthy old antiquary, Hanson, told him that the work at Grimescar was 'a bath, a luxury in which the distinguished Romans greatly delighted.'

A third Roman way touched us as it struck from Cambodunum, Greetland and Caldervale, passing through Lightcliffe to Olicana (Ilkley.) Along this road so many hoards of Roman coins have been found that we are led to the conclusion that the Roman travellers were pestered by sudden surprises from the unyielding Brigantes of the Pennine moorlands. Without referring particularly to the great finds at Morton, near Bingley, and others out of the parish, we have a record that in 1769 a quantity of Roman copper coins were found in Elland Hall Wood, some of which came into the possession of Mr. Watson, the Halifax Historian. These bore the names of the Emperors Gallienus, Victorinus, Tetricus and Claudius. Mr. Richardson, of North Bierley Hall, mentions some found at Greetland and Sowerby, of Nerva, Vespasian, Trajan and Hadrian. He also states (in the letter to Hearne, printed at the end of Leland's Itinerary, Vol. I., 2nd ed.,) that there were not long since divers large copper medals (? coins,) found at Hove Edge in Hipperholme township, in a thick glass vessel. Those Mr. Richardson got, and as this refers to Dr. Richardson we can approximately fix the date, for he died in 1741, were of Dioclesian, Allectus, and Carausius. He adds that doubtless there were divers others though they were dispersed before he had intelligence of them. Mr. Watson saw four of these coins at North Bierley:

(1) Dioclesian;—Reverse, a Jupiter almost naked; in his right hand a Victory standing on a globe; in his left a spear, an eagle at his feet. Motto, IOVI TVTATORI AVGG.

(2) Dioclesian;—Reverse, the above figure sitting. Motto, IOVI AVGG.

(3) Allectus;—worn specimen, bad impressions. Reverse, the figure of Joy or Mirth, uncertain what she holds. Motto, LAETITIA AVG.

(4) Carausius;—Reverse, a female figure in a stola, standing, holding in her right hand an olive branch, in her left a spear. Motto, PAX AVG.

Mr. Richardson had also a Vespasian and a Hadrian, coins found at Warley. Several Vespasians were found during the explorations at Slack superintended by Mr.Barber and others for the Huddersfield (now Yorkshire) Archæological Association, one of them having the most interesting Reverse,—IVDAEA CAPTA, with a palm tree figured, on the left side of which a female captive is seated, reclining sorrowfully. This coin is of special interest to Bible students. Several coins of Domitian and Nerva were also found. But the most important discovery in our district, so far as has been recorded, was made public by the Rev. W. H. Bull, then incumbent of Sowerby, afterwards vicar of Billingshurst, Horsham, Sussex, whose daughter-in-law now possesses some of them, 1892. This discovery took place in a field that was being quarried opposite the old house in Lower Lightcliffe. It has been pointed out to me many times, thirty years ago, and is not opposite Lightcliffe Church and could not have been, but on the right hand side of the road from the Old Church to Bailiffe Bridge, viz. the field behind Upper Smith House.

At Lightcliffe a fourth Iter crossed our township, from Legeolium (Castleford) via Wakefield, Osset Street, Dewsbury, Heckmondwike, Liversedge, (intersecting the great road from Brighouse to Cleckheaton,) Birkby Lane, Bailiff Bridge, and Lightcliffe, to Hipperholme Dumb mill, Barrowclough and Halifax. In the old town's books I have several times met with references to "The Street in Lightcliffe," and a deed quoted by Watson (p. 332) speaks of the Magna Via. Mr. Bull casually heard of the remarkable 'find' at Lightcliffe, and hastened to Bradford and elsewhere to recover as many as possible. He printed an account of the matter in October, 1848, which was reprinted in the *Halifax Guardian* and elsewhere, of which the following is a copy.

"AN ACCOUNT OF SOME GOLD BRITISH COINS AND ROMAN SILVER CONSULAR AND IMPERIAL COINS FOUND IN A FIELD, OPPOSITE LIGHTCLIFFE CHAPEL, WITHIN A FEW YARDS OF THE PRESENT ROAD, IN A ROMAN VESSEL, BETWEEN THE YEARS MDCCCXXVIII. AND MDCCCXXXI."

"The man who found the coins, sold some of them at 5s. per ounce to a person at Bradford, and broke several of them to see that they were really Silver.

The writer of this account was fortunate in obtaining *four* of the British Gold Coins in beautiful preservation, twenty-six of the *Consular* Coins, and five of the Imperial Coins. Some have been purchased by the British Museum, and the Museums of Leeds and York.

The *Consular* Coins have been very much used: many of them have very small letters stamped on parts of the figures on the coins, in the same way as idle people, in this day, disfigure our coinage. But all the *Consular* Coins are from mints prior to the time of Augustus; the latest Imperial Coin in this lot, is one of Caligula, the other four belong to Augustus. Two of the Gold Coins are Boadicea's; and one is very beautiful and very rare, not to be found in Ruding's "British and English Coinage."

BRITISH COINS.

Two of these Coins have on their Obverses; VO..DISI..A. On their Reverses: the outline of a horse. Another, most rare, has on the Obverse: two perpendicular lines in the centre, with dotted lines on their outer sides, next the rim. Reverse: AEL. A horse drawing a war chariot. The fourth has, on its Obverse, a similar device to the last, but blank on the Reverse.

Roman Coins.

The following account of the Roman Coins is derived from Haner-camp's Numismata Aurea, Akerman's Roman Coins, and Ursinus's Familiæ Romanæ.

ROMAN FAMILIES. *CONSULAR.* ACILIA. Head of the Goddess Salus—around it SALVTIS. Rev.: A female figure leaning on a Pillar holding a Serpent—around it, III VIR. VALETV. MV. ACILIVS.

AELIA. Head of Minerva. Behind it, X. Rev: Ρ. Ρ AETVS. The Dioscuri on Horseback: rare.

ANNIA. Head of Juno, before it the Balance, behind it the Caduceus. C. ANNI. T. F. T. N. PRO. EX. S. C. Rev. Victory in a Quadriga, over the Horses Q. in the Exergue L. FABI. L. F. HISP.

CORNELIA. 1. Bearded head with a Diadem. Behind it, a Sceptre. Rev. CN. LEN. Q. EX. S. C. A Sceptre, and a Garland, a Clypeus (shield), and a Rudder. 2. Head of Venus, L. SVLLA. before it, Cupid standing—in his right hand, a palm branch; Rev. IMPER. ITERVM. The Lituus, and the Præfericulum, between two trophies. 3. Laureated head, behind, E. Rev. a Quadriga (or four-horse chariot.) L. SCIP. ASIA. G. The brother of Scipio Africanus, who overcame Antiochus in Asia and was surnamed Asiaticus.

JUNIA. Head of Liberty. LIBERTAS. Rev. The Sons of Brutus guarded by the Lictors. In the Exergue, BRVTVS.

JULIA. 1. An Elephant with a Serpent, in Exergue, CAESAR. Rev. The Pontifical Instruments and the Apex. 2. Head of Venus—Rev. Two Captives sitting under a pile of arms and shields. In the Exergue, CAESAR. 3. Head of Venus. Rev. Æneas carrying Anchises on his shoulders and the Palladium in his right hand. CAESAR. 4. Head of Mercury, behind it, a Trident. Rev. Victory in a Quadriga. L. IVLI. BVRSIO.

CÆCILIA. A Female Head (Africa) covered with an Elephant's Skin, before it, an ear of Corn—under it, a plough—Q. METEL. SCIPIO. IMP. Rev. EPPIVS LEG. F. C. Hercules standing leaning on his Club,—rare.

CREPEREIA. Female bust,—The shoulder exposed: behind it a fish.—Rev. Q. CREPER. M. F. ROCVS. Neptune in a Car, holding his Trident, drawn by two sea-horses,—*very rare.*

ANTONIA. Laureated Head. Behind it, S. C.—Rev. Victory in a Quadriga. Q. AT. BA. B. P. R.

CARISIA. Head of Victory. Rev. A Biga (or two-horse chariot.) In the Exergue T. CARISI.

CASSIA. 1. Head of Ceres, CÆICIAV. Rev. Two Oxen: over them,—M.—Under them,—L. CASSI. 2. Head of Liberty. Q. CASSIVS. LIBERT. Rev. Temple of Vesta; within it a Curule Chair. On one side of the Temple, an Urn: on the other, A. C. on a Tablet, A. C.

CLAUDIA. Laureated Female Head: behind it a Lyre. Rev. M. F. P. CLODIVS. Diana Lucifera, standing and holding two torches.

FLAVIA. Helmed Head. Rev. a Biga. FLAVS ROMA.
LUTATIA. Helmed Head of Minerva.—Behind it, X. CERCO
ROMA. Rev. Q. LVTATI.Q. A Galley: the whole within an Oak
Garland.
NÆVIA. Head of Juno. S. C. Rev.—A Triga. C.NAE.BAB.
POBLICIA. Helmed Head. M.POBLICI.LEG.PRO. Rev.
Victory presenting a Palm branch to a Soldier with his foot on a
Prow. CN.MAGNVS.IMP.
SATRIENVS. The name of the family unknown. Helmed Head
of Minerva. Rev. A wolf passant. above it, ROMA: beneath it, R.
P.SATRIENVS.
SCRIBONIA. 1. Female Head: BON.EVENT.LIBO. Rev.
An Altar, with a Lyre suspended on each side. PVTEAL SCRIBON.
2. Veiled head of Concord. PAVLVS.LEPIDVS.CONCORD.
Rev. Altar, with a Lyre on each side. LIBO.
SERVILIA. Helmed Head, RVLLI. Rev. Victory in a Biga.
In the Exergue, P.SERVILI.M.F.
IMPERIAL. AUGUSTUS. 1. Head of Augustus, without
Inscription. Rev. IMP.CAESAR. A rostral Column, surmounted
by a Statue. 2. Head of Augustus. Rev. a Capricorn. In the
Exergue, AVGVSTVS. Suetonius says Augustus coined Silver
money with the Impression of Capricorn, under which Constellation
he was born. 3. Round the head of Augustus. CAESAR AVGV-
STVS DIVI.F.PATER.PATRIAE. Rev. Caius and Lucius
standing. Two bucklers and pontifical Instruments, AVGVSTI.F.
COS.DESIG.PRIN.IVVENT. 4. Head of Victory. Rev.CAESAR.
IMP. Neptune with the Aplustre in his right hand, and holding an
upright Trident in his left, with his right foot on the Globe.
CALIGULA. Head of Caligula. C.CAESAR.AVG.PON.M.
TR.POT.III.COS.III. Rev. Head of Agrippina. AGRIPPINA.
MAT.C.CAES.AVG.GERM." Mr. Bull added the following Consu-
lar coins to the list:—1. Obverse: Laureate Head, PANSA. Reverse:
a Quadriga, in Exergue, C.VIBIVS.C.F. 2. Obverse: Head of
Juno Sospita: behind it, S.C. Reverse: L.PROCILI.F. Juno
Sospita in a Biga: underneath, a serpent. 3. Obverse: A Female
Head; behind it, PAETI. Reverse: Victory in a four horse chariot.
In Exergue, C.CONCIDI. 4. Obverse: Head covered with an
Elephant's skin: in front, an ear of corn: SCIPIO IMP. on the left:
Q.METEL. on the right. Reverse: Hercules leaning on his Club:
on his right, EPPIVS: on his left: LEG.P.C. It should be mentioned
that, of the coins above described, there were three of NÆVIA, and two
of SCRIBONIA No. 2. Mr. Bull also states, that the coins thus far
enumerated were found by a man employed in opening a quarry, who
struck his pickaxe into the Roman urn which contained the valuable
hoard.

In addition to the foregoing lists, there was dug up in the Chapel
yard, Lightcliffe, in 1833, a silver triumphal coin of L. Scipio Asiaticus; and, a few years since, at a collection for some charitable

purpose, at the same place, there was found in the alms box a fine copper coin of Allectus. The Scipio was given to York Museum by W. Priestley, Esq., then of Lightcliffe.

We can thus form some notion of the great amount and importance of Roman traffic in this district, and we probably owe much to them, besides our indebtedness for the roads they made and which their successors for a thousand years neglected. Some phases of social government can be slightly traced to their influence, but the marvel is that as Hipperholme, Brighouse and Rastrick have been so long under cultivation any traces at all can be found of a military people who left our shores so far back as the year 410, A.D.

Anglian.

FROM Roman hoards we pass to Anglo-Saxon, Pictish and other hordes, and here we have very little in the Archæological way to produce, but we have Anglian life in all its ramifications still, and more proud are we of it than of Norman blood, though they are our distant kinsmen. It is detestable to hear people strain to appear of Norman extraction, whose ancestry stretches to older date than the time of that rhapscalion set.

During the Roman period the brave Norsemen had settled on the British shores, and the mixed British, Romano-British and Anglian peoples who were left here on the evacuation of the Imperial Warriors formed themselves into bands for self-defence, and self-government, and the story of Britain, for a hundred years is one of constant internal, tribal struggles, when ' might was right.' One of the most powerful of these little kingdoms was that of Elmete, with Leeds near its centre as capital, whose dominion extended to this district. Generation after generation, ship-loads of immigrants were arriving from the opposite North Sea shore, of Angles, Saxons, Jutes, and Danes, just as, for many generations past, the American continent has been colonized. Land and sea fights did not check the increase of settlers. The Angles and Danes kept towards the north of the country which eventually took its name Angle-land from the former; the Saxons colonized the south as shewn by the names Essex, Middlesex, Wessex, and others; the Normans vanquished the true Franks in North France. The old Cymri or Celts, mostly known by us as Welsh, were driven to the wall to hide in mountainous Wales, and Cornwall, or succumb to slavery. After long struggles confusion yielded to order, chieftainship gave way to kingship, until eight kings were found in South Britain. Bernicia (including Durham and northwards,) and Deira (Yorkshire,) eventually formed the powerful kingdom of Northumbria, the history of which has been written from tradition, and its kings duly chronicled; but seven kings were too many in so small a country, and sanguinary battle followed battle till about the year 827, England became united under one sovereign. The Northumbrian kings had been the most powerful, but as their prowess began to wane, the Southern kings became supreme. When Egbert had become liege lord of England more than a thousand years ago, another trouble was being felt sorely by the incursions of the Danes whose depredations did not cease until two hundred years had passed, and the Norman Conquest had taken place. Notwithstanding all these wars and struggles for six hundred years, the people were becoming consolidated in nationality, language, interests, and from them the characteristics of the English Nation are to be traced.

It was a sapling of slow and trying growth, and for all we have, and much that we have lost, we must thank our hardy ancestors. They came up the Aire and Calder in their skiffs, built themselves log cabins on the hilly slopes, warded by piles and rails their homesteads from molestation, unitedly cleared the woods of wolves and other wild beasts, pushed their way or were pushed further inland until every habitable hill and dale was dotted with the abodes of these squatters. Some spoke the Danish dialect, some the Anglian, others the Saxon, but they could make themselves understood mostly, unless a Saxon met an Anglian after their ancestors had been separated two hundred miles for as many years. The settler named his abode as the American emigrant does to-day (1) either after the place of his birth, or (2) after his own name, or (3) as descriptive of its situation. We find that the Anglians who settled in the Aire and Calder basins had recourse to one or other of these methods of nomenclature. Near Leeds are some of the first method; Fixby and probably Wadsworth,—with many in Airedale, *Bingley*, *Guysley*, *Ide*-il, *Aikils*-hill, &c.,—are instances of the second, whilst the majority in Halifax parish are examples of the third. Every name was then as clearly understood as we know that Saltaire is named after Mr. Salt and the River Aire, and the great difficulty now is to find the first method of spelling the name. The vast moorlands and forests and marshy dells of Upper Calder became sub-divided by our Anglian ancestors into twenty-three townships, forming probably the largest parish in England, though the ecclesiastical word, parish, is slightly more modern than civil divisions, for English Christianity is not so old as English civil government, though reaching back to 627 in this district. A township is probably identical in most instances with the Saxon tything, which indicated that *ten* free families held a local court or *thing*, and governed themselves locally. Ten of these tythings were constituted into a *hundred*, which was named in Yorkshire and Lincolnshire, a wapontake, or 'weapon touching,' because the freemen of the hundred swore fealty at the Wapontake or Hundred Court to the King's representative or Shire-reeve (Sheriff.) Now as the Yorkshire Wapontakes contain a large number of townships, the earliest townships must have been sub-divided as free families increased, and thus considerably more than ten tythings met at the Wapontake Court, which for this district was held near Morley, (and called Morley Wapontake to this day,) on a mound called Thinglawe down to the times of the Plantagenet Kings, but now called Tingley. Our word R*iding* contains the same root, as do the words *Tyn*wald, where the Manx Parliament still meets, stor-*thing* the name for the Danish Parliament, and hus*tings*. Skyrack Wapontake (Leeds district) was held under the shire-oak at Hea*ding*-ley; Agbrigg Wapontake (Huddersfield,) at the bridge of that name. It is interesting to note that Hipperholme Baronial Court was held under Hipperholme thorn, and the Brighouse Court and Sheriff's tourn were held near Brighouse bridge, whilst general assemblies have been summoned to meet the rulers on mounds and circles in this and other lands, eastern and western, for thousands of years. For comparison, we tabulate the etymologies of our twenty-three Halifax townships, and add similar local examples.

Townships, 5 end in **LAND**, meaning land, namely: Barkis—, El— cum Greet—, Nor—, Soy—, Stain—. These are in the Elland division.

2 end in **FIELD**, trees fell'd; or hilly range, as Dovrefeld in Norway Lang—, Stans—. These are in Heptonstall division; and Wakefeld, Huddersfeld, Mirfeld, (old forms), are similar examples.

2 end in **LEY**, enclosure, Midg—, War—. (Old Linley is included with Stainland.) Feslei = Halifaxley? This ending is very common in Airedale, and we have also several Bradleys, Coley, Copley, Bottomley, Brearley, Exley; without including the lees, as Kirklees.

2 end in **DEN**, dean, vale, Oven—, Erring—. The same is noticed in Ripponden, Luddenden, Shibden, Scammonden, Marsden, Mixenden, Ogden (oak-den), Skirden, Hebden (?).

2 end in **WORTH**, protected, warded, Wads—, Rish—. Other examples—Haldisworth, Illingworth, Haworth, Butterworth, Crimsworth.

2 end in **BY**, Danish for residence, Fekis (Fix)—, Sower—. Another familiar example is Quarmby.

2 end in **AM** (? holme, um), Northour—, Southour—.

1 ends in **HOLME, (UM)**, Hipper—. Also found in two or three Mytholmes, (middleholmes, pastures,) and in Suf, or South, holme.

1 ends in **FAX**, probably meaning a road, Halifax. Fairfax we all remember.

1 ends in **RICK**, either a ric, district governed, or ridge, Rastrick. Similar examples are Lightridge, Sheepridge, Fixby-rigg.

1 ends in **COTE** (coat), cottage, or may be a wood. Skircote. Also Cote in several districts.

1 ends in **STALL**, an abode, Hepton—. Thus we have Kirkstall, Birstall, Saltonstall, Rawtonstall.

1 retains its crude form, Shelf, a plateau, or ledge.

Thus end the twenty-three townships, and it will be noticed Brighouse is left out as it was joined to Hipperholme civilly and Rastrick ecclesiastically, with the Latin word *cum* meaning *with:* Hipperholme-cum-Brighouse which a wag read as Aperums (aprons) and Britches; Rastrick-cum-Brighouse in church matters, until the latter got a church of its own. There could be no district or name Brighouse until a Bridge was erected, and though not early enough nor populous enough to form a separate township, the bridge and its pure Saxon or Anglian name Brig–hus, house near the bridge, will be found to have a very ancient history in our next chapter. For a very long period it will be seen that its name was RASTRICK BRIGHOUSES.

Only five of these townships have churches named after them,— Halifax, Elland, Heptonstall, Rastrick, Sowerby; except quite modern churches. Of the thirteen old churches, eight chapelries are named after some hamlet, as Coley, Lightcliffe, Ripponden, Luddenden, Illingworth, Chapel le Brear (St. Ann's, Southowram), Cross-stone and Sowerby Bridge. Four townships have no hamlets of the name, —Stansfield, Langfield, Wadsworth, and Warley. The great parish is divided ecclesiastically into three divisions,—Halifax, Elland, and

Heptonstall. Brighouse and Hipperholme are civilly in Halifax district, but for convenience ecclesiastically Brighouse goes with Rastrick and is thus in Elland division, often called Elland parish. The three easternmost townships are Hipperholme-cum-Brighouse, Rastrick, and Fixby.

Of Anglian, otherwise Saxon remains, we need not again refer to the Castle Hill at Rastrick which has been generally called a Saxon work. Watson threw out the hint that the name Rastrick from rast, meaning rest, and ridge, may be so named after the place of refuge at Castle Hill. Though the word rast be common to the Anglian races, we doubt the truth of this etymology, and think that there is a British sound in the first part of the name. Watson was struck by this idea in penning the following remarks: "It is certain that all circular forts raised by the Danes were called by the Irish 'Raths' as they were also by the ancient Cornishmen and perhaps other inhabitants of this island, from the word Radt, which in the Celtic signified a wheel, and by adding to this the Danish word Ryg, the ridge of a hill, such as this mount stood upon we have Raths-Ryg, which would easily be softened into Rastrick." The very difficulties of the etymology of Raistrick or Rastrick confirm us in the idea, that we must trace the root back to an earlier people than the Danes. This and a similar earthwork at Lee hill, Slack, are probably British, utilized by the Romans also. Indeed, they are likely to have been utilized long after by great armies such as that under the Danish king, Canute, which must have followed the Cambodunum road in 1017.

The introduction of Christianity into these parts by Paulinus in 627, and kindred topics, and the tracing of any relics of a former Christianity here, are subjects outside our design, but it may be mentioned that Runic remains have been found at Thornhill, near Dewsbury, Bingley, &c., but very sparsely. How many such valuable relics have been destroyed, because they could not then be read, it is impossible to state, but from such records alone

RASTRICK CROSS.

can Saxon local genealogy be compiled. The Crosses already referred to, on the line of the Roman street, are probably our oldest Christian relics.

Great chieftains or over-lords had arisen, some of whom were men of great influence in the state, such as Gamel of Elland. Codes of

RASTRICK CROSS.

laws had been framed by them, and condign punishment awaited any unhappy culprit. Vast tracts of forest land still remained of which we have little more than the names in Brianscholes Forest in Hipperholme, Shelf and Northowram, the name Brianschole still surviving near Upper Brear; and in Sowerbyshire otherwise called Hardwick Forest, connected with which was the notorious gibbet law. Our limits were "Out of Hardwick" so we must simply refer those who desire to know further about the gibbet law and its victims to the book mentioned in the footnote,* compiled from the Halifax histories for popular use.

Of the excellent system of local self-government, and the village community and common land style of living; of beating the parish and township boundaries, and many other Saxon customs we shall have evidence as our story proceeds. We have reached the time when the foundations of our local government were thoroughly established, and upon which a Feudal System was foisted, from whose thraldom the nation has scarcely yet escaped, but the establishment of County

WALTON CROSS.

Councils and decentralization from London red-tapeism are bringing us back to the state of things that existed before the Normans imposed their military tenures.

* HALIFAX GIBBET BOOK, with additions; price 2/-.

Norman Conquest.

WAKEFIELD MANOR.—By the year 1066, when William the Conqueror from Normandy wrenched the kingship from Harold the Saxon, our townships and hamlets were generally speaking as they are to-day. Modifications were adopted, caused by the Feudal System which farmed out the lands from the King to the Barons, and from the latter to Freemen, each on condition that a proportionate military force was at the call of the Monarch, and that certain services to Barons and King were rendered. Hipperholme township at an early date was nominally considered in four parts, (*a*) Hipperholme Quarter, (*b*) Norwood Green Quarter, (*c*) Hove Edge Quarter, and (*d*) Brighouse Quarter. But the whole of Halifax parish, comprising 118$\frac{3}{10}$ square miles, was very sparsely populated, and it is remarkable that none of the old Castle Hills in the district were formed into Norman Fortresses or Manor Halls. The great Barons made their homes lower down the rivers, at Sandal, Pontefract, Skipton, Spofforth. Another peculiarity is that no Monastic establishment existed in this wide domain, though the Knights of Jerusalem held lands here, and some insignificant Nunneries are said to have existed. They chose more genial dales ; Kirklees being the nearest Institution. In the place of great Civil and Religious Houses, we had a number of staunch freemen, kinsmen to Saxon and Norman Barons, whose history is scarcely less glorious, and influence not a whit less beneficial than those of their more privileged Sires. With the Feudal System, it was necessary that an accurate Survey should be made, and this was accomplished by 1087 ; the record, called Doomsday Book, is now exhibited in London. The King held as parcels of Wakefield (Wachefeld) Manor, nine berewicks (sub-manors), Sandal, Sorebi, Werla, Feslei, Micleie, Wadesuurde, Cru'betonestun, Langefelt, Stanesfelt. It was formerly King Edward the Confessor's. Sowerby, Warley, Midgley, Wadsworth, Langfeld and Stansfeld are readily recognized ; the same cannot be said of Feslei, which is more likely to mean Halifax than Fixby, and Crumbetonvtun, ? Crimsworth, Cromwell, Cross-stone, or a lost Crumpton. In Rastric Goduin had ½ car. to be taxed.

Huperun or Hipperholme had two carucates, Fechesbi (Fixby) one, Rastric one, Ufrun (Northowram) two, Scelf one, held by the King. Cliftone had three carucates. In Liuressch (Liversedge) were five villanes (villagers,) and four bordars, (mean farmers with separate bord or cottage, who supplied the lord with poultry and eggs,) and two ploughs. Value in King Edward's time 20s., now 10s. In Wiche (Wike) Stainulf and Westre had four carucates of land to be taxed. Ilbert (de Laci) has it and it is waste. In Elont Gamel had three carucates of land to be taxed, Ilbert has it and it is waste. In the time of King Edward it was worth 20s. There was half a league of woodland. In Ouere (Southowram) Gamel had three carucates to be taxed, less valuable land than that at Elland. Ilbert (de Laci)

c

has it and it is waste; worth 20s. in King Edward's time. Woodlands, three quarants; two long and three broad.

A carucate or plough land was as much land as may be tilled by one plough in a year. It will be seen what disaster had come over the neighbourhood within one generation, in depreciation of property. The idea of a Doombook, or Judgmentbook was not new, for King Alfred had compiled one to rectify disputes as to tithings, and hundreds. The Earl of Warren, some time after the survey, became possessed of Wakefield Manor which included our district, whilst the great Earl Lacy held Elland and Southowram. Between these two great Baronial families a fearful quarrel was afterwards carried on, and the bitterness spread to their tenants, resulting eventually in pitched fights, and dastardly murders, for full particulars of which the reader must consult a cheap popular account in "The Elland Tragedies."* Elland passed to the Elland family and from them, after the murders of two Sir John Ellands and an infant son, to the great Saville family by marriage with the Elland heiress. The Lacy

---

*ELLAND TRAGEDIES. 1330-1350, with recent discoveries of their truth. Edited by J. Horsfall Turner. 2/-

family were represented by a junior branch at Cromwellbottom, which they acquired by marriage with the heiress of Cromwellbottom, of Cromwellbottom, and they also held lands at Leventhorpe near Bradford, whilst an important branch resided in Upper Calderdale till recent times, and a poor branch struggled on in Rastrick. Their history and especially that of the chief line, the Earls of Lincoln, whose home was at Pontefract Castle, is a national one and would fill a large volume. Kirkstall Abbey and other venerable remains testify to their munificence and greatness. Our Halifax, Elland, and South-owram (Chapel le Brear) churches bear their impress.

William the first Earl of Warren married Gundreda, the Conqueror's daughter, and Wakefield Manor was given to the Warrens about 1100. On the 9th of Edward I. there was an enquiry why John de Warren, Earl of Surrey, held the Halifax lands, to which he replied that his ancestors from time immemorial had had free chase in the same, as well in the fees as in demesne lands, viz., . . . Rastrick, Hipper-holme, Northowram, Shipden, &c. He also claimed free warren, in fees and demesne lands in the same, and produced a charter from Henry III., 37th year, confirming him in the possessions. In 1316, John the last Earl of Warren and Surrey, having no lawful issue, surrendered all his estates to Edward II. to have the same regranted to his illegitimate issue. The pedigree is as follows :

William, Earl of Warren in Normandy, Earl of Surrey, died 1088.
⊤ Gundreda daughter of William I., d. 1085.
William, 2nd Earl, Lord of Wakefield Manor, d. 1138.
|
William, 3rd Earl, slain in Palestine, 1148. His sister Ada married
    an Earl of Huntingdon, son of King David of Scotland.
⊤Adela, daughter William Talvas, Earl of Ponthieu; afterwards
  | married the Earl of Salisbury.
Isabel, heiress.
  =(1) William de Blois, 4th Earl, died without issue.
  ⊤(2) Hameline of Anjou, (half-brother to Henry II.) 5th Earl.
William de Warren, 6th Earl.
|
John de Warren, 7th Earl.
|
William de Warren, killed in a tournament 1286, in his father's
  | lifetime. A sister of his married Lord Henry Percy, and
  | another married John Baliol, King of Scotland.
John, 8th and last Earl, died 1347, left no legitimate issue.
  =Joan Barr, grand-daughter of Edward I.
  =Isabel de Houland, both wives living at the Earl's death, but
when Isabel died in 1359, the manor reverted to the crown : and the
King, Edward III. gave it in 1362 to his son Edmund Langley. Earl
of Cambridge. His son Edward, Earl of Rutland, was slain at
Agincourt, 1415, and was succeeded by his nephew, Richard, Duke of
York, slain at the battle of Wakefield in 1460. His son became

Edward IV., and the manor thus came to the crown again, and it seems to have been attached to the Duchy of Lancaster, but was sometimes farmed out, the tenants being free from paying toll, stallage, piccage, pannage, and passage in the Duchy of Lancaster, Hipperholme being one of the towns named in a charter of Henry VIII. In Elizabeth's reign the Tempests farmed the lordship.

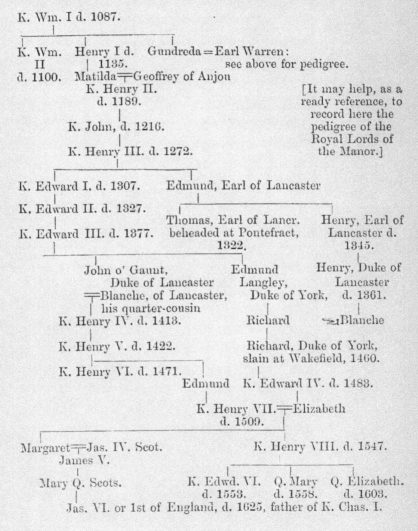

K. Wm. I d. 1087.

K. Wm.　Henry I d.　Gundreda = Earl Warren:
  II　　|　1135.　　　　　　see above for pedigree.
d. 1100.　Matilda ⊤ Geoffrey of Anjou
　　　　　　K. Henry II.　　　　　　　　　[It may help, as a
　　　　　　　d. 1189.　　　　　　　　　ready reference, to
　　　　　　　　|　　　　　　　　　　　record here the
　　　　　K. John, d. 1216.　　　　　　pedigree of the
　　　　　　　　|　　　　　　　　　　　Royal Lords of
　　　　　K. Henry III. d. 1272.　　　　　the Manor.]

K. Edward I. d. 1307.　　Edmund, Earl of Lancaster
　　|
K. Edward II. d. 1327.
　　|　　　　　　　　Thomas, Earl of Lancr.　Henry, Earl of
K. Edward III. d. 1377.　beheaded at Pontefract,　Lancaster d.
　　|　　　　　　　　　　　　1322.　　　　　　1345.

　　　John o' Gaunt,　　　　Edmund　　Henry, Duke of
　　　　Duke of Lancaster　　Langley,　　Lancaster
　　　⊤Blanche, of Lancaster,　Duke of York,　d. 1361.
　　　| his quarter-cousin　　　　|　　　　　　|
　　K. Henry IV. d. 1413.　　　Richard　　⇌Blanche
　　　|
　　K. Henry V. d. 1422.　　　Richard, Duke of York,
　　|――――――――――|　　　slain at Wakefield, 1460.
　　K. Henry VI. d. 1471.　　　　　|
　　　　　　　Edmund　K. Edward IV. d. 1483.
　　　　　　　　　　　　　　|
　　　　　　K. Henry VII. ⊤ Elizabeth
　　　　　　　d. 1509.

Margaret ⊤ Jas. IV. Scot.　　　　　　K. Henry VIII. d. 1547.
　　James V.
　　　|
　Mary Q. Scots.　　　K. Edwd. VI.　Q. Mary　Q. Elizabeth.
　　　|　　　　　　　d. 1553.　　d. 1558.　　d. 1603.
　Jas. VI. or 1st of England, d. 1625, father of K. Chas. I.

On the 6th of Charles I. the manor was
granted to Henry, Earl of Holland in
Lincolnshire, but he was beheaded for his
fidelity to royalty in 1648-9, and the manor
seems to have been granted to Robert Rich,
Earl of Warwick, whose daughter married
Sir Gervase Clifton, of Clifton, Notts.,
who sold the manor of Wakefield to Sir
Christopher Clapham about 1663, whose
heirs sold it in 1700 to the Duke of Leeds.

Dukes of Leeds Crests.   Clapham Arms.

Thomas Osborne, 1st Duke of Leeds, Marquis of Caermarthen.
| Earl of Danby, &c., d. 1712.
Peregrine, 2nd Duke, d. 1729.
|
Peregrine Hyde, 3rd Duke, d. 1731.
|
Thomas, 4th Duke, d. 1789.
|
Francis Godolphin, 5th Duke,
  =Amelia, baroness Conyers, daughter
  | and heir of Robert, Earl of Holder-
  | ness, marriage dissolved by Act of
  | Parliament in 1779.
George William Frederick, 6th Duke, died
  | 1838.
Francis Godolphin D'Arcy, 7th Duke, died
  1859 without issue.

Lane Fox Crest.

The Sixth Duke by will, dated 1836, devised the Manor of Wakefield, &c., upon trust for his son-in-law, Sackville Walter Lane Fox,
Esq., for life, and after his decease upon trust for Sackville George
Lane Fox, with remainder to the other sons, in tail general, the issue
by the 6th Duke's daughter Charlotte Mary Anne Georgiana, who
married Mr. Lane Fox in 1826.

Brighouse Courts.

WE have now reached the point where we have documentary records, half-yearly, of the thousands of people who have figured in the little worlds of Rastrick, Brighouse and Hipperholme, but as Brighouse Graveship had jurisdiction over Northowram, Shelf, Hipperholme - cum - Brighouse, Rastrick, Quarmby, Dalton, Fixby, Stainland, Barkisland and Hartishead - cum - Clifton, persons from each of these places must be occasionally mentioned. Wakefield Manor is one of the most extensive and populous manors in England, embracing the whole of the parishes of Wakefield, Sandal, Woodkirk, Dewsbury, Emley, Kirkburton and Halifax (except Elland, Greetland, and Southowram), and parts of the parishes of Almondbury, Kirkheaton, Huddersfield, Normanton and Thornhill, and was therefore in two Wapontakes—Agbrigg and Morley. The Honour of Pontefract breaks into its contiguity in several places, but it stretches some thirty miles along the Calder from Normanton to Todmorden. Dalton beyond Huddersfield though encompassed by Pontefract Honour belongs to Wakefield, and its people were bound, like those in Quarmby, Stainland, Hartishead, &c. to attend the Court Leet or Sheriff Turn at Brighouse half-yearly. There were and are four Court Leets ;—Wakefield and Halifax with a dozen Constablaries (townships) each, Brighouse with ten, and Holmfirth with eight. No history of any one of these 42 townships can ever be written without a long examination of the Manor Rolls. These Rolls consist of skins stitched together, the earlier ones thirty to forty feet long, written in Latin the full length and partly down the other side. Afterwards, ten or a dozen skins, four or five feet long, are stitched at one end to form a book, and after the year's entries were made, the book was rolled up as before. As population increased, the rolls became thicker. This grand library is preserved at Wakefield, and is one of the choicest libraries in England. A few earlier rolls may have an erroneous date affixed, but I keep to the year assigned to them, and it will be seen they run back nearly six hundred years.

A great Court Baron was held every three weeks at the Wakefield Moot Hall, but the Steward, half-yearly, held his court at the four graveships in succession, the day after each other, and great affairs these events must have been in those times of dangerous and difficult travelling. Brighouse must have been crowded twice a year when ten townships had sent their chief men, and any, which often meant many, unfortunate culprits to the Court Baron or to the Court Leet, the latter court being held the same day immediately after the property affairs were finished by the Court Baron. The leet or tourn was formerly held by the Sheriff, who perambulated the County and held his court in every Wapontake, but afterwards it became stationary, and held before the Wapontake Steward. The King was represented in each Hundred or Wapontake by the chief landowners in succession, and these gentlemen were known down to modern times as Chief

Constables from two Saxon words Coning-Stable, King's stability. The Sheriff (Shire-reeve,) presided at the Hundred Courts, the rolls of which are preserved in London in some measure, but these I have not examined. In 1166, there was instituted, on the lines of the old Tything or Ten-man-tale, the law that four trusty men, that is bye-law-men, should represent each township at Court Leets half-yearly, to report misdemeanours. The township elected a trusty man yearly as Petty or Little Constable. The following pages will shew the power exercised in punishment for offences, at the Brighouse and similar Court Leets, that is, courts of the people. These leets were instituted to ease the Sheriff, and fines could be inflicted, but not imprisonment, for nuisances, scolds, riots, routs, eavesdroppers, barretors, fishing, rescues, unlicensed ale-houses, trespass for game, baking, &c.

A Crowner's or Coroner's Court had to be rapidly assembled on the discovery of any dead person, and the Jury were selected by the Constables of the four townships next adjoining to that spot on which the corpse was found. The constable (or king's stability, king's supporter,) was the man in each tything or township, so far back as Saxon times, who was held responsible for the conduct of the people. In comparatively modern times he paid a deputy to do the work now performed by policemen, "Bobby" Peelers, named after Sir Robert Peel. The Constable for each township was yearly appointed at the Brighouse court, and as these men were always the chief tenants I give the following lists taken from the rolls.

HIPPERHOLME.	RASTRICK.	HIPPERHOLME.	RASTRICK.
1364 Robtus del Rode	Henre Alissaundre	1376 John de Hypom	Thos Gilleson
1365 Nov. Robt del Rode	Henre Alissaundre	1377 Oct.HenMathewson elect	
,, Ap. Robt del Rode	Henre Malinson	1377 Ap. Thos de Ireland	
1368 Thos de Thorp	Thomas fil Julian	1378 Ap. John de Ireland	
,, May ,, John del Rokes elected.	,,	1379 Oct. John de Ireland	Thos Gilleson
1369 Oct. John de Rokes	Thos Gilleson or Julianson.	,, April ,,	
		1380 Nov. ,,	
,, May, John de Rokes	Thos fil Julian	,, Junne Ric de Bentelay	John Hanson
Thos Jonson, elected		1382 Oct. Ricus de Bentelay	Robert Bul
1371 Richard del Clyff		1383 Ap. ,,	
[1370 Thos Jakson	[Thos Gilleson	1383 Nov. ,,	
,, May, Thos de Brighouse	,, Julyan]	1383 May, ·John del Rokes	
Ric del Cliff, elect		1384 Oct. ,,	John Smyth
1370 Ric del Halle		1384-5 Ap. Robt de Wolker	John del ffrith
1372 Ric del Hol[ ]	HenreAlissandre	1386 Oct. Robt fletcher	Henre de Arundell
1372 Ric del Holm	Thos Gillotson	1386-7 Ap.Thos Jacson	
1373 Ric del Halle	Henry Allison	1387 Oct. Thos Johnson	
,, Ric del Halle	John Allissaundre		
1374 Ric atte Halle	Henre Malynson		

HIPPERHOLME.	RASTRICK.	HIPPERHOLME.	RASTRICK.
1387-8 Ap. Thomas del Brighouse		1413 Oct. Robt Jonson John Rokes elect const. & iuratus	
1388 Oct. Thomas Brighouse		1413-4 May, John Rokes	
138⅞ May, Thos Smyth		1414 Oct. John de Thorp	Hugh Tutehill
1389 Thos Smyth		1415 Apr. ,,	
1391 Oct. Thos del Clyf	Wm Alysandre	1415 Oct. John Thorp John Scheplay elect	
1391½ Apr. ,,		1416 Oct. John Schepelay	Hugh Totehill
1393 Oct. Thos del Thorp elect		John Ireland elect	Thos Duke elect
1394 Oct. Thos del Thorp		1416-7 ,,	
1394 Robt Carter		1417 Oct. ,, John Weloweby elect	
1396 Thos Tille	John Taillour	1417-8 Ap. ,,	
1397 John Smyth	,,	1418 Oct. ,, John Manncell elect	
139⅞ May, John Smyth	Thos de Rastryk	1418-9 May John Manneell	
1398 Oct. Thos Tille		1419 Oct. ,, Ric de Thorp elect	
1398-9 Ap. Thos Tylly John de Wylby elect		1420 May ,,	
1399 Oct. John de Wylby	John de Wyndebank	1420 Oct. Ric Thorp Ric Prestelay elect	
1399 May ,,		1421 April ,,	
1400 Oct. John de Ireland		1421 Oct. ,, Robt Walfkerre elect	
140⅖ John Wylkynson		142½ Ap. Robt Walker	
140¼ June ,,		1422 Oct. Rob Wulfkerre	
1401 April, John del Rokes		Thomas Brighous elect	
1402 ,,		142¾ Apr. ,,	
140¾ May, John de Brighous		1423 Oct. ,, Thomas Clyf elect	
1403 Oct. Rich de Prestelay	Thos del ffrith	1424 Oct. John Brodelegh elect	
1403 April ,,		142⅘ April ,,	
1404 -- de Brodelegh		1425 Oct. ,, John Roper elect	
1404-5 Wm de Stancefeld	Hugh ffox	142⅗ Ap. ,,	
1405 John de Brodelegh	Robert atte Tounend	1426 Oct. ,, John Scheplay elect	
1406 Wm de Stanclyf	John de Elystones	1427 ,,	Thos Duke
1406-7 April, Robt de Haldsworth		1427-8 April, Wm Hole	
1407 Oct. Haldeworth		1428 Oct. ,, John Rokes elect	
140⅞ May Henre ffox		1428-9 Ap. ,,	
1408 Oct. ,,		1429 Oct. Wm Hole	Thos ffrith John ffox elect
140⅚ Ap. Thos Mannsel		1429-30 May, John Mylner	John ffox
1409 Oct. ,, John Ireland elect		1430 Oct. Robt Cokecroft	
1410 ,,	Hugh Tothill	1432 Hen Risshworth	
1410 Ap. ,,	,,		
1411 Oct. ,,			
141¼ May ,,			
1412 Oct. ,,			
1412 May, Robt Jonson			

HIPPERHOLME.   RASTRICK.

1433 Oct. John Rissh-
  worth
  Thos Mannsell elect
143¾ Ap. Thos Maun-
  cell   Wm Anyson
1434 Oct. ,,
  John Smyth elect
1434-5 Ap. ,,
1435 Oct. ,,
  John Thorp elect
1435-6 Ap. ,,
1436 Oct. ,,
  John Wyloughby elect
1436-7 Ap. ,,
1437 Oct. ,,
  John Michell elect
1437-8 Ap. ,,
1438 Oct. ,,
  Willm Stokk(s) elect
1438-9 Ap. ,,
1439 Oct. ..
  Ric Clyff elect
1439 ,,   Willm Duke
1440 Oct. John Broke-
  hous: elect   ,,
1441 ,,
1441 Oct. ,,
  Willm Roide elect
144½ Ap. ,,   John by ye broke
1442
  Wm Sheplay elect
1443 (Thomas) Thorpe
  elect
., John Thorpe const.
1444 ,,
., ,, elect Ric ffox
1445 ,,   Wm. Clay
  Oliver Crouder elect
1445-6 Ap. ,,
1446 Oct. ,,
  Robert Haworth elect
1446-7 Ap. ,,
1447 Oct. Robert Clyff
1449 Oct. John Bentlay
  John Michell elect
1450 Ap. ,,
1450 Oct. ,,
,, Thomas Brighous
  Thos Hanson elect
1452 Oct. ,,
  Richard Baroclogh
  elect
1452-3 Ap. ,,
1453 Ric Barocloghe   Hugh Totehill
  Henre Hemming-
  way elect
1454 Oct. ,,
,, Henre Smyth elect

HIPPERHOLME.   RASTRICK.

1454-5 Ap. Henre Smyth elect
1456 Oct. Richd Wodd
  Richd Northclyff
  elect
1457 Oct. ,,
  John Roide elect
,,-8 Ap ,,   John atte Town-
      end
1458 ,,
  Richard Thorp elect
,,-9 Ap. ,,
1461 Oct. Hen Greneall   Wm. ffrith
  Thomas Brighous
  elect
1462 Oct. ,,
  John Hoile elect
1463 Oct. Willm Roide
  elect
,, ,, John Hoile
1464 ,, Wm. Roide
  Thomas Brighous
  elect
., Ap. ,,
1465 Oct. ,,
  John Thorp elect
., Ap. ,,
1466 John Thorp
  Oct. John Thorp
  junr, elect
1467 ,,
  Wm Haldeworth
  elect
1468 ,,
  Oct. Ric Rookes
  elect
  Apr. ..
1469 Oct. Ric. Rookes
  de Rokes
..-70 May, Robt Shaghe
1470 Oct. John Rysshe-
  worth
1471 Oct. ,,   John Hanson
  Peter Thorp elect   John lynlay,
      iunr.
1472 ,,
  Robt Baroclogh elect
1473 Oct. John Halde-
  worth elect
147¾ Peter Thorp
1474 Oct. .,
  Richard Whitlay
  elect
1474-5 Ap. ,,   Richd Duke
1475 Oct. ,,
  John Clyff elect
1476 Oct. ,,
  Wm Chylde elect

HIPPERHOLME.	RASTRICK.	HIPPERHOLME.	RASTRICK.
1477 Oct. Robert Hemingway	Recorded but not copied.	1506 ,, John Michell	
John Hoile elect		1507 ,, Wm Bramhall	
1478 Thos Northclyff		1508 ,, Wm Preston	
1479 Richd Hemingway elect		1509 ,, Robt Whitelay	
1480 Oct. Peter Thorp elect const		1510 ,, Jacobus Bentlay	
1481 Oct. Ric Sheplay elect const		1511 ,, John Thorp	John Goodyere
..½ Ap. John Totehill const		1512 ,, Richd Whitlay	
1483 Oct. John Gledehill		1513 ,, John Whitlay	Richd Hanson
Ric Scolefeld elect		1514 ,, Thomas Nicholl	Edwd Sayuile
1484 John Totehill		(Robert Nichollson const?)	
1485 Oct. John Cooke elect		1515 Oct. John Ho'me	Thos Goodale
1486 ,, John Thorp elect		1516 ,, Richd Waterhouse, iunr	Robt Malynson
1487 ,, Richd Wodd elect		1518 Laur Haldeworth	Edwd Nycholl
1488 ,, John Rideyng elect		1519 Thomas Bentlay	Richd Sundirland
1489 ,, Ric Bairestowe elect	Thos ffletcher elect	1520 Wm Otes	Wm Nicholl
1490 ,, Rad Sayntou elect		1521 Wm Nodder	Edwd ffryth
1491 ,, HenryWalker elect		1522 John Baker	Ric Botheroide
1492 ,, Robt Longeman elect		1523 Wm Rammesden	Ric Hanson
1493 ,, John Baroclogh elect		1524 John Pykhill	John Longewodd
1494 ,, Ric Gybson elect	John Cosyn	1525 Edwd Scolefeld	Rob ffryth
1495 ,, Laurence Haldeworth		1526 ,,	Rob Nicholl
1496 ,, Wmffletcher elect. po lo		1527 John Scolefeld	Jacobus Tolleson
Hen filetcher		1528 Nic Brodelee	Jacobus Ranneshawe
1496-7 Ap. Hen filetcher const		1529 Wm Thorp	Robt Good(ale) (?er)
1497 Oct. Laur Wodd elect const		1530 Wm Thorpe	Thos Nodder
1498 Henry Wodd const	Thos ffryth	1531 Robt VVyears	Wm Smyth
Oct. Lau Smyth elect	Ric Bothroide	1532 Ric Barroclogh	Wm Greue
1499 ,, John Wornewall elect		1533 Edwd Brodelee	Nicholas Batley
,, Richd Wodd const		1534 Ric Rommesden	Gibt Batley
1502 Richd Cowper ..		1535 John Milner	John Hanson
Richd Michell elect		1537 John Watrhous	Xpofer Townend
1503 Oct. Nich Beutlay		1539 ( )	John ffoxe
1504 ,, John Otes		1540 John Wodhede	John Longwodde
1505 ,, Xpofer Walker		1541 Ric Stephenson	John Goodall
		1542 John Wilton	Edwd Nicholl
		1543 John Nicholl	Robt Horcefall
		1544 Wm Beaumond	John Malynson
		1546 John Thorpe	John Goodall
		1547 Wm Thorpe	John ffrith
		1548 John ffletcher	Wm Broke
		1549 ( )	Jacobus Tollson
		1550 John filetcher	
		1551 William Thorpe	John Gledhill
		1552 Elias Nutter	Leonard Longeley
		1553 { Ric Brighous { Wm Deyneham elect	{ Rob Rommesden { JohnGoodar(half)
		1554 Wm Deyncham R(ic) Smythe elect	Rob Rammesden Ric Rawresley
		1555 Thos Bollande	Rob Goodare
		1557 Thos Roide elect	John Watson

HIPPERHOLME.	RASTRICK.
1559 Edwd Sawodd	John Hanson
1560	John Malynson
1562 Thos Pyghilles	John Townende
Robt Haldesworth elect	John ffoxe elect
1563 Geo Scolefeld & Robt Sawodd	} Thos ffrithe
1564 Oct. John Otes elect	Edmd Longewodd
1565 ,, Wm Whytley elect	John Goodale (alias Goodare)
1566 ,, JacobusWaterhouse elect	John Gledehill
1567 Thos Roide elect	John Malynson
1568 Thos Whitleghe	Edwd Malynson
1569 Edwd Hole or (Hoile) elect	Jas Hirst
1570 John Hemmyngwaye	Thos ffirth
1571 Robt Brighous	Robt Rawnesley
1572 Gilbt Saltonstall	Rob Romsden
1573 Thos Thornhill	Thos Hanson
1574 John Smyth	John Goodheire
1575 John Wodhead	John Malynson
1576 Edwd Thorpp, po lo Edwd ill.	Ric Rawnesley
1577 Thos Brighous	John Watson
1578 John Wilton	Edwd Hanson
1579 John Barrowclough	John Hanson, junr.
1580 Ric Scolefeld	John Hanson, senr.
1581 Edne ffairbanck	John Malynson
1582 Edwd Brodeley	Thos Hanson
1583 Ric Kent, po lo Edw Kent	Edw ffox
1584 Ric Northend	{ John ffox const. { John fil John ffox
1585 John Thorpp	John Thornhill
1586 Thos Hoyle	John Malynson
1587 Thos Hoile, Wm Whitley	JohMalynson,jun Edw Malynson
1588 Wm Hoile	John Broke
1589 John Boyth	John Malynson
1590 Robt Brodeley	John ffirth, lynnyn drapr.
1591 Thos Barrowclough po lo Edw Shawe	Edward Jagger
1592 George ffairbanck	{ Thomas Wilson { Arthur ffirth
1593 Wm Barrowclough	Edwd Mawde
1594 John Thorpp	John Tolson
1595 Richd Thorpp	Henry Romsden, gent.
1596 Ric Thorpp const & socii. Wm Hargreaves elect	Thos Bunny elect.

HIPPERHOLME.	RASTRICK.
1597 John Northend	Ric Potheroyd
1598 ,,	,,
1599 Rob Hemingway const	Edmund Broke const
Michl Slater elect	Arthur ffirthe elect
1600 Saml Hole	Gilbert Hoile
1601 Jacobus Rawnsley	Edward Hanson
1602*Thomas Hanson de Brighous	Brian Rawnsley
* From this date to recent times I had compiled a list for Hipperholme from the town's books, before searching the Manor Rolls.	
1603 Edward Hoile	John Holland elect
1604 John Jackson	Edward Hanson
1605 John Brighouse	John Hanson
1606 Richd Brodeley	Wm Mallynson
John Carleton dep.	
1607 John Royd	Thos Hanson
1608 John Wilton	
1609 Wm Northend	John ffox
1610 Jesper Brighouse	John son of John ffox
1611 Mich Slater serr.	
Thomas Smyth	Hen Nicholls
1612 John Waterhouse de Norwood Grene	John Goodheire
1613 Thos Whitley, po lo Thos Hanson de Brighouse	Arthur Hurste
1614 John Haldesworth	John Mallynson
1615 Michael Thorpp po lo Ric Thorpp	Henry Froke
1616 John Whitley	Robt Hanson
[1617 John Hanson for Baroclough. Town's Book]	
1618 Wm Walker po lo Roger Bancroft	Robt Wilkinson
1619 Richd Norclife	Saml Hoile
1620 Andreas Gill	Thos Hanson
1621 Arthur Elmesall (Empson)	Robt Haldesworth
1622 Ric Wison	Thos ffather
1623 Thos Richardson Thos Todde, cep.	Edward ffox
1624 Samuel Hoyle junr	Richd Ramsden
1625 Andrew Marshall	Henry Nicoll
1626 John Thorpe po lo Abm Bridge	Edwd Hanson
1627 Thomas Sugden	John Bootheroide

HIPPERHOLME.	RASTRICK.
1628 { Thos fflather { Arthur Hanson dep.	Roger Hathorne alias Hirste
1629 Wm Hirde	Wm Mallynson
1630 Nicholas Smythe	Edrus Gibson
1631 Wm Birkhead	John Wilson, po lo Timothy Shar-rock and John Windle
1632 Wm Thorpe	Edmund ffox
1633 John Rayner	Edwd ffox
1634 Peter Lee, po lo Matth. Lome	Arthur Hirste
1635 John Appleyeard	John Goodheire
1636 Henry Brighouse	John Crosley
1637 Michael Bentley	Robt Heap po lo Abm ffarrer
1638 Isaacus Broadley	James Lome
1639 Wm Walker	Thos fflather
1640 John Gill	John Kighley
1641 Halifax, Oct.	Md qd sepel villat

de Rastrick, Hippholme, ffekishye, Northowrom, Shelfe, Quernbye, Clifton, Dalton, Hartshead, Stain-land and Barkisland Jurat fuer apud Halifax quia pestis valde grasseabat infra pd. villat de Hipp-nolme et Shelfe.

[No Brighouse court owing to the pest or plague being very prevalent in H. and S., but held as usual in April following.]

1641 Arthur Hanson const	Jas Gleidhill const
1642 Isaac Brodeley Mic Tessimond Anthony fflather & Saml Hoile (4)* ps. qd. Ric North-end elect const est	John ffox elect const

HIPPERHOLME.	RASTRICK.
[Constables of Hipp: from Town's books.	
1643 Michael Bentley, junr. served three months, Henry Brighouse and others served out. Time of Wars.	
1644 Andrew Marshall, but Andrew Gill helped six months.	
1645 Robert Thorp. 1646 Luke Hoyle.	
1647 Robert Hargreaves.]	
1647 Jonas Hemingway po lo Michll	Edwd Hanson Empsall
1648 John Clayton po lo John Hop-kinson	Saml Hoile
1649 Abraham Lome	John Lome
1650 Henry Preistley	Ric Ramsden
1651 Nathan Whitley	John Hanson
1652 Nathan Crosley	{ George Cowper { and John Windle
1653 Saml Clay	{ Wm Steton and { John Bentley

[Hipp. 1653, Ric Thorpe, John Thorppe, John Willson and Robert Smith are appointed Overseers of the Highway for this psent year.]

1654 Brighouse View of Frank Pledge and Court Leet of Oliver Lord Protector of the Commonwealth of England, Scotland, and Ireland, 1654

Joseph Bentley	{ Edward Hanson { gent, Netherwood house
1655 Henry Heming-way	John Boothroid

[•The four men representing the town at the court, present that R.N. is elected.]

The remainder, as I have proceeded no further with the Manorial Rolls, are from the town's-books for Hipperholme-cum-Brighouse only, and will be added afterwards.

Similar lists can be compiled for Fixby, Clifton, &c., from these valuable records.

GREAVES.—A more interesting list even is that of the prepositi or greaves for they were the principal landowners, and the appointments were made in a regular succession according to the land. Watson, more than a hundred years ago saw a list of the Hipperholme Greaves in a drawer at Howroyd, (Mr. Horton's*) that extended from 21 Edwd. IV. to 24 Henry VII, and then the same rotation as to land had to be followed again. He did not print this list, but I have put it into the

* Hortons of Coley Hall, at one time.

shade by extracting from the rolls the lists of Greaves, Graves, or
Prepositi for Hipperholme, Rastrick and Scammonden, from 1300 to
1655, but have not space, nor need, to print them here as they appear
in the *Yorkshire Genealogist.*—The Grave was an Officer under the
Lord of the Manor who had to collect the Manorial rents, and the
name comes down to us from the earliest Anglian times, being found
in all the Germanic nations, like the kindred words—port-reeve, shire-
reeve, translated in these Latin rolls 'prepositus.' Hipperholme
graveship included Hipperholme-cum-Brighouse, Shelf and Northowram, so the list of its greaves includes the property holders of the
three townships. Watson never saw these rolls, and says that the
earliest notices he has seen of Hipperholme Graveship were, 1314 and
21 Ed. IV. He saw at Howroyd the Hipperholme rental for 21 Ed.
IV. and a fuller one 22 Henry VIII., but does not print them, nor
the survey of the copyhold lands as examined by a special jury held
in Coley chapel in 1607. In 1617 another enquiry was held for the
king as to the names of the copyholders, the number of messuages,
cottages, and acreage, and boundaries; also which was oxgangland,
or rodland or freehold. This he does not print either. A great
Court Baron of Thomas, 'Duke of Leedes,' was held at Lightcliffe
Chapel by adjournment, 24 May, 1709, when it was found there were
27 graves who had to serve in rotation, with their helpers. A large
owner might have several times to serve for his several properties.

The Wapentake Court became known in Norman times as the
Sheriff's tourn, torn, tourne. Peers, commoners and clergy had to
attend one or other of these tourns to take the oath of allegiance to
the king, and the sheriff was responsible for the peace of the shire.
Sir John de Elland as sheriff and as a private individual had to attend
the Brighouse tourn :

> These countrymen of course only
> Said Elland kept alway
> The turn of Brighouse certainly
> And you shall know the day. . . .
> The day was set the turn was kept
> At Brighouse by Sir John, &c. . . .
> [Above] Brookfoot a hill there is [Lane Head,]
> To Brighouse in the way
> Forth came they to the top of this
> There prying for their prey.

Sir John coming up to them courteously vailed his bonnet, but was
slain by them "in defiance of the king and his laws, he having that
day, according to the ancient customary law of England represented
His Majesty's person in receiving fealty of his subjects as sheriff." [†]

The sheriff took cognizance of false weights, nuisances, misdemeanours; he held an annual view of the frankpledge—the pledge
every freeman made on attaining twelve years of age that he belonged

Yorks. Genealogist, Vols. 1 and 2, 17 pages ; and *Yorks. County Magazine*, 1893.
† See for full account—The Elland Tragedies, 1300-1350.

to a certain tything, or township. Under some sovereigns, especially when kings were fighting abroad, his powers were very great and the power of hearing and determining criminal causes was not transferred to the Justices at Quarter Sessions until 1461, (Ed. IV.) That relic of superstition—trial by ordeal—was resorted to in early tourns. Even the appointment of a town's bellman can be carried back to those early days when the township meetings were thus called. The reader will know that the testing of weights and measures still appertains to this ancient Brighouse court. It was sometimes spoken of as the Halmote, or Hall moot, that is, the Lord of the Hall's court. The Lord's steward cried out in Norman fashion—"Oyez, oyez, oyez," and then made enquiries as to common lands, deaths of tenants, payment of heriot on taking possession or heirship, waste lands, timber, waifs, strays, turf, trespass, escheats, alienations, lists of freemen, &c. When a tenant wished to dispose of his land to another, he had to appear, or get another tenant as substitute to appear, and surrender up his holding to the lord by yielding a straw, and sometimes this straw was affixed to the new transfer deed.

The Halmote business being concluded each court day, the constable and four men from each township have to be ready to report cases under the Court leet or Sheriff's Turn. The jury is sworn, and the proceedings from time to time may be read in the following pages. In order to crowd as much information as possible we have used abbreviations, *s.* for son; *d.* for daughter; *de* or *del*, for of, of the; *ac.*, acres. *po lo* for pro loco, substitute; *uxor* for wife. All the figures ought to appear in Roman letters xviijd. for 18d., as Arabic figures were not used much before 1600. The extracts are mere pickings, and though many entries are copied that refer to Northowram, Shelf, Hartshead, Clifton, &c., they shew the extent and importance of the court jurisdiction. It will be noticed how gradually Rastrick Brighowses gave way to the name Brighouse.

Rastrick Brighowses Courts, for Hiprome, Rastrick, and Scamonden Graveships.

1272, (1 Edw. I.) (This endorsement is doubtful. It is probably 1307. 1 Edw. II.) Richd. s. Henry de Rokes paid 8s. 3d. for relief of his tenements. Thomas de Totehill, executor of Thomas de ffekisby, and Beatrix de Tetehill appear at court. Henry de Northcliffe gave 6d. for leave to take two parts of an acre in Hiprom from Will. s. Ade. Elias s. Xpiane and Robert his brother of Hiperom gave 2s. for leave to agree with Ric. de Ourom. Henry ffabr (Smith) of Chepedene in Hypm. gave 6d. for leave to take three parts of land in Schepedene from John s. Wymarke. Alexander de Brighouses for cutting green wood paid 6d. Megge de Brighouses for dry wood 6d. Henry s. John de Rastrik 6d., Ric. s. Malin 6d., Will s. Nalle 6d., for green wood. Anote de Rastrik 6d., dry wood. Elias s. Xpiane de Northowram took 12 acres of John de Shawe in N. Owram. William Talvate 12d. for leave to take 6 acres on Clegcliffe. Adam by the

Broke, 4d., Roger del Clyff 6d. thorns. Thomas del Northend, dry wood, 3d. William le Horseknave de Sourby 2d. for a horse's food.

Norcliffe Arms.

Copley Arms.
(Argent a Cross Moline sable.)

Copley Crest.

Court held at Rastrik, feast of St. Barnabas. Will. s. Adam de Schepeden gave 12d. for 1½ ac. new land in Schepden of waste. Jordan s. Adam de S. 6d. for ½ ac. in N.owram. John s. Adam de Hiprom 6d. ¼ ac. waste in Hiperom. John s. Adam del Whytehill 18d. for 2 ac. N.owram. Rich. s. Jordan de N.owm., 6d. ½ rod in N. Thos. s. Xpiane de Linthwaite 2s. land in Quermby. John s. Adam de Lockwode paid xijd. as fealty. Wm. s. Wm. de Hingandrode carried away wood from Rich. del Wode. Thos. s. Modeste fined 12d. Henry Abraham paid 12d. to take 3 rodes of waste in Hipperholm wood. John del Botherode 6d., Henry s. Modeste, Johna d. Xpiane, Sabina wid. John s. Henry, Will Burreheved, Mathew de Totehill, Walter s. Elie

de Ouroni and Thos. his brother, Michael de Haddegreue, Rich. s.
Walter, John le Pinder de Ouroni, Jordan de Haddegreues, Thomas
del Broke, John del Wroo, Eva wife of Thomas le Heyr, John del
Rode, Roger del Brighouses, senior, Thos. s. Roger del Cliffe, John s.
Henry de Astay, John s. Walter, Ric. s. Jordan, John de Whytehill,
Jord. de Hallewaye, Simon s. Jordan, Henry de Coldclay, Henry de
Coppelay and Henry le Marwe, paid from 3d. to 6d. for taking green
wood, dry wood, thorns, wood ; (in Latin form *ririd, sicc, spinis, bosc.*)
Roger del Clifton 6d. 1 rod in Hippm. wood. Henry Abraham 12d. ½
ac. waste.

The Jury at Rastrik *Turn* were—Alan del ffrith, Thos. de Dalton,
fris, Radus (Ralph) de Gouthelaghcharthes (Golcar), Henry le ffrankisse de Staynland, [Ivo] Talvate, John de Bristall, John del Rode,
John clericus de Hertesheved, Henry de Coldelay, John de Percy,
Thomas de Wytewode, Roger de Clifton.

Hipprm township fined 12d. for not being represented at tourn.
The wife (uxor,) of Roger s. John, senior, for brewing, 4d. Magota de
Chepllay, ux Adam Carpentare, ux. Will Molendinare, (the Milner), ux
Ric. le Taillour, each fined 4d. to 6d. for brewing. Alex. the Milner
of Brighouses, not attending the tourn, fined 6d. 'Due pultre wayue'
(two strayed young horses) in the hands of the greave or prepositus
of Hipperom for a year and a day, sold to — del Wode for 7s. 6d.
John Percy of Clifton not attending, 3d. Will le — de Thornhill and
John le Strengfelagh took by burglary from Thos. del Wode's house
goods valued at xls. Hugh s. Will. s. Eve de Wakifeld drew blood
from Ric. del Lathe de Clifton, therefore attached. Rob. Spillewoode
drew blood from Alex. the Milner of Brighouses, fined 6d. Beatrix
wife of Ade le Waynwrith drew blood from Emma Pynder of Hipprom,
6d. ; Alan de Bothomlay blood from Cecilia dau. Will. de Bothomley.
Will s. Robert de Haldeworth 6d. to take 2½ ac. in Haldeworth, formerly held by John de Skircotes. William de Burga was then parson of
Thornhill. Roger de Clifton 2s. 6d., for 2 ac. 1 rod waste in Wolve-
ker. Thos. le Webbester 12d. 1 ac. waste at Underbouth. Math. de
Totehill 3s. for 2 ac. land in le Stede in Hiprum wood. Rich. de
Bosco (Wood) 6½ ac. waste in Chypedene. In Kirkburton district was
a family named Waterhouse. Rich. de Ouerom had a dispute with
Elia. s. Xpiane and Robert his brother.

Court at Brighouses, Feast St. Edmund King, 1st year King Edw.
John s. Walt. de Ouerom assault on Walter s. Elie de Ouerom, and
Matilda his daughter. The said Walter and Matilda had a charge
against Ric. brother of said John. John s. Galfri le Colier gave 6d.
for heriot, for 5 acres in Ourom on the death of his father Galfr.
Will s. Ade de Hipron, 6d. heriot 1 acre on death of his father Ade.
John s. Will. Milner 6d. heriot 3 parcels in Ourom on death of Thos.
his brother. John s. Ade s. John 12d. heriot 4 acres on death of
Adam his father. Will. del Hengandrode 6d. heriot 3 parcels in
Ouerom on death of his father Will. Ric. le Taillour 6d. for half rod
in Brighouse of Roger de Chepelay. The Mill of Rastrick (that is,
Brighouse) farmed to William del Bothes and Alex del ffrith.

Turn at Brighouse. Jury—John de Loewode, Alex. del ffrith, Thos. de Dalton, John le fflemynge, John s. Ade de Loewode, John de Hertesheued, John de Percy de Clifton, Galfri del Dene, John de Bristall, Henry de Coildelay, Henry ffranceys, and Louecok de Nettleton.

Roger s. Hanne de ffekesby drew blood from Agnes d. Thos. de ffekesbye; Adam le ffuller of Goulayecarthes from Allan de Aldelay; Malina de Holewaye de N.owram from Malina ux. Ivon de N.owram; Tho s. of Ivon de Prestley from Will. Coker; Alex le Waynwriht from Henry le Pynder de Hipm; Alcok del Wodehouse from Will. ffoune. Brewers—ux Ric. de Schelff, ux Roger de Brighouses, ux Will Milner, ux Ric. le Taillor. Pannage of the wood of Hippm sold in gross to Will del Bothes and Alex. del ffrith for £6.

1274. This second roll is very imperfect now. Ric. de Thornhill was pardoned for taking a stag in Saltonstall. Alan de ffekisby was a juror at Brighouse. A diverted road had to be restored. Robt. de Saltonstall encroached on Saltonstall waste. Ric. s. Thos. de ffekesby paid 3s. for leave to take 4 acres.

1276. John s. Jordan, Henry de Northend, Peter de Hyprom and Will. Drake broke the pinfold. John de Haylay was fforestar. Will s. Hugh de Schypedene took 1 ac., late Will. del Dene's. Yvo le ffabr (Smith) de Schypden. John le Barn 12d., 2 rods of land in Hyprm-wood. Ric. de Hyprm owes 13s. 4d. to John s. Jordan, bondsmen—Hanne de Nortwode de Hypm, Peter de Hypm. Matthew and John sons of Roger de Bosco (Wood), Rastrick greaveship, paid heriot. Gilbert del Bothes gave 2s. for leave to give his daughter Alice in marriage; bond, Hanne the greave. Year 5 of King Edw. Henry s. Roger de Northwode gave 8d. for relief of his father's lands in Presteley, bonds, Henry de Northwode & Ric. de Coppelay. Alan the priest of ffekisby. Dominus Ingelard the Vicar of Halifax paid 3s. as fealty. Halifax Northbryg mentioned. Adam s. Will. de Hyprm, Alice de Coldelay, Ric. de Hyprm, Will s. Hugh de Schepeden paid 12d. for 1 acre. Radulph de Bayrestowe gave 2s. for 4 acres of John s. Roger and Adam s. Henry, in le Brerechaye, Northowram.

1284. John s. Jordan de Shypedene mortus est (is dead), the lands seized by the lord. Henry de Risseworth a juror at Halifax.

Rastrik *Turn*. Jury—Robert de Stokkes, John de Schelff, Ad. de Ouerom, Henry the Greave of Hyprm, John de Querneby, John le Barne, Henry de Dalton, Robert s. Dolfn, Gilbert Dynes, Robert de Thackmache, Alan de fekesby, Thos. de Nettleton. Peter de Nettleton broke Thos. Edward's head, fined 6d. ux Rob. Bate sold ale, fined 6d., ditto Eva de Rastrik, fined 12d. Gilbt. de Astay gave 2 ac. in Hyprm to Ric. his son. Thos. s. Thos. de Hyperum took a deodand from Jordan the Smith (ffabr). John de Rastrick the greave and Will s. Peter de Hipprum held a house and 4 acres in Hippm. Roger s. John the Milner paid 12d. to take 2 ac. in Hip. of Gilbert de Astay. Will Bercar paid 4d. for 2 hogges in Hyprm wood. John Milner, Henry de Astay, Jake de Halifax, Alice d. Mygeryth, Peter s. Alot de Hyprm

D

owed service to Prior John of Lewys: Hanne the Greave, pledge. Gilbt. de Astey opposes himself against (plaintiff) Thos. de Hylton, an assault in the Wood at Hyprm. John de Stanclyff, and Thos. Hogson taking drywood. Will de Hyprm placed two cows in Hipp. common pasture field at a forbidden time.

1285. Ric. s. Symon del Bothes gave ½ mark to have his lands in peace till of age. Jordan de Bosco (Wood) gave 6d. for relief of ½ ac. to John his son; pledge Henry the prepositus. Adam Here of Hypr. 6d. for greenwood, Roger del Clyff pledge. Matthew de Sonderland, tenant, is dead. Gilbert del Bothes, Bate del Bothes, Hugh le Tinker, Will del Scholecotes and relicta Peter de Haldeworth taking wood. Will of Hiperm quarrel with Thos. le Webester, Webster paid 6d. Walter son of Matthew de Sonderland gave 6d. relief, for 6 acres on his father's death. Henry le Hopper dispute with Eli de Schelff; pledge Geppe del Dene. The lands of Will le Toller taken by the lord. Cristiana d. Ric. de Totehyll and Will. s. Roger de Bosco quarrel; she was fined 6d. for not answering. Adam s. Matthew de Saltonstall appears under Sourby court. Roger s. Walter de Rastrik gave 6d. for 5½ ac. with messuage of Walter his father. Cristiana d. Ric. Quynel gave 12d. for leave to marry: pledge, John the greave of Rastrick. Will. del Bothes, 5s. to take messuage and 20 acres in Hypru' of Alice de Hypru' and Peter her son: pledge, Henry prepositus. Richard s. Walter de Sonderland to respond to Alice de Southourum.

Holdsworth Arms.

Rookes Arms.

Nalle de Dene and Henry de Hip'um mentioned. Adam s. Will le Schapman being dead, the lord holds the lands. John de Coldelay gave 6d. for debt of Thos. s. Alot. Henry le Pynder 6d., 1½ rods in Hypr' of Thos. s. Alot de Hyp.: pledge, Thos. de Hypm. Henry de Risseworth was foreman juror at 'Alifax' turn.

Court at Rastrik, die martis after Nativ. Blessed Mary. Ric. Cade de Schypedene and Bate Bolder had a dispute. Matthew de Schelf gave 6d. to agree in dispute with Alex. and John sons of Walter de Sonderland : pledge, Will. s. Ivon de Hyp'.

John de Hovendene gave 6d. for special trial against Will. Drake. Cecilia de Hyprm plaintiff, *r.* Alice filia Mygeryt, that Nalle her son held in an oat Wynd for ten years. John le Barn gave 6d. for an inquiry respecting a pig killed in Schypeden, Thos. s. Magot rung the pig, and paid 6d. fine. Juliana d. Will de Schypedene 2s. for relief of lands of Adam s. Will. le Schapman. Dispute Ric. del Bothes against Henry de Northwode and John de Bayrstow. Ric. Cade gave 6d. to withdraw in Bate Bolder's case ; pledge, Alcok del Clyff. Ric. s. Adam de Totehyll mentioned under Rastrick. Gilbt. del Bothes plaintiff *rersus* Peter the greave ; pledge, Henry the greave. John Jordan and Jordan Jordan, brothers, *r.* Gilbt del Bothes. Thos. le Spenser disputes with Roger del Clyf and John s. Richard about a quarter of oats. Ric. s. Walter de Sonderland 6d. to agree with Alice wife of Will. de Suthorum.

Brighouse *Turn.* Jury—John de Schelf, Henry de Dalton, John de Quernby, Robt. del Stokkes, Alan del Clyf, John de Lokwode, Gilbt Dynes, Jordan de Rokes, Ad. de Hourum, Will. de Bradelay, Will. s. Vidue, Yvo ffabr (Smith). Robert s. Robt. at Townend (exitu ville) drew blood from Robt. s. John le flemang, in Rastrick graveship. Henry the greave of Hipperholm took from Robt. Cosyn, thief, a blue mantle or watchet. John s. Sybbe and Cecila wife of Ad. Milner carried away oxen at night. Will s. Roger de Wodhouses in Rastrick mentioned. Julian de Scholecotes is pregnant by Hugh le Tynker, and Northowram town knowing it did not report it, therefore fined ½ mark. (A mark was 13s. 4d., a noble 6s. 8d.)

1286. Rastrick village was rated at 13s., and contained only six freemen, the rest were natives, villains, or bondsmen.

1288. 16 Edward I. Geppe de Dene was elected forester of Sowerbyshire and found sureties for his fidelity, Henry greave of Hipperholme, William of Hipperholme, Thos. de Shelfe and Ric. de Schelfe. The foresters were sometimes attacked by gangs of men, and Robin Hood, whose name still lingers in place-names in these parts, could hardly fail to be found amongst the deer stealers. There were also wild beasts, for Alan s. Richard Talvas was imprisoned for taking from William del Hirst six sheaves of oats against his will, alleging that William owed him the same for preserving his corn in the night from the beasts of the woods.

1297. John de Bristall 6d. for green wood ; pledge, Walter de Ourom. John del Wytehill, ditto, pledge, Ric. de Bosco. Will Swyer

paid 6d. for feeding 3 pigs; pledge, Peter del Clif; and Peter de
Sutteclyf, John de Astay, Henry de Coppelay, ditto. Alex. s. Adam
Milner 6d. to agree with Wm. Milner. The cattle of Will s. Nalle
fed on oats on Henry de Hiprom's land, which Will. del Both the
greave sold for 2s. without leave.

Ric. Baton drew blood from Henry de Wyahon; & the said Ric. and
Matilda his mother drew blood from Adam s. Yvon.

Court and *Turn* at Rastrick. Jury—John de Quernby, John le
Barn, John le ftlemyng, Thos. de Dalton, Alex. del ffrith, John Clerk
of Hartisheued, John de Percy, John del Rode, Ad. del Locwod, John
de Locwod, Henry de Hiperon, John de la Haye. Galfri le Colyer
raised hue and cry on William the greave of Hipperom. Eva del
Broke has hand mills to the damage of the lord, as all corn had to be
ground at his mill. Will le piper disputes with Alcok le Waynwrth
and Adam s. John, Henry de Schepden is dead; lands go to the
lord. John del Rode 6d. for drywood, pledge Adam de Brigghuses.
Alcok del Clif 3d. for greenwood, pledge Henry de Northwod. Will.
de Haley food for 2 oxen, 2d., pledge Peter de la Lathe. Walter s.
Macok 6d. greenwood, pledge Will. de Schypden. Malekyn de Haldeworth 1d. for 1 ox's food. Matilda widow of Ivon ffaber, 6d. drawing
blood from Ad. s. Yvon. John son and heir of Henry del Dene, 12d.
relief or heriot, at father's death. Will. de Hagenewrth 6d. to take
Alice wid. Robt. s. Will. le Chapman to wife; pledge William prepositus. John s. John Wyclif of Wakefield relieved his father's land
there. Adam le Waynwrth, John de Holeway, Ad. le Dyr, Hen. de
Coppelay, Thos. s. Elie, John s. Will., Walter s. Elie, Henry del
Rode, Roger s. Walter, Will. Carpenter, Roger de Briggehuses, senior,
Adam his brother, for taking green or drywood 3d. to 6d. each. Will.
s. Walter de Schepden 2s. to take a bovate in Hyp'om of Roger
garcoe Rich. de Clifton for 16 years: pledge, Adam the greave,
Rastrik, and Roger s. John. Ellen d. Matilda de Fixby against
Henry de Fixby that he was a bastard. Thos. de Saltonstall paid 7s.
5d. for bovate and half in Saltonstall. Ric. de Saltonstall 2½ bovates
there 9s. 11d. Leave obtained to build a bakehouse. Ric. de Totehyll
is dead; lands seized.

Court at Rastrik. Beatrix d. and heir of Hugo de ffekesby 12d.
heriot for her father's lands. Thos. del Cote de ffekisbye 12d. for 1
acre; pledge Adam the greave of Rastrik. Cecilia widow of Rich. de
Totehill 2s. for relief. Eli de Benteley owes 5s. to Eve de Hiperm.
Roger s. John Milner 2s. for 1 acre and edifice from Adam his brother
in Briggehuses. Thos. s. Ric. de Totehyll 6s. 8d. heriot on death of
his father; pledge Richd. prepos. Rastrik. Adam s. Henry de Northwod, 18d. for 10 acres from Adam s. Yvon ffabr (Smith) in Breriehaye,
Schepden. Ric. s. Hugh de Schepden gave 40d. for freedom from
service to Ric. s. Yuon de Hypron, John de Ouerun, Simon de Shepeden, Thos. s. Elie de Ouerum, Ad. s. Iuonis and Ric. del Wode. Ric. s.
Yuon de Presteley ordered to scoure his ditches in Shelf. Cecilia wife
of Adam Milner brewing, 6d. Will. s. Radulph de Bayrestowe stole

from the house of Will. s. Oto de Schipden goods to value of 8d., therefore attached. Ric. s. Hugh de Schepden stole 8d. from the widow of Will. de Pudesheye and he is a notorious thief. Ric. s. Thos. del Cote gave 3s. for ingress to a bovate in ffekesby, called Bernard Oxgangs, of Thos. atte Cote, also 12d. for 4 acres, terra nativa, land subject to villein service, and 10 acres of land in Custe rode from Thomas his father. Malina wid. Adam de N.owram conveyed lands and edifice to Ric. s. Jordan de N:owram and John s. Walter. Roger s. Will del Briggehuses, 2s. to take a bovate *ter. nativ.* and 4 acres free land at Longeley in Hiperm. of Will. s. Peter de Hipr. Adam the prepositus of Rastrik 6d. for a rod of new land at Briggerode. Geppe was still the forester of Sourby. Adam s. John de Horton conveyed land in Sourby grave to Rob. s. Will. de Saltonstall.

Horton Arms.   Milner Arms.

Malina de Thyngelawe (now Tingley, near Morley, where the Wapentake court-hill was,) is mentioned. The following paid from 2d. to 6d. for food for their cattle, and were pledge for each other,—Agnes wife Ralph de Bayrestowe, John de B., Geppe le Colier in le Blacker, Will de Halifax, Will Yunghare, W. Balder, Will s. Ede. Roger s. John Molendinare (Milner) gave ½ mark for ½ acre new land adjoining his garden and ½ acre in Smythieker. Ric. s. Hugh de ffekisbye, Gilbt del Bothes, Ric. le Bagger, John s. Thos. the Textor, Alkoc le Waynwrth, Adam s. John the Milner and brother of Hanne the greave, John le Barn, and Ric. s. Yuon de Presteley appeared as plaintiffs or defendants in causes.

Turn at Rastrik. Jury—Robert del Stockes, John le ffiemeng, Ad. de Locwod, Magister Thos. de Dalton, John le Barn, Will. de Bradelaye, Alex del ffrith, John de Herteshcued clerk, Ralph de Goutlekarwes, John del Rod, John de Percy, Thos. de ffekisbye. The lord's seneschall (steward) was John de Doncastre. John s. Will. s. Emme de Staynland drew blood from Will. le Pynder de Staynland. Jack blade alias Mauk had a dispute with Ric. and Hugh de Presteley. Adam the greave of Rastrick 12d. for 3½ acres from Hanne the Milner. For dry wood, Henry del Rode, Thos. de Hipern, Will. de Bayrestowe, paid 4d. each, pledges Peter Suthcliffe, Ad. Brighuses, Ad. fforestar, Peter de la Lathe de Haldeworth and Adam s. John de Hiprom. Adam the Baker having lands in Fixby for not coming to court, 6d., and the township 12d. for not presenting the same. The annual income from Rastrik graveship to the lord was 15s. 6d. ; Hyperom graveship 28s. 5d. (Roman figures are always used, xxviijs. v*d*.)

1306. Cecilia de Brigghuses gave 6d. to hold a toft in Briggehuses and 1 ac. 3 rd. in Rastrik which Adam le Milner formerly held ; pledge, Roger de Briggehuses. Disputes about land &c. by Peter de Suthcliffe *r.* Ad. s. John, Thos. de Totehill *r.* John Spillewod's lands in Briggehuses, Roger s. John the Milner *r.* John s. Ric. Roger, senior, of Briggehuses, took some waste land. Roger s. John le Milner and John de Sunderland paid 2s. each, fine for not serving as greaves. Alcok le Waynewrth 6d. for ½ acre from Adam s. Alote. A colt was in custody of Rob. de Saltonstall, Soureby, and a cow in that of Rastrick prepositus, both waifs. For wood, fodder, &c., Ric. s. Walter, Walter s. Elyot, ux Yuon Milner, Roger de Brigghuses, Henry Milner, Cecilia Milner, Ralph de Shipel, Symon del Dene, Will. s. Ede, Malina ux Yvon, Otho de Heyley, 1d. to 4d. each. Christana d. Ric. de Totehill and Will. s. Roger Wood dispute. Ric. de Wood complains of Will. Saltonstall taking 4 oxen. Saundre (Alex.) de Brigghuses gave 3s. 4d. for messuage and 6 ac. from Hanne s. Will. de Briggehuses ; pledge, John le Barn. For wood, fodder, &c., John del Wro, Will. de Thorp de Hyperm, Malina Peti, Alcok le Waynwrith, John de Holewaye, Henry de Coldelay, Will. Brown de Shelf, Thos. del Broke, Henry de Coppelay, 3d. to 6d. each. John Greteword and Thos. s. Elie, 3d. each, breaking dry wood in Hyprum wood. John s. Hanne de Bayrestowe for fodder in said wood, 12d. John s. Ralph, Will. Milner de Halifax, Roger Milner of Brigghus, senior, Ric. Cissor, John Milner, John del Rode, John de Hastay, Thos. Sourmylk, Bate del Cliff, Alcok s. Walter, Thos. del Northend, the same, 3d. each. Adam s. and heir of Henry formerly greave of Hyprom ½ mark heriot for 2 bovates. Robert s. Capellan. de Eland mentioned.

Court at Rastrik. Ric. s. Jordan de Halifax, 6d., 1 ac. in Okynbank. Will. le Milner, 6d., 1 ac. of waste on Halifax brook bank. Henry de Northclyf, 6d., 1 ac. waste between Willeclogh and lands of Tho. s. Tho. de Hyprm. Roger s. John, senior, 2s., 2 acres waste in Cherpleyker. Ric. s. Adam s. Ionis, 2s. heriot, for 3 acres in Hiprm on the death of Adam his father. Galfri (Geppe) del Dene *versus* Beatrix de Tothill. Gilbert Bridde 2d. per annum for waste land in the Brig-huses. Roger de Chepeley 12d. for waste lands in Brighouses. Peter del Suthcliffe, John fox, Galfri le Colier, answered to charges.

. Annabel d. Henry del Dene paid 12d. for leave to marry as she pleased ; pledge, Simon de Totehill. Sir Ric de Middleton, chaplain, and Will. de Sunderland gave 2s. to take ten acres of waste in Blacker on Clegelyf. Will. de Sunderland, 12d. for 3 acres between Hugh de Ouenden's assart and le Holcan. Bate del Clyf de Ouerom 6d. for toft and edifice and 4 acres in Ouerom from Sir Ric. the chaplain, for ten years. *Turn* at Rastrick. Reign of Edw. son of King Edwd. (1307.) Jury, John de Rodes, Will. del Bothes, John de Locwode, John le ffleminge de Dalton, Henry s. Walter, John de Bristall, Henry de Coildelay, John de Percy, John de Herteshened, Will. de Bradelay, Alex. del ffrith, Simon de Schelfe (? del Dene, or Dean House.) The Greaves were elected as usual—Symon de Totehill for Rastrik, Roger s. John le Milner for Hiprum, John de Sunderland for Sourby, &c. Matilda del Barn, Ric. le Taillour and Will. le Milner for brewing paid 6d. each. Matthew de Totehill breaking the pinfold and taking two oxen out, fined. Alex. late Greave of Rastrik mentioned. Simon de Totehill 6d. for lands in Ouerom from Eva d. Will. le Chapman.

1307. *Court* at Rastrik, die Lune next Feast of Assumption Blessed Mary. Alex. Lucas, seneschal ; John de Stanclyf, Greave for Hiprum. Thos. Miles 2s. to take a toft and 2 acres in N.owram of Henry s. Richard. Reyner the chaplain of Kyrkeleys plaintif *v.* Sus-anna de Brighouses, a shameful dispute about a heifer, letting blood, and using indecent language, though she is defended by all the village of Brighouses, fine 2s. Thos. s. Ric. de Coppelay 1 ac. from Hugh de Stanclyf. Elias de Schelf 2s. to agree with Ric. de Prestlay. Thos. s. Hen. de Coppeley 4s. for lands of Hugh de Suthcliff (? Stanclyf.) Henry s. Thos. del Rode, John s. Alice de Hiprm, Roger de Hiprum, Ric. de Honerum, Will s. Adam, Hudde s. Henry de Stanclyf, Alkoc del Clyf appear in various cases. Ric. s. John del Brickhuses for fell-ing an oak in Bradeley Grange belonging to the Abbot of Fountains' Wood. For wood, fodder, &c., Alice de Coldeley, (pledge, Adam de Coldeley,) Bate de Aldeworth, Henry de Lathe, (Will. Drake, pledge,) Thos. de Coppeley, John s. Jordan, (pledge, Jordan Coleman,) Henry del Rode, (pledge. John de Horton,) and Bate de Halifax.

Turn at Rastrik. Jury—Robert de Stookkis, John de Locwode, Ric. de Hyprm, John de Quernby, Henry de Dalton, Will. de Bradeley, Henry le ffraunceys de Staynland, Adam de Northonru', Jordan del Rokis, Alan de fekisbye, Gilbert le Dyne, Adam de Malleshened and John s. Hugh de Rastrik. Jordan s. Henry removed his boundary marks, fined ½ mark ; Thomas Textor de Hyperum, Simon the Greave, Hugh de Stanclyf and Henry his brother, ditto. Ric. del Wode de Rastrik elected greave. Henry s. Ad. de Hastey 2s. to take 1½ ac. in Camelrode of Peter s. Alice de Hyprum, pleg, Will. de Astey. Ric. del Barn 4s. for 8 acres in Barn from Agnes d. Will. s. John. Thos. s. Ric. de Coppeley 12d. for 1 rod with barn, of Thos. s. Thos. de

Hypm., pleg, John prpos. Hugh s. Hugh de Bothes xxs. vjd. heriot, for his father's lands in Hyperum (graveship, probably Booth's Town.) Hugh s. Henry de Stancliff 2s. for 5 ac. from his father, in Schipden. Thomas the man (serf or slave) of Ric. de Bateley plaintiff, v. John s. Alice de Hyperum respecting nine arrows.

At Halifax Court, next day, the following with numerous others were present, Alcok de Sunderland, Symon the Greave of Hyprm, John de Stanclyf, Matthew de Sunderland, Alcok del Clyf, Ric. de Northorum, Roger the fuller, Walter de Schipley, Ele del Greene, Gilbert del Bothes, Henry s. Ric. de N.owram, Ric. de Thothyll, John del Wode, Roger s. Walter, Ad. Stel, Henry s. Will. Leysing, John s. Hanne s. Ketyl, and Henry formerly greave.

At Brighouse Court, Thomas Undrecliff, Peter s. Adam, and John del Botherode give 20 marks for the Mill at Rastrik (that is, Brighouse,) this year. Agnes d. John del Barn 2s. to inherit 5 acres, her late father's. Jordan s. Thos. de N.owram disputes with John s. Roger de N.owram. Gilbert del Bothes and John le Barn are elected foresters for the woods of Hyperum and Schipden. Jordan del Dene fined ½ mark for breaking the fold and rescuing his strayed beasts. John s. Alote de Hyperm settles his dispute with Thos. the man of Ric. de Bateley. For carrying wood away, Jordan s. Symon, Robt. s. Will. de Schipden, Thos. Bukerel, Hugh de Stanclyf, Roger s. Everilda, 6d. each. Elyas del Grene ¼ mark for leave to take 8 acres in Hypm. of Anabil le Harpr, and Alice and Matilda her sisters : pleg—Symon the greave. John de Stanclyff was elected prepositus for Hipperholme. Hugh del Mire and Yuo de Northwod fined 6d. each for brewing. Richard le Nayler paid 6d. for licence to dig for sea coal this year and make nails. (This is the earliest local instance of coal mining.)

1308. Johan de Danecastre, seneschall. For taking wood, green or dry, and fodder, 2d. to 6d. each, Ralph de Bayrestowe's son, Bate del Bothes, Roger de Brighuse's wife, Ric. Cissor's wife, John del Holewaye, Alcok le Quelewright, Thos. s. Alote, Nalle s. Brown, Will. del Hynganderode, Roger de Brighouses, senior, Will. Scharppe, John del Rhodes, Alex. de Brighuses.

Turn at Rastrik. Jury—Alex. del ffrith, Matth. de Lynthatt, Ric. de Nettleton, John le fflemynge, John Clerk of Hertishead, John de Locwode, Henry le ffrankisse, John del Rode, Henry de Coldelay, Henry Beyontefeild, John de Bristall, Roger de Aula (Hall.) Will. and Robert s. Ade le ffrankisse broke into the house of John del Hirst, burglary. John s. Roger del Clyf drew blood from Roger de Clifton, fined 2d. Will. le Milner's wife, 6d. and Alice le Bagere 4d. for brewing. John s. Adam de Crossland who married Agnes d. Roger de Chepelay, gave 5s. to claim her goods and chattels. Robert the smith (ffaber) of Wollewro, John del Rode and his two sons for contempt of court to answer Roger de Briggehuses, fforester of Hyperum wood, 6s. 8d. There was a Coldley family in Sourby grave, probably a branch of the Hipperholme Coleys.

Court at Rastrik. Johna d. Will Carpenter de Clifton 12d. for ½ bovate and messuage in Rastrik, heriot on her father's death. John s. Walter de N.owram 3s. for ½ bovate, 1 acre, in N. of Matilda d. Hen. de N. Ric. s. Jordan de N. 12d., 3½ acres in N. of Matilda d. Henry. For wood, pannage, &c.—Elias de Skulcotes, Ric. s. Ivon, Alcok le Taillour, Thos. Cocus, Pic. Standwell, Eva del Wolfear, Thos. del Rode and Will. his brother, Thos. del Clyf, Roger del Clifton, Peter del Southclyf, Thos. s. Thos., Henry Horne, John de Astay, Ric. de Hemyngway, John de Bayrestowe, John s. Henry de Bairstowe, Walter de Ouerom, Ric. s. Walter (for thorns), Will. de Heyley (for heybote*), Margaret de Haldeworth, Agnes de Astay and Thos. s. Thos. de Hemyngway, 2d. to 6d. The Abbot and Convent of Fountains were ordered to repair the bridge of Bradelay. Will. de Sonderland gave 10s. for leave to take 17 acres and edifice in Stayncliffe field of Sir Matthew,(Stayncliff),Rector of the Church of Sandale. Will. del Bothes, fforester in Hyperm Wood, fined xs. for not presenting that he had cut 12 oaks. Ric. s. Judde de Halifax took ¼ acre in N.owram for 13 years of Ric. s. Adam. For cutting wood, &c.—Will. Swyer of Hipperom, Roger del Cliff, Jordan de Haddegreues, Thos. de Bellehouses, John s. Walter de Ouerom, Roger de Brighuses, Thos. del Rode, Hen. le Pinder, Henry del Northclif, Will. de Bayrestowe, Thos. del Northend de Ourum, 3d. to 6d.

Turn at Rastrik. Jury—Alex. del ffrith, John le ffleming de Dalton, Thos. ffrankisse de Dalton, John de Locwode, junr., Roger de la Sale, Louecok de Nettleton, John Clerk de Hertesheued, Henry de Coldeley, John de Bristall, John del Rode, John de Sunderland, Thos. del Wytewode. Robt. le Smith of Wollewro drew blood from Roger de Brighuses, junr., fined 12d. The wives of Ric. le Taillour, Roger de Brighuses, senr., and Geppe ffoune for brewing, 6d. each. Sir Hugh de Eland is dead; cried in the court.

Court at Rastrik. Gilbert de Halifax gave 2s. to take 3 acres in Roostorth which Sir Will. the chaplain formerly held. Agnes d. Roger de Chepelay gave 6s. 8d. for leave to marry as she pleased. Simon del Dene is elected greave for Hyprm, and Henry s. John de Rastrik for Rastrik greaveship. Thos. s. Cecil del Holgate 2s. for 4 ac. in le Blacker of Sir Ric. le Chaplain. Henry s. Elie de Rastrik 12d. for 3 acres in Rastrik of Avic d. Richard. John s. Ric. de Rastrik 6d. for 1 acre of the same. Will. Swaype for not attending the court, 6d. Will. ffaber (Smith) de Clifton, cutting greenwood, 6d.; Thos. le Webbester, 6d.; Michael de Bergheye for thorns 6d.; John s. Will. de Ouenden, 1 oak, 2s.; Will. ffox de Ouenden, John Greteword, Ric. s. Walter de Ourum, Ric. s. Jordan, John de Bristall, John le Pynder, Walter de Ourum, Roger de Northclyf, Henry del Rode, Will. Swyer, John del Rode and Thos. his son, Will. Batte, Robert ffabro de Wolwro, Gilbert Bridde, Ric. le Dy'ker, Alcok le Taillour, Galfri le Colier, Eva del Wolfker, John de Bairstowe, John s. Radulph, for green or dry wood, feeding pigs, sheep or cows. Roger of Brighouses, junr.,

* Mending hedges.

gave 18d. to have leave to bestow his daughters Isabel and Cecila in marriage. Will. le Milner de Brighuses and Henry Abraam farm Rastrik Mill this year for x*li*. xijs. iij*d*. ; Will. del Bothes and Alex. del ffrith, bondsmen. Walter de Adderisgate and Simon del Dene farm Chepeden (Shipden) Mill, pertaining to Rastrik Mill.

1311. John de Donecastre, seneschal. K. Edw. s. K. Edw. 5th year. Walter de Ourum 12d. for marriage right of his daughter Matilda.

Court at Rastrik. Will. s. Yuonis, dispute about ½ bovate in Hyprm grave with John the Milner. Mathew s. Bate del Clyf 12d. to inherit 3 acres on his father's death. Matthew de Totehill 2s. for his daughter Alice's marriage rights. John del Holeway elected Hipp. greave, and Alex. del Wodehouses, for Rastrik. Rastrik Mill leased to Matthew de Totehill and Roger de Clifton for 20 marks ; pledges, Simon del Dene, Will. del Bothes, Hen. de Coldeley, and Alex. del Wodehouses. Schepdene Mill let to Simon del Dene.

Turn at Rastrik same day. Jury—Thos. de Dalton, John s. John de Locwod. J. de Nettelton, John del Rodes, John Clerk de Hertesheued, Thos. de Whytewode, Henry de Coldelay, John de Bristall, Thos. de Bosco (Wood), Will. s. Annabelle, Ric. del Hely, Ric. de Crosseland. John s. Walter de N.owram drew blood from Walter s. Elie, fined 12d. Adam s. John de Helagh de Mirfield drew blood from Thomas Clerk of Eland, therefore attached. Will. del Bothe's wife drew blood from Beatrix, wife of Alex. le Waynwrth, fined 12d. Will. de Sunderland 5s. for 14 acres and edifice in Hyprum (graveship) from John s. John le Swyer and Matilda his wife. Hugh de Bothomley, Rastrik graveship, mentioned. Hugh de Rachedale and Matilda his wife paid 6s. heriot for 1¼ bov. and edifice ; her father, Walter s. Elie de Ourom, having died. Ivo s. Will. de Saltonstall 12d. heriot 2 bovates and edifice at Saltonstall on his father's death. Matth. s. Ric. de Bosco, Hiperom graveship, mentioned. Matthew de Totehill, 12d. ; Will. del Castell de Tothill 12d. for cutting greenwood ; Thos. de Astay, Alex. del Brighuses, John de Schepley, Isabell Tilly, Agnes widow of Astay, Henry del Broke, Jordan del Broc, Robt. del Dene, Will Stirk, 2d. each, fodder, &c. Will. de Adderichgate and Alice his wife dispute with Adam de Stayncliff. Henry s. Peter the greave of Rastrik disputes with Auicia d. Thos. s. Ivonis.

Turn at Brighous. Note that the previous half-yearly turn is said to have been at Rastrick, but they both refer to the usual place at Brighouse. Jury—Alex. del ffrith, John s. John de Locwod, John s. Adam de Locwode. Mr. Thos. de Dalton, John the clerk of Hertesheued, Henry de Coldelay, John del Rode, Roger de Aula (Hall), John de Birstall, Thos. de ffekesbye, Robert de Risseworth, Will. Swyer. For brewing, Agnes wife of Ric. de Shelf, Annabil d. Eve de Schelf, and Matilda, widow, 6d. each. Adam de Staincliff's wife drew blood from Adam del Hingandrode, John del Holway from Robert s. Xpiane, Will. s. John from Hugh and Robt. sons of John, 12d. fines. Hugh s. Dobbe de Presteley assaults Ric. s. Iuon de Prestlay, fined 40d., and

Hipprom township for concealing it, 6s. 8d. Simon del Dene not attending court, fined 6d. Roger de Clifton had an oaken scuatn' in his custody, as wayf. The forester states that Cecilie widow of Roger de Brighouses, junr., had the same in Hyperom wood. Symon de Totehill, John le Pinder, Ric. s. Walter and John his brother, John s. William, Thos. Poyde, Will. de Hingandrode, Thos. s. Thos., Will. s. Peter, also mentioned. Thomas Textor of Hiprm gave 6d. for his daughter Alice's marriage-right. For dry wood, fodder, &c., Roger de Brighuses, senr., the wife of Roger de B. junr., Ric. Tyngel, Henry de la Rode, &c. Ric. s. Jordan s. Thos. de N.owram 3s. 4d. for 14 acres new land in Hyprum (11 at Hasilhurst, 3 at Stryndes.) Juliana widow of Walter de Northourum paid 12d. for her marriage right. Robert le Yungr 12d. for 1 acre new land in Hyprum wood. In Sourby grave, John le Walker de Brighouse and Juliana his wife paid 2s. to take 4 acres in Sourby of Robt. s. Roger de Sourby. Henry s. Richd. de Totehill and Bate le Lister de Halifax mentioned. Will. de Adrerichegate and Alice his wife dispute about ½ acre with Adam de Stancliffe, which Sir Matthew de Stayncliffe, brother of said Adam, (p.57,) gave to Alice for life.

Court at ·Rastrick, die Mercure px post festum Sci. Barnabs. Apli. Bate del Bothes 2s. for his daughter Margaret's marriage right. Will s. Bateman de Halifax 18d. for 1 acre in N.owram of Gilbert s. Henry de Halfax. Roger s. Matthew de Wodehouses 2s. heriot, for 6 acres in Wodehouses, his father being dead. John s. Will. Drake, Hyprm graveship. John le Cowhird de Bradley gave 5s. to marry Auicia d. Thos. s. Iuonis. Will. de Retford and Annabil his wife, obtained 4 acres in Prestlay, Hyperum graveship, on the death of Jordan del Broke, uncle of Annabil: Jordan's mother was called Eva. Henry s. Wymark and Thomas his brother, Thos. del Rokes, Hugh de Prestlay, Thos. s. Alot, &c.—a special jury. John s. Henry le Pinder 6d. for 1 rod in Hyprm from Adam s. Henry. Henry de Southcliff 6d., ½ acre in Hyprm from Alex. le Waynwrith. Ric. s. Yuonis de Prestlay had trouble about a thrave of oats. John de Warrena was parson of Dewsbury Church, and Mr. Robt. was parson of [Kirk] Birton Church. John s. Ric. s. Henry de Rastrik 2s. to take 4 ac. ½ rod in Rastrik of Emma de Castro. The agistment of pigs in Hyperom wood brought in 10s. 4d. incusetor; 3s. 11d. forinsecor, (from without), including John del Rode, Thos. s. Thos. de Hiprm, John s. Henry le Pynder, Thos. and John del Cliff, John del Wro, Will. del Rode. Agnes widow de Astay, Widdow de Hekkedene, Bate del Bothes, Henry the Smith, Will. de Bayrstow, Henry de Bothemley, Roger de Brighouses, senr., Wife of Roger de B. junr., Henry Milner, John de Schepeley, Henry del Rode, Will. s. Peter, Alcok de Ourum, Will. s. Adam, Thos. s. Alot, Adam del Bothe, Will. s. Bateman, Will. Hareye, John de Bayrestow, Elyas Waynwright, Jordan de Hiprom, Thos. del Broke de Prestley, Adam del Bothes, Will. del Bothes, John s. Rad. de Bairstowe, Peter del Clogh, Matilda d. Adam, Roger del Northclyff, Adam del Broke.

1312. Cecilia wid. Roger de Brighus junr., Robt de Rysseworth,
Will. del Lee. Ric. de ffekisby, Robert s. Xpiane de N'ourum, John s.
Alex. de Sunderland, John and Henry le Pynder, Alex. de Brighus,
Henry s. Wymark del Broke, Will. s. Peter, Thos. s. Jordan de Rokes,
mentioned. John s. Walter de N.'owram elected greave of Hyprm,
but paid the fine; Symon atte Dene elected. Alex. s. Walter de
Sonderland is dead, his lands are in the hands of the lord. Matilda
and Alice, daughters of John de Sunderland, gave 5s. for their marriage rights: pledge—John their father, and Will. de Sunderland.

Court at Brighouses, feast of St. Dunstan. Symon le Toller 12d.
for 4 acres in Hiprom of Sir Ric. chaplain. Ric. s. Henry le Hopper
land in Prestley, his mother, Alice, having died. Thos. de Totehill
disputes with John s. Henry de ffekesbye about le Oldroide in ffekesbye.
A wayf was in the custody of Alex. of Woodhouse the Rastrick greave.
John the Milner of the Bothes gave 6d. for 1 acre in le Bothes, from
Cecilia d. Elyot de Werlilly. John de Holway 2s. for land in Holkan-
leghes. Rastrik mill, custodians—Roger del Brighuses, senr., Roger
de Clifton, John de Schepeley, Peter de Suthclyf, Thos. s. Thos.,
Will. del Bothes, John de la Botherode, Matthew de Totehill, John de
Rastrick, Will. del Wodehouse, &c. Schypden mill, custodians—Will.
de Sunderland, Symon del Dene, Walter de Aderychegate and John
de Sunderland. Henry de Coppeley elected greave of Hiperom.

Turn at Brighouses. Jury—same persons as before nearly.

In 1314, a very careful survey of the Manor was made. Rents and
services due to Wakefield Lord (Free soccage) from *Fekisbye*—William
fil Tho. de Totehill 4s., Peter fil Will. 3s., Joworthe relict of Robert
3d., Hen. fil Constan 14d., Barnard 18d., Tho. fil Adam 2s,, Rob. fil
Richard 21d., Alan fil Alan 20d., John fil (*i.e.* son of) Rob. 3s.

Rastricke—Will. fil Annabel 5s. 3d., Will. fil Walter, 1d. ob.,
Alexander de Rastricke 2d.

Brighouse—Hugh de Totehill 3s. 3d., Tho. del Roods 18d.

Hipperholm—the free tenants there and in Prestley 3s., Henry de
Northend 4s. 3d., Rich. del Rooks 4s. 1d. ob., Hugh de Prestley, 6d.,
Henry de Copley 2s., Elias de Shelfe 4d. ob., Thos. del Brook 15d.,
Alice de Coldeley 15d.. Thos. de Rookes 3s. 6d., Elias del Brooke 7d. ob.

In *Rastricke*, John del Okes for a tenement and one bovate (oxgang)
of land, 4d. Alex. del Okes, one tenement and 8 acres, 1d., Rich. fil
Maud, 5 acres, 2d. ob., for free lands.

Under the graveship of Fekesbye and Rastricke—Peter fil Will.,
one ten., 5 acres, called bordelands, for homage, fealty, and 3s. yearly.
John fil Rob. one ten. 2 bovates, 3 acres, ditto. Rob. fil Ric. one ten.
one bov. for homage, fealty and 21d. Tho. fil Adam for hom. fealty
and 2s. Alan fil Alan one ten. 2 bov. for hom. fealty and 20d.
Bernard one ten. 1 bov. for hom. feal. and 18d. Henry fil Constance
½ bov. for h. f. 13d. ob. Jowet half tenement, ½ bov. for h. f. 3d. (See
Joworthe, above.) All these were due at Michaelmas, Purification,
and Pentecost, and every one who held the said eight bovates was to
give for a bovate and take, 4½d. at St. Andrew's feast. The said tenants

paid 8d. yearly for two ploughs to plough the bovates, in the time of spring, and if they had more they paid 4d. for every plough, except Peter fil Will. who paid nothing. The above and all other householders who kept fires in the half of the vill of Fekisby gave 3d. each for reaping at Assump. V. Mary, except Peter. There were then five houses which had fires; if they increased they were to pay more at the lord's will. From *Fekisby* wastes, were granted to Richd. fil Thos. 4 acres for 16d., Hen. fil Tho., 4 ac. 12d., Hen. fil Will. 3 ac. 12d., Ric. de Anneley, 4½ ac. 18d., Thos. fil John, 5 ac. 20d., Henry de Totehill, 2 ac. 8d., Will. fil Stephen, 2 ac. 8d., Tho. atWood, 2 ac. 8d., Eve wife of Hugh, 3 ac. 12d., Beatrix filia Tho. 3 ac. 12d., Tho. de ye Litherigg ½ ac. 3d., due as above. The NATIVI in *Rastrick* were, Adam fil Yuon, who held one tenement, ½ bov. 10 ac. for 6s. 4d., and repair of Wakefield mill dam. Roger fil Matthew one ten. ½ bov. 6 acres, 3s., for take 14d., and repair of said dam. Will. de Wodehowses one ten. ½ bov. for 2s. for take 2d. and repair of dam, also for 12 acres he paid 4s. Roger de Wodhous one ten. 5 acres for 19d. and for take 5d. Beatrix wife of Alan, ten. ¼ bov., 12 ac. for 7s. and repair of dam. Matthew fil Rich. ten. ½ bov. 10 ac. 1 rod for 6s. 5d. for take 12d. and dam. Matthew de Totehill ten. ½ bov. and ¼ bov. &c. 9s. 11d. and dam. Will. de Totehill ten. ¼ bov. 3 ac. 2s., Thos. del Okes ten. ½ bov. 12½ ac. 16s. 2d. and dam. John Seele ten. ¼ bov. 7 ac. 4s. 4d. Hen. fil Modest ten. 6 ac. 2s. John de Botherod ten. ½ bov. ¼ bov. 8 ac. for 6s. 8d. and to reap one day and plow as he plowed his own land or give 4d. for a whole plough, 2d. for half, and repair said dam. John Coward ten. ½ bov. 6 ac. for 6s. shall reap to the value of a penny, and repair the dam. John fil Alexander ten. ½ bov. 6 ac. for 5s. 5d. and dam. Henry fil John ten. ½ bov. ¼ bov. 17 ac. 8s. 9d. ob. qa. and dam. Adam . . ten. 9 ac. 1 rod and half for 3s. 4d. Will. fil Henry ten. 8 ac. 2s. 6d. qa. and 1d. reaping. Tho. de Rodes ten. ¼ bov. 6 ac. 3s. 4d. ob., one penny reaping, and dam. Will. fil Hugh 4 ac. 15d. John fil Ric. ten. ½ bov. 10½ ac. 5s. 6d., 1d. reaping, dam. Peter fil Henry, ten. 5½ ac. 18d., 1d. reaping. Margery filia Yuon, ten. ½ ac. 1 rd. 4d. Henry fil Peter, ten. ½ bov. 8 ac. 4s. 1d., dam. John fil Ric. ten. ¼ bov. 1 ac. 3s. 6d. and dam. Will. fil Adam 3 ac., 9d. Roger fil Matthew half of 9 ac., 1d. ob. Alex. Cissor 2 ac. ¼ rod, 9d. John fil Roger 4 ac. 13d. Henry fil Will. 4 ac. 12d. ob. Alex. de Brighouse 1 ac. ½ rd., 7d. ob. John de Shepele 10 ac., 3s. 4d. Roger de Brighowse, senr., 1½ ac., 16d. Peter de Sowtcliff, 4 ac. ½ rd., 16d. ob. Symon de Shipeden, 1 ac. 4d. The FREE TENANTS were, John del Okes, one toft, 1 bov. for 4d., and for plowing, 4d. if he have ale or plough, if not he shall pay nothing, and for reaping, 3d. Alex. de Okes, ten., 8 ac., 1d., reaping, 3d. Ric. fil Maud, 5 ac., 2d. ob. All the nativi shall repair the Wakefield mill dam, and pay marchet* money for said bovates and grind all their corn at the mill of Rastrick (Brighouse mill), and pay for take 6s. 8d.

* The ransom paid by a villein and in some places by a freeman on the marriage of his daughter, grand-daughter or sister.

In the graveship of *Hipperholme*, Tho. s. Thos. was to pay 8d. for the take of hogs for one bovate, for grinding malt 2s. for other lands to plough with 4 oxen or pay 2d. and reap, or pay 1d., and assist the grave in driving cattle taken in making distress throughout the whole graveship, to Wakefield, as often as required by the grave. Several others were bound in like manner, and in case of refusal, fined. Some of the Hipperholm free tenants were bound to give to the lord 4d. for a whole plough, and for as many beasts as they should plough with, two oxen in a yoke, 1d., and for reaping 1d. The pannage* of Hipperholm 4 pounds "comunibus annis," and 4s. 6d. for take, 3s. 8d. for plough work, 2s. for grinding, 3d. for thakstones from Thos. del Northend, 2s. 9d. for reaping, 100s. for court perquisites. Sir John Eland received yearly 19s. 1d. from Will. de Sunderlande, 12s. 10d. from John de Sunderlande, 3s. from Symon de Shipeden, and 6d. from Tho. Bland. These resided in the Northowram portion of Hipperholme graveship. The repairing of the Wakefield mill dam indicated that the land was ancient copyhold or oxgang (bovate) land, whilst newer copyholders were free from it. The former were probably as old as Saxon times. In Rastrick and Hipperholme graveships, 8 bovates, 90½ acres, were so charged; whilst in the time of Elizabeth it had become 19¾ bovates in Hipperholme and 9 in Rastrick, each bovate then paying half-yearly 7s. From 4d. to 6d. per acre with certain services had to be paid by copyholders as rent.

1314. The rolls also record a dispute between Alice de Skrevyn the prioress of Kirkeley and Richard the chaplain of Hertesheued about taking her cattle. Ric. s. Ric, de Saltonstall gave 20s. to take 2½ bovates and edifice in Saltonstall, his father being dead. Jordan de Hiprum 3s. for 6 acres and edifice in Hyperum of Will s. John de Hiperum. Ingolard the vicar of Halifax had a quarrel with John de Bollynges and Alice his wife for detaining a gold ring. John s. Adam de Whithill de N.ourum paid 4s. heriot for 8 acres and edifice in N. his father being dead. Will. del Bothes by Thos. de Witlay his attorney, plaintiff, against Ric. s. Yuon; the latter not appearing was attached. John s. Henry de ffekesby *v.* Alex. del Brighous. Ric. s. Jordan de N.orum *v.* Thos. s. Thos. de Hiprum; they are agreed. John de Sonderland, Hiprum greave, for a false presentment and concealment fined 12d. Disputes—Hen. s. John de Rastrik *v.* Ric. s. Jordan de N'owram; Hugh de Totehill *v.* John s. Henry de ffekisby; Will. Milner de Brighus *v.* Beatrix wife of Alex. de Brighus; John s. Roger del Brighous *v.* Hugh s. Isabel de Lynley.

1314. *Court* at Rastrik. Henry de Saltonstall 20s. for 18 acres and edifice in N.owram from Matth. s. Ric. atte Wode. Thos. de Waddesworth, clerk, 12d. to take lands at Blacker of Sir Ric. de Middelton, chaplain. Henry s. Thos. de ffikisby ingress to 3 acres native land from Alice d. Eue de ffekisby. Ric. s. Matilda de Rastrik obtained a toft and house in R. in the time of Sir John de Doncastre.

---

* Pannage, the feeding of swine in the woods.

Turn, same day. Jury—John de Hertesheued clerk, John de la Rode de Hiprm, Henry de Coldley, Will le Squier de Hiprm, Thos. de ffikisbye, Roger del Hagh, Alex. del ffrith, John filemyng de Dalton, Thos. de Dalton, — ffrankisse, Ivo de Nettelton, John s. John de Lokwod. Ralph s. Vicar de Birstall stole an ox from Robt. de Russcheworth, one from Thos. de Burgh, one from Thos. del Whythill; a cow from Alice sister of Ric. le Bagger de N.owram. The house of Will. s. Adam de Hiperum entered by burglars. John de Schepdene drew blood from Annabil wife of Thos. de Schepden. John s. Roger del Clif de Hiprum a native under the lord, held a tenement and 6 acres. Will. de Sunderland took 12 acres of Matilda his sister. Alex. de Brighous paid 6s. 8d., for 1 bovate and edifice in Rastrik from John s. Ric. for 20 years. In the lord's hands 3 acres in ffikesby of native land, lately held by Hen. s. Thos. de ff. John de Astay held 3 acres native land in Hyp. grave, pledged to build a house. John ffox wrought the forge in Hyperum wood, released it for 9s. Alan Yonghare also had a forge there. Peter s. Henry de la Croiz (*i.e.* Rode)* de Rastrik gave 40d. heriot, 5 acres and edifice, on his father's death. Thos. s. John Reyner paid 2s. heriot for 4 acres in ffikesbye his father, John, being dead. Beatrix de Tothill 40d. to take 16 acres and edifice in Brighous of John de Schepelay.

Turn at Rastric. Jurors—John de Quernby, Thos. de Totehill, John le ffilemyng de Clifton, John le ffileming de Dalton, Alex. del ffrith, John Clerk de Hertesheued, Will de Sunderland, John del Rode, Thos. del Wode de ffekesby, Matthew de Bosco (Wood) de Tothill, John s. Will. de Staynland. The abbot of ffountains to repair Bradley bridge. Roger de Brighouse late greave for Hiperum; Will. de Sunderland, elected. Alex. Cissore (*i.e.* le Taillour) de Brighous, and Cissota widow del Briggehous mentioned. Adam del Wod, Hyprm graveship, is dead.

The mere lists of names of those who took wood, or brewed ale without the taster's sanction we now omit, though exceedingly valuable in tracing pedigrees.

* Proving the existence of the Cross at Rastrick.

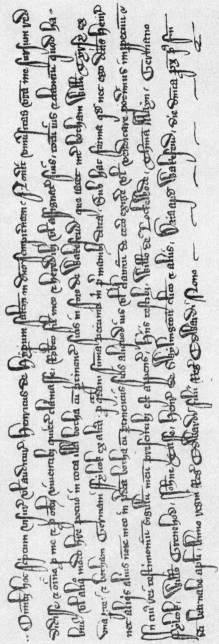

In 1316 Henry de Walda being seneschal, Robt. s. Henry de Hiperum held a booth in Wakefield market.

Long before this date the Hipperholmes had become an important family in Lower Calderdale, and continued to be great men at the Wakefield courts, but their history lies outside our province. The facsimile deed herewith will serve as a specimen of the writing in 1316. It is a quit claim from Henry de Hyprum to his son Robert of a booth in Wakefield Market between the booths of William Tyrsy and German Fylcok. Witnesses, Will. de Lockewode, Thomas Allayn, &c.

Earlier notices of a Henry de Hyperum are:—Henry de Hyperum held 8 bovates with 40/- a year in (Cleck)heton & Ric. de Thornhill 2 bovates there under Sir John de Longevillers, who died in 1254.

Lands of John de Sothill and John de Heton 1266: Jury on Inquisition at their death included Ric. de Hiperum and Thos. Atwell de Hiperum, several Ardeslaws, &c. The lands were in Halifax parish partly, but not in Hipperholme.

1322. *Court* at Brighous. Robert de Risscheworth *v.* Adam Prestman de Eland. Will s. Henry de Goddelay had lands in Schipeden, and John le Webbester a messuage in Hiprm. Ric. de Thorp, Will. Northend formerly forester, John s. Gilbert Bridde, Will de Sunderland, Henry de la Rode pastured two oxen each on waste. Juliana widow Thos. de

Whitehill* drew blood from John Drake. Will. s. Symon Juddeson
of Schelf is an early instance of fixed sirename. Thos. Talvate had a
dispute with Thos. de Totehill about a house at ffekisby. Roger de
Clifton and Thos. his son took 3 acres in Hyperum grave.

1324. Richard de Selby the chaplain of Hertishead, Thos. de
Lightrigge and Will. Pek de Hyprum tenants. Matthew de Totehill
gave 2s. for marriage right of his daughter Beatrix. The town of
Hiperum not being represented at the court, fined.

Turn at Brighouse. Will. de Sunderland took 12 acres of Alice wid.
Matthew de Schepden. Adam s. Elyas and Thos. perpetual vicar of
Halifax held a messuage and bovate in le Bothes (Boothtown ?). Adam
by the Broke held 13 acres in Rastrik grave. John s. Walter de Ad-
richegate paid 2s. heriot for messuage and 7 acres on his father's death.
Henry s. Hugh de Bothomley held lands in Scamonden greaveship.
Peter de Southclife in Hiperum 5 acres to Adam his son. John atte
Northend took 1 rod waste in N'owm, John le Pynder 3 rods in
Hiperum. John of Hiprum hirst (wood) held Schipdene mill. John
del Cliff took 4 acres of waste for 12 years, lately held by Magota
Maure. Some were fined for fishing in Kelder (Calder) without licence;
Annabel Badger for mixing dust with flour, fined.

1325. In Sourby courts, Matilda de Horton, Galfri de Crosselegh,
Hugh de Hillylee regularly appeared.

Court at Rastrik. Adam s. Henry de Hyperum held mess. and
bovate. Will. the Milner de Halifax 6d. 1 rod waste at Blackerheued.
Juliana d. Henry held lands in Rastrik, Will de Sunderland in le
Bothes; Will. de Clayton and Eva his wife 5 acres in Hyp. grave,
lately Adam s. Thos. del Northend's; Roger de Clifton 1 acre in
Hyprm which Adam s. Roger de Brighouse, junr., held; Thos. Baude
1 acre in Brighous. Thos. del Okys was elected prepositus for
Rastrick.

1326. Amongst the chief tenants were Elena de Rastrik, Adam
de Stayncliff, Will de Totehill. To shew the amplitude of these rolls
and the impossibility of giving all the names here, the following notes
are taken from this year's roll.

1326. R. E. fil R. E. xx°· [Copied as a specimen of the Rolls.]

HIPN—Johne de Shepley p. esch. ij d. Rogs. de Brighous p. eodm
iij d. Johne Steuen p. eode ij d. Rico del Hole p. eode ij d. Thoma
del Cliff p. eodm j d. Thoma fil Henr. del Rode p. collect gland iij d.
Sum xiij d.

SOURBI—Wills. de Wolronwal p. esch. best. pl. Rob. freis vjd. Wills.
de Stainland p. esch. bid+ iijd. Hug fil Hug de Northland p. esch. equi.
pleg Petre de Barkesland iijd. Johe del ffrith p. eode i d. Henr. del
Lone p. eode vi d. Johne de Lightesles p. eodm. ii d. Robto. de
Bentelcyroide p. eod. ij d.

HIPN—Ricus del Thorp defend vers⁸ Johem fil Jordan de plito capt
vns vacc.‡ p. Thom. de Totehill pleg. Ada de Heley, js. Et quia deus

* The Whittells of Elland sprang from this family. † Bidens, sheep. ‡ Vacc, cow.
F.

Johes op se Ids dats est dies &c.   Et dcus Johnes po lo suo Adam de Sourbi.

HIPN—Cecil fil Mathi de Sheppeden queres op se vers. Willm de Sondreland de plito tre.   Inquis.

HYPN—Adam del Northende ven in cure & srsu redd in mans dm trtia pte vns mes. & trtia pte vns bouat tre cu p'tinent in Le Bothes in pptura de Hypn que concisse snt. Johi Sutori ten sibi & h. suis p. tota vita Eue vxis Willi de Caiton sedm cons. maner &c.   Et des John dat fine dno. p ingress,   xij d.

HYPN—John fil Rog. de Brighous redd in mans. dm medietate uns. mes & v acras tre cu ptm in Hypn que concisse snt Johi fil Rogi, junior, ten s. & hed suis sedm cons. maner.   Ingress.   ij s. vj d.

HYPN—Willms fil Rogi de Clifton dat dno xijd. p. lic. cap. vna acra noue tre.   xij d.   redd per. anm. iij d.

Sum iiijs. vjd. . . . . de novus redd p. anm. iijd.

SOURBI—For Esch. id. to vid. each.   John le Piper, &c.

Robt. del Okes, Ric. fil Ade de Miggelay, Ric. fil Elia de Hepton-stall, Willm fil Hugon de Heptonstall, John de Hadreshelf, Robt. de Wolronwall, Henre de Holgate, Adam de Kirkeshagh, John de Hipu'hirst, John Culpon, Adam fil Elie, Hugon de Hilelegh, Hug. de Totehill, Adam fil Hugon, Henr. del Bancke.

RASTRIK.—Adam fil Willi quer de Wills del Hill de plito debi, pleg. de ps Thom. de Scamenden.   Re-summoned.

HOLN[OR BURTON].—Jury were Johnes de Shepeley, Adm. de Heley, Willms de Rieley, Ricus de Thornteley, Robtus de Wolwro, Ricus de Birton, Ricus de Heppeworth, Adam Kenward, Adam del Green, Ricus del Both, Henr. Wade & Henre del Lee.

A WAKEFIELD JURY.—Robtus de Stodeley, Henre de Chevet, Thomas Gates, Rads de Kerlinghou, Johnes fil Rici de Osset, Johnes Pykerd Adam de Wodesom, Germ. Cay, Johnes de ffery, Robtus Ilhore, Johnes Dade & Henr. Ganton.

HALIFAX CURE xxvij Octr.

Thomas del Leghrode quer. op se vers. Adam Migge de Warouley, Thomas del Bothem dat iiijs for 2 acres new land in Warouley, xij rent. Ricus Alotson dat xijd. for 1 acre in Sourbi, 6d. p. an.   Thos. s. Henry de Rieuburnden ijs. vjd. heriot mes. v. acres in Sourbi. Adam del Tounende de Miggeley p. Willm fil Hugon ppm. redd in mans dm v acres in Sourbi que comisse snt Thom. fil Will de Saltonstall. Ingress ii s. vid.

Ricus de Loddyngden dat vs. for iiij acras i rod noue tre in le Brodehirst, xxvd. p. anm.

Will. fil Hug. de Warouley dat xii for i acram new land in Warlou-ley, rent 6d., John fil Elie de Warlouley ijs. vid. ij acr. new land in Warlouly rent xiid., John de Elsletburgh 2/6 for 2½ ac. noue tre in Sourbi rent xvd., Adam fil Roger & John frater redd ij acres in Sourbi to John de Elsletburgh. Robtus fil John de Cockecroft redd i ac in Stanyden to Robt fil Wymarke, Robtus fil John de Cockecroft redd iii ac. in Stanyden to Ad fil Will de Northland, Ada fil Roger &

John frater redd iiij acres Sourbi to Wm. del Loyne, Will fil Jordan de Skercote dat xij d ½ acre new land in Warlouley, rent 3d., Willms Mahaud dat xii d. ½ ac. new land in Warlouley rent 3d. p. an., Adam fil Alex 2/- for 1 ac. 1 rd. new land in Warlouley rent 7d., Robt. de Sothill redd 4½ acres 1 rod in Warlouley to John Tailliour ingr 3/-, Adam de Couentre elects. est pptus de Sourbi, & firm molend de Sourbi. Ivo de Saltonstall quers petit vers. Willm Molend de Warlouley, Adam fil Roger redd iij ac. Sourbi to Thom. fil juliane Wade.

TURNUS HALIFAX.—Jury, Ricus de Waddesworth, Thoms. fil Rici, Robtus de Sourbi, Ivo de Saltonstall, Henr. de Holgate, Johnes de Rediker, Willms del Ryding, Johnes de Northland, Johnes fil Robi de Shesewell, Willms del Bothem, Galfrs de Stodeley & Thomas de Sothill.

Ux Bate Tinctoris* de Halifax braciauit contr. assim mia xii d. ux Rog. Spilwode, vx Alex. de Hynggandrode, Matilda que sunt vx Johis Kypas, all for brewing, xii d. each. Willm *strens* vicar txt sangne de (drew blood from) Rog. Spilwod, xii d. & de vx Rog. Spilwode xii d.

Vx Rog. Spilwode txit sangne de Juliana fil Thome fil Cecil, vid. & reverse vi d. John fil Ric de Waddesworth txt sang. de Thom. Culpon xii d. Margia vx Will fil Hugon leuauit vthesur iniste (raised false hue and cry) sup Hugone Wade xii d. Ric fil Thme de Ouenden txt sang, de Thom fil Alex. xii d.

Cure tenta apud Brighous die martis xxviij° d Octobr Anno rre E. ie fil R. E. xx°.

RASTRIK ad cure de Wak. resum.—Adam fil Willi quer de Willmo del Hill de plito debi, pleg. deps Thom de Scamenden Et qa testat est p. pptm de Rastrik cd dcus Willms sum est & no ven ids pre est qd resum qd sit ad pxm Cure de Wakefeld.

HYPN. Inquisic. iiis. iiijd.—Alicia fil Mathi de Totehill quera de Willms de Sondreland de plito tre pleg deps Matho de Totehill & dat dno iijs. iiijd. p. inquis xxiiij hud ad coninicend inquisicoem xij pns capt. Willms de Halifax Molend redd in mans dm diam acram tre cu ptinent in Northouru que comiss est Bate de Halifax Tinctori* tened sibi et hed. suis scdm cons. maner Et dcus Bate fin. p. ingressu vid.

RASTRIK—Thomas fil Willi de ffekesbi dat dno p. releuio duos mesuag & duas bouatas tre in villa de ffekesbi iijs. iiijd. Thoms fil Rogi del Green redd in mans dm. x acras diam acre & duas ptes vns rode tre cu' ptm in Rastrik Que comisse snt Henrico del Okes ad tm. x anos. ten. sibi & hed. suis sdm. cons. maner ad dem tm x anos. Et dcus Henre fin dno p. ingressu xvjd. quia tra debit est & relicta.

Agnes ux Joh fil Henr. de ffekesbi quer de Henr. le Waynwright de plito debi es qd iniuste detinet sibi viijs. quos Henr. pptus, pat. de. Henr. le Waynwright eus hes. & executor ipe est cepit p. manus Thme Alayn balli libe cure de Wakefeld ad differend dce Agnet vt dicit Et Ido cons est qd dca Agn. recupet de dco Henr. Le Waynwright vs. & xd. et dcus Henricus in mia p. fals. detencone, iiijd.

---

* Bate the Lister, or Dyer, was ancestor of the Listers of Shibden.

Hypn—Willms Peck redd in mans dm. vnn mes & x acras tre cu ptm in Brighous Que comisse snt. Johi fil Rogi de Brighous tenend sibi & hed. suis scdm cons. maner Et dcus Johnes fm p. ingressu vi s. viij d.

Villata de Shelf p. contempt quia noluerut eligie sibi constabulare io in mia xijd.

Tra Sesira. Pro est sesire in mans. dm. tciam pte onn tras & tenemens que fuert Ade del Bothe in Northouru p. eo. qd Johnes Sutor emit dcam tcia pte & no' cepit eam in cure & vestura asportavit de dca terra.

Sm. hus. Cure xvijs. ijd. Quibz—Sup. Suiente iii s. iiij d ; Sup pptm de Hypn. xj s. vj d. ; Sup pptm de Rastrik ij s. iiij d.

Turns. Vicecomit tentus ibidem eodem die Anno predco.

xij. Jurat. Henr. de Coldley, Willms de Lockewod, Ricus Couhird, Johnes de Birstall, Thms de Whtewod, Willms de Whitacres, Johnes de Shepden, Ricus de Coluirsley, Johnes de Barkesey, Ricus del Rokes, Ada' de Quernebi et Johnes fil Willi.

Rastrik—Willms del Hill de Berkesland no ven ad turn. ido in mia xijd. Thomas fil Hugon trxt. sangne de Thoma de Wodheued io in mia xijd. Thomas de Wodheued txt. sang. de Thom fil Hugon io in mia xijd.

Hipn—Thomas Molend de Shepden txt. sangne de Thoma Drake io in mia ijs. Johnes Drake txt. sangne de Johne Molend ido in mia xijd. Johnes fil Johis Molend pcussit Thom Drake cu sagitt. & txt. sangne ido in mia ijs.

Smens. Ricus de Skurveton, Idonia vx eius & Wills fil eiusde' Rici occidert felouit Johem de Wraggebi & dimerscrut eum & boua eius ad valent xls. felouit asportauert ido capiat.

Hypn—Johnes de Brighous txt. sang. de Johne de Skercotes io in mia xijd. Thom. le Waynwright txt. sangne de Johne de Brighous io in mia xijd. Johnes Clareson txt. sangne de Johne siuent dm de Clifton io in mia xijd. Johes de Skercotes txt. sangne de Johne de Brighous io in mia xijd. Johnes Dobson de Suthouru txt. sang. de Johne de Skercotes io in mia xii d. Johes fil Rogi de Brighous retexit co filiu sotor suor io in mia iijs. iiijd.

Rastrik—Rog'us del Hirst no ven ad turn io in mia xijd.

Hipn—Johnes fil Robi txit sangne de siuent Rici Gibson io in mia xijd. Thom. le Tailliour no' ven ad turn io in mia vi d. Johnes de Hipnhirst no ven ad turn io in mia xijd.

Sm. huis turni xixs. xd. Quibz—Sum pptm de Rastrik iiiis. ; Sum ptm de Hypn xv s. xd.

Brianus de Thornhill, Thomas the Vicar de Halifax, Robtus de Bellomonte chief tenants. Henre fil John de Heton & Alicia que sunt ux (widow) John de Heton mentioned.

Hipn.—Adam de Sourbi attorn John fil Jordan vrs Ricm de Thorp de plito cap 1 vacc p. Johem de Stansfeld. pleg Ricus de Waddesworth.

Rastrik.—Henre de Welda, Ricus fil Petri, Maths de Totehill, Adam del Rode, Henr. fil Modd, & Henr. fil Henr. op se verss Elyam le

Smyth iniste detinet eis xxx s. quos eis debet vendidit iqmde Elias in Cure tenta hic sursu redd in mans. dm. tra' sua' ad opus Ade del Rode.

HIPX.—John fil Henr de Brighous sursu redd in mans dm. v acras & 1 rod tre cu' ptm in Brighous que comisse sunt Ade fil Rog. de Brighous ten s. & hed suis sedm cons mancr, & Ad. fin. p. ingress iij s.

HIPX.—Ricus fil Jordan de Ouru' qa no ven io in mia iiij d., Adam Poede p. eode' io in mia iij d., John Drake iiij d., Johes Molend de Shepden iij., Symon de Carheued iiij.' Galfrs de Shelff iiij., Willms fil Symon de Shelf ij d., Johnes de Skercotes iij d., Willms de Hynganrode iij., Ricus fil Ade de Ouru' ij d., Rogus pptn de Hypn ij d., all for not attending the court.

Prior de Lewes, mentioned under Halifax.

Thom de Seyuill a chief tenant. Wills de Neuill a chief tenant.

HYPX.—Cecilia fil Mathi de Shepden petens vers. Willms de Sonderland de plito tre no' est ps. Ido illa & pleg eius in mia xij d. Johes fil Jurdan le Milner queres vsus Riem de Thorp de plito capt vns vace no' est ps Ido dicus Johes & pleg eius in mia iij d.

HYPX.—Joh. le Pynder redd in mans dm vnn toftu & vij acre tre & una' roda' cu' ptm in Hypn Que comisse sunt Robto fil Henre de Crumwelbothune s. & hedibz suis et dat p. ingress ij s. vj d. Sup pptm Hypn iij s. ix d.

HYPX.—Adam fil Pet. de Suthcliff redd in mans dm viij acre & di tre in Hypn ad rev'sione viij acre tre & di post morte Petr. pris sui Et dca tra cu reu'sione cocessa est deo Ade et Agn. fil Thom de Warlouley & hedibz cor. legit. Et si obiert. sine hede intr eos legitie p'creat omna pdta ten post morte cor. remaneant hed dci Ade Et dat p. ingress xij d.

FFOR[EST] DE SOURBY.—John de Astey p. 1 equo. vi d. Rog'us de Grenwod p. esch best iij d. Galfro de Crosselegh p 1 quint ij d. Adam de Kerkeshagh p esch best iij d. Johnes Maynard, Willms Horseknaue Robtus de Wolronwall, p. eodm iij d. each.

FFOR'EST] DE HYPX.—Johnes fil Willi de Ouru' p. virid ij d. Johnes Somer, Johnes de Hilton, Willms Le Milner, Johnes fil Henre, Johnes Steuen all for drywood, i d. each. Sm pptm de Hypn xix d.

SOURBY.—John fil Thom del ffeld quarrels with Robt fil John about ½ acre.

RASTRIK.—Johes de Bothrode re in manu' dm. octo acre tre apd Rastrik Que co'cesse sunt Beatr fil Henr fil Margar & hed. sedm cons. Et dat dno p. ingress ij s.

STANELEY.—Duo forg apd Erdeslawe vi d. (Ardsley ironworks.)

SMES.—Alicia p'orissa de Kyrkeleghes p. plibz defalt. verss. Thom de Totehill in mia p. pleg. Robt. de Mora iij d.

RASTRIK.—Thomas de Staynland ven in cure in psent. dm. Phi de Meuwes & pet lic ad assartand & arrand xx acre tra quas cep de vasto dm & concedent ei p. don dm Phm & p. licent. xiij s. iiij d.

HYPX.—p. vire (greenwood), Will fil Thom iij d., Thms fil Henre ii d., Margt del Den ij d., & Thom del Cliff ij d.

Johnes del Northend ijd., Symon del Blacker ijd., Johnes le Milner ijd., John le Bercher ijd., Ricus del Hole ijd., Ricus de Thorp ijd. p. sicc (drywood.)

Rog. del Brighous p j sappelyng iijd. p.viride (greenwood), Henr le Tailliour jd., Matild Tyngel jd., Mich Sutor ijd., Adam fil petr de Southcliff ijd., Rob. de Mora fforester. Sm Hypn ijs. vjd.

HALIFAX—Jury sup articlis psent qd prior de Lewes debet de iure sedm cons. hospitari senescall dm Comit & Receptore & om'es ballies dm Comte qu de ven apd. Halifax bis p. anu ad trnu' tenend Et debet inueire eisdm p se & equie suis omia sua necessare du comorabit. (The Prior had neglected due hospitality.)

Turn tent apud Brighous die mart ante fm sci Marci eu'ng. Anno rre E'tcii post conquest pmo. [1327.]

Jure—Johnes de Berkesley, Johes fil Willi de Steynland, Wills Whitacres, Thoms del Wod, Henre de Coldley, Ricus del Rodes, Thoms de Whitewod, Ricus Couhird, Johes de Birstall, Willms de Steynland, Johes del Hirst & Ada' de Bradeley.

John Clicus de Herteshened stoppan qu'ad fonte coem in Hertesheved io in mia (therefore fined) vid.

Elias Smyth de Clifton vid., Ricus fil Cecil de Eadm vjd., Rogs Percy (iijd) de eadm, Math de Lynthwait xijd., Robt fil Margt. iijd., non ven turn, (not coming to the turn.)

HIPN.—ux Wm. Milner brac. & vend. cont. assm ijs., Agnes ux Rog de Brighous ijs., ux Thos. Baud ijs., ux Ric le Hyne de Clifton iijd., & ux Rog. le Shephird* brac. iijd., vill de Clifton for not presenting the two, xijd.

RAST.—Ricus del Shagh quer de Agnes que sunt ux (widow) John fil Hen. de ffekesby de plito debi. Dis.

HYPN.—Ada' de Eland quer de Robto de Rissheworth de plito debi. Dis.

John fil Alcok de Ouru' querens & Jordan de Hypn de plito debi p. lic. concord iijd. (for leave to agree.)

Johnes fil Jordan quer v. Robt del Rigg & Simon del Kirkeheued.

Wm de Northouru' qui tenuit de vasto dm vna acre tre apud Northouru' obierit est & fil eius & hes ven & fec fidelit & dat dno p. relevio vid.

RAST.—Elena que sunt ux Alan de Rastr tenuit de dno vnn mes. & xij acre tre apd Rastre, John their son fec fidelit & dat dno p releu iiijs. iiijd. Thom fil Robt. de Lightriche ad fec. fidelt.

HIPN.—Thms del Cliff redd in manu' dm vnn mes & vna bovat tre apd Hypn que concesse snt Wills fil Thom del Cliff & hed. suis sedm cons; & dat p ingress iiijd. Rog'us fil Rogr de Clifton cepit de vasto dm apd Hypn vna acre tre Et dat dno p. ingr xijd. Elias de Sculcotes & Willms de Hyngandroides cep de vasto dm. vna plata pti apud Haldworthbroke & dant dno p. anm. de reardt. iiijs. vd. Ricus (de Middelton) Vicar de Coningsby redd vi acres in Hypn. voc Vsterdrodes Que concesse sunt Willm le Milner & Beatrix ux. Ingress xiid.

_____
* Shephird or Bercar.

Hypn.—Alex de Ouenden vid. & Wm. frater vid., John de Astay de Haldworth, Wm. de Hyngandrode, John de Holway, John le Milner de Shepden, Ric. le Badger, John de Northend, Jordan le Pinder, John fil Rog. del Brighous, Wills de Sondreland, all for greenwood.

1327.—This is a damaged roll. Robert s. Henry de Crumwelbothom, Thos. Vicar of Halifax, John s. Jordan Milner, Ric. de Thorp, Cecilia d. Matthew de Schepden are mentioned. Adam s. Peter de Sutchcliffe held a messuage in Hyperum. and Thos. de Totehill was plaintiff against Alice the prioress of Kirkeleghes de plito debit.

1328.—Will de Sunderland felled an oak in Hyprum wood without leave. Will. formerly forester, cut oaks in the same without warrant. John le Pynder enclosed lands sans licence. John s. Roger de Brighous took 16 acres which John de Shepelay had held. Ric. and Peter sons of Adam de Rastrik had lands in Rastrik.

1329.—All the Villata of Hyp'um except Henry Horn and John s. Roger, junior, fined 3s. 4d. for not coming to the election of the greave. *Halmota* held at Brighous. Ric. de Ecclesley (of Exley near Elland), Will. s. Alice de Godelay, Robert le Sagher, Roger del Brighous, John s. Will. le Milner, Sir Will. rector of church of Mirfield, Thos. s. Roger de Brighous, Wade le Harpur, Robert ffaber, Ric. de Thorp referred to. Will. de Hingandrode ½ rod in Hingandrode for 5 years without leave, fined 6d. Cecila and Alice d. Matthew de Totehill took a mess. and 12 acres in Schipden, late Matthew de Schipden's. John s. Jordan had lands at Wildmarker. Will. de Sunderland surrendered the said mess. and 12 acres in Schipedene to Matthew de Totehill, custodian of Cecilia d. and heiress of Matthew de Schipeden. John de Rastrik for contempt of court, 2d. John Malkyn 18d., 4 acres of waste at Clegclif. Adam s. Roger del Briggehous 6d., 1⅓ rod waste in Hyprum. Roger de Clifton late Hiprum greave; John s. Roger de Briggehous was now elected. Henry s. Alcok le Taillur surrendered a cottage and three parts of a rode in Brigghous, which Simon de Lonesdale took. Sabina de Helay (Haley Bank) took 7 acres late John del Cliff's. John le Milner of Schipedene surrendered a cottage and 2 acres in S. to Adam le Shepherd. Adam s. Thos. de Hyprom took of Ric. s. Peter, custodian of the son of Henry Salmon, a mess., 8 acres in Rastrik. Cecil Batt took mess., 6 ac. of said Ric. Beatrix del Rode mess., 6 acres, of John del Botherod. Henry s. Adam Bi ye brook had a rode in Rastrik. Henry del Horsfall, Sourby graveship, fined 3d. for not attending Halifax court.

Halmote at Brighous. John s. Ric. de Waddesworth 1¼ ac. waste at Holcans. Will de la Rode 6d. rode of waste at Brerehey. John s. Roger del Briggehous, senr., and John s. Roger del B. junr., 6d. rode of waste at Calfclif. John s. John s. Walter de Adridgegate, heriot, on death of Julian de A. in Northowram. Roger de Clifton surrendered 1 acre in Wolfker to Ric. del Hole. John s. Thos. de Waddesworth had Blacker in Shipden. John s. John de Lynley elected constable of Staynland, Will de Witacres constable of Dalton. Will. s. Thos. elected for Hyprum at former turn, not appearing, fined

2d. Otto s. Will. de Haldeworth 18d. for 4 acres in Holcans which Adam s. Will relinquished at the present halmote.

Turn at Brighous same day. Adam s. Will. le Milner, Brighous, shed blood of Henry s. Henry le Hird, 12d. Sabina del Dene, brewing, fined 6d.

Henry s. Will. s. Hen. de Eland 12d. heriot, 3 acres in Fekisby on the death of Will. his father. Adam le Shepehird 18d. for waste in Shipden. John s. Ric. de Rastrik, greave for Rastrik; John s. Roger del Brighous, greave for Hyprum.

Halmote at Brighous. Special jury on Schipden lands, Will Sunderland *r.* Matthew Shipeden. Wade le Harpr owes soc to the mill of Rastrik. Thos. s. Juliana had lands in Rastrik, and Simon s. Jordan in Shipden.

1330.—The whole graveship of Hipperholme for not attending the court 2s. Will de Saltonstall elected greave for Sourby.

Halmote at Brighous. Will. s. Will. del Hirst had lands in Rastrik grave. Simon s. Will. Batemanson had 2 acres in Elynrode, N.owram. Will s. Ad. de la Bothe 4s. heriot, mess. 8 acres at le Bothes, his father being dead. Robert de Risseworth comes and owns two stirks found on Bradeforth road. Thos. le Waynwriht surrenders 5 acres in Prestley to Henry del Rokis. Will. s. John de Sundreland 2 acres in Schipden to his brother Henry. Custodians of Rastrik mill—John s. Will le Milner, bonds Adam del Rode, Roger Spilwod, John s. Henry de Rastrik, Alex. de Rastrik, Ad. de Bradley, Thos. s. Roger, Will. s. Thos. de Hyprom, John s. Walter de Adrichegate, Symon del Dene, Will. de Sunderland.

Turn at Brighous same day; brewers, wood takers, &c., as usual. Ric. s. Tille 3s. 4d., 1 acre new land, Hyprum wood. John del Cliff land in Hyprum [grave] to Adam s. Hugh de Ouenden. John le Milner de Hazelhurst took land at Shipedenheued on the death of Matthew s. Adam de Illingworth. Adam s. Hugh had waste land at Blacker.

Court. Thos. le Waynwright 1 rode in Hyprum to John s. Adam de Hiprum. John s. Ric. de Ourum paid heriot for lands in N.owram.

Turn. Agnes Dye*dohter,* (or Dyson we should now foolishly spell it), in Rastrick greaveship, mentioned.

Will. de Sonderland mess. and rode land to Matth. de Ouenden.

1331.—*Hallm.* at Brighous. Henry de la Weld had land at Cleyrod in Rastrik grave. Agnes wid. Adam del Bothes land in Bothes. John de Adrichegate elected greave for Hyprum; but paid 40d. to be freed. Will. s. Roger de Clifton surrendered 12 acres in Calvecliff in Hyprom to Henry s. Roger del Brighous, who paid for ingress 6s. 8d.

Turn at Brighous. Nicholas le flemyng shed the blood of Margaret de Thorp; Roger s. Andrew Alcok ditto of John s. Henry; and Henry s. Adam del Broke of Roger s. Richard. Bate de Rastrik took thackston in the highway of Rastrik. Alice wife of Richard drew blood from Thos. s. Henry de Hyprm, and John Milner del Bothes from the wife of Adam del Bothes. For brewing—the wives of Roger de Brig-

hous, John junior de Brighous, Thos. Baud, W. le Milner and John
Hanneson were called to account.

1332.—Will. s. Thos. del Rodes *r.* Roger del Brighous; latter fined
12d. Will. del Okes was greave for Rastrik. Alex. del Wodhous paid
6d. ingress for lands.

Court at Brighous. Adam del Brighous 4 ac. in Hyprom to John
del B. junr., who paid 3s. ingress. Rastrick mill let this year to
Henry Horne, John s. William, John Willeson, and John de Rastrik
for xiij*li.* vj*s.* viij*d.*; bonds, Symon del Dene, John s. Henry.

Turn at Brighous. John s. Ric. de Ourum shed the blood of John
de Northend. fined 12d., but the wife of Northend drew Ourum's
blood and she had to pay 6d. John s. Symon drew blood of John s.
John del Bothes, and the town of Northowram not reporting it had to
pay 2s. John s. Robert 12d. for cutting an oak in Hyprum wood,
and John de Wolwro, the like. Robert Tyngel paid 18d. for pasturage
at Calcliff, Hyperum graveship. The town of Hyprum for concealing
the case of William Milner's wife. fined. John s. Will. de Haylay
conveyed 1½ ac. to John s. Elie de Sculcotes.

Court. Adam del Birks, a mess., 7 acres in Hyprum to Henry s.
Roger. John s. Ric. de Ourum, mess., 6 acres in Northowrum,
heriot on the death of John de Eland. Thos. s. Simon del Ker 4s.
for 10 acres in N.owram.

Adam de Hyprom, John Pynder, John del Cliff, Ric. de Rokes,
Ric. del Hole, John s. Alex., Ad del Rodes, Will. Swyer, Ivo
Webster, Jordan Pynder, Ric. de Thorp and John Pynder de Ourom
were a special jury on a case respecting Richard le fforester formerly
man (vir) of Matilda widow of John Westwod. Ric. del Hole 8 acres
in Hyprom to his son Wm. Ric. Rokes 16 acres in Hyprom to his
son John. John s. John de Bothes 4s. heriot, mess., bovate in Hyprom (graveship), his mother Matilda being dead. Henry del Broke 5
acres in Hyprom (graveship) to Thos. filemyng. John del Bothe,
mess., 7 acres in Hyprom (graveship) to John his son, who paid 40d.
ingress. Johanna and Matilda d. Ric. de ffekesby paid 18d. for 4
acres in ffekesby.

Court at Brighouse. A two-year old white sheep (unus bidens albus)
sold to John the Molendinare (Milner) de Brighous for 10d. One to
Will de Okes de Rastrick for 6d. Cecilia wid. Simon s. Jordan held
8 acres in N'owrum. Ric. s. Henry de Northcliff 2 acres in Hypr. to
John de Northclyff. Thos. de Wolker 4 acres in Hyperom (grave) to
Ric. s. Jordan and Johna his wife. Jordan Pynder ¼ bovate in Hypr.
to Ric. his son. Adam del Rode had messuage, 20 acres in Rastrik.

1333.—Brighous *Court.* Feast of St. John of Beverley.
John s. Eli de Sculcotes had mess., 16 acres, at Northowram.
John the Milner gave 18d. for 1 acre waste in Hyprum (grave) at 4d.
per annum. The prior of St. Oswald de Nostell had a dispute with
John s. Elye de Scoulcotes and Will. del Hingandrode. John s. Will.
de Astay paid 20d. ingress for 3 acres in Hyprom (grave) on the death
of Margaret wife of Wm. The Ale Tasters of Hyprom fined 3s. 4d.

for not attending to report delinquents. (A Robert de Hiprom resided at Sandall at this time, and Adam le Crowther, or fiddler, at Sourby.) John de Godley disputed with Thos. de Lasci about an oxgang held by John le Aumbler. A special jury, Symon de Dene, John and Matthew del Cliff, Ric. de Schipeden, Henry de Coppeley, Adam de Southcliffe, Will. del Rode, John de Skircote, Henry de Sunderland, John de Holway, John Wylleson and Ric. del Rokes, in a case of John s. John del Bothes, *defore*, and Will. s. Thos. de Hyprom, about the mess., and ½ bovate in le Bothes. Ric. s. Adam de Hyprom had a case against Estiena del Shore after the death of her husband (vir) Ric. del Shore. Robt. s. Henry de Cromwelbotham and Ric. s. Jordan held lands in Hyprm (grave.) Thos. Baude and his wife Matilda had 1 acre, and Roger s. Roger de Clifton 10 ac. there.

Turn. Will. s. Roger de Hyprum and Thos. ffaber de H. drew blood from Ric. Harwer; John s. R. de Rokis ditto from John de Eland's wife; Will. s. Roger de Clifton from John de ffekesby and Ric. de Thorp; Will s. Ric. de Thorp from Rob. Burghclough's son; Annabella wife of Jordan le Pynder from Will. Qwaynt; John (le Colier) de Wolwro from Henry s. Alic; each fined xij*d.* Five women for brewing, 2d. to 3d. each. John le fflemyng fined 40d. for not coming to the Turn. John de Eland concealing 6 denarratas surrendered by Jordan s. Nicholas, fined 2s. 6d.; also same amount against John s. le Milner del Bothes, Adam ·de Hyprom, and John s. Henry. Matthew de Totehill surrendered a mess., xx acres in Rastrik to John his son who paid 13s. 4d. for ingress. Matthew le Taillur surrendered mess., 3 acres in Hyperom. Matth. s. Henry ffaber de Ouenden gave to the lord 2s. for 1 acre waste in Hyp. graveship. John Draak 12d. for assisting to take from the court an ox of Eva de Baristowe.

Turn. Shedding blood cases with usual fine 1s., John s. Roger de Clifton from Thos. de Bromylegh. Thos. de Brighouse, clerk, from Thos. le Waynwriht, Ric. s. Nicholas from same Waynwright, Henry s. Auitia from same Ric., Will Ratheboune from Goderobert de Thornyhales, and Matilda Tyngil from Alice del Parker. John de Shipden, holding 2 acres socc., gave 40d. to be exonerated from the office of greave; John de Holway elected. and Alex. del Wodhouses for Rastrik. John the Milner held mess., bovate, 2 rods rodland, and Hugh le Tailleur 4 ac. in Hyprum (greave.)

1334.—Will. s. Thos. elected greave for Hipr., and John de Rastrik · for Rastrik. Will s. Thos. de Hyperum for mess., ½ bov. in le Bothes, 30s. to John s. John del Bothes. Adam del Rode and Cecill his wife, executors of the will of her father Thos. del Rode, 13s. 4d. heriot.

A special jury about 24 acres in Rastrik, Henry del Botheroide *v.* John del Styghel and Juliana his wife, was composed of Matthew de Totehill, John s. Henry, Alex. de Wodhus, Elias le ———, Peter del Woodhus, Thos. Rayner, Will. Husband, Henry del Broke, Henry Modson, John s. Roger, Henry Horne, and Will del Okes.

Turn at Brighous. Blood drawing by Thos. s. Jordan from John de ffekisby, Hugh le Milner from Estiana wife of Ric., Ric. s. Alan de

Rastrik from Thos. s. ———, and a countercharge, Johanna d. John
Milner del Bothes from Agnes d. Adam; fines 12d, to 40d., and John
s. Ric. de Rokes from Ric. de Thorp 2s. John s. Roger de Brighus 6d,
¼ ac. waste in Hyp. grave. John de Seynell bound to attend Brighouse court. Thos. fleming Taillour surrendered into the hands of
the greave a messuage and 5 acres in Prestlay in Hypron, re-taken by
Henry s. Thos. del Broke.

Turn. Thos. s. Roger de Brighouse shed the blood of John s.
Nicholas, 12d., and Roger s. Wm. s. Henry of Ric. Harower, 12d.
Thos. de Gaytington vicar of John Baptist Church at Halifax, for
lands in Haley, neglected the dues to the mill at Brighus; John Drake
and John de Adrichgate for not repairing with corn to the mill at
Shipden, xij*d.* each. Will. s. Alex. del Wodhous in Rastrik and
Elias ffaber (Smith) de Thornyales had a special jury trial,—John de
Rastrik, Matthew de Totehill, Ric. s. Peter, John s. Henry, Henry s.
Henry, John del Botheroide, Will. del Okys, Henry by ye broke, John
del Brighous, John de Adrichegate, John Stenen and John s. Will le
Milner who say that Alex. del W. and Beatrix his wife held 12 acres in
Rastrik. John s. John del Bothes paid 46s. 8d., mess., 8 acres in Hyp-
erom from John s. Thos. de Hyperon. Adam Nelleson, Matilda his
mother, Adam s. Roger, John s. Henry, and Adam del Rode are not
under the soc of Rastrik mill. Roger de Brighous senior for 2
'porks' and 2 hoggs, in Hyperom wood in the time of feeding, 12d.,
John his son, 2 hoggs, 4d., John de Brighous junr, 2 porcs, 2 hoggs,
12d., Adam his brother 1 porc 2 hoggs, 8d., Thos. Baude 1 p., 1 h.,
6d., John de Hilton 1 p., 4d., Hen. Horne 1 p., John s. Will, 1 h., 2d.,
Hen. de Sunderland 2 h., 4d., Will de Sunderland 1 h., Will s. Ric.
1 p. 1 h., 6d., Will s. Thos. 1 h., Will de Aula (Hall) 1 h., John
de Skircote 2 h. 4d. For cutting greenwood, &c. Will. del Bothe
12d., 14 others 3d each. John s. John del Bothes 2s., for 1 ac. waste
in Holkannes at 6d. per acre yearly. Rastrik mill let this year to
Ivo le Webster and John s. Nicholas for £12, pledge—John de Shipeden,
John de Holway, John de Brighouse senior, Thos. s. Roger. Nicholas
———, Ad. del Rode, Will. del Clif, Henry s. Roger del Brighous and
Will. del Rodes.

Court at Brighous. Simon del Dene for unjust detention of cattle.
Will de Sunderland conveyed 9 acres in N'owram to John his son.
Will s. Thomas de Hyperom, 12d. heriot, mess., ¼ bov. in H., his
mother Cecilia being dead. For not attending the Turn, fined 6d.
each, Adam de Hyperum, Will. s. Ric., John de Adrichegate. Will del
Hyngandrode, John le Pynder, Will de Coppeley, Will del Clyf, Henry
de Coldeley, Rob. le Pynder, Jordan le Pynder, Roger de Clifton, John
Alcokson.

1335.—Henry by thé broke, greave of Rastrik; Matthew de Ovenden
for Hiperom. Hiperom greave for not attending the Wakefield court,
2s. John s. Henry Horn, 12d. heriot, mess., 3 acres in Hyperom,
his father having died. Alex. de Brighous takes Rastrik mill; pledge—
Will del Clyf, Roger de Clifton, Peter de Wodhous. Adam de la Rode

placed his beasts in Hiperom wode at Dedemanclough. Rastrik and
Hiperom bound to repair the mill dam.

Turn. The wife of Nicholas fflemyng de Dalton, Agnes Tyngle de
Hertesheved and three others for brewing and selling fined 12d. each;
seven more for brewing only 6d. each. Adam de Stayncliffe fined 40d.
respecting lands at Shibden head. Matilda wid. Wm. de Sunderland
held from Matthew de Totehill, mess., 10 acres in Hyprum graveship.
John s. John de Haldeworth quit claimed to John del Lathe 15 ac. in
Northourummeire. John s. Wm. de Sunderland conveyed 9 acres in
N.owram to Matilda his mother. Matthew de Ouenden, greave, for
not presenting 4 acres in le Riding which Thos. le Waynewright held
of John del Clif without leave of court, 12d. Thos. le Waynewright
paid 6d. for 4 acres in le Riding. The greave reported 12 acres which
John le Milner de Shipden held of John s. Simon del Dene; Milner
paid 12d. for ingress, to the lord. Will s. Henry by the broke had 4
acres in Hyperum of John del Clif without licence of the court, fined
12d. Ric. Batmanson surrendered 2 ac. 1 rod in N'owram to John de
Breryhaghe and Alice d. Will Batmanson. A red horse strayed, sold
to Thos. Alan for 3s.

Turn at Brighous. 13 brewers, all women, fined.

1336. John del Bothe took a bovate in N.owram paying 2s. ingress.
Adam de Hyprom and Rich. his son took a mess., 7 acres in Hyprum.
John s. Henry surrendered to the lord 1 acre in Hyp. wode, and Wm.
s. Tho. Clerk paid 8d. ingress. John s. Henry de Brighous 1½ ac. in
Brighous, taken by John le Milner, who paid 6d. ingress. Robert,
Abbot of ffuntaynes, and others attached, *re* Bradelay bridge. Agnes
d. Elia de Scoulcote gave 2s. to lord for leave to marry. Ric. s. Jordan
le Pynder held a mess., ½ bovate.

Court held at RASTKBRIGHOUS. Ric. Horne surrendered 11½ ac. in
Hyperm; retaken by Ric. s. Thomas de Halifax. Wm. Benne, mess.,
1 ac. 1 rd. in Hyperom to Johan B. for life, with remainder to Ric. s.
said Johan. John s. Henry conveyed two parts of 2 acres in Rastrik
to Ad. s. Peter de Wodhous; Peter de Wodhous a mess., 14 acres to
said Adam. Henry del Weld 2 ac. to Alex. del Wodhous. Adam del
Birks. Hyp. graveship, held 2 acres of waste land. Cecilia d. John le
Pynder, p. deflorat, 6d., and Ourum town for concealing said Cecilia,
1s. Agnes wife of Thos. s. John de Lockewode drew blood from Ive
Rubilion. The Abbot of ffunteyns for not repairing the bridge over
Keldre between le Couford (the old spelling of Cooper) and the grange
of Bradeley vjs. viijd. The town of Hyprom for concealing John
Benne a common brewer, fined 40d. The usual fine, for wood, fodder,
brawls. John Hanson surrendered into the hands of the lord 2 acres
in Hyprom; retaken by John s. Roger junior, for 6 years, who paid
for ingress, 12d. Adam de Southcliff gave 2s. to the lord that he
might not be elected greave this year for Hyprm; Ric. del Hole was
elected, and John de Rastrik for Rastrik. John Hanneson surrendered
1 ac. 1 rod in Hyprum; taken by Simon del Dene; John de Shepeley
3 ac. in Hyp. to John le Milner. Rastrik Mill let to John le Milner

for 18 marks rent, from St. Michael's Feast ; pledge—John s. Henry de Rastrik, Hen. de Totehill, John de Shepeley, John Steuen, Simon del Dene, Will s. Thos., Galfri de Shelf, and Matthew s. Simon.

Turn at Brighous. For brewing and selling beer, fines as usual. John Milner del Bothes for obstructing the King's Road at Bothes 12d. Thos. s. Roger de Clifton drew blood from Will. del Bothes 12d ; Robt. Tyngel from Tho. de Rauthmel. John s. Henry le Smith, a

Milner Arms (No. 2.)

Hanson Arms.

common (obscene), 40d. Thos. Drake surrendered messuage and lands in Hyprum (grave) ; John Drake gave 40d. for ingress. John de Stancliff conveyed 2 acres to Matthew Bate : 12d. ingress.

⁂ It should be noted that to this date where Hyperum or Rastrik are mentioned, the graveships are often meant, and many of the persons named did not reside in those two townships so named, but the business of the Court Baron, or Halmote, and Leet shews the extent of power over several townships exercised from Rastrick-Brighouse as the centre. Also in these early rolls Rastrick evidently included in many cases the hamlet of Brighouse, and it will be noticed how gradually the name of Rastrick gave way to that of Brighouse for the Courts, but not for the lord's mill which was long afterwards known as Rastrick mill though on the Brighouse side of the Calder.

1337. In this year's roll, the townships are arranged for the first time so that the residences of culprits may be more accurately known; thus—*Turn* at Brighous [mia = fine, brac = brewing, non ven. = not coming, paup' = poor, trax sang. = drew blood, p. qd = constable presents that, cl'icus = clerk, blada = corn.]

Hipn. mia vi d.   *Hertesheued* p. qd Agn. Tyngel brac.

Mia vac. q. paup. *Northourum*, Ric. fil Alice del Ker non ven. turn.

Mia vi d.   ux John de Birstall brac.

                   Alice del Park trax sang. Ellot fil Ric. de Shipden.

Mia vi d.   *Clifton*.   Margeria de Whalley brac.

Mia ij d.   *Shelf*.   ux Galfri de Shelf brac.

                   ux Tho. del Dene mia cond. p. paup.

Mia vi d.   *Hipn*. p. qd Johnes le Milner brac contr. assm.

Mia ij d.   Johna Swyer brac.

    „   ux Henry de Coppelay brac.

    „   ux Will. fil Thomas brac.

    „   ux Ivonis le Webster brac.

Mia vi d.   Thomas clicus de Brighous trax sang. de Willo de Hilton.

    „   Roger Noget trax sang. de John Bolt.

Hiprom.   Ric. Coulird & Robt. de Whitwode.

        Ric. le Stonpotter p. iiij . . in pastura de Hipn. vj d.

        Gilbert de Astey vi d.

The townships in Rastrick graveship are similarly arranged.

    Steynland, ux. Will. Helliwell brac. [of the Holywell, Helliwell, at

    Rastrik, John le Taillour brac.   Stainland.]

    Burksland, Alan de Bothomley at Bothomley.

    Quernby, Elena ux Robt. s. Roger brac.

The towns of Quernby, Berkesland, Dalton for not sending to the court the four men liable to serve on Jury, fined 40d. each township. John de Quernby fined 12d. for not coming ; John de Seynill (Saville) 40d.   John s. Wm. de Staynland, Henry s. Henry de S., Will. s. John de S., and Ric. s. Peter de Ealand gave to the lord 20s. for 'manucapcone* Ric. de Lightriche. Adam de Southcliff is elected greave for Hyperom. Persons mentioned as being called to the wars. John del Rokes made a rescue from Will. Templer the lord's bailiff at Hiperom, fined 40d. [Here we may have the origin of the name Bailiff bridge.] It was found by inquiry that the tenants of Hiperum vill (township) own common pasture in Northouram in Brynscoles wood, to the field fosse of the said town. Thos. le Waynwright being dead, his son Henry paid 12d. heriot for 4 acres in Hiperum. Thos. del Brighous, clerk, paid 2s. for ingress, for 14 acres surrendered by Henry del Hogh, Hyp. greaveship. Lands of the Hospitallers at Dalton are referred to. Henry s. Henry de Rastrik took 6 acres in R., John s. Henry de Weld 6 acres. Adam Batte 1 acre in mortgage from Henry by the booke, and paid 6d. to the lord. Roger ffox had 12 acres in Rastrik grave. John Pynder of Hyprum and Jordan his brother 'Carinfex'† made bad use of the office. Matilda and Margaret

_____
        * Pledge, supposed felony.   † Executioner.

d. of Wm. de Helliwell and Thos. s. Alice d. said Wm. paid heriot on the death of Henry s. said Wm. for 7 acres in Scamonden. Two of the three daughters were evidently married, for William de Waterhous and Margaret his wife, and Matilda her sister surrendered the messuage and 7 acres in Scamonden to the use of Henry s. Wm. de Waterhous.

Wm. de Helliwell	Wm. de Hepworth and
	Adam his son held lands
|———|———|	in Rastrik grave. John
Alice Matilda Margaret	del ffrith had 1 acre in
=== ==Wm. de Waterhous	Scamonden.
Thos. Hen. de Waterhous.	

John de Heley had 3 acres in Hiprom grave, surrendered to John s. Elene de Sculcotes and Margaret widow of Eli Stevend. John s. Henry de Brighouse surrendered 3 ac. 1 rd. in Hiperom to John del Brighous for 12 years : ingress 12d. John del Both gave to the lord 6s. 8d. p. manucapcone, pledge—Thos. de Lascy.

Turn at RASTRIK-BRIGHOUS.

Shelf. Cecilia de Bentley brewing. Beatrix de Thorp drew blood from Alice d. Brown. Hipn. Adam de Southcliffe not coming, 4d. Cecilia wife of yong John, ux Henry de Coppeley, ux Will. de Coppeley, Ad. del Rode, ux Jordan le Pynder, brewing. Northourum, Johna d. John Milner, deflorat, 40d. fine. The Town of Clifton 40d. and Northouram 12d. fines for not being represented at the Court. Northouram brewers—Eglentyn del Bothe, the wives of John de Birstall, John s. Henry, Henry de Sondreland, and Isabel d. Simon.

1338. John s. Wm. del Brighous and Wm. Baude broke the lord's (pin)fold at Hipron. Hen. s. Robt. de Rissheworth to respond to Robt. Taillur, Hip. graveship. de plo debi. Thos. s. Juliane de Rastrik v. Abbot de fontibz and Brother Will. de Bradeley. Will. de Totchill and Thos. de Lightriche taking ' blada et herbam ' at ffekesby. Will. del Bothes conveyed 6 acres in Hypron grave to Ric. del Hole. Ric. de Kerheued returned to the lord 2 ac. 3 rodes in Hipron ; retaken by John le Milner. John del Cliff cutting an oak and stubb, 12d. ; Will. de Haldeworth an oak 12d. ; Roger ffox a stubb 6d. Certain of town (vill) of Brighous breaking the fold 6s. 8d. Tenants of Hiperom for removing the former hedge at Brynscoles, 2s. Ric. s. Nicholas Ters cutting underwood in Shipden, 2s. Blood-drawing brawls, Robt. s. Ric. Sisson from Robt. de Dalton, John de Popilwell from John Tyngil, John s. Matilda de Popilwell from John Tyngel, Thos. Hare from Robert Tyngel, Galfri de Shelf from John del Rokes and vice-versa, each 12d. Ric. del Ker not coming to court 4d. Isabel d. Simon s. Jordan de Adrichgate, nativa, deflorat, 12d. Simon del Dene for selling wood on virgin lands that he holds, 12d. ; Will. the clerk, Will. del Hole, John de Stayncliff, and Wm. del Both for the like.

Turn at Rastrik. The Molend (mill) let this year to John le Milner. John Emson de Mirfeld, Hugh de Astay, and Adam s. Wm. de Shagh for xiiij marks.

1339. Seizure in lord's hands of 6 acres with appurtenances in
Hyprm. which Ric. del Hole held per charter, said Ric. to respond to
Wm. del Bothes, and special jury. Will. Tilly and Margaret his wife
took a messuage and 1 acre in N'owm.

Court at Brighous. Scamonden tenants to pay 24s. for enclosing
lands.

Turn—Goderobert de Thorneyales, Clifton, drew blood from Thos.
s. Robert; and Henry s. Alice de Hyprum from Thos. Hare. Ric. de
Thorp not attending court, 12d., and John fflemyng, Knight, 2s.
Henry del Weld conveyed a mess., 14 acres in Rastrik Wodhous, to
Robert de Bollyng and Beatx his wife. Robert de Wyndhill 18d. for
land in Hyprom (grave) at Blacker and Drakerode of John ffigge and

Hoyle (de la Hole) Arms.   Hoyle Arms.

Johanna his wife for 10 years. Ric. de Thorp, Hyprum, had been
breaking down hedges. Ric. Knight ran the chief fulling mill at
Wakefield. John s. and executor of Matthew de Totehill and Modest
wid. and executrix of the will of Thos. de Totehill attend court to
make their claims. John de Haldeworth 4 acres in Hyprum (grave)
to Ric. his son, who paid 12d. ingress. Special jurors concerning
6 acres, Ric. del Hole, *v.* Wm. del Bothes, were Ivo le Webster, Will.
del Cliff, Will. del Rodes, Henry s. Elene, Robert Pynder, Henry del
Rokes, John del Rokes, John s. Wm. de Ourum, John le Pynder,
Adam de Hyprum and John de Whithill.

Court and *Turn* at Rastrik-brighous. Henry del Weld surrenders a
messuage and 24 acres at Wodehous to John s. Henry, and Margaret

his wife. John s. Hugh de Bothomley held 7 acres in Scamonden.
Will. del Rode 5 acres at Brerehay in Northourum to Adam del Wro.
Blood drawing—Ivo le Webster from Thos. s. Henry, John Milner
from Henry de Hoo, Robt. de Rissheworth, and his son Henry from
Wm. and John de Coppeley, brothers, Roger de Clifton from Thos. s.
John de Newal. Ric. del Rokes levavit hittes, (raised hue and cry,
roused the neighbourhood), about a loss. Rastrik mill let this year to
John Milner for x*li :* xs., pledges—Robert del Haigh, John s. Elena de
Rastrik, Matthew de Totehill, Henry de Totehill, Jankyn de Rastrik,
Wm. de Hepworth, Alex. de Wodehous, and Adam Shephird.

1340.—Robert Pynder took 2 acres of waste in Hyprom at 8d. per
ann. paying 6d. for ingress. Henry del Hill not coming to tourn, 2d.
Rastrik mill let to John Molendinar (Milner), and Robert Pynder this
year ; pledge—John s. Matthew, Thos. le Clerk, Hugh s. Ric., John s.
Walter. Wm. le clerk de Sunderland, conveyed a messuage, ¼ bov.
3 ac. 1 rd. in Schipedene to Matthew de Ouendene, 4s. ingress.

Court at Brighous. John s. Wm. del Rodes paid 5s. heriot, for a
mess., bovate and 6 acres in Hyprum ; Ric. s. Wm, atte Cliffe paid 4s.
heriot, for mess. and bovate in Hyprom,—their fathers being dead.

Turn at Brighous. Brewers and ale sellers as usual. Brawlers
drawing blood,—Adam del Rode from Johanna Swhier, (6d.), Wm. de
Hilton from Will. s, Jordan, John s. John Milner from Roger Taillur
at Clifton. John s. Matthew de Totehill elected greave for Rastrik,
and Wm. del Bothe for Hyprum.

1341.—Thos. s. Simon de Kerhead surrendered 5½ acres waste land
(cepit de vasto) in Hyprum (grave) to John s. Robert de Halifax, 2s.
ingress ; the latter conveyed it to Wm. s. Alex. de Hyngandrode.
Thos. de Lascy 6 acres in Hyprum to Robert s. John de Clif. Wm.
Nalson del Brok and Wm. s. Roger de Clifton not coming to Turn, 4d.
each. John de Holway, junior, 2 acres in Hyprum (grave) to Matth.
Bateson and John his brother, ingress 16d. Matthew de Yllyngworth
1 ac. 1 rod in Hypr. grave. Robert Alcokson, called in another place
Robert s. Alex. de Northourum, conveyed a mess. and bovate in N. to
John his son, and Agnes wife of (? Robert).

Turn at Brighous. Jury, Wm. ffrannk, Henry de Coldeley, Wm.
de Bradley, Thos. de Loewod, John de Birstall, Ric. Cowhird, Thos.
del Wodheued, Ric. del Rokes, Robert de Whitwood, Hugh le Shephird, John s. Thos. de Dalton, and John fflemyng. The mills of
Rastrik and Shipden let this year to Sir John de Eland.

1342.—*Turn* at Brighous. Jury, Ric. del Rokes, Henry de Coldeley, Thos. de Wodhead, Henry s. Henry ffrankys, Galfrid de Shelf,
Robert de Whitwod, Wm. de Whitecres, John de Birstall, Ric. Couhird, Thos. de Loewod, Thos. del Stockes, Wm. de Staynland. John
s. Wm. reports that Roger s. Richard formerly greave of Rastrik had
6s. 8d. due to Rastrik mill. Wm. del Both surrendered 4 acres in
Hyprum (grave) and Thos. Lascy gave 18d. for ingress. Agnes wid.
Wm. Vaysor and Wm. his son surrendered 1 acre to Thos. Alcokson
de Ovynden. John s. John de Wales paid 18d. heriot for mess., 4

F

acres in N'owram. John de Shipden's trial, v. Ric. de Kerheued and
his mother Alice about the field formerly John de Kerhead's, father
of Richard. Roger de Spilwod took plots in Hyprum called Mickel-
blakker and le Lytilblakker of Wm. s. Gilbert de Halifax. Elizabeth
d. John Clerk a plot in Bothefield from Agnes at Both and Wm. her
son. John Sagher and Matilda his wife, daughter of John del Bothes
v. Robert del Cliff about a bovate in Hyperom. John de Wales conveyed 1 acre to John Dykson de Shipden.

Turn. Jury, Thos. de Locwod, Wm. de Staynland, Thos. del Stockes,
Ric. de Herteshead, Will. de Whittacres, Henry de Coldley, Hugh de
Bersland, Will de Bradley, Thos. de ffekisby, Thos. de Wodhead,
Ric. de Rokes, Galfri Shelf. Hyprum—Hen. Amson by the broke,
Wm. del Houe, Wm. Nalson by the broke, not attending turn 2d.
each. Blood brawls—Hen. Alison from Wm. Judson, John Nalson
from Ric. Judson, Will. del Bothes from John s. Adam, Dyonis de
Roe from Cecilia del Rode, Henry and Robt. sons of Matthew Yllyng-
worth from Ric. and Matth. sons of Simon del Dene. For brewing,
the wives of John Milner, John del Brighous junior, Wm. del Rode,
John del Hall, Henry de Shepden twice, Thos. de Hiperum, and
Henry de Coplay. Ric. s. Adam de Hypr. paid 20d. for mess., 3 parts
of a bovate and 4 acres rodeland from Eglantine his mother. Alex.
de Wodhous conveyed a mess., 8 acres in Rastrik Wodhous to John
his son. Ric. Yonghare gave 10d. to the lord for a rode of waste in
Ourum. Cecil d. Matthew de Shipden part of a bovate, and 2 acres
of rodland to John de Howe, who paid 5s. ingress. John Clerk de
Brystall 1 acre in Hyp. grave to Roger Spillewod. Thirty persons
fined 2d. each for not attending the turn. Hyperom forester reported
Margery de Ovendene, Thos. Mortimer, and Thos. Shephird for cutting
green wood; fined 2d. each. Cecilia ffox, for taking greenwood from
Rastrik wood, 2d.

1343.—Michael Jonson Willeson de N'owram heriot for a mess., 1
bovate in N., John his father being dead. Matthew de Yllyngworth
a mess., bovate and 8 acres rodland to Henry his son. John del
Northend took a rod of waste in Ourum.

Turn at Brighous, Robert de Rissheworth, Nich. de Hellywell, John
Tomasson de Dalton, Ric. de Rokes and others previously named were
jurors. God-Robert Colyer drew blood from the wife of John Milner.
John de Wales 2 acres at Wynnyrode with edifice in N'owrum to
John Symson del Dene, paid 12d.; John atte Northend and his wife
Anabill gave evidence in the case. John s. Symon del Dene 2 acres
at Whynnyrode in Nm. to Annabill atte Northend. John Symson
Judson paid 2d. for greenwood.

Turn at Brighous: Jury, John Seyvyl, Thos. de Locwod, Thos. del
Stockes, John Thomasson de Dalton, John de Birstall, Henry de
Coldeley, Ric. del Rokes, Thos. Jonson de Dalton, Wm. del Grene,
Robt. de Whitwod, John Elyson de Rastrik. Elene Jondoghter de
Dalton was one of the defaulters. Drawing blood cases were—Henry
de Shipden from Ivon Webster, John Milner wife from Isabel del

Stones, Matilda del Halle from Beatrice Alcok wyfe. John s. Adam de Stayncliff took 10 acres which Matthew the chaplain, brother of said Adam, had held. John Robynson Alcokson of N.owram, 1 ac. 1 rd. to John Sysson de Eland; he appears as John Robtson Alcockson in the same roll. Symon del Dene a bovate to Mathew his son. A plot called Hadgreves in Hyprom grave, from Andrew le fforester to Margary d. Robt. de Rissheworth. Adam del ffeld of Sourby was a principal tenant in that district, and John del Kerkeschagh in Warley district. Henry de Tothill and Cecilia his wife to John s. Matthew de Totehill, a mess., 7 acres in Rastrik which Cecilia had from Matthew de Shipden. Eglantine del Bothes in her widowhood surrendered 3 parts of 5 bovates, (12 acres and edifice) and 9 acres of rodland in Nm. to Ric.Maunsel, senior. Wm. s. Symon Judson, 40d. heriot for a cottage and 6 acres in Hyprom grave, Simon his father being dead. Roger s. Wm. le Smith took 1 acre of waste in Ourum ; Ric.

SAVILLE ARMS.

s. Adam de Hiperum 4 acres in Hyp. which Eglentyne del Bothes held.

1344.—*Turn* at Brighous. Jury, Thos. de Locwode, Thos. del Stockes, Wm. de Staynland, Wm. de Bradeley, Robt. de Whitwod, Ric. de Rokes, Ric. Cowhird, Thos. de Whitacres, Galfri de Shelf, Adam del Hirst, John Tomesson de Dalton, Henry de Rissheworth. Henry Jonson del Cliff de Hiperum held 10 acres, late his father's, paid 6d. ingress. Seizure of messuage and 4 acres in Hiperum which Robt. s. Hugh de Ovynden held.

Turn, Jury, Henry de Rissheworth, Thos. Hughson de Bothomlay, Nichs. del Helliwell, &c. Henry del Cliff took 10 acres and edifice in Hiperum which Ric. s. Ric. had held. Margaret wife of Wm. Tyllye held a cottage and 1 acre in Northourum which her mother Sabina de Skulcote had held.

1345.—*Turn* at Brighous, Oct. 27. Jury—Wm. de Staynland, John de Dalton, Thos. Locwod, Wm. del Grene, Robt. Whitwod, Wm. de Bradley, Henry de Ryssheworth, Ric. del Rokes, John del Brighous junr., Thos. de Whitker, Nichs. del Hellywell and Galfri de Shelf. Hen. s. Matth. took a pasture in Hyperum of Wm. s. Agnes. John s. Thos. Milner de Ovenden 1 acre of waste in Clegcliff in Hipron at 6d. per ann., ingress 12d. The officer of the turn for Hyperum says that Ric. le Smith de Warlilley got sea-coals without leave, fined 12d.; that the Vicar of Birstall dug peat without leave, fined 12d. Henry del Cliffe and Wm. del Hoghe not attending the turn, 3d. each. Blood drawing—John Milner from Wm. de Hilton, 6d., Wm. de Hilton in self defence from John Milner. Ric. and John brothers of Wm. de Hilton from John Milner, John Milner's wife from Adam de Hilton, each 6d. Roger s. Roger de Clifton broke the fold at Hyperum. John del Clif took a rode in Hyprum. John Alcokson of N'ourum to John his son, 3 parts of a bovate, paid 40d. ingress. Hen. s. Thomas, 2 acres in Shipden to Richard and Thos. del Kerr, brothers.

1346.—Ric. Littelwright de Brighous carrying away wood from Rastrik to the value of 2d., Isabel Horne ditto, 3d., wife of John Abraham, 2d. Robt. del Cliff 1 acre in le Bothes to John his father, ingress 8d. John del Cliff gave 6d. to take 1 acre for 17 years from Henry s. Matthew. Ric. Mansell, 7 acres of rodland, and 3 parts of a bovate to John del Both. John de Wales ½ acre and edifice in N. to Ric. s. Symon del Dene. John del Godhour 7 acres and edifice in Rastrik for 16 years to Robt. del Okes.

Turn at Brighouse. Jury, nearly as before. Particulars of waste land in Hiperum entered on the roll. Galfri de Shelf had an action against Ellotte de Ormerode. John s. John Cliff held 2 acres in Ourum.

Turn. Jury. Thos. de Lockwod, Thos. del Stocks, Wm. de Staynland, Ric. de Hertsheved, Wm. de Bradlay, Robt. de Whitwod, Ric. del Rokes, Thos. de Whitacres, Adam del Hirst, Henry de Rissheworth, Nich. de Hellewell and John Enotson de Skamonden. John s. Ric. de Shipden *r.* Henry the servant of John Symson, and Margaret wife of Ric. s. Jordan de Hyprom.

1347.—Mutilated roll. Jury at Brighous, as last time. Ric. de Thorp drew blood from Hen. Sklater's wife, Hyprum. Brewing ale— the wives of John Milner, John de Brighous junr., Thos. Clerk, and Rich. s. Nichs. Ters. John fligge and Johan his wife held a plot of 3 acres in Blakker.

1348.—*Turn* at Brighous. Jury, Thos. de Locwode, Wm. de Staynland, John de Hopton, Ric. de Herteshead, John de Dalton, Henry de Rissheworth, John de Stayncliff, Adam del Hirst, Nich. de Helywell, John del Brighous, Ric. de Rothelset and John s. Eve de Scamanden. Juliana widow of John de Adrichegate took a mess, 8 acres, in N. Johna and Sabina daughters of Robt. Pynder de Cromwellebothom paid 2s. heriot for 20 acres in N. on the death of John de Adrichegate their uncle, with reversion to a mess., and 8 acres on the death of

Julian his widow. They gave also 1s. to heriot a mess., 7 acres in Shipden on the death of John s. John de Adrechegate their cousin. Matilda and Elizth. d. Adam del Bothe for a messuage and 10 acres in Hyprum on the death of their brother Wm. paid heriot, and John s. Ric. del Hole 12d., 8 acres in Hyperum on the death of Wm. del Hole his brother. John son and heir of Robert del Cliff paid 3s. 4d. heriot, for a mess., bovate, and 4 acres of Rodland in N. on the death of John s. John del Cliff his cousin. John s. Henry de Totehill, 3s. 4d. heriot, mess., bovate, 4 acres of Rodland in Rastrik on his father's death. Annabil widow of Wm. del Bothes, and Matilda and Elizth. d. Adam del Both in virginity, surrender a mess., 11 acres, 3 rodes in le Bothes to Ric. Mansel, who pays ingress 3s. 4d. Adam s. Wm. 12d. heriot a mess., and bovate in N. on his brother John's death. John s. Thos. Rayner 8d. heriot, mess., and 3 acres in Rastrik at his father's death. Agnes Benne 12d. heriot, mess. and part of a bovate in Rastrik at her uncle John Steel's death. Ric. Gryve, 8d. heriot 3 acres in Hiperum greave at his cousin's death, Wm. s. Ric. de Shipden. John de Hilton executor of the will of Wm. de Hilton gave 12s. 5d. to Matthew Illingworth for 'blad,' pasturage. Ric. Maunsel for unjust detention xs. from Henry s. Matthew, exec. of the will of John del Cliff. Peter de Barne surrendered a bovate and edifice in N'owram to John String. John s. Wm. del Rode and John s. Simon del Dene farm the mills of Rastrik and Shipden this year for 28s. It is presented by the tenants of Hiprom that 'tenta tre iacet ibm vest. moult qd solebat reddere p. ann. Ivs. xd. ob. qe ut p. capte p. eodem hic in cure libat.' John Wynter took an assart in Hyprum of 3 acres formerly Ric. de Byrc's. Elyas s. Symon Judson and Thos. Culpan executors of the will of Sir T. de Gayton formerly vicar of Halifax gave 2 stirks, 5s. 6d. John s. John Souter de Halifax 6d. heriot, 8 acres in N'm. at his father's death. William de Lokyngton and Beatrice his wife 12d. heriot, 3 acres in Shipden on the death of John de Godley her brother. John s. Robt. del Cliff ½ bovate, 2 acres rodland in le Bothes, paid 12d. heriot on the death of his uncle John del Cliff. John s. Ric. Symson, heriot, 5 acres and mess., in Shipden on his father's death. Isabel d. Symon del Ker, 18d. heriot, mess., 8 acres in Shipden on her brother Thos. del Ker's death. Alice d. Wm. Symson 18d. heriot 8 acres and messuage in Shipden at her father's death. John Symson, 2s. heriot, 10 acres and messuage in Shipden on the death of Matthew his brother. John Alcok messuage and 8 acres in Nm. to John de Whittill. John s. Wm. de Hyngaudrode 4d. heriot, 1 acre in Shipden at his father's death. Robert s. Ric. del Wolfeker 18d. heriot, 8 acres and a messuage in Hyprum at his father's death. Robt. del Cliff surrendered 10 acres oxgangland, 4 acres rodland in le Bothes to John s. said Robert junior, who paid 3s. ingress.

1349.—The fearful array of deaths in the last year's roll will have aroused attention to an unusual occurrence. Never in the history of England has a more terrible event happened than the **BLACK**

DEATH. It swept away whole families, and one half the priests in England fell victims. In 1349 it reached its climax in this country, and labourers became exceedingly scarce, the cattle died, taxation arose to unbearable figures; Justices of Peace were first appointed, and the poor were ordered to work for such wages as were paid before the plague. Sir John de Castleforth, then Senescall for Wakefield Manor, and his servants, ran great dangers in attending the courts, for the Turn was held at Brighouse as usual during the plague time. Edward III. had taken the finest young men for ten years past to fight in France, and resumed his French war as soon as the plague was over. Hen. s. Matthew, the greave of Hiperum was fined 3d. for absenting from the Brighouse *tourn*, which was held Jan. 9th, when the Jurors were, Thos. de Locwod, Wm. de Staynland, Wm. de Bradeley, Thos. del Stocks, Thos. de Whitacres, Ric. de Herteshead, Robt. de Whitwod, Ric. del Rokes, Henry de Rissheworth, John de Brighouse, junr., John s. Ric. de Hopton, and John de Stayncliff. It seems that the richest people came off best, and this is not surprising when we remember what unsanitary mud huts the poor dwelt in. For drawing blood, Henry de Risseworth from Wm. del Bothes, and Wm. s. Hen. de Coppeley from John Whitehead, were fined. Ric. de Thorp and John his son had a dispute with Henry s. Thomas; the Abbot of ffountains with John s. Matthew de Totehill; John de Northcliff with Henry de Seyvile; Wm. Smith de Eccleshill and Ric. Maunsell with John del Cliff of Hyprum, when Priour-rode in Hyperum is mentioned. Maunsell had a dispute with John s. of Sir John de Eland; and John del Cliff was fined 4d. for not presenting Sir Thos. vicar of Halifax, who held lands in Nm. John s. John de Haldeworth gave 18d. heriot for 2 acres in Hyprum at his brother William's death. John s. Walter surrendered 2 acres in Hyprum to John del Hyngandrode. Margaret de Sculcotes surrendered 6 acres to Agnes wife of Ric. de Haselhirst, and 6 acres to Cecil wife of Wm. de Hailay. Thos. Smith of Halifax took a rode of nativa land of John de Godeley. Ric. s. Jordan Pynder and Ric. s. Symon del Dene for not attending the court 2d. each. Wm. de Bristall gave 18d. heriot, for 3 ac. in Nm. at the death of Agnes his mother. Galfri de Coppeley yielded part of a bovate in Hyprum greave to John de Coppeley. John Drake took 2 ac. 1 rd., and Matilda widow of John Sagher paid 40d. for lands. Otes Haldeworth paid heriot for 2 acres in Hyperum greave, on the death of Wm. de Haldeworth his father.

Turn at Brighouse held May 13th. Jurymen mostly as before. Fines for brewing as usual, generally the same women.

1350.—The turn held 22 Dec. at Brighons still in plague time.

This roll is unfortunately mutilated. Henry del Cliff, Henry de Coppley, Adam del Wro, John s. Matilda, Ric. de Skulcote, Elyas s. Simon, Wm. de Godley, John de Illyngworth, Thos. Smith, Ric. Bateson, John Wynter, and Henry s. Wm. for not attending to elect the greave fined 1d. or 2d. each. Ric. s. Ric. Magson de Halifax paid 3d. heriot, for 1 acre in Hyperum grave, his father being dead.

Henry s. Matthew de Yllyngworth held 10 acres. John s. Ric. del Hole, John s. Thos. Milner, and Ric. s. Matthew de Illingworth attended the tourn.

1351.—*Turn* at Brighous, names of Jury not given. John de Holway gave 12d. to have Henry s. Matthew as greave in his place this year. 4 acres and edifice in Nm. late Roger Smith's conveyed to Cecilia d. John de Wales. Ric. s. Henry de Sunderland paid 2s. heriot, for a bovate and edifice on his father's death.

John Bateson took of the waste in Shipden 1 rod formerly Adam de Stancliff's. Henry de Bentley, Shelf, ¼ rode of waste. John de Haldeworth senr. an assart under Solhill, 4 acres. Ric. s. Wm. del Cliff, part of a bovate which Roger s. Roger formerly held. John the chaplain of Hertishead drew blood from John de Thirsk, chaplain; Henry de Lascy from Robt. s. Wm. Tomson ; John Alcok from John del Hill; Henry de Bentley from Henry de Ryssheworth and from Nicholas de Ryssheworth. Robt. Pynder fined 3d. for not attending the turn. The greaves of Rastrick and Hyprum for not going to Wakefield court 2d. each. John Bateson and John de Sculcotes took Priorrode at 4s. 6d. per ann., and Haylayrode at 12d. Mill of Rastrik let this year to John Hilton for 2 marks, 26s. 8d. [It will be noticed that 12d. is always given, not 1s. The payment would be in 12 silver pennies.] Shibden mill was let to Robt. Hare for 3s. 4d. Thos. Smith de Halifax had a bovate and edifice, and 3 acres of Rodland in le Bothes of Henry de Altonlay custodian for John s. Robt. del Cliffe. Thos. Shentogh to cut wood in Hiperum, paid 4s.

1352.—Sir Wm. ffrank was then senescall. Sir John de Eland, John de Bollyng, Adam de Bateley, John de Quernby, Thos. de Lascy and others, chief tenants. Henry s. Matthew, greave of Hiprom, says he paid the greave of Ossett ¾d. towards repairs of mill dam at Wakefield. Elizth. d. Adam Moke, in virginity, surrendered 1½ ac. in Hyprum which Henry s. Matthew holds, with usual manorial customs. Le Strindes, in Nm., formerly Nich. de Haselhirst's, reverts to the lord.

Turn at Brighous, Jury not named. The towns of Dalton, Rastrik, ffekesby, Barsland, Shelf, fined for not being represented. Wm. Waynwright de Stainland, 2d.; Henry del Hagh 3d. and Tho. de Rothalfold de Quernby 2d. for not coming. The town of Herteshed presents that John de Tresk (Thirsk), capellanus, and Henry Mynsmith not coming, 2d. each. John Sprent 6d., for drawing blood from Agnes Tyngill, and Agnes Tyngill 4d. for brewing and selling contrary to assize. Clifton presents that Wm. de Qwalley &c. Northourum that Henry s. Matthew forestalls &c. Hiprom that John Milner (4d.), Henry Gybson (6d.), and John Percy wife (1d.), brew and sell, and John Dykson (4d.), bakes and sells bread against the assize. The wife of Ric. del Thorpe fined 12d. drawing blood against peace from Henry del Cliff's wife, and Thos. Shentlogh (12d.) from Margaret Wyldblod. Total income 3s. 3d. Wm. de Qwalley had 10s. due from the district, for some court fees he had farmed, and

Henry de Risheworth, Henry de Bentley, John de Stancliffe and Robt. Pynder were fined 2d. each for not having paid. John Wynter made a rescue from Henry s. Matthew, the lord's servant; fined 7d. John de Eland *v.* John Wilkynson Tomson: latter fined 2d. John del Northclif *v.* Wm. de Mirfield. John s. Wm. del Bothes 3s. 2d. heriot, mess., 20 acres with appurtenances in Hiprm (grave), his father being dead. John del Hingandrode heriot, for a bovate, messuage thereon, &c., in Nm. on the death of Thos. de Whithill, he being cousin of Juliana relict of said Thos. Elizth. d. Adam del Bothe, in her virginity, surrendered mess. and one acre in Bothes to John de Haylay, who paid 18d. ingress. Ric. del Botherod gave 40d. heriot for a bovate, and messuage thereon on the death of John his father. The four men in the Qwalley case above, appealed against Henry de Lascy, who did not attend next court and was fined 2d. My ancestors in Stansfield had not learnt to keep the peace, for at Sourby court Alice the wife of Adam of the Horsfall drew blood from the wife of Henry del Horsfall, and had to pay 4d. fine. Thos. de Sayntswythanes in Sourby district, *v.* Robt. de Adrerichegate, about lands. The 4th part of the mill of the lord in Rastrik was farmed this year to John de Hilton for 26s. 8d., and the 4th part of Shipden mill for 3s. A Robert de Hiprom resided at Rothwell at this period, and John de Hiprom at Lofthouse.

John de Seyuil, Brian de Thornhill, knight, John s. Elene de Rastrick, Henry del Weld were chief men at this time and John Laysingcroft was seneschall. An inquisition was taken by twelve jurymen of Hiprom, (as also in Rastrik graveship,) who say that John de Eland, knight, held in his lifetime in the graveship of Hiprom, xx marks, xxxij s., a plat called townstigh, 2s. from a plat called preisthead, 5s. from a plat called Sondrelandfeld, 3s. from a plat called Priorrode.

1353.—The roll for this year is missing, a loss to be specially deplored, as there ought to have been some further reference to Sir John de Elland in it. Having printed in 1890, as full an account, both prose and poetical, as can be obtained respecting this great worthy, we must be content here to refer the reader to "The **ELLAND TRAGEDIES**," viz., the Murders of Sir Robert Beaumont of Crosland, Hugh de Quarmby, John de Lockwood, Sir John Eland senior, at Lane Head, Brighouse, when returning from the Sheriff's tourn, Sir John Eland junior, and his son, at Eland, with notices of the families connected with the long continued feuds. All the men concerned in this awful struggle were well known at Brighouse Tourn as will be seen in the foregoing pages. The whole account was supposed to be a myth by some, but its veracity is proved by writings recently found in the Record Office, London, by Mr. Paley Baildon, and Mr. H. J. Barber has a very ancient poetical account in manuscript. In 1353 Robert del Bothe of Holmfirth and Ric. his brother, Matthew de Hepworth of Hepworth, Thomas the Litster or dyer of Almondbury and Ralph de Skelmanthorp were

seized because they had harboured Wm. de Lockwood and Adam
Beaumont knowing that they had slain John de Elland, knight, and
were outlaws. Edmund de Flockton was seized also for harbouring
Beaumont at Flockton, and Thomas Molot of Wakefield for giving

Thomas son of
Thomas Lacy of
Cromwellbottom
40s. knowing he
had slain John
de Elland, knt.
The jury pro-
nounced them
"Not guilty." At
York Castle de-
livery in 1355,
John de Shelley
was tried and
found "Not
guilty," having
been seized by
order of the
Sheriff, because

CROMWELLBOTTOM HALL.

CROMWELLBOTTOM, (Back View.)

he received at Brighouse, William de Lockwood, Adam Beaumont and
others who had feloniously slain John de Elland, knight, knowing of
the commission of the felony. As there was no bridge at Elland

then, Sir John was accustomed to return from the Brighouse court by the old road (now John King lane) to Lane Head, via Elm Royd lately known as Dick Hodgson's lane, to Brookfoot, Purlwell, and the old or upper road to Cromwellbottom, where the Lacy family lived. To our own day, nearly all the hill slopes down to the river from Brighouse to Elland, save the marshy valley, have been well wooded, and in this wood the gang hid themselves. From this time the Saviles take the Ellands' place as owners of a sub-manor here.

1354.—*Turn* at Brighouse, jury not named. Ric. s. Ric. Magson 1 acre in Hyprum (greave) to Henry s. Matthew. John Robertson 6 acres in Nm. to John Symson. Margaret d. John Coppelay 5s. heriot, mess., bovate and half of land in Hiperum on the death of Henry de Coppley (her uncle). Alice, Isabel, Matilda, Johna and Margaret daughters of Alex. de Hengendrode 15d. heriot, 15 acres in le Blakkerre, their brother Wm. being dead; Isabel surrendered her fifth in her virginity to Wm. de Helay. Robt. s. Robt. del Wode paid heriot, for lands in ffekesby, his uncle Henry del Wode, being dead.

John s. John Spilwood 6d. heriot, for an acre in Hipr., his uncle Roger S. being dead: he surrendered it to John Drake. Robt. Hare and Thos. Milnerson conveyed a plat called Hustardrode, 5 ac., in Hyprum grave to Wm. Yonghare. Blood-drawing brawls by Wm. Whittle from Wm. Locus; John del Thorp from Henry de Shipden. Ale brewers and sellers were—Matil. Hare, Robt. Wilkynson Tomson, Isabel Tomwife, John Milner, John del Clay, John Percy, Thos. Shenthogh, Robert Shortanhaw. Wm. Jonson Milner 18d. heriot, mess., 6 acres in Nm. his father, John, having died. John Symson 2s. heriot, mess., 6 acres in Hyprum, his cousin John s. Ric. Symson being dead. Wm. del Lee gave 6d. to the lord, to take mess., 20 acres in Hiperum greave from Wm. del Kirk and Margaret his wife, custodians for Robt. s. Ric. de Wolkerre, for 12 years.

1355.—John del Clay 2s. to take a mess., a bovate in Hyprum (grave) of John Willeson del Halle. Henry Alisandre surrendered a garden (1 acre) in Hyprum to John Milner. Thos. Milnerson 1 acre in Hustardrode to Elene d. Elie Walker. Matilda d. Alex. del Hingandrode, in virginity, 2 ac. 1 rode in Blaker to Wm. de Helay: John Webster and Margaret his wife gave evidence. Otes de Haldeworth de Ovenden mentioned. John Symson 3 acres in Sonderland to Matthew Bateson. Margt. d. Matthew de Ilyngworth, in virginity, mess., 8 acres in Sunderland to Henry son of Matthew. Johna widow of John del Northcliff, part of messuage and 8 acres in Adrichegate to John de Haldeworth. John de Whittel 4 acres in Hyprum (grave) under Solhill, now Swill-hill, to Wm. s. Ots de Haldeworth. Henry de Risheworth and Adam de Calys drew blood from Ric. de Herteshead, fined 12d. each; Thos. de Sheplay from Johana del Hole. Fourth part of Rastrick mill let for 26s. 8d., ¼th of Shipden mill for 3s.

1356.—A Thos. del Brighous was residing in Sourby district. John de Hengandrod 2s. heriot for rodland in Ourum, his cousin

Thos. de Whithill being dead. Isabel del Kerre, 7 acres in Ourum to Henry s. Matthew. Ric. Jonson Adamson 3d. heriot for a rode in Ou'r Shipedene, his father John *de Staynclif* being dead. Robt. de Adrichegate and Julian his wife, held a bovate in Nm.

Turn at Brighous, jury not named. Wm. de Mirfield had succeeded Ric. s. John as senescall. Ric. ffox drew blood from John Hanson of Rastrik. Ric. del Thorp paid 6d. to take 3 acres from John Lascy. Matilda and Ellen d. Wm. Batemanson paid heriot for 2 parts of 2 ac. 1 rd. in Nm. on the death of Ric. Batemanson their uncle. Robt. s. John ffygge heriot, 3½ acres pasture in North Blakkerre, his mother Johna being dead. John s. Robt. del Cliff and Ric. Mansel held in le Bothes, Hiprum graveship, a mess., and 14 acres. Alice Jondoghter Symson, called also *Alice d. John Simson Judson Nerooman*, gave 3s. 4d. heriot mess., 6 acres, her father John, and Juliana de Aderichegate both dead. John del Hingandrode asked for an inquisition against Robert de Adrichgate and Juliana his wife, respecting a mess., and a bovate, on the death of Thos. de Whitill. Henry de Ryssheworth took ½ acre of waste in Hiprum, between Collarhousted and Hekdenbrok, paying for ingress, 3d., and an assart called Henrerod which the said Henry paid heriot for in the last turn at Brighous. Hiperum greave not going to Wakefield court fined 6d. John s. Wm. del Rode, a bovate and rodland in Hyperum to Henry de Ryssheword, for 9 years. Henry de Ryssheworth surrendered a tenement and croft

COLEY HALL GATEWAY.

called Dogatrode to John Wilkynson. Henry de Ryssheworth [of Coley Hall] paid heriot for 3 acres and pasture and an assart called Henrerod his uncle Henry de Coldlay being dead. From this time the Coleys of Coley cease, and the Rishworths follow for two centuries. Adam s. Adam s. Thomas de Hipperum attended the tourn. Rastrick mill (¼th) let for 26s. 8d.; Shepden ¼th., 40d.

1357.—Beatrix Lascy conveyed to John del Thorp a plat in Hiprum called Longmere. Margaret and Mgt (?) d. Adam Judson de Ovynden paid heriot for an acre on their father's death.

Turn at Brighous, in November, names of jurors not given. Matilda and Elena d. Will. Bateman lands in Blakker to John del Wro. Rastrik mill (¼th part) let this year to Robt. de Coventre for 27s. 3d.; pledges, John del Clay, Thos. de Shepley. Shipden mill (¼th) to Rob. Hare : pledge, John de Whitill.

John s. Rob. de Cliff returns to Ric. Mansell the cottage and 14 acres in le Bothes. Ric. s. Matthew held 3 acres in Nm. Henry del Cliff took mess., and 20 acres in Hyprum of Ric. del Cliff for 9 years, paying 12d. to the court for ingress.

1358.—Twenty seven from Hiprum greave fined 1d. each for not attending the tourn. John Wynter surrendered an assart in Nm. to Thos. del Cliff; John de Haylay mess., 7 acres in Nm. to Hen. s. Matthew; Roger Tayllor paid 2s. 6d. to take mess., and 24 acres in Tothill of Hugh s. Stephen custodian for John s. John s. Matthew. Rastrik mill let to Roger Cowhird and John Stre'gg for 26s. 3d.; Shipden mill to John Drak and John Tomson. Cecilia de Wales sur. a cottage, 4 ac., in Hyprum grave to Robt. Hare ; regranted to John s. Wm. de N'ourum. Wm. de Hemingway 4 acres in Hiprum to Robt. Pynder. Wm. de Hemingway, senior, 1 acre called William-

SIMPSON. RHODES (DEL RODES.)

ryding to Wm. de II., junior. Robt. s. John ffigge de Rothwell, surrendered lands at Blakker to Thos. Smith. Robt. s. John del Halle, paid 3s. 4d. heriot, mess., bov., 3 rodes of Rodland in Nm., his father being dead.

1359.—Alice Nellmayden holds 1 acre in Shipden milne estate for 20 years from Henry s. Matthew. John del Hengandrode 2 acres to John Symson. John Symson 2 ac. 3 rods to Ad. Willeson de Shelf. Beatrix d. Wm. de Hepworth paid heriot for Estridding in Rastrik.

Turn at Brighouse. Jury named,—Will de Bradelay, Henry de Ryssheworth, John de Stancliff, John s. Ric. de Hopton, John s. Thos. de Dalton, Wm. de Staynland, Adam del Hirst, Nichs. de Halywell, John de Brighouses, Ric. de Gledehill, Ric. de Hertesheued and John del Rode. Galfri de Welberton, knt., and Alma his wife *r*. Wm. del Dene. Alice de Leyrode, Sourby, was eight years old when her father died of pestilence. John de Hyngynrode, by John Drake the greave, sur. to John s. Simon del Dene 1 ac. 1 rod. John Thomeson de Haldworth *r*. Ric. s. John de H. about 4 acres ; special jury, viz., John Symson, John de Staynclif, Ric. de Birstall, John del Strong, John de Wythill, Ric. Maunsell, Hen. Mattheuson, John Bateson, John del Northend, John Drake, John Wylkynson, Hen. de Cliff, (Northowram men evidently.)

1360.—Brighouses *Turn*, Vigil St. Katrine. Jury, Henry de Ryssheworth, John de Staynland, Thos. del Wodeheued, Nic. de Halywell, Wm. de Bradelay, Adam del Hyrst, John s. Thos. de Dalton, John de Stancliff, John del Rode, John Drake, John del Brighouses, and John Elynsone de Rastrik. Henry de Rysshworth paid 1d. to take a rode of waste at Hill in Hyprom. Under Hiprom township, John de Wyloghby not attending fined 2d. John Milner, 6d., Ric. de Whalley 3d., Hen. de Clyf 2d., for brewing and selling against assize. Thos. Hunter of Clifton not attending the court 2d. Herteshead, Thos. Chaplain of the parish of Hertshead 'abduxisse vol. Alice d. Johanna pette contr. voluntatem suam,' 2s.

Turn, April 13th. Jury as before, except Halywell, Stancliff, Drake; replaced by Wm. de Ryley, Ric. de Herteshead, John s. Ric. de Hopton. John Percy, Henry s. Enot, and Adam de Blakeburn not attending the court, 2d. each. Ric. Mohaut (Mawd) *r*. Adam Shelf. A John de Brighouse resided then at Pontefract. Henry Matthewson took of waste land 4 ac. 3 rd. in Hiprum (grave) which Ric. his brother held since the pestilence at 12d. per annum. Ric. Mansell took 5 acres in Priorrode which John Bateson held since the pestilence at 20d. per annum. Hen. Matthewson executor of John del Cliff's will, *r*. Ric. Mansel. Matthew Bateson after enquiry by special jury, took 12 ac. 3 rods in le Holkans at 3s. per. ann. John Drake took 1 acre of waste in le Scotchlane. Henry de Ryssheford took 3 rodes at Hyprum grene at 3d. rent, paying 6d. for ingress.

1361.—Rastrik Mill. Henry Mwson (Matthewson) farmed ¼ pt. from feast of St. Michael, at 25s., and Shepden mill at 3s. 6d.

MAUDE ARMS.

Turn Nov. 16. Jury named, as before. Townships in each greave arranged : Barkisland, Dalton, Quernby, ffekisby, Rastrik and Staynland under Rastrik. Under Hyprm, Shelf, a clean bill ; Clifton, three brewers, Haket, Whalley, Whytewod ; Hertshead, Agnes Tyngil as usual for brewing ; Northourum, Robt. Hare, brewer ; Hyperum presents that John de Wyloghby (whose family founded the Willoughby chantry at Halifax), Henry Dmteson, Robt. s. Wm. did not attend court, fined 2d. each ; John s. Wm., Henry del Cliff, John de Wyloghby, John del Hole, Matilda Smythsone, fines 3d. each for 'semel' brewing, and John Mylner 6d. for brewing and selling. Ric. Johanson 12d. for drawing blood from Thos. s. John Alcok. Henry Adekynson of Scamonden by John del Hole, greave, surrendered 12 acres in S. to Ric. del Heye. Thos. By the water *r.* John del Rokes. John del Smaleleghes *r.* Johana wid. John Matthewson. Found by inquisition that Thomas le Smyth cut down 20 young oaks on virgin land held by him, and carried them to Halifax, fined 10s., also Henry Matthewson had cut 6 oaks from lands formerly Robt. Hilleman's, fined 6s.8d. Ric. de Sculcotes *r.* Ric. Drake. Hen. de Ryssheworth and John del Scoles *r.* John de Wyloghby. John Drake surrenders 1 ac. 1¼ rd. in les Holmes to John Tylly. Hen. s. Matthew requires 5s. from John Boy due to the graveship account when he was greave. Wm. de Helay, 6 ac. in Nm. to his wife Johana. John Milner drew blood from Henry de Yorkshire, but Emma wife of Henry retaliated. Alice d. John Milner del Bothe *r.* John s. Robt. del Cliff, re messuage, ½ bovate, 2 ac. rodland in Nm. Alex. de Hengandrode 7 ac. in Nm. called Cowrodes to Isabel his daughter. Wm. vicar of Hodresfeld church appears in a case. Ric. de Stayncliff being dead, a mess., 36 acres relieved by John s. Elye Adamson, for 9s. Beatrix Souter daughter, 1½ ac. in Hyprum (greave) to Hen. s. Matthew. Wm. de

Mekesburgh, by John del Bothrode the greave, conveyed ¼ rode to John del ffryth.

1362.—John de Seyvill de Eland regularly appears. Wm. s. Ric. de Saltonstall held a mess., 23 acres in Saltonstall. Henry de Rishworth took 2 acres, formerly waste, in Hekden near Mathewgrene at Hyprum. Rastrik greave not attending Wakefield court fined 2d.

Turn at Brighouses, 19 April. Jury, Henry de Rissheworth, Wm. de Staynland, Ric. de Hertshead, John Thomassone, John de Hopton, John Percy, John Enotson, Ric. del Gledehill, John Milner, Adam del Stockes, John de Stancliff, John del ffrith. Ric. de Baildon sub-bailiff of Morlay came to Barksland Dec. 10 last, and took Ric. del Heigh without warrant to Sandall Castle. Johanna d. and heir Wm. de Birstall held mess., 2 bovates in Nm. Ric. de Thornhill appears

THORNHILL ARMS.   THORNHILL ARMS.

for land in Rastrik or ffixby. Henry de Rishworth took 2 acres at Prestlay. Adam de Topgreve, Rastrik paid heriot for mess., 15 ac., 1 rod. Thos. de Saltonstall and Matilda his wife were executors of the will of Thos. s. Thomas Smith de Halifax. John de Wyloby 'summonsed' by Wm. del Both for 3s. 4d. for cart tymber. Ric. s. Ric. Magson 6 ac. 3½ rodes in Hyprum (?greave) to John del Hill his cousin. John del Northend, 1½ ac. in Nm. to Rob. Hare. Henry de Bentley, John de Wyluby and Alice del Brook, *r.* Henry de Rishworth re Nm. lands. Thos. By the Water and John del Wode, greave of Rastrik, take ¼th Rastrik mill. Ale Tasters appointed for each greaveship. John de Haldworth had 4 ac. in Nm. John Symson yielded mess., 18 ac., in Nm. to John de Shipden. Henry Shiphird took 2 acres waste in Hyprum in Hekas near Falrode, at 4d. per annum each. Wm. de Prestlay resided in Sourby district; Wm. s. Adam de Crossleghe, constable of Stansfield, John Robynson of Sourby, John del Brodeleghe, Ovenden. John de Rillyngton vicar of Birstall and Adam de Heton chaplain make ffidelity for Herteshede lands. Ric. Maunsell, Hyprum greave, and nine others fined for not attending, 2d. each.

1363.—*Turn*, Oct. 16. John Elynson for a tumult in the court, 3d. John de Bretton capellanus (? chaplain of Rastrik) mentioned under Rastrik. John de Stone de Heightmundwyk mentioned. Stray cattle, John de Wylouby lost a heifer, Ric. del Hole found a stirk, in Hyprum; in Rastrik five were fined for allowing hogs to stray,—Henry Alisaundre, Roger Diconson, John Hansone, Hugh Stevensone, and Adam de ffernley. Brewers as usual.

Court and *Turn* at Brighous, 17 April. John Bateson took 1 acre of new assart in Shipden at 4d. per ann., paid 12d. ingress; John de Holway 1 rode at 1d., ffine 4d. Ric. de Birstall paid 6d. to take 1 acre of Henry Matthewson and Isabel his wife, custodians of John s. Matthew. John at Bowes had 2 ac. at Blacker, and Wm. Milyas and his wife Alice 4 ac. in Lowroyd in Hyprum.

1364.—(See full account in *Yorkshire County Magazine*.) Roger s. Ric., messuage and 4 acres in Rastrik to John del ffrith and Margaret his wife and their heirs. Ingress 8s. John Elinson fined 2d. for not attending the election of greave. Six fined in Hyprum for absenting.

Brighouses Turnus tent die Martis xix die Nouembre Anno R. R. E. ter. post conquest xxxviij°. Each township had to be represented by four men, those from *Hiperom* being Thomas fil Johis, Robtus del Rode, Johis de Rokes, Wills de Hogh; iure p'sentam qd. Johes Milner (viijd.) bracavit et vend cont. assm. Itm Matill Gibdoghter ij d., Johna Gibdoghtr ij d. messere in antupno exa villam contr. statutu. Inquis magna p'sentat qd Johes de Wilghby debet adventu & non ven quem. Thomas fil Joh xij d. & soc. sui concelauernt.

Brighouses Court, 19 Nov., die Martis. Ric. de Haldeworth being dead, John his son took 4 acres in Nm. paying 18d. heriot, whilst Juliana, John's mother, paid 6d. for his custody during his minority. John Milner of Wodehouses, Rastrik, had killed five 'nilton' (? what) value 20s., has to make satisfaction to John de Wodehouses., and fined 3d. Rastrik grave yielded 18d. this court, Hiprom 2s. 11d., and Scamonden 6s. 8d. Halifax court was held next day; Kirk Birton or Holm court was held on the 18th. Under Rastrik for Wakefield court appears the name John de Colereslay. capellanus, (chaplain.)

From *Rastrik*, Henry Allison and his three companions say that John del ffrith (ij d.) sold Ric. o' bothcroid lands without leave, Rog. Taillur sold John Milner (ij d.) a half acre, and Rog. Taillur (ij d.) for selling 13½ acres. The figures in brackets are the fines.

From *ffekisby*, Willm. de Lightriche and his three companions have nothing to present. The sum from this Turn xiiij s. ix d., viz., from Hip'om grave ix s. viij d., from Rastrik v s. j d.

Brighouses Turn, 7 May. Robt. del Rode, constable of Hyperom, with his four companions—Robt. ffletcher, Ric. del Hoile, John Webster, Henre del Cliffe, present that John de Wilghby (3d.) owes ' adventu' & did not come; John Milner (12d.) for brewing; Matill Gibdoghter (6d.) is a common litigatrix, therefore fined as above, total xxj d. There seems to have been no ducking scolds in the river then. ffekesby, villata there have nothing to present. Wm. de Whallay of Clifton fined 4d. for tanning and shoemaking; and 6d. for brewing. For Rastrik, Henre Alissaundre, constable, & his companions present that Alicia Turnur brewed and sold against the assize, fined 2d. Rastrick graveship yielded 3s. 4d., Hiprom 4s. 3d., this Turn. Court at Brighouses, same day. Roger Dikson of Rastrik had a dispute with John de Totehill about deducting a rode from 9 acres he had bought. John de Wilghby surrendered a mess., 1½ bov. in Hiprom to Elena his wife, who gave 6s. for ingress. John Aumbler gave to the lord 18d. to take of Ric. de Sunderland a mess. ½ bov. in Nm. for 6 years. Rastrik yielded 9d., Scamonden 4d., Hiprom 7s. 9d. this court. The Halifax court for Sourby greaveship was held May 8th. Thomas de Lodingdene one of the lord's natives begs for a tree to repair his house with, he being poor. Hugh s. Stephen, and Margaret wife of Hugh, held a mess., 16 acres in Rastrik. John de Holwaye, who held by right of his wife Mergerte 6 acres and 2 houses in Nm., surrenders them to John Boy: ingress 2s. John Bosville held the agistment at Sandal Castle for 13s. 4d. (He was chief forester for Wakefield in 1368.) Ric. de ffinchendene held Wakefield mill & town farm for £66 13s. 4d. Hypron—John s. Wm. de Hypron took to farm ¼th mill of Rastrik for the year for 21s. to be paid half-yearly at Pasch and St. Michael's. Robt. Hare took Shepedene mill for 3s. The tolls of Halifax were farmed to Rog. Edeson for 26s. 8d.

1365.—Rastrik mill to John s. Wm. de Hiprom; and John Aumbler took Shepdene mill.

Turn held Nov. 13. Constables' names are now given for all the townships; Will de Weteacre for Dalton, Will. Wrigth for Hertshead, John Chapman for Clifton, Ric. de Heliwell for Stainland, Robt. del Rode for Hipron, Will Dobson for Berkesland, Ad. Willeson for Shelf, Henry del Hagh for Quernby, John de Whitelee for N'ourum, Wm. lyghtriche for ffekesbye, Henry Allissandre for Rastrik. The Hiprom Constable and his companions report that John de Willoby is away, (3d.), Ric. Webster brewed (4d.), Ric. Michel (12d.) drew blood from Tho. de Brighouses. Robt. ffletcher complains that Matill de Shepelay had taken his garden produce at Brighous: fined 3d. Roger Taillur yielded 3 ac. 1 rd. called Brigrode to Magote wife of John Elisson, who paid 2s. John Milner ½ ac. called William Pighel in Rastrik to John de Boderode. The three daughters of Wm. de Coplay, viz. Johna, Margaret wife of John del Hingandrode, and Alice wife of

G

Robt. Hare, plaintiff, *v.* John de Wilghby and Elina his wife *re* a messuage and 2 bovates in Hiprom. Matilda d. John de Sculcote, mess., 10 acres in Sculcote and 1 acre in Priorrode to Ric. Drake; ingress 4s. Ric. s. Adam de Hiperum quit claimed to John del Cliffe mess., 8 ac. in Ourum; ingress 2s. Rob. Pynder, a mess., 5 acres in Hiprom, 5 ac. in Brethhay, and ¼ ac. in ffalbank to Alice his wife.

1368.—Henry s. Wm. de Hyprm took ¼ Shipden mill for 4s.; and Robt. Pynder of Hiprom, Rastrik mill at 24s. yearly for four years, Rog. Edeson is pledge.* Wm. de Estfeld was then senescall. Brighouse *Turn,* Nov. 2. Rob. Wilkynson Dykson de Hiprom taking brushwood from Roger de Rastrik, called at the next court Roger Diconson de Rastrik, but Robert surrenders a mess., 1½ bov. in Hiprom which Wm. (or Wilkyn) father of said Robert had held, to Roger. John Couper *v.* Simon the chaplain of Heptonstall, and the capellanus was fined 2d. A Robert de Hiprom lived at Alverthorp.

Turn at Brighous, die Lune, 28 May. Jury, Wm. de Bradelay, Henry de Rissheworth,—de Stokes,—de Lockwode, John de Hopton, John Drake, John Jagger, John de Brighous, Ric. de Halywell, Rob. Pynder, Thos. de Dalton, Ric. Lassels.† The old constable reported his cases, and a new constable was elected at the Spring Turn. Thomas del Crosse, capellanus, Rastrik (graveship), *v.* Henry Robynson de Berkesland; Thos. paid 2d. Thos. Walker being dead, his cousin Wm. Casseson paid xxd. heriot, for 4 acres in Hiprom, but surrendered them to Wm. de Hemyngway. Robt. Aumbler, a mess., ¼ bov. in Hiprom to his son John for 7 years. John Denyas *v.* Nichs. de Herteshede capellanus; John pays 2s. John del Rokes drew blood from Adam del Dene of Shelf who made hue and cry, and Margota del Dene raised hue and cry, fined 4d. each. Alice d. John Symson surrendered by the greave, 1 ac. 1 rd. in Nm. to John Symson. Alice d. John Symson de Adrichegate held a mess., 9 acres in Shipden, for which Elyas Symson her cousin pays 3s. 4d. heriot. She is next called Alice d. John de Adrichgate and had held for life with Juliana de Adrichegate a mess., bov., 3 acres of rodland in Hiprom (grave) for which Elyas paid also 3s. 4d. as heriot. In a trial, mention is made of a turf spade, a plogh staffe, a swyvel, a feiriren, a chail, 2 strokes; total value 6s. 8d. The usual fines for taking wood, brewing, brawls, and non-attendance occur.

1369.—Brighous Turn, Oct. 1, Monday. Robt. de Morton, senescall. The widow of Galfri de Werberton sold to Thomas de Brighouses an oak growing on the lord's waste at Brighouses grene, which Thomas cut without leave, valued at 15d. John Milner, who is now dead, built Brighouse park boundary. Ric. de Botherode de Hudresfeld had pasture in ffeksby. Wm. Drake is dead, and John s. John s. said Wm., his heir, paid 18d. heriot for 3½ ac. in Nm. called Blakker. Diota or Dionisia wid. of John Milner de Brighouses, *v.* John de

---

* The sub-manors seem to have held ¾ths of the mills. † From whose family Lascelles Hall, near Dalton, is so named.

Stokes and Ric. or Dicon de Blakhale. Her husband had held a mess., 24 acres in Brighouses. Juliana de Adrichgate who held mess., bovate, in Nm. from Thos. de Whitel, is dead, Alice dr. John Pynder brother of said Thos. pays heriot, 3s. 4d. John Bateson, 6 ac. in Shepedene to Ric. de Heton, ingress 12d. Elena d. Nelle 1 ac. in Halay to Margt. wife of John de Haylay; ingress 6d. Ric. de Heton vicar of the church of Halifax made homage to the lord for a messuage and 2 bovates in Shepdene. Brian de Thornhill, chevalier, not attending Wakefield, fined 2d. It was found that this great "sect-ator" (follower, or head man,) was dead. Rastrik mill, ¼th part, to Ric. Machon for 16s. 8d.; ¼th of Shepdene mill to Robt. Hare for 40d. To Wakefield courts came John the Abbot of Cristal, John the Prior of Monkbretton, and other ecclesiastics who owed service. John s. Thos. Alcok being dead, Johna wife of Hen. de Rothelay, his sister, paid 2s. heriot for 6 acres in Soilhill, Nm. Brighouses *Turn*, May 20, John de Wiloby objected to a house being built by Ric. de Bakhale. Ric. del Brig, 10 acres in Cleg Clif to John de Haldeworth; ingress 2s. Ric. de Bratwhait took 3½ acres in 'Venella' called Breryhaylone of Robt. Hilman. Diota wid. John Milner *v.* Margaret wid. and executor of the will of John de Percy (of Clifton) about 4 cows. Margaret de Botherode let to John de Stokkes for 20 years a mess., 24 acres in Rastrik. For fishing in Keldre in Sourbyshire 24 paid 6d. each. Hyperom wode hewers were Robt. Pynder, John s. Wm. de Hyprom, Robt. s. Wm. de Hypr., John s. Hen. de Hypr., Alice Nale doghter, Henry del Clyf, Isolda de Prestelay, Roger de Rastrik, John de White-hill, Roger de Bratheywhate, Henry Batte, John s. Symon, John Strong, John le Boye, John s. Wm., Henry de Bentlay, Ric. de Birstehall, Ric. Bateson, Thos. del Clyf, Henry s. Mathew, 2d. to 3d. each. John s. Henry de Hyprm *v.* Alice Naldoghter about a cottage, croft &c. in Hyprum held by Anabilla sister of said Henry.

1370.—Matthew Bate having died, Elizabeth his daughter paid 3s. heriot for mess., 12 acres in Shepedene. Ric. Drake and Matilda Sculcotes, mess., 12 acres in Sculcotes to John Aumbler. Alan Goidair de Scamonden not attending the court, fined 2d. John de ffery (Sourby) *v.* Elizth. de Staunton exec. of the will of Johna widow of Bryan de Thornhill, knt. Halifax tolls were let to Henry de Risseworth for 26s. 8d. this year, who also leased Sourby and Soland mills for 73s. 4d. The 4th part of Shipedene mill let to Rob. Hare for 3s. 4d.; of Rastrik mill to Ric. Machan for 16s. 8d.

Bryghouses Turn, Monday, 18 Nov. The constables were—Robt. Milner, Dalton; Wm. de Ravenslawe (Rawnsley), Berkisland; Nich. de Lum, Staynland; Thos. de Bentlay, Shelf; Wm. de Stonlee, Quernby; Wm. Lightrich, ffekesby; Thos. Gilleson, Rastrik, from whence Wm. Colier was fined 2d. for not attending; Thomas Jakson, Hiperum, who with his four companions report John de Wiloby for absence, 3d.; Thos. Jonson (8d.), Ric. Machon (8d.), John Smith (4d), Ric. del Halle (4d.), Isolda de Wiloby (3d.), Matil. (d. Gilbt) de Astay 3d., for brewing. Thos. Cosyn, Clifton constable, reported Margaret

Percy for absence, 2d., Wm. de Whalley as a tanner and sutor, 3d.
Henry Bat was Northourum constable, and Wm. Wright for Hertshead. John de Haldeworth conveyed a mess., ½ bovate, called Adrichegate for 11 years to Henry Wilkinson. Elias de Northeues to John
del Bank, mess., 8 acres called Adrichgate for 7 years. John Boy *r.*
Henry Matthewson about a cow sold 'qd horet villm infra xv. dies
post fm. Pentecoste ad da'p. que taxant xij *d'.* Wm. del Broke broke
into the house of John de Rokes at Hiprom, and took a coverlet, some
silver goods, &c. His body to be taken, that is, imprisoned. John
Symson of Ourum, 3 ac. at Hingandrodefeld to Ric. de Heton, vicar
of Halifax church, and his heirs for ever. John de Wodehede de
Cliffehous in Hiperum greave *r.* John Boy. Brighouses *Turn,* May
5. Robt. de Morton, senescal. John de Hiprom, 6d. for drawing
blood from Ric. del Halle. Adam Jankynknave died seized of a mess.,
15 acres in Rastrik, for which John s. Wm. de Hiprom his cousin and
next heir, paid 2s. heriot, but surrendered the same to Wm. de
Shepeley. Elyas of Northeves *r.* Rob. Pynder and Alice his wife,
about a messuage, bovate, and 3 acres in Nm.

1371.—Shepden mill (¼th) to Rob. Hare for 40d., Rastrick mill, ¼th,
to Roger Milner, 16s. 8d. John del Bothes, Will. del Bank, Henry
Milner del Cliffe, all of Hiperum ; and John Elison, Henry Allissandre,
Alice de Botherode, Robt. Bul, John de Wodehouse and John de
Stokkes, all of Rastrik, fined 3d. each for not attending the turn, 20
Oct. In Northourum there was a stray cow, value 5s. Matil de Astay
was fined 4d. for brewing and 2d. as a litigatrix. Fines in Hyprum
for brewing—Janyn Rissheworthman 6d., Rob. Carter 6d., John
de Wyloby 6d., Isolda de Hiprom 4d., Alice del Roidehouses 4d., Roger
del Hoile 6d., Thom Jonson 4d., Ric. Masshon 6d., John Smith, 2d.
Henry del Okes, conveyed a mess., 18 acres in Rastrik to John his son.

Turn, April 5th. Henry de Risshworth, 2 acres at Wynterege to
John de Wyloby, who paid 8d. ingress. John Drake 6 acres in Blakker
and Heye to John his son. Repairs to Rastrik mill, 20s., paid out of
the greave's fund.

1372.—Ric. de Thornehill paid his fine to this court for his lands
in ffekisby and Totehill ; John Drake for Nether Shipden, and Ric.
(Heton) vicar of Halifax for Over Shipden. John Mohaud (Mawd)
was greave for Sourby. Mill of Rastrik (¼th) non potest dimitor ad
antiquam firma hoc anno Ideo Hen. Matthewson, John Staincliffe,
Roger Diconson, Johnnes Symson overant indulgere eidm molend vt
respondeant dno de porc'one dno p'tinenti in app'amentes hoc anno.
Shipden mill the same.

Turn, Oct. 18. John s. John paid heriot for 9 acres in Rastrik,
Isolda his mother being dead. Elena de Kighley de Airdale *r.* John
de Wyloby, re nilton,* sold for 4s. 4d.

Turn, May 9. Robt. de Morton seneschal. Hipron constable and
his four companions present that Adam Lauerak† drew blood from

---

* I am unable to explain this.　† ? of Laverock (or Lark) Hall, Hipperholme.

Adam Taillur; also four brewers reported. Matill. Astay, litigatrix &
rixatrix, (scold and brawler), 2d. John s. Simon del Dene, a rode
called Baro, and 6 acres at Shortrode to Beatrix wid. John Pristson.
Thos. s. John s. Isolda de Wodehouse, 9 acres in Rastrik to John
Matthewson de Wodehouse, who paid ingress 12d. Henry de Rissheworth, Hiperum forester, presented 25 persons for taking away wood,
2d. to 12d. each. Roger filemyng and John de Cogcroft were sub-
foresters for Soureby and Werlullay (Warley).

1373.—Rastrik mill (⅓th) to Robt. ffletcher, for 16s. 8d., Shibden
mill not able to be let this year, the same four persons responsible as
last year.

Turn, Oct. 24. Wm. Lightriche, ffekisby constable, with his usual
blank list. Hip. Robt. ffetcher's dog had killed Adam Taillur's pig,
worth 6d., Robert says the dog did not kill his pig, and demands an enquiry, and pays 2d. to have one. Adam's wife was fined 3d. for taking
away Robert's herbage, and she was fined 4d. also for being litigatrix;
poor Emma! John Boy died, and John his son and heir, aged 10, gave
2s. to heriot the third part of a bovate in Hiprom. Thos. de Dalton
bought two wrecked trees on his land near Kelder for 2d. Ric. de
Thornhill took of the lord 14½ acres in ffekesby. Ric. del Halle, the
Hiprum constable, had to report himself (4d), Thos. de Brighouse (6d),
Adam lavrok (8d), Ric. Machon (6d), John Smith (2d.), brewers; that
Wm. de Shepelay (8d) had enclosed a common well, and Henry de
Benteley (8d) had enclosed a plot of common pasture at Heli Welle
Seik* to the hurt of the tenants. Margt. del Dene's cattle had trespassed
on Roger de Rastrik's land: fined 2d. Adam Taillur's horse had been
eating Will Hunter's oats to the damage of 2d. value. Ric. Bateson
had died, and Johna wife of Ric. de Sunderland, his daughter and
heiress, paid 3s. heriot for a grange and ¼ bovate in Clifferode in Hiprom
graveship. The Brighouse Jury varies very little yet: Wm. de Bradelay,
Henry de Rissheworth, Adam del Stokkis, Thos. s. John de Dalton,
John Drake, John del ffrith, Wm. de Stokkeis, John Jagger, John de
Berksay, Rob. Pynder, Ric. de Heliwell, Thos. de Lokwode. All the
Rastrik, Hiprom, Osset, &c. &c. tenants to repair their share of Wake-
field mill dam. The prioress of Kirkelghes *r.* Esmon son to the noble
Richard of England and Earl of Kent, by Robt. de Morton, seneschal,
about 18 acres in Hertshead of the prioress and noueynes: Jury, Thos.
Hunter, Ric. de Hertshead, John ffletcher, Thos. Cosyn, Adam de
Walton (cross), Adam Blakburn de Clifton, Roger Milner de Cliffeton,
Ric. de Cogcroft, John atte halle de Clifton, Ad. de Wodeshagh, Ric.
del Milne and Wm. Wright de Clifton, who say on oath that Thos. de
Malhum, capellanus, Ric. Brand, capell., Ric. de Calthorne, capell.,
and Nichs. de Estrik, capell., held the said mess., 18 acres and third
part of a mess., in Herteshede of the gift and feoffament of Henry de
Risshworth and his wife by fine in the king's court.

---

* Helliwell Syke, near Priestley Green. There was evidently a holy well here
from Saxon times. Richard de Heliwell, juror, resided at Stainland Holywell.

1374.   Hiperum greave fined 2s. for not attending the court.

Bryghouses *Turn.* 16 Oct. Thos. Smith flees from the court, 12d. Thos. Otes 12d. for drawing blood from Thos. Smith. John Drake and Ric. de Sunderland had made 2 lideyates* at the ends of the road between Cliffehouses and Horlawegrenehouses to the hurt of the people; inquiry to be made. John Milner of Halifax for selling flesh against the assize, fined 4d. Henry Rissheworth and Roger fflemyng farmed Sourby mill for 76s. 8d. this year, Rastrik and Shipden mills (¼th) for 22s. in half-yearly payments, Halifax tolls for 26s. 8d. Rastrik mill cost £9 15s. 6d. repairing, when John Boy was greave.

Turn, April 24. Thos. Sharp of Nm. *r.* John Wilcokson. John ffox being dead, Hugh his brother paid 5s. heriot, for mess., 24 acres in Rastrik. Ric. del Cliff has stopped the highway between Wherolay and le Bailibrigge (? Halifax). Wm. del Hoof (Hove Edge ?) made a ditch west of Hallecrofts, fined 4d. Thos. de Thorp obstructs Lyesgate, 4d. John de Bates vicar of Dewesbury and Robt. de ffreaston *r.* John Drake, about 6s. 8d. detention. John de Stayncliff for pious uses surrendered to Roger del Clay a messuage and 28 acres in Northourum. Robt. ffidge, sur. 3½ acres in Blakker to John Milner. Wm. del Bank and Isolda his wife took a mess., 6 acres in Ourombanke. John de Staincliffe surrenders to the lord a mess., 23 acres in Shipden, and retakes it for his life, and then to the use of his son Wm.

1376.   John Tylly, chaplain, took 1 acre called the Holmes in Hiprom grave. Robt. ffletcher took the lord's portions of Rastrik and Shepden mills for 24s., pledges, John Drake and John s. Wm. de Hiprom. Rissheworth and fflemyng took all the waifs and straies of the whole lordship, except Wakefield town, for 33s. 4d. this year; also Halifax tolls for 20s., and Sourby mill for £4.

Brighouses *Turn,* 6 Oct. Henry Mallinson paid 4d. for brewing, at Rastrik. Wm. Lightriche was ffekesby constable. At Quernby, Hugh Souter (suter) paid 4d. as tanner and sutor (shoemaker.) Nicholas the capellanus (chaplain) at Hertshedd fined 3d. for closing a common road.

Turn, 4 May. John Hanson 8d. for drawing blood from Rob. Bul. John de Wyloby being dead, John his son and heir, aged 13, gave 3s. 4d. heriot for a mess., bovate, and a rode in Hiprom at 7s. 7d. yearly rent. Robt. Walker conveyed a roide, containing 2 acres, in Hiprom, to Robt. s. Wm. Thos. Taillur took at foldestede a plot with house in Rastrik.

1377.   *Turn,* Oct. 19. Jury, Thos. de Dalton, John Drake, Nichs. de Risshworth, John del Rokes, Ric. de Sunderland, Robt. del Roide, Ric. de Haliwelle, Thomas Cosyn, Wm. del Hirst, Henry de Risshworth, John Gagger, John de Berkesay.† Wm. Chullur of Hertshead for brewing, 6d.; thieving, 3d. Henry Matthewson is dead and Ric. his brother paid 10s. heriot for mess., 5 acres, called the Lee in Shepden, mess.

---

* I take this word to mean a 'swing gate,' to prevent cattle straying from the common fields. Lidgate, in Lightcliffe, and many other places of this name have this origin.   † Barkesay in Barkisland; pedigree in Watson's *Halifax.*

called Nicher, 6 acres at le Ryding, 2 acres called Surdeland, ½ bovate
and cottage of Elias de Northend, 4 acres &c. in le Bothes, &c. &c.

Turn, April 26. Jury as last nearly. John de Rastrik being dead,
John Hanson his cousin and heir paid 5s. heriot, for a mess., croft,
half bovate, 6 acres of roideland in Wodehouses.

1378. John Symson paid heriot 6s. 8d. for mess., ½ bovate, 12 acres
of assart in Shepeden, his father John S. having died. Thus the name
Symson had now got fixed, or the son would have been called John
Johnson. Robt. Fletcher took Rastrik and Shepden mills as before,
for 20s. per ann. Adam Hanson and John atte Vikers, executors of
the will of Wm. de Isle, vicar of Hodersfeld, *v.* Adam Dikson, Rastrik
graveship.

Brighouses *Turn*, 18 April, Robt. de Morton, senescal. Jury, Henry
de Rissheworth, Thos. de Dalton, Ad. de Stokkes, John Drake, Thos.
del Hirst, Ric. de Helywelle, John de Rokes, John del More, Robt. del
Rode, John Jagger, Rob. Pynder, John de Hepworth. At Quernby,
Hanne Souter paid for his privilege as tanner and sutor. Ric. Matthewson to Matilda Colier, a mess., 4 acres in Shepdene, for 10 years.

1379. John del Bothes, senr., and junr., Ric. Matthewson, John
Simson, Ric. Symson, John Boy, John Wilkinson, Rob. Pynder, Rob.
de Wolfker, Henry del Cliffe, Henry de Rissheworth, for not attending
the election of greave, 3d. each.

Turn, Oct 24. Jury as last, except John de Calthorne for Rob.
Pynder. Ric Peres-son was constable for Clifton, Wm. de Bothomley
for Barkisland, Thos. Gilleson for Rastrik, Robt. Hare, Shelf; John
s. Wm., Northourum, who reported that John de Illingworth had carried 16 loads of sclatestones to Halifax from Bothes. John de Ireland
the Hiperum constable, reported John Annson, Matil de Sculcotes,
Elena de Wyloby, and Ric. Masshon for brewing, fined 4d. each.
Robt. flletcher takes the mills at 21s. 6d. Sourby and Soland mill as
before, but Warley mill is to be removed and a new one built at
Ludingdene, John Maude a supervisor for it. Robt. Hare *v.* Ric.
Jonson Simson; Rob. del Crosse, capellanus, *v.* Rob. flletcher; Wm.
de Sugden *v.* Thos. Sharp; Adam Lister *v.* Ric. del Halle.

Brighouses *Turn*, 16 April. Jury as last nearly. Wm. Lightriche,
the ffekesby constable, says there are two stray stirks in John Couhird's
custody. Ric. del Cliffe, Hiprum greave, surrendered for John Drake,
4 acres in Kowrode to Isabelle Alkok.

———————→>◇<←———————

I have now reached another breathing space, where we can take
stock of the population, though the amount of information now
brought to light for the first time makes me chary in taking up any
space in reflections. The observant reader will be able to judge for
himself how important the half-yearly meetings at Brighouses were,
but as the tenants and freemen from all the townships had to attend,
and the exact township was seldom indicated in the early rolls, the

foregoing notes afford a history of Rastrick and Hipperholme greave-ships, as well as the two townships. In 1379, to add to the great local burdens of the people, a capitation or poll tax was imposed by Parliament, ranging from 4d. to £6 13s. 4d. per head; and next year a more rigorous exaction of 12d. per head was voted on every person above 15 years of age. Goaded by these taxes, and by the indecent manner that the tax-gatherers in some cases tried to discover the age of youths, the great insurrection, under Wat or Walter the Tyler and others, broke out around London. With these difficulties, the spread of Wickliffites or Lollards, the invasions of Scots, the growing power of the yeomanry class, the young king, Richard II., had his hands full, but he managed to become almost an absolute monarch, only to fall a prisoner when Henry IV. wrenched the throne from him in 1399. The names of the inhabitants, except children, of each township were entered by the poll tax collectors, and those for parts of Yorkshire have been lately printed in the *Yorks. Archæol. Journal*, from which we take the following lists, though the reader will be familiar with each person already. Married people were counted as one for taxation.

RASTERIK: 4d. each.

Thos. fil Julian and ux
John de Wodehous ,,
John Stokkes ,,
John de Tutill ,,
Wm. Tinghill ,,
Henry Alisaundre ,,
Wm. Scheplay ,,
Ric. Buthrode ,,
Robt. Bull ,,
John Hanneson ,,
John del ffirth ,,
Henry Malinson ,,
Henry ffox
Alice del Hall
Margeria Walker
Wm. Alynson
Isabella de Scheplay
Beatrix dau. John
Johanna dau. John
Total, 12 married,
7 single; 6s. 4d.

SOUTHOUROM had John Lascy, franklain, 3s.4d; Exley, Haldworth and Pek, tradesmen, at 6d; 16 others married at 4d; a widow and two single women.

MIRFELD, had Wm. de Mirfeld, Knt., 20s., John de Boulton, franklayn, 3s. 4d., two at a 1s., four at 6d., twenty married couples, and 44 un-married payers at 4d.

SCHELFE, 3s. 4d.

Thos. de Wyke and ux
Wm. Carter ,,
Thos. de Bentlay ,,
Robt. Hare ,,
Wm. de Dene ,,
Adam Wilson ,,
Ric. del Carre ,,
John Dicson ,,
Robt. Carter ,,
Magota del Dene

BARKESLAND had Wm. de Wodhed, carpenter, 6d. John Barkesland, 6d., 12 other married couples at 4d., 5 single payers.

QUERNBY paid 18s. in fourpences

ffEKESBY.

Wm. de Lytherige & ux Anabilla dau. Wm. Magota dau. Wm.
Total, 1 married, 2 single; 1s.

HALIFAX had 25 mar-ried, 13 single, all at 4d.

NORTHOURUM had 21 married, 7 single, all at 4d. Roger de Ras-trik was married and settled there; also families of Elland, Batt, Milner, Drake, Stancliff, Simson, Sunderland, Godlay, Sclater.

CLIFTON had four tradesmen at 6d. and 14 others married at 4d. and 18 unmarried or widows.

STAYNLAND had 3 at 6d., 12 married at 4d., 3 single at 4d.

HYPRUM:

HYPRUM:

HYPRUM:

Henry de Rysseworth, mercator, & ux, 1s.

Thos. de Thorp, mercator, & ux, 1s.

John de Byrkes, sissor (tailor), & ux, 6d.

Ric. de Bentley, carpenter, & ux, 6d.

Thos. de·Thorp, ffaber (smith), & ux, 6d.

Robt. Pynder, sutor (shoemaker), & ux, 6d.

Thos. de Birkhous and ux, (wife), 4d.

Robt. ffletcher and ux

Wm. Scheplay   ,,

Adam Tailour   ,,

John Smyth and ux

Richard Machon ,,

Thos. Tolour   ,,

Roger de Hoyle ,,

Richard de Cliff ,,

Thos. Smyth   ,,

Wm. de Huff   ,,

Thos. Tilli   ,,

John s. Wm.   ,,

Robert Walker   ,,

Robt. s. Wm.   ,,

Janyn de ffraunce ,,

John Yrland   ,,

Ric. del Halle   ,,

Wm. s. Agnes   ,,

Matilda de Scheplay

Kateryna   ,,

Johanna de Scheplay

Isabella Machon

Ric. de Brighous

Henry del Rodehouse

Alice del Hill

Elena de Billay (?)

Elena de Prestelay

John de Prestelay

John s. Henry

Total, 25 married,

11 single ; 14s.

HERTESHEAD, 7 married, and Brig's 4 daughters unmarried ; 3s. 4d.

We miss the names of Wyloby and Rookes in the Hipperholme list for which we cannot account.

Whilst Halifax township had only 12s. 8d. to pay, say 30 houses, Elland township had Savile, Knight, at £1, a franklain at 3s. 4d., 2 merchants at 1s., 6 tradespeople, two being Websters (women), at 6d., 24 others, married couples, and 27 unmarried, at 4d. With these figures there is no difficulty in arriving at the population. Rastrick had about fifteen houses, Hipperholme-cum-Brighouse thirty, or equal to Halifax. There is no wonder that Wm. de Lightriche was always the Fixby constable, but there is a wonder that the Thornhill, or some other Fixby family, is not mentioned. Elland slightly outstripped Mirfield, with nearly forty houses each. Having given up to this date as complete an account as possible, without knowing the exact township in which many of the persons lived, we must now only refer to those of our particular townships, and as briefly as possible.

1380. Ric. Milner took Rastrik mill at 18s. 4d. ; Rob. Hare that at Shipden at 20d.

Bryghouses *Turn*, Nov. 5. 4 brewers in Hiperum. Hugh Stevenson, mess., 16 acres in Rastrikmere to Cecilia his wife. John del Northend de Ourum dead, Ric. s. Peter de Thorneals his cousin and heir paid 20d. heriot, for 6 ac. 1 rode in Clegcliffe in Hiprom. John de Eland held 2 mess., 40 acres in Nm., his daughter and heiress, aged 12, takes them. Ric. de Thorneals conveyed 6 acres 1 rode in Clegcliffe to John Jankson de Ouendene.

Turn, June 3. Jury as before nearly. John Wilkinson de Hiprom dead, Robt. his son paid 6s. 8d. to heriot, a mess., ½ bov., 6 acres of roydeland in Hiprum. Ric. del Cliff is dead, Henry del Cliff his cousin paid 6s. 8d. heriot, for a mess., a bovate in Hiprum. John Hanson and Alice his wife took a mess., ½ bovate, 7 acres of roidland in Wodehouses late John de Rastrik's, with Tontoft and Northtoft.

1382.   Ric. Machon and Rob. Hare took the mills this year, 20s.

Turn, Oct. 20, Jury as before.   John, vicar of Dewsbury, *v.* Robt. ffletcher de Brighouses and John Smith de Brighouses about debts. John Thomasson Gilleson is dead, Wm. by the Broke paid 4d. heriot for his land in Rastrik.   John del Wro 1½ ac. in Hyprum to John s. Thos. del Cliff.

1383.   *Turn*, Nov.   Jury, Hen. de Risshworth, Wm. de Whitil, John Drake, Roger de Wodhede, Thom. de Dalton, John de Rokes, Ric. de Helwelle, John de Calthorne, Thos. del Hirst, John de Hepworth, Robt. Daweson, John del More.   Robt. de Parys, 3 acres in Clegcliff to Alice Taillor wyfe de Haldeworth.   John del Rokes, Hiperum constable, reported Janyn ffrankysman (called also Janyn, servant of Hen. de Rissheworth), Ric. del Halle, Matilda gentilwomman, John de Ireland, Ric. Machon, Ibbota Machondoghter, for brewing; fined 2d. or 3d.   Hugh s. John de Totehill paid heriot for a mess., 1½ bov., 6 acres rode land in Rastrik, his father being dead. Robt. Pynder and Alice his wife surrendered an assart, 6½ ac., called Beryroide to John de Haldeworth de Astay; released to them next year.   Ric. Machon took the mills as before; and next year at 19s.

1384.   *Turns* and Jury as usual.   John del ffrith de Rastrik took of the lord one acre, and had to make the hedges from Rastrikbryg to Scolaybrig.   Brighouse turn was followed by Halifax, then by Kirkburton on following days.

1386.   Richard the vicar of Halifax fined 12d. for not attending Wakefield court.   Constables' names are all given; brewers, absenters, &c. fined.   Thos. Sherpe was constable of Northouram, Roger de Woddeshed of Hertshead, Thos. Coweper for Wherneby (Quarmby).

1387.   Machon took the mills again.   Henry and Thos. del Cliff conveyed ten acres to Janyn servant of Henry de Ryssheworth or Janyn Ryssheworthman.

1388.   *Turn*, Oct. 20.   Thos. Smyth de Roidehouse not attending the election of greave, 3d., for brewing and selling 4d.   John Weloby 4d. and Ric. Machon wife 2d. for brewing.

1389.   Fourth parts of Rastrik (14s. 2d.) and Shepden (2s.) mills to Ric. Machon for 16s. 2d.   Magota de Anelay conveyed to John her son 3 acres in Rastrik called le Brydrode (? Birdsroyd).   Ric. vicar of Halifax surrendered 9 acres called le Ou'Shipden to Wm. his son, and after his death to Wm. Hanson brother of said Richard.   Richard son of Henry de Heton became Vicar in Nov. 1362.   Watson mentions a deed of 1389 from the Vicar to his son William Heton, Esq., granting Over Schipden Hall and Hyngandrode.   His arms on the roof at Halifax Church are: Argent, on a bend sable, three bulls' heads, cabossed of the first, half faced looking to the left.   He died March 9, 1389, (or 1390 according to the present style of commencing the year with Jan. 1, whilst the old style began with March 25th.)   Note also that the Vicar's brother is named *Hanson*, son of Henry.   John Smyth de Bryghouses fined 2d. for fishing.   Beatrix prestson wyfe conveyed a parcel called Eustroide in Hiprom to Simon de Whitlay.

John de Rastrik conveyed le Londymere assart and a rode in Nm. field to Ric. Symson, and a bovate in Hiprom grave to Henry Boy.

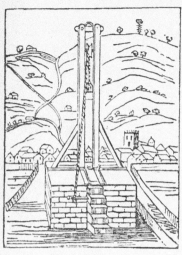

HALIFAX GIBBET.

It is as yet unaccountable that Sourby graveship should have exercised the 'privilege' of gibbetting thieves caught within its boundaries, whilst Hipperholme and Rastrick graveships seem to have had no such privilege. Even the Sourby culprit was free if he could escape across the Halifax beck, so long as he did not return. The custom must have come down from Saxon times before the Manor of Wakefield included the Halifax portions, or all would have had the same rigorous treatment. The 1360 roll mentions the custom. Mr. Lister finds in the Assize Rolls of 1391 several cases of murder in Halifax parish, and four or five persons so convicted were outlawed for not answering to the charges. In 1337, Robert and John sons of John de Copley were indicted at York for slaying John s. Bate le Lister at Woodkirk, possibly at the great fair. In 1378, Richard de Sunderland was indicted for slaying Henry Matthewson, whose name so often appears in our pages. The pol-axe with which the deed was done was valued at 3d., and like all deodands was forfeited to the lord of the manor. John Cockcroft of Wadsworth stabbed Adam s. William of Marsden, at Christmas, 1379. He was a fugitive till Candlemas, 1391, when Thos. s. Thos. de Hylelegh of Sowerby shot him with an arrow, which was valued at 1d. The said Thos. of Hilelegh, junr. shot with an arrow, at Hylelegh Place, John Hardery of Bingley shortly before, for which he was indicted. Four more cases of murder occur in 1390-1. From this time we find a branch of the Hileleghs at Hilelegh or Hiley Hall, Clifton.

1391. Ric. de Hylelegh was constable of Clifton. John de Roides conveyed one acre in Hiprum to John de Ireland. Sibilla wid. John de Haldeworth conveyed a mess., ½ bov., 4 acres of fforland in Hiperum to Wm. s. John de H., who released it to Sibilla (his mother) for her life. Henry de Risheworth, fforester of Hyprom, presents that Robt. Carter, 12d., John de Ireland. 12d., Roger Trnor, 2d., Robt. de Haldeworth, 6d., Robt. de Wolker, 12d., Robt. Wylkynson, 6d., Alice wife of John Wylkynson, 12d., Robt. Johnson, 12d., John de Hepworth, 12d., John Straunge, 3d., Ric. Symson, 3d., Henry Boy, 12d., Thos. Sherpe, 12d., Wm. de Hemyngway, 6d., Ric. Tylly, 6d., John del Bothe, senr., 6d., junr. 6d., Ric. del Vikers, 12d., all cutting greenwood

in Brynescoles forest. (Hipperholme Commonwood is all that remains
of this forest.)

1392. Brighous *Turn*, Oct. 15, Jury named, having been omitted
a few years: Henry de Ryssheworth, John Drake, John de Rokes,
Ric. de Heliwell senr., Wm. de Steinland, Thos. del Hirst, Wm.
Woddhed, Thom. de Lockwodd, John del ffrithe, Wm. de Steghill
(Steel, or may be Staghill, near Outlane), Ric. del Haye, Thom. de
Gledhill. The Gledhills were noted Barkisland people.

Turn, April 29th, Adam del Skoles, Thomas de Dalton, John de
Hepworth, Wm. de Lokwodd, take the place of four of the above.

1393. The 'hawking' in the common fields of Herteshead, Rastrik,
Brighous and Hiprom, let this year to John Piper, capellanus, for 6d.
The same occurs next year; and for Sourby &c. to John vicar of
Halifax for 6d. John Piper was curate of Rastrick chapel in and
before 1411. John Kyng became vicar of Halifax in March, 1389, (or
1390 we should now say.) An artist may here draw the burly priests
mounted on horses, attended by gay ladies and squires, with the
hawks perched on their shoulders ready to pounce upon unwary birds.
A savoury smell at the Rastrick parsonage would repay the 6d. outlay.
Rastrik and Shipden mills: no name or amount opposite for two years.

Turn, 15 Oct. Thos. del Crosseland was a juryman; others as
above. Isabella de Brighouse fined 6d. for raising an unjust hue and
cry against her daughter-in-law. Alice de Haldworth conveyed an
assart of 4 acres formerly Ric. de Haldworth's to John s. Ric. de H.
Isabella Alcokdoghter paid 3d. heriot, for part of Blakker, Alice Melias,
her sister, being dead. John Stronge one rode in Pyndercroft in
Hiperum to John Boye. [An assart is a 'clearing,' or new land.]

1394. Robt. Stronge 3s. heriot, for bovate in Nm., John his father
being dead. Rastrik mill, ¼th, 11s. 8d., Shipden 3s. 2d. Wm. del Ker,
Shelf constable; Wm. Johnson Malynson for Northouram. Janyn de
Hyprom, Matilda de Stancefeld, John Smith's wife, Ric. Machon's wife
were brewers. John de Wilby absenting from the turn, 3d. Janyn de
Hyprom r. Thos. de Thorp. Isabel, wife of Thos. Johnson, drew blood
from and raised unjust hewes (hue) against Matilda, wife of John
Tomson, fined 6d. and 4d. Wm. Hanson and Ric. de Kent for digging
coal in Nm. Henry Risshworth was fforester of Strangstigh wood in
Rastrik grave. John de Botheroide had a mess., edifice and 16 acres
in Rastrik, which Alice his daughter, wife of John Bramde, paid 12d. to
inherit. Wm. de Godley being dead, Ric. his son, paid 6d. heriot for
2½ acres in Shipden. (Godley Lane bears the name still.)

1396. Jury, Dalton, Steinland, Crosseland, Hirst, More, Heliwell,
Drake, Wodehed, W. and T. Lokwood, Thos. Smyth de Hiprom, and
John del Rokes. Henry Brodelegh says that John s. Henry de Rysshe-
worth senior had owed him ijs. (2s.) for a toga (cloak) for ij years.
Ric. Strange or Strungge conveyed a mess. and bovate in Hiperum to
Thos. Otes. Thos. Percy, Knight, r. John de Calthorne and Robt.
Bull of Rastrik. Jury, April 22, Thos. de Bothomley, Smyth, Rokes,
&c. Robt. Johnson de Hiprom and Cecilia his wife conveyed 11 acres

in le Holcans to John Jacson Milner de Halifax; the same Robert disputed with Wm. de Hemyngway about detaining Robert's cattle.

1397. 'Hawking' (sporting with 'hawks') in Sourby and Hiprom let to John Kyng, vicar of the church of Halifax, for 6d. this year. Rastrik mill 11s. 8d., Shipden 3s. 2d. this year: lessee's name not given.

Turn, Oct. Jury, as before. Wm. de Deyn capellanus, *r.* Thos. Leche, and Thom. de Bretteby for 17s. 6d. for a horse which Bretteby bought of William at Halifax (fair), Feast of Nativ. St. John Baptist. Isabella wid. Thos. del Bryghouse *r.* Thos. del Cliff, about a quadrant of false gold. Henry de Rissheworth, by the hands of John Drake, surrendered a bovate and half of land, formerly Henry de Coppelay's, and a plot called Hekdeyne in Hiprom, to John son of said Henry senior: ingress 40d.; also a plot, formerly taken from the waste on west of Coldelay to said John s. Henry de R.; ingress 6d.; also mess., edifice, 1½ bovates formerly Wm. del Bothes, and 1 acre in les Hilles in Hiprom to Henry s. said Henry. In Halifax district, Ric. de Holland, John de Eikeroide and Alicia del ffield resided. Ric. Matthewson surrendered 4 mess., a bovate, and 20 acres of roidland in Hiprom to Henry his son, who paid for ingress 10s. Tenants of Rastrik, Hiprom, &c. bound to repair the dam of Wakefield ffulling mill.

Turn, May 14. Jury, Dalton, Stainland, Hirst, More, John del ffrithe de Bothomley, Heliwell, Drake, W. & T. Lokwodd, Calthorne, John del Rokes and Thos. Smyth de Hyprom.

SMYTH ARMS.

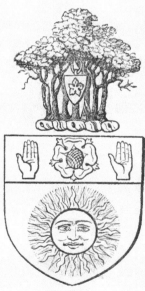

HIRST ARMS.

1398.—Robt. Derwhit, senescall. Jury panelled were as before, but Thos. Smyth de *litheclif*, (not Hyprom, though the same man, after whom Smith House is named), and John de Haldeworth de Hiprom, Henry de Bibby de ffekisby, John Taillur de Rastrik, take ffrith, Drake, and Calthorne's places. John Brodelegh, of Hiperum, being absent fined 4d. Rob. de Prestelay *v.* Henry Matthewson capellanus. Ric. Hylelegh constable of Clifton reported John Taylor's wife of Wolrow for brewing. Rob. Hare conveyed a mess. 11 acres, called Whithillroide in Nm. to Henry de Rastrik. [The Rastrik family gradually migrated towards Calverley, &c., at this time, where their descendants, known by the name Raistrick, are still numerous.] John de Haldeworth gave 2s. heriot for mess., part of a bovate, and an acre of fforland in Hiperum, his brother Wm. being dead.

1399.—John King, vicar of Halifax, still paid 6d. yearly for Sourby and Hiperum 'hawking.'

Turn, 13 Oct., Jury as last. Hugh de Totehill of Rastrik for not attending the turn, 3d.

Turn, May 10th, Jury as before. Ric. Tilly was Hiperum forester. Thos. del Cliff conveyed an assart called Ellenroide (Nm.), and 15 acres, to John Gibson. [The second turn should always be reckoned as belonging to the succeeding year.]

1400.—John de Wakefield alias Sir John ffitche de London, surrendered waste lands in Kergate, &c., Wakefield, the ceremony being performed in the church of St. Paul, London. Opposite Rastrik and Shipden mills, no name or rent given.

Turn, 18 Oct., Jury panelled by the turn,—names as before. John de Holway conveyed a messuage and 8 acres to Johan his wife ; John de Haldeworth 5 acres in Clegclif to Thos. de H. Jury at *Turn,* W. Lokwodd, Staynland, Hirst, Wodhed, ffrythe, More, Rokes, Smyth, Taillur, Helywell, junr., Robt. de Haldeworth, and Wm. de Wolverwall. John Drake had received 23s. 4d. of Thos. Smyth for a 'lumis' cross, in Halifax Church, and 15 years have since elapsed : fined 12d. Ric. Tilly was Hiperom forester.

1401. Rastrik and Shipden mills : no rent or tenant named. John King, vicar of Halifax, paid 6d. yearly for Sourby and Hiprom 'hawking.'

Turn, Oct. 18. Jury, W. Lokwodd, Steynland, Rokes, Haldeworth, More, Taillor de Rastrik, John de Hepworth, Thos. de Crossland, Wolverwall, Hirst, Wodhed, Ric. de Sunderland. Thos. s. John del ffrith de Rastrik made fidelity to the lord for lands purchased of John de Anneley in Rastrik. Wm. brother of Henry Matthewson, capellanus, surrendered mess., ½ bov., 3 acres called Sundirland to Ric. de Sundirland. John Brande and Alice his wife surrendered a mess. and 20 acres of pasture and wood, called Botherodes, formerly Ric. de Botheroid's, her uncle, and 10 acres there formerly John de Bothroide's, her father, to the use of John Piper, capellanus, who paid 4s. ingress. The same John and Alice conveyed 10 acres to Thos. del ffrith.

Turn, April 17. Jury as last. Thos. de Mirfield, ½ rode at Okes in Rastrik to Hugh Couper.

1402. Rastrik mill, nil, Shipden ($\frac{1}{4}$) let for 21d.

Turn, Oct. Jury as before, with one different name. John s. Henry de Brodeleigh took of the lord a parcel of waste land at Prestelay grene, in length iiij^{xx}x (*i.e.* 90) feet, in breadth 40 feet. Ingress, 4d.

Turn, May 7. Jury, the same.

1403. Edm. s. William, seneschall for Wakefield Manor. For the first time instead of Rastrik we have Brighouse Mill; no tenant nor rent named.

Turn, Oct. Jury, Thos. de Crosseland, Wm. de Lokwod, Wm. de Wodhede, Thom. del ffrith, John del More, John del Rokes, Robt. de Haldworth, Wm. de Woln'wall, John de Hepworth, John de Bothomley, John de Calthorne, Thos. de Gledehill. Constables sworn as usual, John Clerk for Hertshead, Wm. del Ker for Shelf, Henry del Holynes for N.ourum, John de Hemingway for Clifton, &c. John Thomson of Brighouse fined 3d., being absent. Ric. de Sunderland *c.* Thos. Jacson de Brighouse. Wm. de Stancliffe, mess., $\frac{1}{4}$ bovate in Nm. to John his son and Elizabeth, John's wife. Johna d. Gilbt. Otes paid 3s. heriot for 16 acres and edifice in Hiprom, her father being dead. Trespassers in Hypromwode and Brynescholes fined as usual.

Turn, April. Jury, Crosseland, Steynland, Hepworth, More, Calthorne, Woodhead, Lokwod, Rokes, Haldeworth, Wm. de Longley, Thos. del ffrith (Rastrik), Thos. del ffrith de Scamynden. Alice de Cownall of Hiperum raised hue unjustly on her son John, fined 2d. John s. Thos. de Thorp paid 12d. heriot, for 4 acres in Longmarsche, John his uncle being dead.

1404. Shipden mill $\frac{1}{4}$th, let for 21d. Rastrik stands, rebuilding. John de Wylby inclosed a parcel of waste without leave, in Hiprom. Henry Sayell, now the forester, presents John del Bothes, senr., junr., John de Holway, John Roper, Rob. Johnson, John Hare, Ric. Bate, Thos. Otes, Ric. Symson, Hen. Sherpe, Robt. Walker, Alic. wid. John Wilkinson, Robt. de Haldesworth, Robt. Carter, John de Ireland, John de Wylby, John de Brodelegh, John de Ryssheworth, John del Deyne, John Sherpe, Wm. del Ker, Ric. de Totehill, and Ric. de Prestelay for carrying away greenwood from Hiprom wood.

1405. Shipden mill, 21d. *Brighous* mill, nil: stat.

Turn, Oct. 20. Jury the same. Hen. s. Roger de Rastrik surrendered Whithill in Nm. containing house and 12 acres to John s. Rob. Hare; ingress, 4d. Matil. wid. John Symson, mess., 10 acres, in Hyprom (? greave), to Ric. de Mekesburgh for 10 years. Ric. had been indicted in 1390 for murdering John Dell at Halifax on the Feast (Thump) Sunday.

Turn, May 4. Jury as before.

1406. Mill of Brighous nil this year, stat. in facture; Shipden 21d. Tolls of Hiprom let to Thos. del ffrithe for 6s. 8d.

Turn, Oct. 6. Jury, John de Ryssheworth, Lokwod, Wodhed, Thos. del ffrith, More, Rokes, Haldworth, Bothomley, Wm. de Denton, Calthorne, Hirst, John del Haghs. John de Brighouse 2s., Henry ffox 2s., John Smythe de Brighouse 12d., Wm. de Staneefeld 2s., Janyn de Hyprom 2s., Ric. de Thorp 2s., John de Thorp 2s., Roger Mauncell 2s., and Thos. Tilly 2s., all of Hiperom, brewing helpales against the statutes. Janyn de Hiprom was fined at Halifax turn for selling meat.

Helpales were harvest or feast-time jollifications. John de Hemyngway, the Clifton constable, was fined 40d. for concealing Helpale brewers there. John del ffrith, senr. conveyed a mess., and 30 acres in Rastrik to his son Henry, with remainder in case of Henry's death to Hugh his next son.

Turn, April 19. Jury, as before nearly, except John Lascelles. John de Wylluby brewed a helpale, and sold, fined 2s. John de Ireland conveyed to himself and wife Isabella, 3 rodes, called Hilles in Hiprom.

1407. John Roper, Northouram constable, took Shipden mill at 21d. Hiprom and Rastrik tolls, with waifs and strays, let to Thos. del ffrith for 6s. 8d. John King de Halifax, vicar, paid 6d. as usual for Hiprom and Rastrik 'hawking.'

Turn, Oct. Jury as usual; same at the following *May* turn.

1408. John s. Robt. atte Tounend, Rastrik graveship, fined 40d. for drawing blood from John Piper, capellanus, de Herteshede. (Was he a pluralist? see 1393, 1401.) John King, vicar of Halifax church, executor of John de Burgh's will, *v.* Roger Maunsell, about 10s. 6d. for a bovate of land.

Turns, Oct. 21, April 29. The Juries were the same persons as previous year. John Tilly conveyed 1½ acre in Tillyholmes in Hiprom to John de Brodelegh.

1409. John de Risshworth, Henry his brother, Galfri Warde, and John Willby fined 4d. each for not attending the election of greave.

Brighouse *Turn*, Oct. 7. Jury, John Rissheworth, Thos. Crosland, Wm. Wodhed, Thos. del ffryth, John del More, John Rokes, Wm. Staynland, Robt. Haldeworth, John Hepworth, John Bothomley, Wm. Denton, Thos. del Hirst. This list is remarkable as *de* (for *of*) is left out for the first time, whilst *del* (of the) is still inserted. Brighous Mill (⅓th) let to — Stok for 16s. 8d. this year; Shipden to John Roper for 21d.; Rastrik and Hiprom tolls, waifs, and strays to Thos. ffirth for 5s.; the 'ancupac,' or leave to take 'p'dices' (hawking) to Sir John Kyng, vicar of Halifax church. John Wodhous paid 18d. for leave in 1411.

1410. Brighous Mill to John del Stokkes at 16s. 8d., rest of lettings as before.

Turn, 13 Oct. Jury as before. John Wodhous, senior, conveyed a mess., 40 acres in Wodhouse to John his son; ingress 3s. 4d.

Turn, April 21. Jury, the same. Wm. Hemyngway abdux. vnn bordor, fined 12d. The constables were—Thos. Otes for N.owram; John Hemingway, Clifton; Ric. Totehill, Shelf; John Tynglle, Harteshead, &c. Thos. Lascy conveyed 6 acres at Randes in Nm. to Ric. Batt for 20 years.

1411. Brighouse *Turn*, Oct. 12. Jury as before, with remarkable regularity. If they had not been rich men we might expect that a substantial feast followed the two courts—Baron and Leet. Ric. Sundirland and Johne his wife conveyed a mess. in Sundirland and a bovate, and an assart called Bareroyde and Simonroide to Ric. their son, and Margaret dau. of Ric. Simson ; and a mess. and 10 acres called Clifroyde to Ric. their said son.

1412. *Turn*, Oct. 17. Jury as usual. John Avisson was constable of ffekisby, Ric. Stheghell (Stighel, stee-hoil we now say) for Stainland, John Lassels for Dalton, Ric. ffaldyngworth for Barkisland, &c. Hen. s. Ric. de Godley paid 18d. heriot, 1½ acres in Shepden, called Smethecroft, Pygrene, and Ympyerd, his father being dead.

1413. Brighouse mill—blank. Shipden mill, ¼th, to Robt. Eland for 21d. The Hyprom and Rastrik " ancupaco' ad p'dices " let to the vicar of Halifax and John by the broke de Hodresfeld for 12d.

Turn, Oct., same Jury. Amongst the Hiperum brewers is Alice del Milnes for brewing and making a new ale-house, fined 2d. Wm. Stancliffe conveyed Newhey to Wm. his son ; Hagstokes to Henry his son, whilst John paid heriot for a mess., and 13 acres of roydland, his father and mother Wm. and Elizabeth being dead, and he was also heir appt. to his younger brothers Wm. and Henry just named. John also paid heriot for 20 acres between Scowt and Shypden browk on the death of Wm. his father. Ric. Sundirland junr. and Johne his wife conveyed a mess., bov., croft of 6 acres in Nm., to his father Ric. and mother Agnes, for their lives.

Turn, May 1. Jury named, as before nearly. In Hyprom, Ric. de Thorp fined 4d. for making a Newe alehous. Wm. Thornhill de ffekesby took some waste land at Okesgrene.

1414. Brighous mill—blank ; Shipden to Robt. Eland. Wm. s. Ric. de Horsfall and Wm. s. John de Eikrode fined 12d. each for fishing Kypers, Sourby district. It is seldom such an entry occurs for this part of the Calder, [see 1439.]

Turn, 23 Oct. Jury, John Ryssworth, Wm. Stainland, John More, junr., John de Bothomley, Wm. Wodhed, John Hepworth, Rob. de (H)Aldesworth, Wm. Denton, Thos. Hyrst, Wm. Lokewodd, Wm. Longlay, John Rokes, John Drake, Adam Beamound. John Avysson was ffekesby constable, Robt. Sharp for Northourum, John del Hyrst for Quernby, Ric. de Bentlay for Shelf, John del Roydhouse for Clifton, John Williamson for Dalton, Wm. Moldson for Staynland, John de Tyngel for Herteshead, Wm. del Hole for Barkisland.

1415. *Turn*, April 16. Ric. Simson, Ric. Sunderland, Thos. ffrith de Rastrik were on the jury. In Holmfirth district was the family of Josep or Jessop at this date. Robt. Haldworth and John Ireland *v*. Thos. Tilly and Ric. de Thorp for not repairing the hedges, called Kyngshard in Hiprom. Robt. Wulfkerr, greave of Hiprom, for not attending Wakefield court, 6d.

1416. Arabic figures first occur but very rarely. One-fourth the Water cornmill at Brighous let this year to Robt. Eland for 16s. 8d., Shipden water mill for 21d. Hyprum and Rastrik tolls to Thos. de ffryth and Ad. Makreth for 3s. 4d. Hiprum ancup. (hawking)

H

to John Kynge, vicar, for 6d.; Rastrik ditto to Thos. Duke, Rastrik constable, for 8d.

Turn, Oct. 6. The prioress of Kyrkeles had been having some Thakestones led from a Rastrik quarry. Thos. s. John Rishworth, the Lord's day after the feast of S. Michael, at Hertshed church, assaulted John Rodehouse and made a great affray, therefore is attached. John s. John Blakeburn and others are common players at unlawful games at Clyfton; Janyn de Hiprom and John Brodele, drapor, the same at Hiprom, therefore attached (summoned).

Turn, April 28, Jury as usual. Thos. Tilly of Hiperum brewed a helpale, 18d. John Wylcok held mess., 20 acres in Rastrik greave, for which Alice his daughter, wife of Henry Bothom, pays heriot. Ric. Bentley, Shelf, broke and carried away the hedges of Thos. Cowper at Engesall. Henry Seyvill, forester, presents a long list of culprits for Hiprom, &c.

1417. Brighous water mill (¼th) to Robt. Eland, 16s. 8d.

Turns, Oct. 13, April 19, Juries as usual. John Sharp was constable for Shelf. John Boy, the Hiperum greave, presented John Rishworth, John Weleweby, Thos. Clyf, Ric. Bates, John Bayrestowe for not attending the election of greave, each fined 4d. Henry Rischworth formerly held of the lord a mess., and edifice in Hiprom in which Robt. Carter lived, a mess. and edifice there, and part of a mess. formerly Alice Naldoghter's, two bovates in Hyprum, a close called Osbarne rode, a close of rodeland, called Breryhay, 20 acres of rodeland in Southegge, Collay, and elsewhere; his nephew Henry, son of Nicholas de R., next heir, paid 10s. for heriot. Beatrix wife of Hugh ffox, daughter of John Hanson, paid heriot for a mess. and 24 acres in Rastrik at her father's death.

1418. Brighouse mill as before. Shipden mill and Rastrik and Hiprum tolls left blank. Janyn de Hiprom conveyed a mess. and 11 acres in Hiprum to Henry de Risshworth, junr. John son and heir of Henry de Rischworth paid 4d. heriot for a cottage and a rode in le Hey in Hiprom.

1419. Mills and tolls as last year. Jury also. In Hyprum, Alice Mylne and Cecil d. John Smyth brew helpales. Wm. Peresson, constable of Clifton, presented John Hemingway of Thornyals for not attending the turn, 4d. Thos. Duke of Rastrik and his son Ric. took 16 panstres (loads) of Thakstones without leave, therefore summoned to appear.

1420. Mills as before; also John Kyng's 6d. Jury, 23 Oct., Thos. Crossland, John Haldesworth, Thos. ffyrth, Thos. Hyrst, Wm. Denton, Wm. Longlay, John Haigh, John Rokes, John Hepworth, John Taillior, John Jagger, Ric. Helywell. John Smyth's wife of Brighouse made and sold bread against the assize, fined 2d.

Turn, April 15, Jury as last. Robt. Rischworth de Lev'segge brewed a helpale and sold in Hiprom. Robt. Johnson, John Scharp and Robt. Haldeworth, junr., are common players at 'tales and teril'* against the statute, therefore to be summoned. Henry Sayvyll,

*Dice.

forester for Hiprom and Rastrik, presented a long list of wood takers. Galfry Warde having died, his son Thos. paid 4s. heriot for mess., 1½ bovates, 12 acres of rodeland called the Legh in Nm. He died this year, and an enquiry was held before Robt. Waterton, chief senescall, at Wakefield, when it was shown that Wm. Burgh was cousin and next heir of said Thos. Ward, thus, Wm. was son of John, son of Wm., son of Robt., son of Radulph, son of Roger brother of Hugh, father of John, father of Wm., father of Galfrid, father of said Thos. Ward, therefore Wm. Burgh paid heriot, 10s.

John Kynge, vicar of Halifax church conveyed 9 acres in Ovyrschipden to Wm. Otes, drapor, ingress 2s. 6d. The vicar received from John Jacson 12 acres called Holkans in Nm., ingress 18d. Ric. Sculcotes, senior, conveyed a close containing 12 acres in Nm., with an 'Ovil' (hovel) within it, to Ric. Rokes ; ingress 2s.

Roger	Hugh
Radulph	John
Robt.	Wm.
Wm.	Galfrid
John	Thos. Ward
	Wm. de Burgh.

1421. Mills let for 16s. 8d. and 21d. to Robt. Eland. Vicar King and Thos. Duke take respectively Hiprum and Rastrik ' Ancup,' (hawking).

Turn, Oct. 21. Jury as before, except John Taillor de Clifton is one. John Weloweby enclosed waste land at Brokehous near Holden broke, 40ft. by 20, therefore summoned (attached.) John Smyth of Brighouse brews ; also bakes and sells bread against assize.

1422. Brighous mill to Robt. de Eland for 16s. 8d. Shipden mill 21d. but no name opposite. Henry Risshworth lets Hollmyres close in Hyprum to John R. for 6 years. Ric. Rokes re-conveys Sculcote-rode (12 acres) with Ovil thereon in Nm. to Ric. Sculcote, junr. Henry Saynyll paid 3s. 4d. for the waifs and strays in Rastrik and Hiperum. Robt. Johnson of Hiprom conveyed a mess., bovate, 18 acres of rodeland in N.owrammere and Hiprommere to Richard his son : ingress 6s. 8d.

1423. Brighouse mill (⅛th) to Rob. Eland, 16s. 8d.

Turn, Oct. 13. Jury as before recorded. *Turn*, May 17th. John s. John Mylner at Kyrkeleis drew blood from Thos. Brighouse, therefore attached : no fines being now imposed at the turn as were formerly. Alice widow of John Hanson surrendered a mess., 16 acres in Wodhouse to John their son ; court fine 3s. 4d. John ffrith de Rastrik conveyed an acre at Wodhouse croft and a rode below Scolaybrigg to Thos. ffrith of Rastrik.

1424. Imperfect roll. Brighouse *Turns*, Oct., April. Juries as usual. Wm. Steyncliffe paid 3s. 4d. for Hiprum ways and strays ; and Henry Sayvill, the fforester, reported numerous cases.

[1400.—Lumis rood, under this date, p. 110, means rood light for Halifax Church.]

1425.—Brighous water mill let to Rob. Eland for 16s. 8d. Schipden mill 21d., no name opposite. Vicar Kynge pays 6d. yearly for the sport of hawking.

Turn, Oct. 22, Jury, Thos. Crossland, Thos. ffryth de Bothomley, Thos. ffryth de Rastrik, Wm. Langley, Thos. Hirst, John Woodhed, John Hepworth, John Hagh de Hagh, John Royks, Robt. Haldesworth, John Hirst, John Taillur. Hiperum constable reported that Walter Merchaunt drew blood from Wm. Totehill, (no fines here now.)

Turn, April 22. Henry Strunge was Hiperum greave. Thos. Clyf, present in the court, conveyed a mess., and bovate in Hiprom to his son Robert and Johna, Robert's wife.

1426.—Mills as before. Henry Risshworth and John Barowclogh of Hiperum brewed helpales and sold contrary to statute; attached. The latter baked and sold bread, fined 2d.

Turns, Oct. 15, May 22. John Barowclough's wife at the latter turn fined for baking and brewing, 2d. each offence. Alice Brighous,* Robt. Cokcroft wife, Henry ffox wife, all of Hiperum, brewed helpales; attached. Robt. Johnson, the greave of Hiperum, presented John Weloweby, John Rischworth and John Holloway for not attending the election of greave; fined 4d. each. John de ffryth de Rastrik paid 4s. heriot, for mess., 30 acres in Rastrik, his father Henry having died. Johna d. and heir of John Haldisworth de Erdislaw (Ardsley), paid 20d. heriot 10 acres in Clegcliff. Johan d. Wm. s. Thos. Holdsworth de (Holdsworth in) Ovenden paid 12d. heriot for 5 acres in Clegclyff, her grandfather being dead. John s. Thos. Haldesworth de Ovenden took 100 ft. by 80 of waste at Ovendenbroke in Nm. between Bradford highway on north, Batehayne on south, to erect a fulling mill; rent of waste 1d. per annum, ingress 2d. John Haldisworth of Astay conveyed 16 acres in Sourebymere to Robt. his son.

1427.—*Turn*, Oct. 16. Jury, Thos. ffryth de Rastrik, Wm. Langley, Wodhead, Hepworth, Hagh, Royks, Haldesworth, John Hyrst, John Taillior, John brodelegh, Wm. Denton, John Jagger of Stainland. Jury, April 27, instead of Brodelegh and Jagger were Ric. Longbothom and Thos. ffrith de Bothomley. Assessment of 20s. on Hiprom tenants to repair the highway in a road (venell) leading from Balybrigg to Barowecloghbrigg. John Weloweby, who held a mess., bovate, 9 acres, 3 rodes in Hiprom, being dead, John his son, aged 12, paid heriot 3s., and Margaret his mother paid 12d. to have the wardship. Wm. Hole, who held ½ bovate in Lyghtclyf, being dead, John his son paid 16d. heriot. Wm. Stayncliff farmed Shipden mill, but no name is put against it in the rolls. Robt. Eland paid 16s. 8d. for Brighous mill (¼). Vicar King paid 6d. yearly as before.

1428.—Mills, &c., as just named, Stayncliffe is inserted. Robt. Rysshworth drew a dagger to attack John Symson, therefore summoned. John Hole paid 9d. for Wayfs and Strays of Hiperum. Ric. s. Thos. Gypson paid 12d. heriot for 5 acres called Elynrode in Nm., his father being dead. John Brodelegh conveyed a parcel 60 ft. by 40, called Haylathe in Prestelay to John Bentley; ingress 4d.; also Tillyholme to ——— (unfinished.)

* Possibly this means Alice Milnes; 1413.

1429—Mills as before. Jury at Oct. *Turn* as before. Wm. Hawme was constable for ffekesby, and John Wod newly elected; for Staynland, Wm. Moldson, John Bothomley newly elected; Dalton, Thos. Snape, John Dighton newly elected; Quernby, John Drake, Ric. Wylson elect; Barkisland, Thos. Wodhede, Thos. ffirth elect; Clifton, John Smyth, Wm. Bartrem elect; Northourum, Wm. Ellysson, Thos. Otes elect; Hertshed, Ric. Norclif, John Tyngill elect; Schelf, Hen. Scolefeld, John Leche elect. Each constable presents his complaints, if any. For Hiperum, John Stansfeld was generally fined 4d. for not attending, and four women 2d. each for brewing, viz., Alice Brighouse, and the wives of John Barowclogh, Thos. Hanson, and Wm. Stokkys. The greave had generally ten absentees to report at 4d. each, for Hiprum graveship, for not attending the greave election; and the forester a longer list of greenwood delinquents at 2d. to 6d. each. These are nearly the only lists we have to show who the inhabitants were, as parish registers did not come into vogue until 1538, the date of the first Halifax book, whilst Elland starts with 1558. John de Methley paid 3s. 4d. for Hiprum graveship waifs and strays. Surrenders and heriots for Northowram are numerous, thus affording complete family histories for that township. Clyfhouse so often mentioned before was in Nm. I think, and named after a family of Cliff whose original name was probably derived from the cliff in Lightcliffe.

1430.—*Turn*, Oct. 17. Jury as before. Henry ffox's wife, John Drake's wife, and John Smyth are to be added to the last list of Hiperum brewers. Margaret Malbon of Hertshead at Kyrkley had sent away two hens value 6d. to Hampole priory, therefore attached. Hugh ffox and his wife Beatrix conveyed a cottage and garden in Rastrik to their son Robt., who paid 6d. ingress. Thos. ffryth of Rastrik surrendered 8½ acres, and ¼ acre in Brigge Pighill to Thos. Hanson. John Hanson paid 6s. 8d. heriot, for a half messuage, and 22 acres in Wodhous, his parents John and Alice being dead. John Wodhouse junr., being dead, his son John paid 13s. 4d. heriot for a mess., and 40 acres in Wodhous. Thos. Aynelay conveyed Briggeroide close, 4 acres, to Thos. Hanson.

1431.—*Turn*, Oct. 16. Jury, Thos. Littlewod *vice* John Wodhed. *Turn*, May 7. Jury, John Rishworth, Thos. ffryth de Bothomley, Thos. ffryth de Rastrik, John Wodehede de Hartishede, Ric. Symson del Owrum, John del Schagh de Bothm Hall, John Jagger de Staynland, Thos. de Wodehede, Wm. de Longelay de Dalton, Thos. Clyff de Hiprome, John de Hepworth de Dalton, Ric. Gledehill de Staynland and Wm. Rodes.

A new hand writing commences here. Hiperum constable presents that John Roks had stopped a common way called A bridull Way at Pristelay grene, therefore summoned. Wm. Schippingdale alias Schipden *v.* Wm. Turnor de Schipdene. Wm. Awmbler surrendered ½ rode in Hiprum to Wm. Deyne, capellanus. Ric. Pristelay of Hiprome *v.* Wm. Brodelee for stopping a road, or stighway, at Hiprom, to the Flatt, having been a road time out of mind. The special jury on this case, being township men, is here added: John & Henry Rishworth, Robt. Walker, John Stansfeld, Robt. Thorp, Ric. Thorp, Wm. Rode, Thos. Clyff, John Brokehous, Henry de Scolesfelde, Thos. Mauncell, Wm. Awmbler.

1432, imperfect roll. Henry de Scolesfeld, Hiprom, brewed a help-ale. John Stayncliffe conveyed a mess., 15 acres of roydland to his son Wm., and a mess., ½ bovate and 20 acres of roydland to his son John, each paying 6s. 8d. ingress.

1433.—John Otes, Hiperum greave, reported John Ryshworth, John Boy, Robt. Awmbler & John Stanclyf for not attending the greave election ; fined 4d. each. Wm. Stokks conveyed mess., 7 acres called Stysroide to Rob. Berstawe ; Ric. Vycars, 5 acres of roidland to his son John ; John Symson a mess., new edifice, ½ bov., 15 acres of roidland to Ric. s. Robt. Symson ; and John Drake did homage (made fidelity) for his Northowram lands.

1434.—*Turns* as usual, Juries the same. N.ourum constable pre-sented that John Wyloughby, Peter Crowder, Thos. Batte, Rob. Carter, Ric. Wylughby, John Wylughby de Este birle, Robt. Nettleton and others, in Westercroft, by force of arms with arrows and swords, drew blood from John s. John de Ryssheworth and Ric. Hoile Taillyor, and made a great affray. John Northend was then Nm. constable. He also reports that John Hoile of Lyghtcliffe, Ric. Thorpe, Wm. Roide, Ric. Prestelaye, John Roper, John Stancefeld, Hiprum men, dug and took away turves from Nm. moor or marsh, in great contempt of the lord. John Lynlay paid 2s. heriot for mess., 11 acres in Rastrik, Alice his mother being dead. John Notyngham and Johna his wife, by Robt. fflemyng steward for John Harryngton senescall, conveyed 3 closes called Coweroide, Laweroide, and Horlawegrene feld, (16 acres and edifice,) to John Lassye, John & Henry Rissheworth, and Henry Clay ; ingress 10s. Brighous *Turn*, April 26. Thos. Emeson and others unknown came to Brighous and assaulted John Smyth. John Barocloghe brewed a helpale. Wm. Burgh conveyed a mess., bovate, &c., to Thos. Bothe.

1435.—*Turn*, Oct. 19. Jury, Henry Risshworth, John Drake, Thos. fflrthe de Rastrik, Wm. Longlay, John Haghe, Thos. Haghe de Skyres, Wm. Denton, John Hirst, Thos. Wodhede, Ric. Gledhill, Thos. Cliffe, John Bentlay. Wm. Heylelee (of Cross Hall, now Hiley Hall,) was Clifton constable. Clegcliffe in Northourum now is written *Gled*cliffe. John Thorp conveyed 4 acres in Longemarshe to his son John, and Ric. uncle of the said John junr. gave 6d. to have the custody till the boy was of full age. Thos. fflrth of Rastrik conveyed mess., called Botheroide, and 34 acres (excepting 1 acre in Wodhouscroft and 8 acres in Rastrik fields held by John Wodhede and Ric. Botherode,) to Wm. his son, who paid 5s. ingress. Ric. Prestelay had taken 30 oxen from the Hiprum pinfold to the great contempt of the lord.

1436.—Henry Sayvill, custodian of Brynescoles, presented a long list of woodgatherers. The mills and tolls not recorded for some years.

1437.—John Hanson quit claimed to John ffoxe and Johan his wife a close called *Chapelcroft* in Rastrik. Ric. Symson conveyed a mess., two bovates, 2 acres of oxgangland, 8 acres of roideland to Ric. Rooke, with remainder to the heirs of said Ric. Symson ; also Smythyecroft, 2½ acres, to Wm. Sunderland. John Ekecopp, 1½ ac. in the Hilles to Wm. Roide. Henry Sayvill being dead, his son John paid 6d. heriot for the Randdes, 5 acres, which he conveyed to Nicholas Sayvill and Johne his wife, daughter of John Lassye. Ric. Godlaye being dead, his son Henry paid 6d. heriot for Smythyecroft in Shipden, 2½ acres, but conveyed the same to Ric. Svnderland. Wm. Turnor conveyd a mess., 7 acres, to Wm. Otes, capellanus, Ric. Batte, and John Drake. John Smyth of Brighous cut greenwood in Strangstyes in Rastrik. Ric. Batte took and carried away by force of arms from Isabella Totehill of Shelf, a horse worth 13s. 4d. Ric. Sunderland conveyed Smythyecroft to his son Wm. John Rawes surrendered Haggstokks to Wm. s. Wm. Stayncliff. Thos. Hanson took ½ acre of waste, east of Newland and [River] Kaldre.

1438.—Thos. ffrith and John s. Henry ffrith exchanged 4 acres at Heelay for 4 acres called Esteroide from John ffox. Henry ffirth being dead, John his son paid heriot for a mess., and 30 acres in Rastrik. Brighous *turn*, Oct. 14. Jury, Henry Rishworth, John Drake, Thos. ffirth de Rastrik, Thos. Wodhed, Ric. Thurgurland, Wm. Longelay, John Haghe, Wm. Denton, John Hirst, Ric. Gledhill, Thos. Cliffe, John Hepworth. Hiperum constable presents that Thos. Moodye's wife baked and sold, and Wm. Stokks' wife brewed, and that Thos. Maunsell obstructed a highway in Hyprome with a dung-hill (fimario.) Ric. Swift of Nm. fined 12d. for being a common forestaller of victuals.

1439.—Matilda Symson conveyed a mess., 11 acres, in Totehill to John Lynnelay ; ingress 3s. 4d. Henry Smith of Brighous and others fined for taking kepirs from the Keldre River. Henry Risshworth conveyed the Hilles, 3 acres, to John R. Adam Totehill was constable for ffekesby. A score pay 2d. each for taking wood from Brynscoles in Hiperum. John Stancefeld and Robt. Thorp of Lightcliff fined 2d. each, not attending the court. Proclamation in Wakefield court three times for a tenant for Horlawe grene close, 4 acres, lately held by Ric. Lister, none appearing it was taken by John Lassy and John Rysheworth senior, as ancient land ; ingress 12d.

1440.—*Turn*, Oct. 12. Jury as before. Constables are regularly recorded. Robt. Woleker senr., being dead, John Rydeinge of Hyprome paid 5s. heriot for a mess., bovate, &c. in Hyprom, and John Rideyng of Ovenden gave 20d. for custody during the minority of the first named John.

Turn, April 23. Jury, John Drake, Ric. Rokes, Ric. Batt, John Jagger, John ffrith, John Hepworth, John Bentlay, John Hirst, Wm. Denton, John Hagh, Wm. Longley, Thos. ffirth, Rastrik. Wm. Otes conveyed two closes, Littilroide and le Pighill, 3½ acres, to his son Robert in Hiprum.

1441.—Hiprom constable reported that John Wylby of Birstall parish and Henry Thornhill came into the lord's warren and took hares, therefore attached. Thos. ffirth being dead, his son John paid 5s. heriot for a toft and bovate in Rastrik. Wm. Wodd was ffekesby constable.

1442.—John Thorp of Lightcliffe took turf from Northourum marsh; Thos. Sklater, Hiprom, brewed a helpale; both attached, *i.e.*, arrested. Ric. Rokes was constable of Shelf; Rob. Totehill succeeded him. Adam Bemonde conveyed a mess. and 31 acres in Skamenden, (successively failing issue to one) to his children, James, Nicholas, Richard, Johane wife of Laurence Wodd, Johane (another sister of the name), and finally to Thomas the oldest son. Matilda Symson surrendered lands formerly her husband's, Gilbt. Otes, to John Otes of Halifax, *walker*. (Walker means fuller; he ran the Halifax fulling mill.)

Turn, April 30. The town of Clifton to repair the highway at Thorneyalls before next turn on pain of 6s. 8d. Agnes d. John Ryssheworth of Coley, wife of Ric. Longbothom, conveyed Warley property to their sons Ric., Rob., and Edmund L.

1443.—Thos. Anelay surrendered 4 acres between Newlande and Keldre to Thos. Hanson; John, s. Henry ffrith ½ acre there called Willepighill, to same Thomas; Johan Alisaundre, widow, ½ acre at le Toft to same Thomas; Hugh Totehill 2 acres on the ffalogh called Meylemakerflatt to the same Thomas. Wm. Brodelegh, Hiperum, conveyed Tillyholme to Wm. Lister de Halifax. John Stansfeld, of Hiprom, surrendered the Royd in Sourbyshire, to Thos. Wylkynson, vicar of the church of Halifax, and Thomas Strenger, capellanus.

1444.—Tenants of Hyprome to repair Hypromloyne on pain of 6s. 8d. Brighous *Turn*, April 6. Jury, Henry Ryshworth, Ric. Dalton, John Drake, Ric. Rokes, John ffrith, John Wodhede, Wm. Longley, John Hirst, John Hepworth, Thos. Haghe de Skyres in Quernby, John Haghe de Bothomhall, John Jagger, John Bentley, Ric. Anelay.

1445.—*Turn*, Oct. 19. Ric. Rokes de Rokes, and Ric. Rokes de Northourum were jurymen. Robt. and Ric. Cokcroft took hares in Hyprom warren. The Brighouse tenants were to repair the way between Brighous and Cliftonbrig under penalty of 6s. 8d. John Wylughby surrendered lands to John Otes for life, remainder to Ric. son of said John Otes and Margaret wife of Richard, daughter of John Lynnelay, and remainder to Thomas, brother of Richard.

1446.—Several are presented for playing at speres and other unlawful games. No games were allowed after 9 p.m. Rob. Haworth of Hiprom brewed a helpale; he was constable. The common way in Hypromloyne to the boundary of Brighous town (that is, to Slead Syke) to be repaired on pain of 6s. 8d. by the tenants.

1447.—In Hyprum, Thos. Bryghouse, Rob. Haworth and Wm. Totehill brewed helpales last year. People from Okenshagh, &c., had fetched Thakestones from Smalecloghegge, Nm. Henry Ryssheworth being dead, his son John R., senior, paid heriot for a cottage and closes called the Hey and the Hilles, and a close in Nm. called Wharllers. Ric. Northend greave of Hiprom and others come before John Sayvill, senescall, and pay taksylver for 12 good and faithful men to have special inquiry: the 12 jurymen chosen were, Ric. Rokes, Ric. Symson, Henry Strange, John Otes, John Stancliffe, John Haldworth, Ric. Haldworth, John Hoile, John Wylogheby, Rob. Cliffe, Ric. Sunderland & John Bentlay, who say that the tenants had pasture for pigs in the time of pannage in Hyprome wodd, and that John Ealand, knt., yielded to Earl Warrenne 4s. 6d. in former times.

1449.—Woodcutters fined as usual. Thos. Populwell de Scoles took hares from Hiprom warren. John s. Robt. Clyff paid 40d. heriot for a mess., and bovate at his father's death, and conveyed them to himself and Elizabeth his wife, daughter of Wm. Haldesworth.

1450.—Ric. Saltonstall was greave for Sourby. John Mawde of Hiprom was presented for brewing, and he and Ric. Wodd for not attending the turn. John Bentley obstructed the way between Longstobynge and Brehous in Hypprome to the hurt of the tenants, especially of Ric. Northend, and contempt of the lord.

1452.—John ffirthe of Brighous and John Mawde brewed helpales. Thos. Brighouse drew blood from Oliver Milner in Hyprom; attached. Henry Rysheworth conveyed ½ bov. for 12 years to Ric. Shaghe. Proclamation made against brewers, lndeness, illicit games, bowls, &c. Matilda Symson, widow, quit-claimed to John Lynnelay a half messuage and 11 acres in Totehill. Hiperum tenants pay 6s. 8d. towards Wakefield mill dam repairs; Rastrik ditto. Brynescole forester reports as usual.

1453.—Elena wife of Henry Rysheworth a certain day last year in the church of Halifax made an assault on Alice d. John Smyth de Lyghtcliffe, therefore attached; also John Townend on Ric. Shaghe (an under tenant of Henry Ryssheworth's), in the Halifax cemetery (churchyard); and John Milner on Rob. Thorp.

Turn, Jury as usual, two Ric. Rokes, Wm. Cosyn, Laurence Newall, Rich. Northend. Margt. ffernelay of Dewsebury broke into a house in Hyprom; and Agnes wife of John Smyth of Lightcliff and her son harboured and received into their house the said Margaret, knowing what she had done: therefore attached. Wm. Holloway by John Otes, walker, surrendered mess. and ½ bovate in Hyprome to the use of the said Wm., and Johanne his wife. John Sunderland was constable of Fikesby. Henry Smith of Hiprom baked bread, fined 2d.

1454.—Wm. Sheplay was ordered to cleanse his ditches at Brighouse, on pain of 12d. John Jacson, Thos. Brighous and Ric. fletcher ditto at Clifton brig, pain 2s. John ffrith of Rastrik being dead, Thos. his son paid 10s. heriot for a mess., 74 acres. Brighous Turn, April. Jury, Ric. Dalton, John Drakys, Ric. Rokes de Rokes, John ffrith de Barkesland, John Wodhede, John Bentlaye, John Hepworth, Wm. Cosyn, Laurence Newall, Ric. Northende, Ric. Aynelaye, Ric. Thurgurland. For brewing a helpale and selling, Ric. Thorp was attached. Thos. de Roide, also of Hiprom, for absence, fined 4d.

1456.—In Hyprom, Thos. Sclater, John Shippyngdale and John
Smyth brewed helpales.　Johna Bryg with palings has enclosed the
way in Herteshede between the Rectory and the Church.　Thos.
Haldeworth conveyed lands formerly waste (100 ft. by 80) in Hyprome
to Thos. Awmbler.　John Brodeleghe being dead, Ric. his son gave
3s. 4d. heriot for 16 acres in Hyprom.　Thos. Populwell of Scoles
(near Hartshead), and Ric. his son took hares from Hyprum warren :
summoned to appear under pain of 40d.

1457.—Edward s. Henry Rishworth in Hyprome for lying in wait
for and drawing blood from Ric. Northcliffe, attached.

FIELD ARMS.　　　　　　　　　　RADCLIFFE ARMS.

Turn, Oct. 3.　Jury nearly the same as before, Wm. Lokwodd
instead of Dalton.　Peter Thorp to remove obstacles from a field east
of Hyprom, pain 6s. 8d.　Wm. fflecher to cleanse the ditches in Park-
croft in Brighous before the next turn, pain 3s. 4d.　John, Agnes,
and Alice Smyth to remove the palings, ditches, &c., in Woodhall
flatts, Hyprom.　Jas. Ermytage had to cleanse the running water at
St. Mary's Yng in Dalton.　John Thorp, harper, and his mother
Johna, widow, convey to Robt. Thorp, senr., Longmarshe close for
80 years.　Ralph ffourness and his son John, Thos. Populwell and
his son Ric. had been " Traseyng " hares in the warren ; attached.

1458.—John Wilby, John Boethe, Ric. Rokes de Rodeshall, Ric. Northend, Ric. Stancliffe, junr., Wm. Holway, 4d. each, for not attending the greave election.

Turn, Oct. 10. Ric. Dalton, Ric. Rokes de Rokes, Ric. Thurgurland, John ffrith de Barkesland, John Jagger, John Hepworth, Thos. Longley, John Wodhede, John Bentlay, Ric. Aynelay, Wm. Lokwodd, Wm. Cosyn, Ric. Northend, Wm. Shepley, John Hey were Jurymen. John Clyff and John Clay, both of Hyprom, brewed helpales. Ric. Smyth, Thos. Roide, and Henry Hemingway, all of Hiprom took turves from Shelf waste. John Chaloner of Anelay in a place called Knolles in Fekisby took carriage and goods over a "bridyll way"; attached. Wm. Clay and John his son quit claim to John ffox the lands formerly of Hugh ffox and Beatrix his wife. Wm. Lister, Halifax, conveyed Tillyholme to Thos. Neleson, of York, merchant. Thos. s. John ffirth de Rastrik now being 22 years old takes certain lands.

1460.—Ric. Staincliffe surrenders a mess., 1¼ bov. in Hyprum (grave) to Thos. Bates, for 30 years. The roll this year is mutilated; it may have been at the battle of Wakefield fought this year.

1461.—1st Edw. IV. The *Battle of Wakefield*, and a new royal line do not interfere with these courts. Brighouse *Turn* was held Oct. 13, the Jury being Ric. Dalton, Ric. Rokes de Rokes, Ric. Rokes de Nm., John Drake, John Hepworth, Thos. Longelaye, John Wodhede, John ffrith, John Bentlay, Laurence Newall, Thos. Brighous, Wm. Cosyn, Ric. Northende, Ric. Aynelaye. Ric. Scolefeld, Rob. Thorp, and Ric. Wodd to cleanse the ditch on the road towards Brighouse mill, on pain of 3s. 4d. at next turn. Thos. Woodd was constable of Fekesby. Henry Rishworth being dead, Edmund his son, paid 6s. 8d. heriot, for a mess., 2½ bovates, 7 acres of roidland.

1462.—Amongst the great men who did homage at Wakefield court, paying 12d. each, were Brian Thornhill, Ric. Longbothome, John ffrith de Rastrik, heirs of John Drake, Wm. s. John Prestlaye, John s. Ric. Prestlaye.

Turn, Oct. 19, as usual. Thos. Sklatter had to turn the water into its proper channel at Hiperum.

1463.—*Turn*, April 10. John Smyth de Lyghtcliff on the jury. Thos. Horton was constable for Barkisland. Gilbert Lacy and his wife Johna, dau. Gerard Sotehill attend Wakefield court. Ric. Whitelay to repair the fences of Hyprome field on pain of 3s. 4d. Ric. s. Rob. Wodd, of Hyprum, fined 4d. for not attending the turn. All and singular of the tenants of Hiprom to ring their pigs on pain of 4d. each. Hyprom tenants obstruct a way at Northegegate, and trespass on Shelf mores to the detriment of Shelf tenants. Rich. Brighous built a house on the grene, Hyprom township, without leave. Peter Thorp broke the common law made by common assent.

1464.—John Appelyerde of Hiprum, is a common forestaller. Ric. de Leeroide of Hiprome and John Haldeworthe, junr., brew helpales. At Clifton many were reported for playing at Karddeyng (cards), and at Speras (bowls) at their houses, and Thos. Darynelaye is a vagabond, and John Cosyn had harboured the vagabond, (wanderer).

Turns, Oct. and April 29. Juries, John Rishworth, Ric. Dalton, Ric. Rookes de Rookes, John Hepworth, Thos. de Longlaye, John Wodhed, John Bentlay, Thos. Brighous, Wm. Cosyn, Wm. Lokwod, Ric. Northend, John Drake, Adam Hirst, John Smyth de Lyghtclyf, Wm. Roide. Richard Whitlay to cleanse Hathelay dike, Hiprum. All field enclosures to be repaired.

1465.—*Turn*, Jury, Oct. 9, included Ric. Sunderland, John Hylelee, Ric. Aynelaye.

1466.—Ric. Whitlay and Ric. Wodde broke Hiprom pynfold. Robt. Helywell at Thurcroft, Hyprum, obstructs the footpath. Edmund Ryshworth and Elena his mother make a nuisance in the common way. Ric. and Wm. ffletcher are to purge their ditches; John Scolfeld and Robt. Thorpe to cleanse the stream at Marshe.

1467.—Wm. Brodelee, at Presteley, took 3 oxen from John Bentlay by force of arms. Tenants of Hiprum to repair their boundaries and palisades, (metas and cippos); to repair the common way at Hylle-myers. Bryghous tenants are not to take wood from Rastrik common lands. John Hanson paid 8s. heriot for a messuage and 32 acres in Wodhous, John his father being dead.

Rookes Hall

1468.—Brighous *Turn*, Oct. 18. Jury, Ric. Dalton, John Hepworth, Ric. Rookes de Rookes, Thom. Langley, Wm. Lokwod, Ric. Northend, Wm. Bentlay, John Drake, Adam Hirst, Wm. Roide, Ric. Sundirland, John Thewles. No mills are mentioned now. Robt. ffox conveyed a toft and garden in Rastrik to Brian Thornhill. Edmund Rishworth, Ric. Otes, and the heirs of Wm. Holway, fined 4d. for not attending the election of greave.

1469.—Robt. Smyth to cleanse the running water at Bryghous. John Thorp, junr., Hyprum, allowed his cattle to trespass. John Hanson, Hiperum township, to cleanse the running water.

1470.—*Turn*, May 7. Jury, Ric. Rookes de Rookes, Ric. Aynelay, Wm. Bentlay, John Drake, Adam Hirst, Wm. Roide, John Haldworth, Thos. Wodhede, Ric. Sheplay, Thos. Bythebroke, John Hepworth, Ric. Dalton. Ric. Scolefeld to cleanse the stream at Tukroid and Haythelay (Hiprum). Robert Shaghe's wife and Thos. Brighouse's wife, for brewing, 2d. each. Bryghouse tenants cut wood on Rastrik moor without leave.

1471.—*Turn*, Oct. 15. Jury, Dalton, Th. ffirth, John Smyth of Lightcliffe, Ric. Longbothom, Ric. Sunderland, Bentley, Drake, Roide, Haldworth, Wodhed, John Cowper, Thos. Gledehill. Thos. ffrith, constable for ffekisby, was succeeded by Ric. Botheroide; Shelf, Rob. Thorp by Ric. Roide; Clyfton, Wm. Blakeborne by Ric. Mankinholes; Hertshead, Thos. Bryg by Rob. Arundale; Northourum, Rob. Awmbler by Ric. Northend, junr.; Dalton, Adam Longley by Geo. Bothroide; Barkesland, John Ravenslawe by Wm. Townend; Staynland, Robt. Aynelay by Wm. Priestlay; Quernby, Wm. Dawson by Wm. Bothomlaye.

1472.—Elena Rysshworth to clean the running water below Hiprom hills. Wm. Raumesden, Hiprom, brewed a helpale. Hiprom tenants to repair the way to Balebrig. Brynescole wood list as usual.

1473.—John Rissheworth and John Staincliffe not attending the greave election, 4d. each.

Turn, Oct. 12, Ric. Rookes de Rookes, John Smyth de Lightcliffe, John Wilby, Ric. Sunderland, amongst the jurors.. John Brodelegh, Wm. Marshall, capellanus, and John Lyster, for Ric. Northend deceased, surrendered a mess., edifice, 1½ bov., 12 acres roidland in Nm., and a messuage, edifice, bovate and 8 acres of roidland in Hiperum to John Northend his bastard son de corpore Elisote Otes. Jas. Halywell, of Hyprome, and Jas. Witley brewed helpales. Hiprum and Rastrick tenants paid 2s. each township to repair Wakefield mill dam.

1474.—Hiprum tenants to repair their part of the way from Nm. to Wakefield. Ric. and M'eriori Sunderland being dead, their son Ric. paid 2s. heriot for Sunderland, Clyffroide, &c. Hyprum constable presents that all is well, (omnia bene.) Rastrik constable reports that John Shaghe and Thos. Sheplay, both of Brighous, pasture horses and cows in Rastrik common lands; therefore summoned to appear.

1475.—*Turn*, Oct. 3. Hyprum constable reports Wm. Bentley and John Schofeld for not attending, 4d. each; Jas. Whitley and Robt. Strangefellow for brewing helpales; John Hanson de Rastrik senr. and junr., Alex. ffirth, Ric. Ravneslaw and others for pasturing cattle within Bryghous town; also all inhabitants to have their pigs rung. John Clyff, constable of Hyprum, April *Turn*, gives Thos. by the Broke and John Wood, as not attending, 4d. each; the Northloyne to be repaired, the Brighous lane to be repaired, each on pain of 8d. John Townend deputy of John Woderove, Esq., custodian of Brynescoles, gives his list of culprits. John Shaghe of Brighouse had obstructed a road, and Ric. Rooks of Roidshall, John Stancliff, and John Ryssheworth had absented themselves at the election of greave ; fined 4d. each. Robt. Thorp conveyed Longmarshe 5 acres, to Ric. his son.

1476.—All the inhabitants forbidden to carry unreasonable weapons, as, sword, axe, bill, spear, on pain of forfeiting it to the lord and paying 3s. 4d.   Affrays were common at Halifax feast.   Jas. Whitley's wife brewing ale (cervis) fined 1d., John Thorp brewing a helpale, arrested.   John s. Ric. Duke did homage and paid heriot for 10 acres on the death of his father, and his mother Johne Duke, d. of Wm. Alisaundre.   Injunction against Hiprom Northloyne again.   John and Cristofer Haldworth, Ric. & John Scolefeld, John Ryding, Robt. Otes and John Wilby, all of Hiprome, took turves from Shelf.

1477.—Edm. and John Ryshworth and John Hoyle, absent at the greave election, 4d. each.   Alice, Margt., and Johna, daughters of Wm. Roide hold Jakwyfroide for 20 years at 2d. per ann., and John Smyth de Lightcliff holds the land at 5d. per ann., called Ploghsilver, (in lieu of plough duty to the lord,) for 12 years.   Edm. and John Ryshworth and Ric. Longbothom have not made fines for their lands.   John Bekwith, Hiprom, absent from the turn, fined 4d.; Christopher Haldworth brewed a helpale.   Wm. Sayvill was deputy for John Sayvell, knt., the senescall.

1478.—John Ryshworth being dead, his son John paid heriot, 6s. 8d., for 1½ bov., formerly Henry Coplay lands, a plot called Hekdeyne, and another formerly waste, east of Coldelay.   John Wodhouse quit claimed to Thos. s. Thos. Sayvell, formerly of Holynegge, a mess.,

COLEY, FROM ROYDS HALL.

called Wodhous, with 48 acres. John Gledehill and John Sharp made an affray at Lightclyff. Thos. Lacy, Esq., comes and takes of the lord to farm the fourth part of the mill of Brighous for 40 years at 15s. per ann. and 4d. p. novo moru', paying 8d. ingress. It had evidently been on a long lease before. Thos. s. John ffrith de Darton and Elizabeth his mother quit claim to Thos. s. John ffrith de Rastrik a mess., and 30 acres in Rastrik; ingress 2s.

1479.—Wm. Sunderland, John Boethe, John Northend, and John Boy surrendered Hasillhurst close in Nm., formerly waste, to Ric. Barestowe for the use of the town of Hyprome. Ric. Rookes of Roideshall, greave for Hyprum, for not attending Wakefield courts, fined 8d., 12d., 12d., 6d., 4d., &c. John Sharp, Hiperum, brewed a helpale; attached, that is, arrested.

1480.—*Turn*, Oct. 9. Jury, Henry Longlay, Ric. Rooks de Rooks, Ric. Longbothom, Ric. Sunderland, Thos. ffrith, Wm. Lokwodd de Collenly, Thos. Gledhill, Wm. Thewles, W. Bentley, Adam Hirst, Ric. Sheplay, John Northend, John Bentlay, John Haldworth. Agnes, wid. of Ric. Scolefeld, and John Leeroide, both of Hiprom, brewed helpales, fined 4d. each, and Ric. Wood's wife brewed ale (cervis), fined 2d. The road in Hyprome field to be repaired. Ric. Longbothome took 1 acre of waste near Shipdeyne hall without leave. Ric. Thorp took of the waste near Estfelde liddeyate (that is, Lightcliffe Lydgate) of Hyprome ½ rode at 1d. per ann., ingress 4d. Ric. Wodd took ⅓ rod between Ovirflatt and Cloghebrooke in Hyprum, rent 1d., ingress 4d. Wm. Baytes conveyed a mess., 3 ac. in Cloghroide in Hyprum to his wife Katrine for life, remainder to Laurence, John, Thomas Baytes, (probably their sons.) Brynescole custodian presents John Haldworth, John Rideyng, John Scolefeld, Ric. Townend and Rob. Helywell for cutting greenwood, fined 2d. each.

1481.—Ric. Gledehill took 1 acre of waste abutting Rakesclogh, S., Wm. Burgh's close called Rydeyng, N., Drawstones close, E., Jclnnroide close, W., in Hyprome. John Thorp, Hyprom, to repair the highway called Ebestoneloyne. Alice, wid. of Ric. Gledehill conveyed a mess., and 15 acres to their son Wm. She was daughter of Wm. Stayncliff and paid heriot for 1 acre in Nm. this year.

1483.—Henry s. Thos. Sayvell, of Holyngegge, surrendered his lands held of the king, in Horbury, Halifax, Sandall, Hyprum, Rastrick, Holme, Erlesheton, and Osset, to Elizth., wid. of Robt. Waterton, Esq., and Thomas Sayvell his brother: ingress 20s. A mess. and 24 acres in Rastrik conveyed by Thos. Totehill to John Clayton, ingress 6s. John Lynlay, mess., 11 acres in Rastrik to his daughter Alice, wife of John Wylkynson.

Turn, Oct. 14. Jury, same as 1480, except John Boythes, Thos. Wodhede and Ric. Aynelay instead of Sunderland, Sheplay and Northend.

1484.—Thos. s. Thos. Neleson, formerly of York, paid 4d. heriot for 5½ rodes called Tillyholme in Hyprum, his father being dead; but surrendered it to Gilbt. Lacy, Esq. John Hanson, senr., conveyed a mess., edifice, and 12 acres in Rastrik, to John his son. Amongst the Brynescole wood depredators were John and Adam Wilton. Elizth. d. Ric. Thorp, aged 1 year, by Thos. Holleroide, paid 12d. heriot for 5 acres in Longemarshe, her father being dead. John Clyff surrendered a mess. called Clyffhous with its lands, pastures and wood in Hyperum to Ric. Clyffe, ingress 3s. 4d.

1485.—Rob. Burgh, capellanus, conveyed a mess., 1½ bov. in Hyprum to Rob. Otes, for 40 years. Halifax *Turn* held Oct. 7, Brighous Oct. 8, Holm Oct. 9. Brighous jury, Ric. Rookes de Rookes, Henry Longlay, John Haldworth, John Bentlay, Thos. ffrith, Wm. Denton, Thos. Gledehill, Ric. Aynelay, Thos. Hawme, John Wornewall, John Ramsden, Gilbt. Wodhede, Wm. Bentlay. Next *Turn*, April 10. Cristopher Brodelegh, Hiprum, absent from turn. Wm. Sundirland being dead, Ric. his son paid 7d. heriot for Smythie croft, 2 acres. John Sunderland of Sourby, being dead, Thos. his son paid heriot.

1486.—John Duke conveyed 10 acres in Rastryk to Thos. Goodheire. Robt. Hanson ordered to cleanse the ditch in Brighous on pain of 2s.

1487.—John Sayvell, knt., chief senescall. John and Edm. Ryshworth, and Ric. Rookes of Roides Hall, not attending the greave election, 4d. each. John Brodelegh took 1 rode of waste at 1d. per ann., ingress 2d., between Edw. Otes land, E., highway, W., John Haley's land, S., in Hyprum. Thos. Sowodd, 2 acres of waste between Blakelclough and Knightroide. Ric. Gledehill being dead, Wm. his son paid 4d. heriot for 1 acre formerly waste. John Northend, bastard, surrendered mess., edifice, bovate, 8 acres roideland to Thos. his son ; and 10 acres of roideland at Brerehay.

Turn, Oct. 14. Jury, John Rookes de Rookes, Henry Longlay, John Haldworth de Hyprome, John Hoile, John Hanson, Ric. Rookes de Roidshall, &c.

LISTER ARMS.   LISTER ARMS, (Hull Branch.)

1488.—Thos. Lister conveyed 1 acre formerly waste in Hyprum to John Shore ; Thos. Sowood and Isabella his wife, 4 acres at Dykonfeld, (Nm.) to Gilbt. Saltonstall : who took also 2 acres of waste under Boltshaghefoote.

Turn, Oct. 7. Margaret wid. Ric. Thorp fined 12d. for not repairing the highway at Eastfield gate, and John Thorp 6d. for uncleansed ditches at Hathelaylayne. Edwd. and John Cosyn fined 6d. each for affray with Laurence and Agnes Scholefeld.

1489.—*Turn*, Oct. 20. Jury, Ric. Rowkes, John Rowkes, H. Longlay, W. Bentlay, Ric. ffourness, Ric. Aynelay, Thos. Gledehill, Rob. Dawson, John Boy, John Hoyle, Thos. ffirthe, Laurence Barestowe. Edward Hirst was ffekesby constable, Percival Rayner for Hartishead. Henry Walker of Brighous fined 2d. for taking green wood from Rastrick wood. John Walker of Barkisland and Wm. Moregateroid, 12d. each for an affray at Rybornedeyne chapel at Easter.

1490.—John Wilby absent from greave election, 4d. The forester of Strangsty in Rastrik presented a list of delinquents.

Turn, 18 Oct. Jury, an unusual list, who mostly formed the Halifax jury next day; Wm. Mirfield, Esq., Wm. Scaregill, junr., Esq., Rob. Pilkyngton, Esq., Ric. Wodrofe, Esq., Rob. Gargrave, Esq., John Burton, Wm. Wilkinson, Edwd. Rysshworth, Adam Hirst, Hen. fferror, Wm. Drake, Ric. Aynelay, John Wilkinson, John Miggelay. John Rydeyng conveyed a mess., bovate, in Hyprum to his son John; Thos. Lister, a house called Barkhouse, and garden in Hyprum to John Shore for 18 years. John s. Wm. s. John Gybson, 20d. heriot for 5 acres and edifice at Ellynrode, Nm., his uncle John G. being dead.

1491.—Jury, Longley, J. Rookes, John Haldworth de Hyprum, W. Bentlay, John Boy, Thos. ffirth, Ric. Lokwod, W. Cowper, Ric. Waterhous, W. Drake, W. Thewlis, Ric. Sunderland, Jas. Otes, Thos. Gledehill.

1492.—Special Jury, Ric. Rookes de Roideshall, John Boy, Ric. Northend, Jas. Otes, John Ryding, Peter Thorp, Ric. ffourness, John Stanclyff, Wm. Scolecote, Wm. Awmbler, Ric. Townend, Wm. Boethes, about a close called Winters, whether it is free land, or copy hold, when it was found that 1¼ rodes on the north side are free, and the rest is held of the lord by copy of Court Roll; the close being south of John Rysshworth's land at Coley. A greater finding took place this year when Columbus discovered America. How proud Americans would be to trace a town history four hundred years back! Ric. Symson *alias* Ric. Symmes, vicar of the church of Halifax, paid 6s. 8d. heriot for mess., edifice, ½ bovate, 15 acres of roidland in Hyprome (graveship), his father Ric. Symson or Symmes being dead. Egidius Hoppay fined 20d., for affray on Thos. Boethe with a 'sithe.' Gilbt. Lacy, Esq., conveyed Tilleholme to his sons Edw. and Christopher. John Thorp of Southcliffe (Hyp.) placed his cattle in Shelf common pasture, fined 8d. See view of Thorp's Cottages, next page.

1493.—*Turn*, Jury as before, Hirst, Lokwod, Bentlay, Gledehill, Ric. and John Rookes, Aynelay, Drake, Boy, Haldworth de Hyprome, ffirth, Ric. Northend, John Hoile, Thos. Brigghous. The previous jury only differed in the names Ralph Stancefeld, Thos. Smyth, Lightcliffe, John Wilby, Hiprum, Robt. Dawson, John Thorp.

1

Robt. Smyth, Wm. Brook for his boys, Henry Walker, all of
Brighouse, 4d. each for breaking and carrying away hedge stakes.
The lads could not have been keeping Gunpowder Plot then; nor
would hedge stakes be big enough for yule logs. We next get a
tasty bit of English amongst the ocean of Monk Latin : Ad hanc cure
Domin. Rex. Mandavit John Sayvile, milit, capitl. Senl. Domij de
Wakefeld ;—Trusty and welbeloued we grete you wele and bee credibly
enformed that certain our officers called Greves within our lordship of
Wakefeld being bounden by reason of thair tenures to gadre our Rent
there wil nat of thair obstynances bring in the saide our Duties at
suche tyme as hertofore vvas appointed afore our auditour and Richard
Cholmeley our Receyuor there and namely oon Gilbert le Greve of

THORP'S COTTAGES, SUTCLIFFE WOOD.

Ossett with diu'se other Greves of our saide lordship wherefore we
vvol and desire you and nev'thelas comaunde you straitly to see that
hasty payment bee made of all our said Rents by the said Gilbert and
other our like officers there, accordeing to thappoyntment aboue
lymyted, and where as it is shewed vnto vs that after the custome and
vsage of our said lordship the lands of diu'se such Greves bene seised
vnto our hands for nonpayment of our said Duties We charge you
to see that they, and namely the said Gilbert Legh, of Ossett, be not
admitted to thair fynes therein hereaft. but that other ffolk rather
than they may have the same lands like as to your discrecion shalbe
thought moost for our prouffite and avauntage whiche wol bee an
example and fere vnto them and all other like officers there to comitte

semblable offences in tyme comynge and cause theym to bee the more redy to kepe thair dayes appoynted for the said payment hereafter. Yeuen vndre our Signet at our palace of Westmr. the xxth day of Nouembre.

Rob. Hemmyngway took ½ acre of waste in Nm. and Hip. having Yvynear W., Bryndescolebrooke E., Robt's. lands S., Yvynearcloghe N. John s. Peter Thorp broke into Nm. pinfold; fined 4d.

1494.—John Weloweby (by his substitute John Haldworth of Hiperum,) surrendered a messuage, bovate, 9 ac. 3 rods, to the use of John Nevile, knight, Thos. Nevile his son and heir, Mr. Ric. Symmes, vicar of church of Halifax, Wm. s. and heir of the late Wm. Symmes, John s. and heir of Thos. Lacy, Esq., Mr. Thos. Sayvile, vicar of the church of Braithwell, Wm. Rookes of Roydeshall, John Stanclyf, Laurence Barestowe, Thomas Smyth, Thomas Weloweby, Rob. Otes, and Thos. Oldefeld and their heirs on trust, who paid for ingress xxs. This refers to the founding of the Willoughby Chantry at Halifax. Ric. Clyff and Thos. Brighous were summoned for making a Bowlynge Aley at Halifax against the statute.

John Willoughby founded the Chauntry of the Trinity at Halifax, of the yearly value of £4. Watson states that ——— Willeby founded a chauntry on the south side of Halifax church, and to endow it feoffed Sir John Nevil, knt., Thomas Nevil, Esq., his son and heir, Thomas Willeby, his kinsman, and others in lands in Priestley in Hipperholm, to the yearly value of six marks, June, 9 Henry VII." In Halifax Register is the entry: "Dom. Thomas Gleydehyll cantarist. in cantar. voc. Wylbe Chantre, ac quondam Vicarius de Cunnesburghe, sepult. 12 Maii, 1541." The lands belonging to this Chauntry were granted by Edw. VI. to Thomas Gargrave, knt., and Wm. Adam, jun. In 1553, (Willis's *Mitred Abbies*, vol. ii.,) Richard Northend received £3 12s. 0d. pension, as Incumbent of Wylby's Chauntry. The south or Holdsworth Chapel at Halifax Church was the favourite burial place of many old families, and there was interred the body of good Oliver Heywood, of Coley. In Watson's *Halifax* will be found a long Latin record of the foundation of this Chauntry. John Willebye, in the name of the Father, Son and Holy Spirit, by charter tripartite enfeoffed John Nevil, knt., Tho. Nevile son of said John, Mr. Richard Symmes, Wm. s. Wm. Symmes, John s. Thos. Lacye, Esq., Mr. Thos. Savile, Vicar of Brayvell (sic). Wm. Rookes, John Stancliffe, Laurence Bairstowe, Thos. Smith, Thos. Willeby, Robt. Otes, and Thos. Oldfeld in his messuages, lands, &c., in Hipperholm, and appointed Thos. Gledhill to be first chaplain. The lands were to be held and occupied by 'Thos. Willobye consanguineum meum, et heredes suos,' on paying six marks at Pentecost and St. Martin's in Winter in equal portions. Provision was made for the support of Johanna wife of the donor, during her lifetime. The chaplain was required to pray for him and his family in this form:—Ye shall praye for the soule of John Willebye, founder of this Chauntrye and Service, and for the soules of his two wives, his children, his fader, his moder soules and all his elders soules," and say immediately De profundis, &c. Dated and sealed 10 June, 9 Henry VII.

In less than a generation these religious benefactions were interfered with by a rapacious Monarch, and the Reformation followed. The lights at the altars in the churches were extinguished, and the morrow mass, sung at 5 a.m., silenced. Winteredge, Coley Hall gateway, Coley Chapel House (the public house adjoining the graveyard), and other properties in Halifax parish, bear the double cross, still carved on them, shewing that the Knights of St. John of Jerusalem derived certain rents therefrom. At Howroyd, in Barkisland, the home of the Hortons, (who resided at and owned Coley Hall for some time,) Watson saw a rental of the sums paid to the Knights from Halifax parish in 1533 : John Rushworth of Coley for certain lands and tenements in Coley, 5s. Richard Sunderland for lands and tenements in Shibden, 7½d. Henry Batt for tenement called Hayley Hill, 6d. Richard Saltonstall for Godley in Shibden, 2d. John Northend for lands, &c., in Shibden, 1½d. Edward Kent for Wheatley in Ovenden, 1d.; and for Shelve-park, 4d. Robert Deane for Ekersley (Exley) Hall, near Eland, 6d. Rob. Northend for Horner's in Shibden, 2½d. Total 7s. 6½d.

1495.—John s. Robt. Brodelegh conveyed to himself for life and to his son John, lands in Hyprum. The said Rob. B. senr. yielded 14 acres in Hyprum to John and Thos. B., charged with 23s. 4d. yearly for Robt's. life. Ric. Bairestawe took 1 rode of waste in Hyp., a marsh on the N., Ric. Thorp's land on W. Proclamation at three courts that the Hiperum greave has the Boythes (bovate and 8 acres) formerly held by John de Boythes in his hands. John Haldeworth of Sourby and John Waterhous senr., paid 13s. 4d. ingress for the same. Constables —Wm. Thorp, Shelf; Gilbt. Rayner, Hartshead ; John Shore, N'ourum ; Ric. ffletcher, Clyfton ; &c.

1496.— Jury, Rad. Stancefeld, John Rookes, Thos. Smyth, John Boy, Gilbt. Saltonstall, Ric. ffourness, John Haldworth, Gibt. Wodhede, Ric. Waterhouse, Thos. ffrith, John Thorp of Sutclyff, John Hoile, Thos. Hanson. Nich. Bentlay took 1 acre of waste in Hyp., having Bryndescoles E., Rad. Saynton's lands W., Westroide S, Rideynge N., Rad. Saynton took 1 rod in Hyp., with Walleloyne W., King's way E., Walclogh S. Wm.Bentlay being dead, his son Laurence paid heriot 20d. for waste land called longestubbynge, Jakstubynge and little pighill.

STANSFIELD-ROOKES ARMS.

1497.—Ric. Aykeroide surrendered Shugden Hall, Nm., to Wm. Aykeroide, rector of the church of Marston, Thos. Yongesmith, vicar of Dewsbury church, Robt. Burgh, chaplain, John Yorke, chaplain, Thos. Sayville de Bladeroide, John Waterhous, senr., and Brian Otes. Ingress 6s. 8d. W. Akeroide was a great benefactor to Grammar Schools. Vicar Symmes of Halifax, being dead, Wm. s. Wm. Symmes paid 8s. 2d. heriot for mess., edifice, ½ bov., 15 acres roideland, and 4½ acres lately waste. To this court comes John Northende, Bastard, in his proper person, and in these words " To the Stevvard of the lordeship of Wakefeld, Humblely shevveth vnto yore maistrship yore dayly orator and bedeman John Northende, Bastard, hovve that afore thys tyme it was agreed and com'ited betwixe yore seide Orator and one Thomas Nayler, yt one Thomas Northende, son and heir appar- int of the seid John, shuld wed and take to wife Johnet Nayler doghter of the seid Thomas, for whiche mariage to be hadd the seid Thomas Nayler payde to yore seid Orator 1 *li.* of money, and because bothe the seid Thomas Northende and Johnet Nayler were within yeres of consent and was doutefull whedir thay wolde agree to the seid mariage att yeres of consent the seid John Northende made a surrendre of Diu'ses p'cells of land ligynge in Northeourome in the graveship of Hyprome halden by Copie after custome of the maner of Wakefeld to thuse of the seid Thomas Nayler and his heires vppon condicion yt yff the seid Thomas Northend disagreed to the seid mariage att yeres of consent yt then the said Thomas Nayler shulde hafe the seid p'cells of land to hym and his heires in recompence of the seid some of 1 *li*, payde to the seid John Northende like as in the Court Rolles more playnely apperith. So it was yt the seid Thomas Northende hath disagreed to the seid mariage and also hath caused a diuorce to be mayde betwixe hym and the seid Johnet as apperith in the concistorie of the holy fader in God Thomas Archebisshop of Yorke. After which disagreement and diuorce by mediacion of frends of the seid Thomas Nayler and John Northend it was agreed betwixt the seyd Thomas and John by thaire aboue assent or agrement yt the seid John Northend shulde repay agayne to the seid Thomas Nayler the seid 1 *li.* and yt the seid Thomas shulde make a surrendre agayne to the seid John Northende and his heires of the seid land the which 1 *li.* the seid John hath repaid to the seid Thomas and the seid Thomas refusith to make the seid surrendre agayne to the seid John accordynge to his seid agrement contrie to lavve and consiens, Wherefore please it yo'e goode maistreship call the seid Thomas affore youe to answer to yo'e Orator of the p'misses and also to compell hym to make the seid surrendre for that yo'e seid Orator hath no remedie accordeyng to the ordre of the Co'em (common) lawe and he shall dayly pray for yore goode maistership." The whiche Thomas by a Iniunccion to hym mayde by Sr. John Sayvile knyght, Styvvard of of the lordeship of Wakefeld appered afore the seid Styvvard att Wakefeld atte Courte halden there next after ffest of Seynt Michell in the xiij yere of the reigne of Kynge Henry the vijth Att which Day

the seid bill atte instance of the seid John Northende was redd vnto
the seid Thomas Nayler and he couth not with say the content of the
seid bill bott yt itt was true in all thyngs accordeynge to the shevv-
ynge of the seid John Northende Wherefore the seid Styvvard awarded
yt the seid Thomas Nayler shulde make agayne a surrendre of the
seid land to the seid John Northende and his heires vppon payne
of seiser of all his copylands and also vppon payne of a C m'rks.
The aforesaid Thos. Nayler surrendered the mess., edifice, 1½ bov., 12
acres roid!and in N'ourum to the use of John Northende and his heirs,
who paid 8s. ingress. At the next Brighous court he surrendered
the same to his son Thomas, who paid 5s. ingress. John Rydeynge
of Hyprome took ½ rod of waste, Symondroide being on the W.,
Marshes E., Hypromfeld N., Lyghtclyff S., which with Calfcroft and
edifice in Hyprum he conveyed to himself for life, and to his daughter
Margaret. Laurence Haldworth of Hiperum took ½ acre of waste at
Northmarshe, with Syndirhills on N. and John Haldworth close on S.
Ric. Clyff took 1 ac. 1 rd. of waste between Lyghtclyfbroke W., Ric.
Wood's close N., Ric. Clyff's messuage E., and Doggehous, S. at 6d.
per ann.; ingress 6d. Ric. s. and heir of Wm. Sundirland paid 20s.
heriot for Sundirland, Bareroide, Symondroide, Clifroid; his uncle
Ric. S. being dead. Laurence Bentlay took ½ acre of waste in Hyp-
rum; Oldeerthe E., Highway W., Waste N., Braynyngeley S. Ralph
Roides took 1 rod in Hyp. near Hillez; Thos. Ecclesley's close on E.,
Hypr. to Brighous highway W. Ralph Saynton 1 rod in Hyprum
waste; Halifax and Wakefeld highway S., Walloynes close N., Hyp-
romegrene W. John Wilby took 1 acre of waste, half at Prestlay
greene, near Calderfall close, John Risshworth's, N., John Wylby's
Marsfelde W., Priestlay to Halifax road, E., and S.; and half in the
Marshe, with Wynters on E., Laurence Bentlay's new close S.,
Synderhills W., and Shelf road N. John Otes of Southourome took
3 acres of waste, next Hypromefeld S., Synderhills N., Highway to
Shelf Colepitt, W., Wynteregge E. at 1/- per ann. and 1/- ingress.
Wm. Otes took 1 acre of waste abutting on the hill called Wynteregge
E., Commonfield of Hiprome S., Highway W., John Otes' close N.
Laurence Haldworth took 1 acre in Northemarshe, with Wynteregge
E., Northegge S., Rryndescoles eves W., highway N. Clyfton com-
plained that Bryghous inhabitants had interfered with boundary
hedges. At the Brighous turn, feast of Apostles Phil. and James,
Elena Hudson, widow, of Brighous, Rob. Smyth, Wm. Brooke, for
breaking and carrying away Clyfton fences were fined 12d. each, and
John Turnor of Bryghouse 4d. for using Clifton common pasture.

1498.—Elizth. Bynnes, widow, took 1 rod of waste near Hilles,
Southegge. and Walloynes, in Hiprum; and Ric. Wodd a ½ acre in
Lyghtclyff, with Hallcroft E., Calfcroft S., Symondroide W., late
wasteland N., at 2d. Laurence Bentlay of Preestlay, John Hoyle of
Lightcliffe, John Rydinge of Hyprum, &c. were on a special jury.
Ric. Gepson, constable of ffekesby, was succeeded by Edm. Hirst;
Wm. Blakburn, Clifton, by Wm. Clay. All the rest of constables are
recorded. *Turn,* April 16. Jury as before.

1499.—Jennings or Janyns of Hyprum has descendants at Sourby. Brighous *Turn*,—Jury, Wm. Rookes, Laur. Bentlay, Gilbt. Saltonstall, Ric. Dalton, Hen. Longlay, Ric. Lokwod, Adam Hirst, Thos. Hanson, Ric. Sunderland, Wm. Thewles, Thos. Wilkynson, John Hellywell, Ric. Waterhouse.

1500.—Imperfect roll. Johanna d. and h. Ralph Saynton paid 4d. heriot for three roods formerly taken from the waste. John Otes being dead, his son John paid 12s. heriot for messuage and two bovates in N.owram, Hipp. graveship. John Lacy, Ric. Peck, Thos. Grice conveyed an acre called Rydeynge between Westroide, Ralph Saynton's land, Bryndescoles, and Hipperholme, to Ric, Bentley; also the Hilles to Ralph Roydes, ¼ acre between Synderhills, Hipromfelde, the highway and Wynteregge to John Otes; ¼ acre in the Cloghe in Clyffcroft, east of Symondroide, to Thos. Smyth, ¼ acre between Hipp. and Coley Hall Lanes and Wynters, to John Wilby; and a rood called Hilles near Southegge lane and Walloyneynge to Elizbth. Bynnes, widow.

1502.—A letter by the King's authority, in English, about the murder of Thomas Norton, Wakefield. Brighous *Turn*, Oct. 5. The town of Clyfton and Hammelet of Brighous to repair the highway at Clifton brig on pain of 12d.

1503.—Edward Stanhope, knt., head senescall. Elizth. d. Ric. Thorp, in virginity, surrendered ¼ rod, formerly waste between Estfelde and Liddeyate of Hyprum, and 5 acres in Longemarshe to her mother, Margaret, wife of Ric. Miggelay, with remainder to Edwd. Sheplay. Wm. s. and h. John Stancliffe paid heriot for roidland in N.owram. Ric. Fourness and Robt. Northend conveyed a mess., 6½ acres, &c., to Thomas son of said Ric.

1504.—Wm. Savage, Esq., head senescall. John Otes, Hyprum, conveyed land, 15 by 17 yards, to his brother Wm. Edwd. & Christr. sons of Gilbt. Lacy, deed, conveyed Tilleholme to Jas. Oldefeld.

1505.—Thos. Smyth being dead, John his son paid heriot 3d., for ¼ acre formerly waste. Ric. Barestawe conveyed 1 rode, late waste, at Hypromeyate, and Longmarshe to Wm. Holleroide of Warley. Jas. s. Wm. Otes paid heriot for mess., ½ bov., 6 acres in Whynnyrode, his father being dead. Lawrence Bentlay conveyed Longstubbing to Gilbert his son. Christr. Walker made a 'rupture' in the common road, Hyprum, fined 4d. John Cooke of Lightcliffe, 4d., for mischief by his pig.

Turn, April 28. Jury as last list. Thos. Lister conveyed 1½ ac. in Nm. in trust to Thos. Jenkynson, capellanus, (curate of Halifax, afterwards vicar of Ilkley,) and Ric. Longbothom.

1506.—Margt. wid. Ric. Miggelay and Edw. Sheplay convey Longmarshe to John Lacy, Esq., and he to Henry s. Edmund ffairebanke, each time paying 40d. ingress, and Wm. Holleroide ½ ac. formerly waste, and an edifice at Hypromyate to ffairbanke. Alice wife of Gerard Lacy, Esq., Isabell wife of John Sayntpaule, and Johna wife of Thos. Tryggot, paid 40s. heriot for mess., edifice, ½ bov., 15 acres

of roidland, 4½ ac. formerly waste in Hyprum (graveship); Wm.
Symmes (brother of Alice and Isabella, and uncle of Johana) being
dead.   Ric. Clyff of Halifax, conveyed mess. and bovate in Hipp. to
Wm. C. of Halifax ; Wm. Burgh, a mess. and bovate, &c., called Legh,
in Shibden, to Robt. Burgh, chaplain.

1507.—John Rideynge being dead, Ric. his son paid 9s. heriot for
a messuage and a bovate.

Turns, Oct. 26 and May 9.   Juries, Ric, Dalton, Wm. Rookes, Ric.
Lokwood, John Rookes, Ric. Longbothom, Gilbt. Saltonstall, John
Batt, Thos. Priestley, John Rammesden, Ric. Northclyff, Ric. Aynelay,
John Hanson de Woodhous, John Thorp, Ric. Jagger, Ric. Sunderland,
Rob. Hemingway, Henry Sharp.   Elizth. Bynnes, widow, conveyed
½ acre formerly waste to John Rysshworth, Esq., and John Wilby.
Ric. s. and h. John Rideing paid 9s. heriot.   Wm. Skoldcote conveyed
edifice and lands in Hyp. to himself and wife Johanna.

1508.—Ric. Cliff, John Hoyle, and Jas. Otes fined 4d. each for not
attending the greave election.   John Ryding, Hyperum, and Margaret
his daughter, conveyed ¼ rod, late waste, Symondrode E., Hypromfeld
N., Lightcliffe S., Marshes W., to Henry Smith.   Nic. Bentlay, 2 acres
formerly waste, and edifice, to Laurence B., Jas. Shaghe, John
Waterhouse of Skircote, Ric. Longbothom, Wm. Illingworth, Ric.
Waterhouse, Shelf, W. Baroclogh, John Rooks of Rooks, and Brian
Otes.   Robt. s. John Brodelegh, mess., and 16 acres to Thos. Brodelegh,
John brother of Thos. B., Ric. s. Thos. Haldworth, and Gilbt. s. Rob.
Otes ; ingress 9s.   John Wornewall, senr. formerly of Lightcliffe,
surrendered lands in Warley to his son Wm.   For using the common
pasture of Shelf, the following Hiperum men were fined 8d. each ;
Nic. Kytson, Ric. Haley, Edm. Stokke, Rob. Bryghous, Wm. Hoyle,
Rad. Roide, Chas. Haldworth, Wm. Brodelee, Thos. Boethes, and
John Estwod of Lyghtclyff.

1509.—Brighous *Turns*, Oct. 23, April 16.   Jury, Wm. and John
Rookes, &c.

1510.—Ric. Tempest, Esq., dep. senll. of Thos. Lovell, knt.
Rysshworth and Wilby regrant to Alice d. of Elizth. Bynnes, part of
an acre.   Rob. Bryghous took of the waste 7 acres in Nm., called
Grenesykes.

Turns, Oct. 22, May 13.   Hiperum, Umfrey ffrith, for not repairing
a commonway, 8d.; Gilbt. Saltonstall, junr., and John Baker for
breaking wood at John Tykhill's house, fined.

1511.—Henry Smyth took 1 rode of waste, E. of Brodegatehed, W.
of Hypromwodd, S. of Moorroid.

Turn, April 27.   Jury, John Risshworth, Esq., John Thornhill,
Esq., Ric. Lokwod, John Wilby, Gilbt. Saltonstall, Thos. Hanson,
John Booth of Boethes, John ffrith of Baresland, Ric. Sunderland,
John Hanson, Laur. Bentlay, Christr. Bentlay.   Fekisby constable
was John ffrith.   Thos. Thorp of Lyghtcliffe, Ric. Barestaw, Wm.
and John Awmbler, 3/4 each for taking Sklatston (slates) from
N'ourum.

1512.—Umfry ffirth conveyed ½ ac. lately waste, to Rob. Sayvill, and he granted it to Ric. Brodelegh. John Hoyle took of waste in Hyprum greave, 3 acres, paying 60s., at 12d. per annum, lying between a running spring, and Ric. Barestawe's land on W., High cross on the E., Grenedyk close on N., Wm. Northend's close, S. John Lacy, Esq., leased ¼th of Brighous mill at 15s. 4d. per annum for 46 years. Humphry ffirth and Johana his wife, dau. of Ralph Steynton deceased, conveyed 3 rods formerly waste to Ric. Brodelee; and Thos. Northende ½ acre to said Ric. John Boethes of the Boethes surrendered Hassilhurst in Nm., formerly waste, to Ric. Longbothom, Ric. Sunderland, junr., Christr. Boethe, W. Stanclyff, John Drake, junr., John Boy, John Awmbler, John Northend, Henry Batt, Brian Otes, John Sharpe, and Ric. Haldworth for common use of Northowrum. Probably connected with endowing Coley chapel, see next year.

COLEY CHAPEL FOUNDED.

1513.—*Turn*, April 28. Wm. Rookes of Roides Hall, Ric. Rookes of Rooks, Gilbert Bentlay, Humphry Waterhous, Ric. Haldesworth de Asseday, John Bentlay de Hybentlay, Ric. Sundirland, junr., John Bryghous, Wm. Saltonstall, Thos. ffourness, Laurence Haldeworth, John Roides and John Smyth de Lyghtclyff came into court before the senescall and took of the lord one acre of land de solo and vasto (waste) between a close called Wynters on E., Wm. Otes' land on W., the Kirkegaite from Coley to Halifaxe on S., and Jepgreve on N., for a CHAPEL upon the same acre to be newly built, paying 4d. per annum of new rent, and giving to the Lord 20s. for fine for ingress.

Richard Sunderland and Laurence Bairstow, greaves.

Laurence Bentlay conveyed Jakstubbynge, 2½ ac. to Christr. Bentlay. Ric. s. James Stanclyff surrendered a mess., 7 acres, to Laurence Barestowe, Ric. Waterhous de Nm., Ric. Stanclyff de Halifax and Wm. Ambler. Brighouse *Turn*, Oct. 19. Jury, John Rissheworth, Esq., Thomas Longeley, John Rookes, Ric. Lokwodd, Laur. Bentlay, Thomas Preistley, Ric. Norclyff, Ric. Sunderland, John Hanson, John Wilby, Gilbt. Saltonstall, JohnHaldeworth, Ric. Waterhouse, Chrs. Bentlay.

Under Rastryke, the six townships or constableries south of the Calder are arranged, Rastryke, Ffekesby, Stayneland, Dalton, Barkesland, Querneby. Edmund Goodheire, constable of Rastryke, reported that Ric. Hanson was nominated his successor, and

RASTRICK BRIDGE.

that Wm. Nicholl made an affray on Alice wife of Thos. Goodeheire and Isabell their daughter and Robert their son at the end of the Bridge of Rastryke by force of arms against the King's peace; the fine 20d. was inflicted. Under Hyprome were arranged Hyprome, Shelf, Clyfton, Northourome and Harteshede. Clifton constable reported that Wm. Brooke of Bryghous and John Batley of the same had broken the fencing at Clifton, fined 8d.

1514.—Thos. Northend conveyed Walloyne in Ric. Brodlee's tenure, to sd. Ric. John Hoyle being dead, his son John paid 6s. heriot for ½ bovate for 40 years. Robt. Swayne (? of Northowram) being dead, John his son paid heriot for 1 rode and edifice, 6d., but conveyed them to Isabel his mother. John Hanson of Wodhous conveyed 4 ac. 3 rds. at Vnderbanke to Ric. his son, with remainder to his other sons, Robt., Thos., and John. Ric. Lacy took 1 ac. of waste between Hyprum and Shelf highway E., Shipdeyne broke W., le Heght of Hyprome banke S., Northourum banke N., paying 30s., also 6d. rent. Brighous *Turn:* Jury, John Risshworth, Esq., John Gledehill, John Rammsden, Ric. Sunderland, Laur. Bentlay, Ric. ffourness, John Hemmingway, Ric. Clyff, Ric. Northend, John Wilby, Ric. Waterhouse, Ric. Botherode. Edward Marsshe, ffckesby constable, was succeeded by Robt. Hardegreves; John Woode, Clyfton, by John Pereson; Wm. Rayner, Hertshead, by John Rayner; John Sundirland, Shelf, by Rob. Gybson. The inhabitants of Hipromethorp and of Lyghtclyff not sufficiently repairing a highway, fined 6s. 8d. Ric. Sunderland, junr., and Margt. his wife, regrant lands in Nm. to Ric. father of said Ric.

Turn, April. Jury, Thos. Longeley, Thos. Hawme, Rob. Hemingway, John Haldworth de Astay. Edm. Hanson, Thos. ffryth de Rastrik, Wm. Rayner de Hartshead, John Wilby, John Rammesden, Laur. Bentlay, Ric. Boothroid, Ric. Sunderland. Wm. Whitlay at Yate fined for his wife breaking the pinfold of Hyprome. John Estwode and Jas. Waterhouse, Hiprum graveship, for not attending, 4d. each.

1515.—Geo. Barestawe took 3½ ac. waste between Dyconfeld E., Pokelandnase W., Mekilmosseford N., John Haldworth's new house S. John Haldworth de Asttay conv. mess., ½ bov., 4 ac. roidland, 7 ac. roidland, and Grenewayclogh 1½ ac. in Hyprum grave to Ric. his son. Wm. Erle took ½ ac. waste between cartegaite from Hyprum to Heebarnes, Whynnyroides S., Longsheghgate N. Laur. Bentlay took ½ ac. waste between Carwodde E., Hellywells S., Wykeclose N., and ½ acre between Bryndscolesbroke W., Synderhills N., paying 10s. for each, yearly rent 2d. each.

John Hanson being dead, John his son paid 16s. heriot for 32 acres in Wodhous. Cristofer Walker of Hiprum fined 5s. for affray by force of arms, and drawing blood from W. Whitlay. Edm. Stokks fined 40d. for breaking into Hiprum pinfold. Cristofer Bentlay to remove a Qwykesett* at Wyldemarecarr which obstructs the way, on pain of 10s., and for enclosing the waste 20s. John Rissheworth, Esq., took

---

* Thorn hedge.

3 rodes, waste, between Collay slak E., highway W., Kirkeway S., Shelf township N. Ric. Clyff (by John Smyth of Lyghtclyf, a tenant of the lord's) conveyed a mess. called Clyfhous, lands, pastures, woods, to Ric. son of said Rich.

1516.—Adam Wilton (Nm.) being dead, Ric. his son paid heriot for 2 acres, 12d. Ric. Lacy took 8 acres of waste between Newlandwodde close E., highway from Rastrik to Totehill N. and W., and Thos. Sayvill's close S.; paid 8 li. and 2s. annual rent: *Chapel* croft and *Scolc*house croft are mentioned. Thos. Boethe conveyed 1½ ac. to Ric. his son ; remainder to John s. John Boethe of Wynteregge.

1518.—Robt. Haldworth clerk, (Vicar of Halifax afterwards, where he was murdered), took 6 acres of waste in Hyprum, 4 being between Hyprum and Shelf highway and Brynescolebroke, 2 acres between said brook W., highway to Hypromwodd E., John Hemingway's sprynge (plantation) S.

Turn, Oct. . Jury, John Sayvile de Hollynegge, John Gledehill, Ric. Botheroid, Ric. ffourness, Ric. Lokwodde, Wm. Awmbler, Rob. Brighous, John Otes, Jas. Bothes, John Wilby, Geo. Hellywell, John ffrith. Nich. Kytson broke Hiprum pinfold 3s. 4d. Laur. Bentlay is dead, Gilbt. his son paid 4d. heriot for ½ acre formerly waste. Three proclamations made respecting Shipden mylne, ¼th part of Bryghouse mylne with a fulling mill newly built there in the tenure formerly of

BRIGHOUSE LOWER MILLS. 1885.

East view ; the long chimneys belong to modern mills, of course.

Robt. Eland, Esq.   Ric. s. John Rookes of Rodeshall paid 16s. heriot for a mess., 2 bovates, 2 acres of oxgangland, 8 acres 1 rod of rodeland, his uncle Wm. Rookes being dead.

[An interesting entry from "Durham Sanctuary Book," published by the Surtees Society, vol. v., 1837, may be given here.   1522, Oct. 21.   A certain Roger Tempest came to the Cathedral Church of Durham, from the parish of Bradford, in co. York, and begged immunity because that, at *Brighouse* on the 21st April, 1518, he had feloniously struck a certain Thos. Longley, of the parish of Heton with a sword upon the thigh, of which he died on the next day.   For which he begged immunity.   There being present Thos. Sanderson, chaplain, and Henry Fetherstonhalgh, and John Bukley.   For notices of Sanctuary, see "Dumb Steeple," *postea*.]

1519.—John Lacy, Esq., paid £1 for an acre of waste in Hyprum near the Kirkgate leading from Coley.   Henry Smyth took ½ ac. and running water between Wynteregge E., Bryneskolebrook W., Synderhill N., Brodegatehead S., paid 11s.   Ric. Hanson took 1 acre at Shipdenbroke near Ourumfelde, Baterydinge and Kirkegate.   Robt. Eland, Esq., took Shipden mill, ¼th the Brighous corn mylne with half the running water of Caldre, and a fulling mill newly built,

BRIGHOUSE LOW MILL (fulling.)   From the West side.

which he had held 10 years without leave of court and in contempt of the lord, fined x*li*, and to pay 12d. per annum.   Robt. Eland, Esq., conveyed the Brighous mills to John Lacy, Esq., for 45 years; thus 170 years had healed the family quarrels.   Edwd. Waterhouse had to repair the highway from Ric. Stephenson's house to Thorneal Bryg, or pay x*s*.

1520.—John Lacy, Esq., conveyed 1 ac. formerly waste to Umfri Rysshworth. Ric. Hanson, ½ ac. in Nm. of waste to Ric. Rokes of Roideshall. Bryghous *Turn*, Oct. 17. Robt. Brighous conveyed 7 acres formerly waste in Nm. to Ric. and John his sons. Edward Saltonstall was constable of Shelf. John Cowper of Rastrik greaveship, being dead, Edwd. Cowper his father paid 4d. heriot for Grenehousyerde. Rob. Herdgreve was constable of ffekesby.

1521.—John Burgh being dead, Rob. his son paid 14s. heriot for a mess., 1½ bovates, 7 ac. roidland, in Shipden, called Leghe. Ric. ffourness being dead, Thos. his son paid 2s. 6d. heriot for Meresyke, 2 ac., and 4 ac. waste. Jas. Oldfeld conveyed 5½ rods at Tillyholme to Edwd., Edmd., Jas., Christr. and John his sons. Gilbt. Bentlay surrendered Jakstubbyng, Little pighill, &c. in Hyprum, to Wm. his son. Rob. Preestlay and two other Halifax men fined 20d. each for an affray on the king's watchmen in Halifax.

Turn, April. Jury, John Thornhill, Esq., Ric. Northend, Ric. Gybson, Rob. Brighouse, John Thorp, G. Hellywell, Ric. Botheroide, Ric. Hey, Ed. Hanson de Linlay, W. Hanson, senr., Hen. Sharp, and Wm. Hylelee. Nic. Eland, gent., (by John Savile of Lupset, Esq.,) took Shipden mylne, ¼th Brighouse mylne (corn), ½ running water of Caldre, and the fulling mill newly erected: ingress 6s. 8d.; but surrendered the same to John Lacy, Esq., 6s. 8d. de firma. Ric. Hanson, Taillor, made an affray on Rob. Pek at Hyprome; fined 20d. Edward Waddington took waste land at Clifroid and Blakkerwood, Nm.

1522.—Ric. Wylton and Johana his wife conveyed 2 acres formerly waste, to John their son. John Milner of Pudsay surrendered Blakker to Ric. Awmbler of Brokehous. Margt. Croslee of Halifax kept a brodelhous and receives persons of bad life. Brighouse *Turn*, Oct. Jury, fourteen or fifteen names now appear instead of twelve as before. John Thornell, Esq., John Gledehill, John ffrith, John Hemingway, senr., Ric. Hanson, Thos. Northend, John Drake, Ric. Botheroide, junr., Rob. Drake, John Thewles, Rob. Brighous, John Haldworth, Galfry Ramsden, John Preestlay. The constable of ffixbye was John Woode; of Clyfton, Robt. Drake. John Milner, of Pudsey, held Blakker in N.owram.

1523.—Wm. Otes, capellanus, surrendered the Pighils, Hyprom graveship, to Bryan son of said Wm., who conveyed them to Wm. Haldworth. John Wylton and Elizth. his wife, 2 acres to John Townend. Ivyncar or Grenewayclogh in Nm. is laid under proclamation, but Sir Rob. Haldeworth, clerk, professor of Sacred Theology, paid ingress for it by Ric. Haldeworth of Hiprome. Ric. Brighous took ¼ acre at Horwithynges, Nm.

1524.—Ric. Scolecote, 26 Hy. VI., surrendered Priorrode, Haldworthbroke, in Nm. to his children successively—Wm., Ric., Alice; and Thos. Wadlovve son of Alice paid heriot 3s. 4d., his uncles having died without issue; but surrendered the same now to Thos. Rawson, Warnefeld. Ric. Haldworth, Ralph & John Roides, and Nic. Kytson, fined 4d. each for cutting greenwood in Brynscoles. Ric. and Robt. Bayrestawe 12d. for taking Slatestones out of N'ourum.

1525.—Rob. Brighous and Ric. his son took waste lands at Barmes. (Nm.) Ric. Northend being dead, John his son paid 12d. heriot for 2 acres in Brynskoles. John Hoile being dead, Edward his son paid 5s. heriot for ¼ bovate.

EDWARD HOIL, of Hoil House, Lightcliffe, living there 20 Henry VIII.

```
                    │
    ┌───────────────┴────────────────────┐
 John, of Hoyle House.        Margaret = (1) Mallinson.
    │                         d. 1614, = (2) Edwd. Hanson, in
 ┌──┴───────┐                 aged 87.    1590, of Nether Wood-
 Saml. of   Mary = John s. John Drake     house.
 Hoyle House, bap.     by Grace, d. John
 bap.  │  d.   1564.    Bairstow.
 1569. │ 1644.
       │ Will 1644.
```

┌─────────────────────────────┬──────────────┬──────────┬─────────┐
Saml. of Hoyle House, living 1651.   John.   Grace.   Mary.

Hyprome fined 20s. for not repairing the highway at the Townend. Ralph Rodes, John Hoile, Edwd. ffarebank, 8d. each for not resorting to the lord's mill at Bryghous. John Bunny (by Wm. Otes, chaplain,) conveyed after the death of his mother Elizabeth, Meggeroide in Hyp. to John Lacy, Esq.

1526. Nic. Eland conveyed Shippeden mylne (corn) with running water to Ric. Gybson for 46 years. Ric. Haldworth 5s. for an affray on John Thorpe at Hyprome. Jas. Shagh, John Waterhouse, Wm. Yllyngworth, Ric. Waterhous, and Brian Otes convey 2 acres and edifice formerly Nicholas Bentley's in Hyprome to Rob. Waterhous de Shipden and John his son, John s. Wm. Murgaitroide, John Waterhous de Woddehous, Gilbt. Otes, Thos. Shaghe, John Brodelee, Wm. Yllyngworth, junr., John Deyne, Edw. Waterhouse, junr., Wm. Wodd, Arthur Bentlay, Umfri Waterhous, and George Boethes. Possibly this may refer to Lightcliffe Chapel foundation.

1527. Johanna d. Arthur Nottyngham being dead, Elizabeth wife of John Hoyle, dau. of Gilbt. Nottyngham, paid heriot 8s. for a mess. 16½ acres in Hyprum (? grave); Elizabeth the wife of Edwd. Hanson was formerly the wife of the said Arthur Nottyngham.

Turn, Oct. 16, John Thornell, Esq. and 14 others on Jury list. John Lacy, Esq., conveyed the 4th part of Brighouse corn mill and the fulling mill to himself and wife Alice for life, with remainder to Leonard their son. Ric. Waddington and Johanna his wife, conveyed lands to Edward Waddington and his son Edward.

1528. Brighouse *Turn*, Oct. 14. Jury, John Sayvile de Hollyng-thorpe, Esq., John Sayvile de Newall, gent., and 11 others as usual. Ric. Sunderland and Margary his wife, conveyed lands in Sunderland, &c. in Nm. to their son Ric. Wm. Otes regrants lands to John and Ellen, his father and mother.

1529. Thos. Lyster and Alice d. Edw. Hoppay convey a mess., &c. in Hyprom grave to John, father of said Thos. Edwd. Waddington being dead, his son Edward paid heriot.

1530. *Turn*, 26 Oct. Jury, Thos. Sayvvell de Copley, Esq., and 13 more. One acre near Coley Chapell formerly in the tenure of Ric. Roks, John Smyth, and others, having yielded no rent for 10 years to be seized. John Wyloby being dead, his brother Edmd. paid 6d. heriot for 1½ ac. Cristofer Bentlay surrendered Stubbynges in Shipden to his wife Margaret, with remainder to Edwd. his son, and Edward's sons—Henry, a bastard, and Christopher, legitimate. Wm. Rydeyng being dead, his sister Agnes, wife of Henry Cokcroft, paid 6s. heriot for lands in Hyprome grave; regrants to her mother Isabel. John Rysshworth, Esq., surrendered to come into force after his decease 1½ bov. at Hekden, west of Coley, &c. to Wm. ffrost, Esq., Ric. Rooks de Rodeshall, Robt. Ryssheworth, Rob. Waterhous, Wm. Sayvile and Ric. Stanclyff, for ten years, to perform requirements of his will. Laur. Haldworth conveyed a mess., 2 acres, &c. to John his son. Gilbert and Wm. Sunderland regrant Highfield, &c. to Ric. their father for life. John s. John Hemingway paid heriot for 3 roods.

1531. Ric. Lacy being dead. Thos. his son paid 4s. heriot for mess., 9 ac., &c. Thos. Sayvill being dead, Thos. his son paid 20s. heriot for lands in Ossett, N'ourum, &c. Ric. Sunderland leased Clyffroide in Nm. to Rob. Gregg, who had to yield a red rose yearly, if demanded in the time of roses.

1532. John Rysshworth conveyed 1 ac. 1 rd., and Umfri R., 1 ac. to John s. and heir of Alexr. R. Leonard Lacy, gent., surrendered the reversion of the ¼ Brighouse mill, &c. after the death of Alice his mother, to John Lacy, Esq. Dr. Rob. Haldworth, Vicar of Halifax, conveyed Ivynear, Nm., to himself for life, remainder to John s. Ric. Gybson. Edwd., Edmd., Christ., and John Oldefeld (Sourby district) convey Tillyholme to Jas. their brother; remainder to John. Thos. Goodheire being dead, John his son paid 5s. heriot for ten acres in Rastrik. John Lacye of Crumwelbothome, Esq. surrendered all corn mill dues from the inhabitants of Northourome living west of Shipden-broke, to do service at the mill of Rob. Waterhous in Halifax, to said Robt. who paid 12d. fine for ingress.

Turn, Oct 23. 13 Jurymen, Ric. Longley, gent., Nic. Brodelee, John Boy, Thom. Northend, Ric. Haldworth, Edw. ffirth, Ric. Botheroide, John Bairestowe, Ric. Sunderland, John Otes, Thos. Wodhede, Ric. Saltonstall, John ffirth. Wm. Hylylee was constable of Clyfton.

1533. John Croser, John Wodde of Yllyngworth, and John s. Laurence Wodd, at the special request of Ric. Wodde, surrender a mess., 7 rods, to said Ric. Wodde of Lyghtclyff. Thomas Northend surrendered roidlands to his children, Robt., Chris., Margaret and John, with remainder to his eldest son, Richard.

Turn, Oct. 15. 13 Jurymen, Henry Batt, Galfri Rommesden, jun., &c. Robt. Brighous for not removing a wall at the highway in

Hyprome, fined 6s. 8d.   Rob. Boy had surrendered an annual rent to
ffeoffees for Halifax Church, and Gilbert Otes for 7 years had made no
acknowledgment to the court, therefore it was seized.   Margaret wid.
of John Hoile, and Henry, Edwd. and Thos. their sons, take the lands
the father had held.

Turn, April 22nd.   Robt. Brighouse and Ric. his son had encroached on the waste of N.ouram.   Elizbth. and Isabell daughters of
Ric. Whitley paid heriot for lands in Nm.

1534.   Ric. Sunderland, Ric. Clyff, Thos. ffourness, Jas. Boethes,
Christr. Boethes and Edwd. Hoile fined 4d. each for not attending
the election of greave of Hiperum.   Alice wid. Garrarde Lacy, Isabell
wid. John Sayntpoule, and Johanna wid. Thos. Trygott surrender 2
mess., edifice, ¼ bov. 15 ac. roid, 4½ acres formerly waste in Hyprum
grave to Wm. s. John Sayntpoule ; ingress, 8s.   Edm. ffairbank, (by
Ric. Horsfall a tenant,) ¼ acre &c. to Hen. F. his son.   Leonard Lacy,
gent., took 1 acre at Newlandwodde close, bounded by the Caldre, and
lands of John Hanson of Wodhous, and John Hanson of Brigroide.
John Mitchell, Gilbt. Best, Ric. Leirode, Wm. Lome, John Hoile's
wife and Ric. Brighous fined 8d. each for not repairing the highway
at Hiprum Marshe.   John Thomson and Thos. Craven fined 20d. each
for encroaching on the waste, Hyperum.   Ric. Wodde de Lyghtclyff,
conveyed a mess. 7 rods, to John Smyth de Lighclyff.   Ric. Rookes
being dead, Wm. his son paid 16s. heriot for a mess, 2 bovates, 2
acres oxgang land, 8 acres 1 rod roidland, in Hiperum.

1535.—John Hoile and Elizabeth his wife conveyed 5 acres at
Horleygrene to Elizth. wife of Edw. Handson for her life, it having
been her former husband's, Arthur Nottyngham.   John s. John Lacy,
Esq., paid 8d. heriot for land at Strangsty in Rastrik.   John Lister
conveyed lands in Nm. to his son Thomas and to Elizth. d. John
Waterhouse of Skircote.

1537.—Wm. Sayntpoule of Camsall, clerk, having conveyed the
lands in Shipden to Ric. Bentley without fine, they are seized.   He
and John S. of C., Esq., paid for ingress 20d.   Rob. Kent took ½ rod
of waste between Wynteregge E., Brankscolesbroke W., Synderhill N.,
Moreroide S.

Turn, May 7.   Jury, Henry Batt, Ric. Botheroide, Hen. Sharp,
Ric. Stanclyff, Galfri Rammsden, Thom. Wodhedd, John Drake,
Nich. Brodelee, Edwd. ffirth, John Clay, John Preestlay, Ric. Bentlay,
George Thewles, Thos. Gledhill.

⁎.⁎ From this date we can refer to the Registers preserved at
Halifax Church for baptisms, marriages, and deaths of Hipperholme
people.   Elland Registers commence with 1558, and record those for
Rastrick and Brighouse.

1539.—Fourteen on jury as last : new names, Christr. Boethe, Thos.
Stanclyff, Brian Wormall (written Wormwell previously,) Jas. Hagh,
John Hirst, Wm. Haghe, Ric. Saltonstall, John Hawme, Ric. Clyff.
John Otes of Synderhills surrendered an annual rent charge of 20s.
from 3 ac. in Nm. to Jas. s. Ric. Waterhous.   Gilbt. Otes, of Halifax,

conveyed Holcannes in Nm. to his children, Anne, Grace, Alice, Gilbt., Wm., Michael, George, and Robt. Robt. Eland, Esq., sub-let Shipden mill and its lands to Ric. Gybson and his son Edw. for a year.

1540. Robt. Neville, Knt., was deputy seneseall for Thomas, Earl of Rutland. Thos. and Hugh Sayvell, gents, surrendered 2 mess., 66 acres in Rastrik to said Hugh and Anne his wife, and their heirs male. John Hanson de Rastrik, junr., by John Hanson of Wodhous, conveyed lands in R. to said John junr. and Anne d. Rob. ffirthe, and failing their issue, to heirs of John H. of W. Ric. Northend surr. the great close in Estfeld (Lightcliffe) to Wm. Whitley at 25s. 4d. yrly. rent. John Rysshworth's lands, formerly Hen. Copley's, and a plot east of Coldley formerly his uncle John's, held 8 years without fine, therefore seized. Wm. Bentley's 2 parcels from John Wylbe to Ric. Waterhous not recorded, therefore seized. Thos. Sayvell holds and occupies 22 acres and edifice at Totehill, formerly his father's (Thos.), two years without fine; seized. Edwd. ffirth being dead, Thos. his son paid 23s. 4d. heriot for 72 acres in Rastrik. Jas. Waterhous takes Wilby's two parcels; Thos. ffoxcroft takes Totehill formerly Thos. Savell's of Ecksley; John Rysshworth takes the Coley lands formerly his uncle's.

1541. Brighous *Court*. Oct. 19. Jury, (14,)—John Smyth de Lyghtclyff, Gilbt. Rommesden, John Townend, Brian Wormewall, Ric. Bentlay, Tho. Gledehill, Christr. Boethe, John Otes, Rob. ffirth, Ric. Clyff, George Hoile, Ric. Hanson, Rob. Northend, John Hirst.

Edwd. Gypson *v.* John Tillotson, Hyprum greaveship.

1542. Wakefield great Court held at Sandall Castle. Elizabeth wid. John Hoile being dead, her son Robert Childe paid 8s. heriot for mess., and 16 acres. Wm. Smyth being dead, Thos. his son paid 3d. heriot for ½ acre, Hyp. graveship. Rob. Bryghous surr. Bolleshey and 6 acres to Rob. s. Ric. B. Sir Rob. Haldeworth, S.T.P. surr. Yvynear or Grenewayclogh to John Gybson.

1543. John Lacy Esq. took mess., 12 acres, called Brygroide in Rastrik, formerly John Hanson's. John Haldworth being dead, Ric. his son paid heriot for mess., bovate, 7½ ac. roid, &c.

Brighouse *Turn*, Oct. 17. 14 jurymen. Edwd. Cooper being dead, Edw. his son paid heriot for Harshawynge, Rastrik graveship. Brian Haldworth conveyed ½ acre to John s. John Roide de Hyprom.

1544. Ric. Hanson being dead, John his son paid 2s. 4d. heriot for Underbanke, Rastrik. Edwd. Longbothom, senr., of Shypden Hall, surr. mess. in Nm. to his son Edward, and Alice his son's wife, dau. of late Wm. Sunderland of Nm. John Wodd, Hyp., and Ric. Wodd, Southourome, convey lands, messuage, to Tho. Smyth for 10 years. Rob. Handson, John Broke, Wm. Broke, and Rob. ffirth paid 12d. for special jury "to inquire for land devidyd by the said ten'nts in Rastrik hauyng a joynt asyate and one Edw. ffirth dyed and the other lyffed, wheder the survivours shall haue the hold of thoes lands or that the heire shall inheret his pt whyche yt his father dyd occupy by reson of the devysion maide of the saide land emong their selff." Evidently

J

the bad Latin has given way just once again to bad English.

Brighous *Turn*, Oct. 15.　Edm. Wilby conveyed a cottage, &c., in Hyprum to Henry Kent for 21 years; Mathew Oglethorpe, gent., a messuage to Edwd. Brodelee for 60 years.

1546.　Ric. Brodelee conveyed a mess., 8 acres and rod, to his son Robt.　Wm. Awmbler of Awmbler Thorn, Nm., being dead, 16s. 6d. heriot was paid by those whose names are in italics:

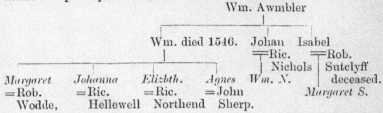

Wm. Awmbler

Wm. died 1546.　Johan Isabel
　　　　　　　　　＝Ric.　＝Rob.
　　　　　　　　　| Nichols | Sutclyff

Margaret　*Johanna*　*Elizbth.*　*Agnes*　*Wm.* N.　deceased.
=Rob.　　=Ric.　　=Ric.　　=John　　　　　*Margaret S.*
Wodde,　Hellewell　Northend　Sherp.

John Hanson, senr. Rastrik, conveys 34 acres to John his son and Margaret d. Thom. Wodhede, intended wife of John the son.　Edwd. Oldfeld conveyed Tillyholme, Hiprum grave, to John and Jas. Oldfeld, his brothers.

Brighous Turn, Oct. . . 15 names on jury: John Rysshworth Esq., Thos. Drake, Nich. Brodelee, Thom. Gledhill, Jas. Otes, Ric. Northende, John Preestlay, Ric. Bentlay, John Hanson de Wodhous, John Haldesworth, Wm. Thorpe, John ffirth, John de lez Strenes, Robt. Sutclyff, Geo. Hoyle.　Brighous is entered under Rastrik greaveship this time as if it were a separate township, but no constable is named. Its ecclesiastical relationship to Rastrick may account for this exceptional mention.　Christr. Boethes obstructed the highway at Highrode, Hyperum; fined 6s. 8d.　John Tempest, Knt., chief senescall.

1547.　John Rysshworth took 3 rods of waste in Copley (? Coley) layn, butting on Copley broke, ffalrend, Newynge and Towlerynge; paid 15s., rent 2d.　John Northend surr. 2 acres land and wood in Brynescholes and edifice to Brian Otes.　John Hanson being dead, Ric. his brother paid heriot 2s. 4d. for Vnderbank in Rastrik greaveship.　John Brokesbank conveyed his third of 6 acres 1 rd. and edifice in Hyprum to Ric. and Edw. his brothers: Henry Hoile his moiety of 4 ac. and edifice to Thomas his brother.　Bowling alleys at Halifax, &c., caused a little trouble at this time, or at least, they added to the court income by fines.

Turn, April 18.　Jury, Ric. Brighous of Hyprome, Edw. Thorpe, John Boy (Bois, Bosco, or Wood—in earlier times,) were on the jury. Nearly all the constables reported " All well."

1548.　Ric. Bryghous and John Northend conveyed messuages in Hiperum to Ric. s. Edwd. Brodelee.　There is a long account in English about lands belonging to chantry priests in the manor, which reminds us we have reached the period of the REFORMATION.　In Rastrik, Robt. ffox, Jas. Tolson, Thos. Hanson, and Robt. Nicholl were fined 4d. each for not ringing their pigs,—putting rings in their noses to prevent them from grubbing.

1549. Ric. Brighous surr. 4 ac. in Nm. to Rob. s. John Brighous; Henry Bentlay a half-rod and edifice, Hiperum, to Rob. Sowodd. John Lacy holds land and water of Mill and Calder between Strangstye and Rastrik brigge.

1550. John Mitchell, Hiperum graveship, surr. 2 ac. 3 rd. formerly waste to his wife Isabel (dau. of Thos. Crosselee,) and their son John.

Turn, April 15. Jury, 14 as usual. Margaret Malynson, Rastrik, fined 4d. for a Ridlynge, (?) on the common pasture. John Otes of Synderhill, Coley, surr. land at Brynescolebroke to Henry Kent; John Brighous conveyed Bolshoue and 6 acres to Ric. his father.

1551. Henry Batt surrendered a mess., 1 ac. 3 rods, formerly Ric. Wodde's, to Thos. Smyth of Lyghtclyff; John Otes, junr., 3 acres and edifice at Synderhill to Henry Kent.

1552. Ric. Haldworth de Astay being dead, John his son paid heriot for waste lands in Hiperum. Rob. s. Ric. Brighous, of Hiprum, surr. mess., 6 acres, at Bolleshaie in Nm. to George Whytlee.

Turn, Thos. Thorpe, Hiperum constable, presents that Elles Nutter is nominated successor. Thos. ffirth surr. mess., 5 acres called Castilhill, in Rastrick, tenure of Leonard Longley, to George Longley for 20 years ; ingress 16d.

1554. Robt. s. John Brighous surr. lands in Nm. to Wm. s. John Sherpe. It will be noted that we are using the words 'surrendered' and 'conveyed' as synonymous.

Brighous *Turn*, Oct. 9. Jury—15, John Handson, John Claye, Ric. Brighous, Edw. Thorpe, John Wodde, Ric. Bentlay, John Townende, Edwd. Hey, Ric. Haynley, Edw. Denton, John Rommesden, Thos. ffirthe, John Hemmyngwaye, Wm. Haigh, John Roide. The old and new constables for each township are recorded. Brighous village is placed under Rastrik greaveship again ; no constable, of course, is named for it, but 'all well' is reported. Rob. Childe takes 16 acres and edifice in Hiperum grave to himself and wife, Margaret d. John Boy. ffixby had 'a spring watter that was to be suffered to run in *her* olde course.'

Brighouse Curia cum turno tent ibm 16 die Aprilis An. Dm. *1554* primo Marie Regine, Jacobus Waterhouse et soci present

ffirst the said jurye do present that there is within the precincts of the said Turne three greaveships, viz. Hipperholme, Rastrick, and Scamonden.

Item, they present that there is within the greaveship (not the township alone) of Hipperholme above xl acres of waste, being heath, moss and turbarye.

Item, that there is within the greaveship of Rastrick above xxx dwellinghouses which are inhabited with much people and they have not of waste above (blank) acres, being heath, moss, and vent, and being in diverse parcells, lanes and wayes, and so default of sufficient waste and comon the auncestors of the inhabitants of the same town in times past have leyd forth of their arable lands above xxx acres to enlarge the comon with, which their auncestors in tyme past have both plowed, sown, and tilled, and for which as well the freeholders as customarye tenants of the same graveship do both pay yearly rents, suits, and service on this present tyme.

Item, they do present that within the greaveship of Scamonden there are above xx acres of moss, heath and turbarye.

Item, they do present that to their knowledge the same graveships are ancient demesne and parcel of the Lordship of the Mannor of Wakefield, and according to the use and custom of the same Manor the copyholders of the said graveships do hold their lands.

Item, they do present the copyholders or customarye tenants of the said graveships have a custom within the said Manor of Wakefield that they and their auncestors, tyme of remembrance at the change of tenants else by death or surrender, have paid for heriot or fyne to the Lord where the lands be holden by oxgang on estymacion about a year rent and when the land be holden by acres take about iiiid. the acre or thereabouts as by the discretion of the Steward.

Item, they do present that to their knowledge the Queen's Majesty hath no demesne lands within the precincts of the said Turne. ffynally they do present that there is within the precincts of the said Turne one messuage or tenement with the appurtenances in Shelf of the yearly valewe of xxxiiis iiiid now in the tenure of one Rich. Waterhouse, which before tyme was gyfen to certain feoffes of trust to the intent the same feoffees should stand seized of the same tenement to the use of a Chappell called Colley Chappell or to the use of mendyng the hyeways and bridges next adjoining to the said messuage or tenement, or to the maryinge of pore maydens* thereabout inhabiting.

1555. Ric. Brighous of Hyprome, senr., surr. Belshaye and 7 acres in Nm. to Robert a younger son of his, with remainder to Robert's brothers, Edwd., Martin, and Jesper. John Lacy of Cromme-Welbothome, Esq., surrendered Soland mylne to John Waterhous of Sourbybrigge. John Hanson of Wodhous took of the lord the King and lady the Queen (Philip and Mary) ½ acre, with John Hanson's close at Mylneclyff S. & E., Totehill and Brighous road W., Water of Calder N.; paid 10s. John Lacy, Esq., took 1 rod waste butting on Caldre N., Edmd. Malyson's land W., Rastrik S., Brighous Milne Dame E.; paid 5s. John Brighous, son of Ric. B. of Hyprome, deceased, for £17, sold his share of Bolleshey, and 6 acres, to Robt. his brother. Thos. Drake, conveyed Cloughroides in Nm. to Umfri his son; Brian Otes 2 acres in Brynscoles, 2 closes called Darlyngland and ffoxhoiles at Brynscoles in Nm. to John s. John Northend. John Northend de Shipden surrendered his 4th of 2 mess., bovate, &c. in tenure of John Saltonstall and Agnes Brighous, widow, to Robt. s. Ric. Brighous. John Otes and Eliz. his wife surr. 1½ ac. between Shelfsyke N., Brynscolebroke W., John Otes close E., Laur. Bentlay close S., to Ric. Sunderland. Wm. Beamonde was ordered to pay 3s. 4d. or amend the dam of the fulling mill at Oldeford between Rastryke and Brighouse.

---

* We fear the 'pore maydens' seldom got a marriage portion.

1557. Brighous *Turn*. For Rastrik, John Watson, John Hanson, John Gooder, Thos. Hanson, John Malynson report to the turn. Ralph Roides, Hiperum graveship, being dead, Thomas his brother paid heriot. for 3½ acres and edifice, which he conveyed to Isabel Mawde, widow, his sister, remainder to John their brother. Rastryke people have to repair the ' stoks,' on pain of 6s. 8d. For Hyprome, Thos. Bolland, Ric. Brighous, Laur. Bellynge, Henry Haighe, John Brodeley (constable, and the four men,) present the report.

1559. Brighouse *Turn*, May 5. Jury, John Rysshworth, Esq.. Thos. Smyth of Lightcliffe, &c. John Lacy and Ric. Rokes surr. mess., bovate, 9 ac. 3 rds. in Hiperome to Henry Kent. Edward Horton and Wm. his son held lands in Sowerby district.

From 1559—Dockets, that is, indexes to the names of parties surrendering or receiving lands have been made—for easier reference. John Lacy, Esq., surrendered into the hands of the lord a fulling mill on the water of Caldre, and ⅓th pt. of corn mill called Brighous mylne, to the use of Jas. Waterhouse for 21 years.

Turn, April 30, Jury, John Risshworth, Esq., Edmund ffairebank, John Wodde, John Clay, Edwd. Thorpe, Ric. & John Barystall, Thos. Gledehill, Thos. ffirth, Wm. Cowper, Edwd. Marshe. Henry Kent conveyed ½ bov. &c. in Priestlay, and 1 rod formerly waste, &c. at Synderhill, to Ric. his son.

1560. The road from Rastrik to Rowndehill named. Thos. Smythe of Lightcliff conveyed 1 ac. 3 rods formerly waste to his son John. Jas. Hoyle took ½ acre of waste in Hiprum graveship.

1561. This is a paper copy. Edmd. and George ffairebank, Edwd. Hoile, and Jas. Woodhead report for Hiperum.

1562. *Turn*, Oct. 12. 13 jurymen, John Rysshworth, Esq.. John Hanson, John Gooder, Ric. Sunderland, Edwd. Thorpe, &c. 'Omnia bene' is Hyprum constable's report.

1563. Henry Kent de Priestley and Ric. his son and heir surr. 3½ acres at Synderhilles to Thos. Whytley of N'ourum ; Robt. Sutclyffe 1½ acres in Hiperum to Adam his younger son. Ric. s. Henry Kent surr. a bovate in Prestlay, and other lands to Edward his son, and Anna wife of sd. Ric.

Turn, Oct. 12. Edmund ffairebanke, Isabell Scolefeld, Ric. Gill, fined 3s. 4d. each, for not repairing a bridge at Lidyate. (There is no stream now.)

1564. John Haldesworth de Astay and his wife Elizth, dau. John Hopkinson of Sourby, conveyed mess., 11 ac. roidland, cottage and 2 acres in Hyprum, to Robt. son and heir. Henry Kent de Prestley and Ric. his son and heir convey a mess., a cottage in tenure of Wm. ffoldes, and Longynge, Rowdeclose, Gunuscroftflatts, Ou'wynters, Nethyrwynters (5 acres) in Prestley to Rob. Rayner for 10 years. John Risshworth de Standeroide, co. Loncastre, Esq., surr. ½ ac. in Nm. to Rob. his son. John Otes, constable of Hyperom, presents that Wm. Robynson made affray on Christr. Waterhous in the house of John Longbothom by force of arms, and shed blood. Edward Hole de Lyghtcliff surrendered reversion of ½ bovate in Lyghtcliff to John his son and heir, and to Agnes d. John Walker, intended wife of John H.

HIGH SUNDERLAND, HALIFAX

1565.   John Hemingway and his wife Johanna, dau. of Ric. and Elizth. Sunderland, take lands.   Ric. s. Brian Sunderland, deceased, formerly of Halifax, surr. Highfield in Nm. to Ric. S. of High

Sunderland. In Hiperum for affrays, by force of arms, Robt. Dobson fined 40d., Ric. Dobson 20d., John Baroclough 30d., Wm. Baroclough 20d., Thos. Taillor 40d.

1566. Robt. Rayner of Ricroft (by Jas. Waterhous of Prestley) surrendered a mess., held by court roll in Hyprome, to Thos. Dobson. Henry Batt de Birstall, gent., surr. 6s. 8d. yearly out of Boythe to Anthony s. of late John Waterhous de Hollyns. Ric. Bawmfurth de Lightcliffe, a tenant. Halifax vicar fined 5s. for making a rescue from the bailiff.

. Brighous *Court with Turn*, Oct. 15. Jas. Hoile being dead, Ric. his son paid 3d. heriot for ½ acre of waste. John s. Ric. Thomson and his wife Isabel, d. and heir of John Whitley, pay 2s. heriot for 5 acres and edifice—except Shaysike, Isabel mother of the said J. Thomson being dead.

1567. Ric. Sunderland, Edwd. Hoile, John Smyth, Edw. Gibson, Edw. Longbothome, Jas. Oldfeld, and seven others from Hyperom greave fined 6d. each for absence at greave election. John Armytage was constable of Clifton.

Turn, Oct. 9, Jas. Waterhouse, Edwd. Thorpe, Henry Haigh, Wm. Hoile, and Wm. Michell represented Hiperome at the turn.

Court with Turn, May 4, Jury, John Hanson, John Gledehill, Thos. Wodhede, Geo. Hellywell, Ric. Brokesbank, John Woodd, John Townend de Sowodd, Leonard Denton, Thos. Rayner, Edwd. Thorpe, Wm. Haigh de Skirehous, Wm. ffourness, John Clay, Edwd. Hoile.

1568. Rob. Whyte *v.* Ric. Barestowe, Hiperum, about price of a chymney. John Crowder's cow, worth 18s., mentioned. At Halifax 26 persons had 1s. each to pay for making weddyng dinners.

Court and Turn, May 10, Thos. Whitley, constable for Hiperum. Hugh Rommesden for affray, 40d.

1569. Clement Oglethorpe being dead, his son and heir Wm., gent., paid 12s. heriot for a mess., 1½ bov., and 12 acres in Hyperome (greaveship). Ric. Northend of Hyprome surr. messuage in Hyprome ville to Martin, Michael, Andrew, Isabell, Sibell, Agnes, Grace, Alice his children for 12 years, with remainder to Ric. his eldest son. At Halifax *Turn* is a Memorandum; It is laide in payne by the Jurie that if any landlordes do kepe in theire houses any prsons after Michaelmes next not beynge able to lyve by their awne labor and not havynge dwelled by the space of three yeares last passed or hereafter shall receyve any to dwell or any suche lyke evill disposed prsons to forfeyte to the Quene Ma'tie vse xxxviijs.

Brighouse *Court with Turn*. Jury, names as before. The year's roll at this time was composed of a dozen skins 3½ ft. by 2 ft. written on both sides. The spelling Hipprholme gradually becomes adopted.

1570. Ric. Sunderland complained of his obligation as Greave, which will be found in the list of greaves, (*Yks. Genealogist.*) Ric. Northend being dead, Ric. his son paid 7s. 4d. heriot for ½ bovate, 6 acres, see 1569. He settled lands on Agnes, d. Edwd. Stancliff deceased, his intended wife; ingress 4s. 8d. Certificate in English on

Wakefield Milnes' dammes repairs : Item frome th'endes of the said
ffifthe Roode measuringe alonge the damme as aforesaid The Quenes
Mats. tena'nts of her bond oxgange lande lyenge wthin the Grayve-
shipps of Sandall . . .   Hippholme and Rastrick hathe by right
by reason of the tenure of their said lands at all tymes vsed to repaire
and mayntene ffifteen roodes of the same damme enyone of them
equallie accordinge to the rate and nomber of their oxgang. John
Haldworth, brother and px. heir Robt. H. defunct, paid 6s. 8d. heriot
for messuage in Hipprome (graveship). Brighouse *Court and Turn*,
Oct. 10, Jury, Gilbt. Saltonstall, John Goodall, John Barrowclough,
twelve more names.

    1571.—Rob. Boithes, of Leedes, s. and heir of John Boythes of Old
Temple, in Whitchurch, deceased, and Sibella wife of Rob., conveyed
lands at Booth in Nm. to Ric. younger son of Ric. Sunderland. Robt.
Overall surr. mess., in Lightcliff, in tenure of Edwd. Hemmyngway,
Margt. Hemmyngway, widow, Rob. Hole, Ric. Barrowclogh and Thos.
Hanson, and 20s. yearly rent from lands of Edwd. Sowod in Light-
cliff, to himself and ffrances his wife, ingress 20s.

    Turn.—Oct. 9. John Drake for Margaret his mother, widow,
granted 33s. 4d. yearly out of Creswell and Brestland in Hipp., to
Homfrid, Margt., Sibill, and Alice his brother and sisters. Ric.
Bairstow, Hipp., being dead, John his son paid heriot for Hessil-
hurst.

    1572. Rob. Sowod, senr., surrendered lands in Hipp. to Robt. his
son. Wm. Oglethorpe of Roundehey Graunge, gent., surr. a messuage in Hipp. to Ric. Saltonstall of London, skynner ; ingress 13s. 4d.
Thos. Whitley surr. annual rent of £3 6s. 8d. from house, cottage,
garden, 3½ acres close, at Synderhill, to Margaret his wife, dau. of
Edwd. Boythes, and Edwd. their son ; remainder to Thos. their son
and heir. The clerk at this time wrote fine initials for each para-
graph, and adorned them with grotesque faces ; the tongue well
protruding. John Bairstow of Thorpp Hall, Hipp. (graveship), surr.
lands in Nm. to Wm. Deane of Eckesley (Elland) ; confirmed by Anna
B., widow of John. Galfri Redmoke of Quernby fined 20d. for keeping an alehouse without leave.

    1573. John Haldworth, defunct ; Ric. his son paid 14d. heriot,
Hipp. Johanna wife of Thos. Rishworth, cousin and heiress of John
Thomson, viz., dau. of Ric. Whitley, brother of John W. father of
Isabel, Ric. Thompson's wife, parents of John Thompson, paid heriot
20d. for lands in Hipp. (grave)—except Shaysike. Long account in
English of Ric. Townend's gift to Halifax Grammar School from lands
in Nm. The town of Brighouse to amend the bridge between Clifton
and Brighouse, penalty 6s. 8d. John Armytage, of Kirkelees, to mend
Nunbroke lane, penalty 20s.

    1574. Ric. Haldesworth de Ossett, s. and heir of John H. decd.,
surrendered mess., croft, 3 closes, in occupation of Wm. Medley, to
John Hoile of Hoylehouse. Robt. Mawde sold to John Hemingway, of
Mytholm, lands at Grenewayclogh, Ivyncarr, &c. Thos. Whitley surr.

MYTHOLM.

33s. 4d. annual rent from Hipp. lands to Margt. wid. of Wm. Otes of Shelf. Henry Kent of Prestelay and Ric. son and heir, surr. 23s. 4d. yearly from lands in Hipp. to Thos. Whitley of Synderhills. Ric. Saltonstall of Saltonstall and his sons, Gilbt., Ric., Edward; and dau. Agnes transfer lands.

Court and Turn, Jury, John Gleidhill, Jas. Stancliffe, John Goodheire, Robt. Bryghouse, John Romsden, John Hemingway, George ffirth, Wm. Boy, Wm. Haighe, John Clay, Ric. Bairstowe, Edw. Hey, John Drake, Thos. ffirth, Ric. Gomrsall. Ric. Sunderland of High S. surr. 1½ bovates formerly Henry Copley's in Coley to his children (in succession failing issue), Ric., Abraham, Johanne (wife of John Hemingway), Agnes (wife of Gilbt. Deyne), Marie, Grace, and Sarah. Wm. Oglethorpe gent., quit claimed to Ric. Saltonstall, citizen and skynner of London, lands in Hipp.

Turn, Jury, Gilbt. Saltonstall of Godley, Rob. Romsden of Clifton, &c. Rob. Whitley, of Lightcliff, broke Edward Thorppe's hedges; fined 12d. John Milner of Pudsey, Anna his wife, and Rob. their son surr. Blacker in Nm. to John Northend of North Byerley. Thos. Rishworth and Johana his wife surrender Shaysike, Nm., to Thos. Michell of Oxnopp, near Haworth.

1575. John Northend, s. and exec. of Christr. N., surr. Northwolley close to Rob. Brighouse of Hipperholm. Wm. Whitley, senr. and junr., surr. the great close adjoining Wakefield and Halifax Rd. in N., and Ric. Cliffe's lands S., to Isaac s. and heir of W. W. junr. Robt. Overall and ffrees. his wife, surr. lands in Hipp. graveship to Edwd. Hemingway; and Allenroyde and Wharlers to Thos. Hanson of Wike. Fined 6d. each for playing at bowls at Hipperholme,—Jas. Haldesworth, Rob. H. junr., Rob. Smyth junr., Geo. Waterhouse junr., Thos. Barrowcloghe, John Rawnsley, Christr. Bolland, Henry Wilson, Thos. Judson, and Gilbt. Barrowclough. Robt. s. and heir app. Rob. Sowood of Hipp., conveyed 4 ac. 3 rds. to himself and Margaret d. Wm. Lawe, his intended wife.

1576. Ric. Sunderland of High S. being dead, Abm. S., son and heir, paid 20s. heriot for High S. Agnes wid. Ric. Northend surr. messuage, mistall, ffold, garden and 4 closes to Wm. Stancliff during her lifetime.

Turn, Oct. 9. Jury, John Gledhill, yoman, (Barkisland), John Gleidhill of Rastrick, Gilbt. Saltonstall, Homfry Armytage, John

Hoole, John Smyth, Ric. Waterhouse, Jas. Otes, John Haldesworth,
John Hogg, W. Boy, Geo. Firth, Geo. Hellywell, Edw. Denton. Rob.
Sowood of Hipp., carrier, son of Rob. S. surr. messuage, 4 ac. 3½ rods
in Hipp. to Rob. Bentley. Ric. Kent surr. 2 parts of bovate to Ric.
Waterhouse de Presteley and Ric. Gomrsall, for 20 years.

1577. *Turn*, Jury, Robt. Brighouse, John Hoile, Ric. Beamont,
Leonard Crowder, Wm. Presteley, Ric. Soithill, Geo. Wibsay, John
Hanson of Lynley, Edw. ffairbank, the 2 Gledhills, John Romsden,
Leonard Denton, G. Firth, W. Boy. Jas. Waterhouse of Priestley
surr. Bridgroid to his three daughters, Mary, Grace, and ——. Jas.
Waterhouse gave 1 acre called Snakehill in Rastrick to Thos. his son,
formerly parcel of Earl Leicester lands ; Ric. fflather of Brighouse
tenant. Wm. Taylior for affray at Hipp. on Mich. fflather, fined 20d.

Queen Elizabeth granted to Earl Leicester, in 1566, amongst other
lands, 221 acres, 2¼ roods, and a plot 50 yds. by 20, with a watercourse in Hipp. graveship, and 12 acres, ½ rood, in Rastrick graveship,
under Wakefield manor. These lands he granted next year to Sir
Thomas Gargrave, and Henry Savile, Esq., of Lupset. The rent was
4d. per acre to the crown, 4d. fine or heriot on the death of each
tenant, and 4d. on every alienation, and suit of court.

1578. Thos. s. Edw. Hanson of Netherwodhouse and Roger s.
Thos. Hanson of Rastrick, landowners. Ric. Saltonstall of London,
skynner, (by Gilbt. S.,) conveyed his Hipperholme copyhold lands to
his son Ric. in the event of death of Richard, the father. Wm.
Horton of Sowerby greave being dead, John the son paid heriot.
Ric. Saltonstall of High Saltonstall, and Gilbt. his son, of Godley,
leased lands in Saltonstall to Jas. Bawmfurth for 21 years.

Turn, Jury, Thos. Thornhill, John Ramsden of Bowers, John Clay
of Lynley, John Hoile, &c. Ric. Shepley held land and water called
Oldforth (the *old ford* at Snakehill,) in Rastrick, his son Owyn S.,
gent., paid heriot. John Armytedge of Locwod, in Rastrick greave,
takes rogues and vagabonds into his house ; fined 12d.

1579. Owyn Shepley, gent., surrendered Oldforth, and damm and
fullingmill in R. (properly Brighouse,) to John Armytage of Kirkelees.
John Stocke *v.* John Stones, Wm. Whitley *v.* Brian Wilson, affrays at
Hipp., each of the four fined 10d. The court revenue was improved
by fining both sides, and probably they deserved it.

Court and Turn. Jury, Rob. Romsden, gent., John Hanson senr.,
Wm. Presteley, John Romsden, Thos. Bothomley, Rob. Brighouse,
Thos. Whitley, John Bentley, Michl. Drake, Ed. Wodheade, &c. all
yeomen. Rastrick-cum-ffixbye are sometimes thus coupled together.
John Smythe of Lightcliffe and Isabella his wife surrendered 2 ac.
1rd. in the occupation of Robt. Smyth, senr., to John Booth. Thos.
s. Thos. Broke of Newhouse, marriage settlement of lands in Toothill
on Elizabeth, d. Ric. Horsfall, deceased.

1580. Hipp. Edwd. Sowod, Rob. Horsfall, Ric. Brokesbank fined
for brawls. Rob. Burgh of Flansall, Wakefield, conveyed Hipp.
lands to Henry his son. Agnes wid. Ric. Bawmeforth of Lightcliff,

ARMYTAGE ARMS.

RAMSDEN ARMS.

dau. of Henry Hemyngway, decd., for 20 marks surrendered West
heighley (5 acres) in Lightcliff to John Woodhead. Ric. Kent (by
John Hoile of Lightcliffe, one of the Queen's tenants) conveyed a
mess., lands, woods, water, &c. in Presteley in tenure of Ric. Mitchell,
to Wm. Hoole, of Sleadhall, wooldriver: agreed to by Anna wife of
Ric. K., and by Edwd. son and heir. Edwd. Hemyngway fined 3s. 4d.
for not mending the highway to Roger fowte. Hugh Romsden to
make apology for crossing Thos. Thornhill's lands. John Armytedge
of Kirklees, gent., and Hugh Romesden, Rastrik, to amend the Nether
Mylne dam; pain of 13s. 4d. laid. Ric. Best being dead, his son Ric.
paid 2d. heriot for ½ acre of Rob., Earl of Leicester's lands. Wm. s.

SLEAD HALL.

John Northend formerly of Nm., surr. 1½ rods in Hipp. to his brother
Edward. Wm. Hoile of Slead Hall surr. Bridgroid in Rastrik to John
Hanson senr., of Wodhouse, and Nicholas his son.

1581. Alex. Rishworth, Esq., and Beatrix, wife, took Harwithings in Nm. of the Queen; ingress £6. Henry fferror of the Ewodd, gent., took mineral coal, (colebeddes,) in Hyperholm for the year, for 5s. John Lacye of Leventhorpp, Esq., (nr. Bradford), surrendered the Brighouse fulling mill, and ¼ of the water corn mill, with goit, damme &c. to John Lacye, junr., Esq. son and heir of Ric. L., Esq.

Turn, Oct. 10, Jury, John Smyth of Lightcliff, &c. Rob. Waterhouse of Presteley surr. 1 rod in P. to Thos. Walker on lease. Roger s. and heir of Thos. Hanson of Rastrick held lands.

1582. Rob. Boythes of Boythes towne and Elizth. his wife, surrendered (by John Boyth of Hipperholme,) a mess. in Boythes to Nic. Kay. Robt. Hemingway of Walterclough took Overnewark in Nm.

Turn, Oct. 9. Jury, Rob. Romsden, gent, Hen. Burgh, gent, John Romsden, Thos. Hawme, Wm. Hoole, John Smyth, Gilbt. Rayner, Edw. Clay, Ric. Aneley, W. Presteley. Rob. Romsden of Clifton, John Wilkinson of Staynland, Edw. Denton of Stainland, Edwd. Denton of Scamonden; yeomen. Margt. younger dau. of Jas. Waterhouse, defunct, surr. messuage, garden, &c. at Brigroid to Thos. Walker and Marie his wife. Edwd. Carye, Esq., had been head senescall some years.

1583. In Hipp'holme graveship 19¾ oxgangs bound to the repair of Wakefield mill dam; in Rastrick grave, 9. Ric. Stancliff of Esington, York, clerk, son of Jas. and Elizth. S., paid 20d. heriot for Nm. lands, his mother being dead.

Turn, Oct. 5. Jury say upon their oth that John Romsden of the Boyth, and Whitelees of the hie mosse and moslyngden ought of right to have a way for bride and corse over ye ground of Thos. Bothomley in ye accustomyd place wthout licence askinge. Ric. s. and heir of Henry Kent formerly of Prestelay, and Edwd. K. son and heir of said Ric., conveyed 4 closes in Ric. Pighells' tenure, viz: Inge under the house, Netherfeild, Newfeild, Whynnybancke; also Knollhey wood (1 rod) at Coleybroke to Gilbert Saltonstall of Rookes, who paid 10s. ingress. Wm. Lawe and Margt. his wife surr. £1 per annum out of wastelands in tenure of Robt. Sowood senr. and his son Robt. S., to Thos. Whitley, senr., of Synderhills, chapman; ingress, 4s. 6d.

1584. Thos. Walker of Hipp' and Maria his wife, Wm. Hoile and Isabel his wife, quit claim Brigroid to John and Nicholas Hanson; and the Walkers (by John Hoile of Hoilehouse, a tenant of the lord,) surr. the mess. and garden at Brigroid in John Watson's tenure, which was obtained from Mary W's. sister, Margaret younger dau. of Jas. Waterhouse, to Gilbert a son of Gilbt. Hole, defunct, who intends to marry the said Margaret. Proclamation respecting Wynteredge and 8 acres received by Gilbt. Saltonstall of Rooks from Kents: G. S, paid 18s. ingress. Geo. Haldworth of Hipp. fined 2s. for unlawful games at Halifax. At Rastrick for playing at globes (bowls), John Batley, Leond. Boothroyd and Jas. Bartle of Brighouse, 1s. each.

1585. Ric. Sunderland of Grays Inn, London, surr. Highroide at Boythes, received from Rob. Boyth of Leeds, to John Cosyn. John

Wodheade, of Norwodgrene, surr. Westheathley, with edifice, 8 acres in tenure of Rob. Hargreaves and Thos. Hollyns, to John Scolefeld of Coley hall. Anna Kent, her son Edw. K. of Presteley, and Agnes his wife surr. a cottage and the common croft, and Oldroyd close adjoining in Prestley, to John Stones for 21 years. Thos. Brodeley of Lightcliffe, and Michael King of Hipp' for an affray on Ric. Nicoll, junr.

Turn, April 19. John ffairebank, John Northend, Ric. Northend, Ric. Brodeley, John Medley, and Edw. Nicholl fined 4d. each for not mending the way between Hiegreave Ing and High Street. Edwd. Hemingway of Shelf surr. Marland and Intack to Ric. Scolefeld, junr. of Lightcliffe.

1586. Edw. and Agnes Kent of Priestley surr. the Wynters to Gilbt. Saltonstall; Edw. s. Ric. Kent also conveyed Knowlehey wood, Knowlynge, and Brokehousbottom, to John Scolfield of Coley, and Rob. Waterhouse of Priestley, after the death of his mother Anna now wife of John Haldsworth. John Lacy of Leventhorpe, gent., (son of Ric. L. Esq.,) and Helena now wife of John, surr. Brighouse Milnes to John Lacy of Brereley, gent. John Hoile, of Hoile House, surr. mess. in Lightcliffe called Soperhouse and 2 acres in tenure of Wm. Medley, to Henry Hoyle of Halifax and Michael Smith of Skircote. Abm. Sunderland of High S. being dead, Ric. his brother paid 20s. heriot. Edw. Kent surr. Brokehousyng, Presteley, to Ric. Sunderland of High S., ingress, 1d. John Hanson of Wodhouse, senr., Michael Hanson younger son of Edw. H., Netherwodhouse, and Thos. H. of Brighouse, surrendered Bridgroid, in tenure of John Watson, to John Hanson, junr., son of said John H., senr.

ROOKES PORCH.

1587. Ric. Waterhouse, John Hoile, Ric. Jagger, fined 12d. each for not attending the Brighouse court on the mandate of Edwd. Shaw, deputy-greave. John Batestow of Hipp. fined 4d. for damaging a tenter-row in Nm. Ric. Saltonstall of Middle Temple, s. and h. Ric. Saltonstall of Minchin Lane, London, merchant, (by Gilbt. S. of Rookes,) surr. messuage, cottage, &c., in Hipp., to the use of his father. Gilbt. Saltonstall of Godley, s. and h. Ric. S. of High Saltonstall surr. ⅞ths part of Saltonstall in Warley to Robt. Milner of Pudsey, Rob. Waterhouse of Harthill, Saml. Saltonstall of Rooks, and Geo. ffairbanke of Lightcliffe for 20 years in trust for the education &c. of his children. Rob. Grenewod of Inner Temple, gent., was appointed dep. steward of Wakefeld and Bradford manors, under John Savile and Edwd. Carye.

Court and Turn, Oct. 3. Jury, Rob. Romsden, gent., Edw. Stancliffe, W. Presteley, John Hanson, junr., Rob. Haigh, Ric. Tempest, Ric. ffirth, Thom. Aneley, Rob. Brighous, Gilbt. Rayner, Rob. Waterhous, John Killingbeck, John Hylileigh, Thos. Hawne; all yeomen.

The old and new constable lists, as usual, are given :

HIPP.	Thos. Hoile—Wm. Whitley.	RASTK.	John Malynson, jun.—Edw. Malynson.
NORTHOW.	Leon. Crowther—Ric. Bentley.	FIXBY.	Edw. Marshe—John Wilton.
SHELF.	Ric.Sunderland—Jas.Brokesbanke.	BARKSLD.	Ric. Romsden—Gibt. ffirth.
		STAYNLD.	John Jagger—Anth. Romsden.
HARTSHD.	Gilb. Rayner—Oliver Haughton.	QUERNBY.	Edw. Hurst—Geo. Haworth.
CLIFTON.	Hen. Beaumont—John fforness.	DALTON.	Hy. Beaumont—Ric. Broke.

Ric. Best and Kath. his wife, of Barmes, Nm., Jas. Otes, Nm., Ric. Sunderland of Shelf surr. Barmes to Gibt. Saltonstall of Rookes. Ric. Northend, Hipp. surr. 2 ac. near Over Northedge formerly in Wm. Stanclyff's tenure, to Thos. Stancliff of Hipp. Wm. s. and h. Ric. Northend, deceased, surr. bovate and 6 acres to Rob. Brighous his cousin, for 10 years. Edw. Kent and Rob. Hargrave had an affray at Hipp. fined 10d. each.

1588. Robt. Mawde being dead, Saml. son and heir, paid heriot for Ivynear alias Grenewayclogh, Nm., but with his wife Susanna, and mother Grace, conveyed it to John Scolefeld of Coley on lease. Thos. Hanson of Totehill, s. of Edw. H. of Nether Wodhous, took a mess. in Bryanscoles of the lord. Thos. Hoile of Halifax, clothier, Matth. H. of Hx., Thos. Hoile of Hipp. son of sd. Thos. H. of Hx., and George Hoile of Scamonden took lands in Scamonden. Edw. Kent of Presteley surr. four closes, Knollheys, Carrynge, Brodehousynge, in Presteley, to Gilbt. Saltonstall of the Rooks, yeoman. Thos. Hoile fined 20d. affray on Jas. Oldfeld, Hipp. Wm. Broke, Henry Scolefeld and Thos. Hanson fined 12d. each for not repairing the roads.

1589. John Hoole of Hoolhouse and Saml. Hoile his younger son, take Bolleshawe, in tenure of Rob. Bentley, quit claimed to them by John Savile of Bradley, Esq., Elizabeth his wife, and Elizth. his mother. Edwd. Brighous and Mary his wife one of three d. and co-h.

of Ric. Boy, held Wilkinheys in Nm. John Gybson, Hipp., 3s.4d. for not making his gates secure; John Naylor of Clifton and John Drake of Nm. for breaking into Hipp. pinfold, 40d. each; Wm. Broke, 20d., Henry Scolfeld, 20d., John Waterhouse, 2s., John Hemingway 12d., John Haldworth 12d.. John Hoole 2s., John Royde 2s. Rob. Brodeley, 2s., Thos. and John Barraclough 8d., John Mitchell 4d., John Mitchell of Rouks 12d., Wm. Haldworth 12d., John Snell 4d., John Appleyard 12d., Thos. Pighells 4d., John Pennygton 8d., for not mending the highways.

THORPE ARMS.   SAVILE CREST.   APPLEYARD ARMS.

1590. John Greenwood of Bradford takes Nm. lands of George Boothe, clerk, vicar of Kirkebye. Edw. s. and h. Robt. s. and h. Jas. Waterhous claimed his lands in Priestley. Wm. s. Robt. Brighouse took lands in Nm. Thos. Whitley of Synderhills surr. 4 ac. 3 rds. edifice &c. in Synderhills to his sons John, Michael, Matthew and Samuel. Thos. Bolland of Priestley, clerk, and Grace his wife, (d. of Jas. Waterhouse of Priestley, deceased,) surr. Briggeroid, Rastrick, to John Hanson of Wodhous, junr. and Gibt. Hoile of Lightecliff. Thos. Savile, Soc. Coll. Marton, Oxon, a younger son of Henry S. of Bradley, gent., decd., at the request of his brother John quitclaimed Briauscoles, lands, woods, &c. formerly in Ric. Pighells' tenure, now Edw. Presteley's tenure, to Thos. Hanson of Totehill, s. Edw. H. of Nether Wodhouse. Ric. Sunderland, gent., held Olde Hyghe Sunderland. Rob. Rishworth was one of the chief creditors of John Bairstow of Nm., a great debtor, cheat, bankrupt: a long account given in English. John Medley of Hipp. fined 10s. for not permitting the water to run in its right course to Rob. Wodhead's house. Thos. Waterhouse s. of Jas. W. of Presteley, decd., surr. Brigroyd, formerly in John Watson's tenure, to his sister Grace Waterhouse. John Booth of Lightcliffe conveyed 2 acres, 1 rod to Hugh his son; released to Mich. Scolefeld for 21 yrs. John Hanson of Wodhouse, junr. and Johanna his wife, quitclaimed to Gilbt. Hoile of Lightcliffe and Margaret his wife, the ffoldesteade, Brigroidynge, and Weteynge in Rastrick.

1591. List of free tenants given each year. Rob. Overall of Rotherham, yeoman, and ffrances his wife, surr. messuage, le Royd,

Marland, Intack, le Banke, Parocke, &c. to John Hoole, Lightcliffe, and Saml. his son, for 24 years. Special jury report that Gilbt. Saltonstall of Rookes, and Samuel his son and heir, rented to John Hogge a mess. in Priestley grene; they paid 20s. to Savile and Carye, chief seneschals, for the same, viz. a bovate, and 4 ac. 3½ rods formerly Ric. Kent's, called Knollhey, Knollwood, Brokehousebothom. Rob. Brodeley of Hipp. and John Haldeworth of Hoole quitclaimed to Ric. Brodeley of Hipp. three closes called Welleyses and one called Claybutt. Rob. s. and heir of John Hemyngway of Mytholm, his father having died, paid 16d. heriot, for Bothomhouse, garden, parocke, three closes called Stonehope, Skarrbancke, Hawkroyd; and Shelf colepitt.

Court and Turn, Oct. 5. Jury, Rob. Romsden, gent., Thos. Thorppe, &c., yeomen. Edw. s. and h. Ric. Kent surr. woods, underwoods, at Presteley to Saml. s. Gibt. Saltonstall of Rookes. Brian Otes and Hen. Lister 3s. 2d. each for affray and blood drawing at Hipp.; Thos. Thornhill, gent., 39s. for not placing two 'steles' for footpassengers at Netherend of the Ridinge next the road, and a gate at the ffleake* required by the Brighouse inhabitants when conveying grain, coal, &c.

1592. John Booth of Ouer Crowe Neste and Hugh Boothe his son, and Mary wife of Hugh, surr. a garden, close, a new barn, in Lightcliffe, (at le fflatte near Browncroft, Michael Scolefeld, senr., tenant,) to John Hoile of Hoilehous. Thos. Hanson of Brighouse and Nich. Hanson of Eland, younger son of John H. of Wodhouse, senior, held lands in Okesgrene. George flairebanke of Lidyate, senior, and Geo. his son conveyed a mess., called Lidyate in Lightcliff, also a parcel with oven built thereon, a fold, barn, a 'fflore' to purge grain, the Greateynge, Lathecroft, Longmarshe, running water, to Hugh Norcliffe of Sowerby, clothier. Rob. Brodeley, of Hipp. Lane-end, surr. Little Southedge (¼ acre) to Ric. B.; John Hoile, of Hoile House, a bovate to his son and heir Saml. Gilbt. Brokesbanke broke the lord's fold at Hipperholme. Henry Musgrave fined 5s. for affray at Hipp., drawing blood from Edwd. Shawe, constable. Rob. Brodeley and Anna his wife, surr. a house at Lane-end, Hipp., called Oldhouse, a barn called Oldlathe, a croft called Croft under the Lathe, and Wodclose at Brianscole wood, to his son Robt. and himself; and a mess. at Lane-end, called New Parlor, a shoppe and gallery, to Ric. his son; and Whalloyne to Edeth d. John Bairstow of Northbrigge.

1593. Thos. Hanson of Brighouse and Margaret his wife, held Okesgrene lands in Rastrick.

1594. Johanna d. and heiress of Rob. Hemingway paid 2s. 8d. heriot for Mytholm lands, Bothomhouse, &c. John Booth, and Hugh his son, of Over Crow nest, let the long and two little parocks to John Cowper of Deanehouse, Shelf. Nic. s. Ric. Stayncliffe of Essington, Cleveland, clerk, and Elizth. his wife, paid 12s. heriot for Nm. lands.

1595. Thos. Smyth of Smythhouse, Wm. Robinson, John Appleyard of Presteley, Geo. Hargreaves, Tempest Rookes, Rob. ffairbank, Arthur Elmsall, Hugh Ramsden, and Ric. Duckesburye fined 2s. 6d.

K   * Fleak means 'a gate in a gap.'

each for playing at bowls in Hipp. township. John Romsden, Edmd.
Broke, Saml. Smyth, John Otes, Wm. Pollard, Saml. Bairstow for
affrays, 20d. to 40d. each.

1596.   Robt. Crowder of Ealand, a younger son of Leonard Crowder,
decd., of Nm., surr. lands in Nm. to Thos. Bunny, Rastk., and John
Bunny, Ealand.   Ric. Saltonstall, Alderman of the City of London,
(by Gilbt. S. of Rooks) surr. (after his death,) 3 mess., a cottage, and
all his lands in Hipp. to Saml. S. son of said Ric., reversion to Edward
another son, and failing issue, to Peter, another son.   His mansions
were at Mynchenlane in London and South Workenden in Essex.

Turn, Oct. 5.   Jury, Robt. Ramsden, gent., John Broke, Ric.
Tempest, John Haldworth of Hoole, Thos. Hanson, Rob. Thorneton,
of Quernby, Ric. Haldworth, John Roide, Thos. fflather, John Ratcliffe,
Ric. Rayner, John Wormall, Rob. Haigh, W. Drake.   John Scolefeld,
of Coley, conveyed Grenewayclogh in Nm., which he had of Saml.
Mawde of Altofts, to John Wood and Susanna his wife, daughter of
his brother Robt. Scolfeld, with remainder to Samuel s. said Robt.
Robt. s. Rob. Boothe, of Mixenden, conveyed Holcannes, Nm., to his
brother Geo. B., clerk.

1597.   Rob. Ou'all being dead, his son Wm. paid 11s. 4d. heriot
for 1 ac. 1 rd. at Lightcliff broke, and a mess., called Cliff house 1½
bovates, and for lands in Sowerby.   Ric. Sunderland of Coley, gent.,
had 1½ bov. formerly Henry Copley's in Newynge, Copleyinge,
Osburneroyd, Northroyde, 3 rods at lower end of Coley lane, abutting
on Coley broke E., ffalroyd, W., Newynge, N., Tollerynge, S., also
Hekden, east of Copley broke; another parcel east of Coldley alias
Coley; 3 rods between Coley Slack alias Wynter Slacke, E., and highway from Coley chappell to Shelf, W., abutting on cemetery of said
chapell, S., and on Shelff town on N.; also a mess., 2 acres and house,
Thomas Lombe former tenant, Thomas fferneside present tenant;
and all copyhold lands formerly held by John Rishworth of Coley,
afterwards of Parkehill, Lancashire, Esq., deceased. All were seized
by the lady, and Ric. Sunderland of Coley, gent., and John Rishworth
of Shibden, clothier, came before the seneschall and paid 30s. ingress.
Edw. Kent and Agnes his wife quitclaimed John Stone's tenures in
Preistley to Saml. Saltonstall. Rob. Hemyngway of Mythom, and Jas.
Oldfeld of Southowram surr. Tyllieholme (Nm.) to Thos. Savile, gent.,
of Whitlee, and Thos. his son, who reconveyed it to Ric. s. Hen.
Northend. Rob. Smyth of Lightcliff bought lands in Sowerby of
Miles Brigge.

Turn, Oct. 11.   John Haldesworth of Asday conveyed 6 acres in
Hipp. to Simon ffairebank.   Geo. Booth, M.A., of Ovenden, held
lands in Nm.

1598.   Ric. Saltonstall, Knight, Maior of the City of London, was
elected greave for Hipperholme this year : see *Yks. Genealogist* for full
list.   John Butler was his deputy.   Wm. Overall of Eastwod surr.
messuage called Westheathley in Lightcliff, with house, garden, fold, .

easements, 6 acres, to Rob. Hargreaves and Hannah his wife, at £4 13s. 4d. rent yearly. Isabella widow of Gilbt. Saltonstall, of Rookes, quit-claimed their lands to Saml. S., gent., son and heir. Anna Haldesworth of Presteley, widow of John Haldesworth of Hoole, formerly wife of Ric. Kent of Preistley, surr. all copyhold lands to Saml. Saltonstall of Huntwick, gent., s. and heir of Gilbert. Wm. Ouerall of Eastwod conveyed Warleys and Allynroides in Nm. to

SIR RICHARD SALTONSTALL, Lord Mayor of London.

Saml. Saltonstall gent., for 20 years. Michael Bairstow and Bridget his wife, 1 ac. in Bryan Scoles, in John Sharpp's tenure, to Michael younger son of John Northend of Fold. John Barrett 3s. 2d., and John Brodeley alias Denholme, 10d. for affray at Hipp., the latter losing blood. John Malynson 12d. for not mending the highway at Hipp. John Haldesworth of Hoyle, s. and h. of J. H. of Hoyle, paid 7d. heriot for edifice and land 17 yds. by 15 ; homage or fidelity. Nathl. s. Edw. Sowod formerly of Hipp. paid 2s. 9d. heriot for Netherhilelee,

Crosseroyd, and Crosseclough. Saml. s. and h. John Hoyle of Hool-
hous paid 2s. 6d. heriot for mess., croft, 3 closes, in occupation of
Wm. Medley; also garden, close formerly in two, a new barn, 1 ac.
1 rd. called the flatt in Lightcliffe at Browncroft, in the tenure of
Michl. Scolefeld. Ric. Sunderland of Coley, Gilbt. Deane of Allerton,
and John Rishworth of Nm. senior, surr. £4 yearly from lands in
Nm. to Thos. Cosyn of Halifax.

1599. Amongst the Free Tenants or Freeholders are John Armytage of Kirkelees, Esq., John Hanson, Nich. Hanson, yeoman, John
Thornhill, Esq. Wm. Whitley and Isaack his son, of Lightcliffe,
convey the great close in the Eastefeild now made into separate closes
to Geo. Dickson of Crawelshawes, Sowerby. John Lacye of Brereley,
Esq., (by Thos. Hanson of Brighouse,) surr. the fulling mill and a
grain mill called Brighouse Milne, formerly in the tenure of John
Holland, to Jas. Hilles formerly of Ribonden, ffuller, for ten years.
Gilbt. Saltonstall of Rookes being dead, Saml. his son paid 30s. heriot
for Wynteredge and 8 acres in tenure of Rob. ffairebancke; 3 closes in
Preistley called Wynters, 1 rod at Knowleheywod; Knowleheys,
Carrynge, Brokehousynge, 4 closes; Barnes in Nm.; and for lands in
Horbury. Geo. ffairbank being dead, his son Geo. paid 2s. heriot.

Turn, Oct. 16. Robt. Ramsden of Rastrick is dead since last court,
Robt. is his son and heir; John Hanson of Wodehouse, senr., is dead,
John is his son and heir. Under Hipperholme, John Roydes, Wm.
and Jasper Brighous fined 20d. each for affrays. Ric. fflather, of
Brighouse, dug and led away slatestones from Rastrick Common.
Thomas, Arthur, Ric., Joseph, sons of Thomas Hanson; and Robt. s.
Nicholas Hanson of Ealand, take lands in Brighouse lately held by
John H., senior. Roger s. and h. Thos. Hanson of Rastrick, deceased,
surr. lands to John Hanson of Wodhouse junr., and Thos. Hanson of
Totehill. Robt., John, Thos., brothers of Roger, obtain land also.
Edward s. Arthur Hanson, decd., ditto. Thomas Hanson and his
nephew John s. John Hanson of Netherwodhouse, decd., the nephew
being 51 at the time of his father's death, ditto. Robt. Romsden of
Rastrick being dead, Henry his son, gent., paid 6d. heriot for a house
called the Chappell,* and gardens. Ric. Brodeley of Hipp., and
Margaret his wife, surr. Little Southedge, ¼ ac., in tenure of John
Horsfall, and Willeyses, 4 ac., to Rob. s. Robt. Brodeley, deceased.

1600. John Savile of Howley and Edwd. Carye, Knts., Head
Senescalls. Henry Burgh being dead, Robt. his son paid 40s. heriot
for lands in Hipp., &c. John Armytage of Kirklees, Esq., and
Margaret his wife held lands in Holme graveship. Henry Savile, pre-
positus (provost) of Eaton, Eton College, surr. by Nicholas Hanson,
Boldshaw and lands in Brianscholes formerly his brother's. Thomas
S., deceased, to Samuel Hoile and Thos. Hanson of Totehill. John
Wod of Coley and Susanna his wife, d. Rob. Scolefeld, surr. Grene-
wayclough in Nm., 6 acres, to Ric. his son.

---

* Restored to its proper use afterwards, see 1605.

HENRY SAVILE, Esq., Bradley in Stainland.
= Ellen d. Robert Ramsden, Esq.

Sir John, born 1545, Steward of Wakefield Lordship, Baron of the Exchequer 1598, Justice of Assize, Knight 1603. Died 1606, buried in St. Dunstan's, Fleet St., his heart was buried in the south aisle of Methley Church, where is a monument with his effigy in stone, in his judge's robes. In 1675 one of his law books, " Reports of Cases, &c.," was printed in old French.

Turn, Oct. 7. John Hanson held Little Milnecliff, butting on the highway from Brighous brigge to the town of Rastrick. In Hipp., Jas. Oldfeld and Arthur Emson fined 20d. each for not ringing their pigs. Ric. Norcliffe, Percivall Steade, Thos. Smyth, Wm. Walker, all of Brighouse, fined 6d. each, for placing their horses in the pasture of Rastrick Common.

Sir Henry, born 1549, Greek and Mathematical Scholar, Warden of Merton College, Oxford, Provost of Eton in 1596, Knight 1604. His only son died about 1605. Founded Professorships at Oxford University, and a Library, and enriched the Bodleian Library. Buried at Eton College. Author of Chrysostom's Works, &c.

Thomas, was admitted to Merton College, Oxford, in 1580. Proctor of Oxford in 1592, died Jan. 12, 1592-3, buried in Merton College Church. Author of "Letters" to Camden, &c.

Sir Henry Savile.

A scabbed horse on Rastrick Common reported. Michael Waterhouse of Shelf, surr. lands in Nm. to Thos. Whitleye of Synderhills. John s. and h. John Haldeworth of the Hoile, deceased, and Susanna

SIR JOHN SAVILE.
(Copied from Oil-Painting.)

Priestley his intended wife, marriage dowry.

1601. Michael Bairestawe of Wakefeld, s. and h. Wm. B., defunct, of Mount Pellan in Hallifax, and Brigitta wife of Mich., convey lands in Nm. to John Thorppe of the Ewetrees in Lightcliff. Ric. Sunderland of Coley Hall, gent., surr. 1½ bov. formerly Henry Copley's, and Heckdeyn, and other lands of John Rishworth, Esq., decd., and of Rob. Sowood, in Hipp., to Mary his wife, d. Ric. Saltonstall, Knt., citizen and Alderman of London, deceased, for her lifetime. Jas. Oldfeld and Alice his wife of Preistley quit-claim to Ric. Northend a close in Nm. Lands of Saml. Saltonstall of the City of London, seized by the lord. At Hipp., Jas. Oldfeld and Simeon ffirth made rescues from the pinfold, fined 40d. each, and John Wood for shedding John Michell's blood, paid 5s. Ric. Norclyff, the milner at Brighouse, was fined 40d. for placing his cattle on the common of Rastrick. Ric. fflather hathe cutt brakyns on common of Rastrick, and carried them to Brighous, fined 12d., and placed his cattle on Rastrick Common, fined 2s., and cut wood in Healey bancke and carried it to Brighouse, 3s. Shocking, Flather! Wm. Midgley and Rob. Hargreaves, junr., fined 30d. each for shedding blood of Robt. Feilde.

1602. Saml. Saltonstall of City of London, Esq., and Elizth. his wife, took of the lady (Queen Eliz.) of the manor, messuages occupied by John Northend, Ric. Brodeley, Isaack Brodeley, Widow Brighous, Gibt. Barrowclough, and John Butler, paying 40s. to Humphrey Cheke, gent., Clifford Inn. Thos. s. Edwd. Hanson of Netherwodhous paid 6d. heriot. John Lacye of Brereley, Esq., surr. fulling mill at Brighouse, ⅓th water corn mill, called also Brighous milne, to Thos. Pilkington of Nether Bradley, Esq. Henry Tylson was constable of Waddisworth, but the family was of older standing there. Rob. Booth of Booths town being dead, Daniel his son paid 16s. heriot. Geo. ffairbanke of Lidyate and his sister Anna broke the pinfold, fined 40d.

1603. Ric. Sunderland of Coldley Hall, gent., surr. Osburnes, 6 acres, in John Bancroft's tenure, to Saml. Saltonstall of Huntwick, gent. R. Sunderland and John Rishworth of Shipden surr. Knowlhey, after the decease of Anne now wife of Wm. Watmough, and lately wife of Ric. Kente of Prestley, and also Knowleynge, Brokehousbothom, to same S. Saltonstall, gent., who surr. Barnes in Nm. to Sunderland. Rob. Hemingway of Mitholm, fined 5s. for breaking trees, &c. of Rob. Hemingway of Netherbrea. Saml. Saltonstall of Kirkestall, lately of Saltonstall, son of Gibt. S. of Godley, and cousin and heir px. of Ric. S. of Saltonstall, surr. Saltonstall to Christr. Wade's sons, of Warley.

Turn, Oct. 11. Jury, Geo. ffirth of ffirthhouse, John Drake, John Waterhouse, Ric. Brigge, Saml. Hoole, Thos. Smythe, Rob. Hurste, Thos. Denton, Thos. ffirth de Lynley, Arthur Gawkroger, John Hylilee, Brian Mawde, John Gleidhill, Matth. Longley, John Goodall, Ric. Waterhouse, Ric. ffirth. John and Wm. Hogg fined 40d. each, for breaking open Hipp. pinfold ; W. Stevenson ditto. Isack Brodeley, Rob. Barraclough, and Ric. Brodeley fined 40d. for not scouring out the Sopr loyne wells. Ric. Sutcliffe and Ric. Norecliffe both of Brighous, fined 12d. each for placing horses on Rastrick Common. Rob. ffirth of Boothroyd being dead, Thos. his brother, of Haighhouse, paid 10s. 6d. heriot for Boothroyd and 20 acres ; which Elizabeth wid. of Robt. also surrendered to him. Ric. Boothroyd fined 40d. for permitting unlawful games in his house in Rastrick; John Blackburn for harbouring dishonest people in his house there, 20d.; Thos. Stansfeld for working on Sunday, 6d. From Northourum, several were fined 2d. each for practising archery on Sundays.

1604. Rob. s. and h. Rob. Hemingway of Netherbrea surr. le Pighells in Nm. to Rob. H. of Mytholme. Hugh Norecliffe being dead, John his son and heir paid 16d. heriot for mess., east end of Lidyate in Lightcliffe from the 'fflore' of said messuage, and a furnace called an oven built thereon, half a fold for thrashing and winnowing grain, a barn, a close called Lathe croft, now held by his mother Sibille N., wid. John Haldworth broke Hipp. pinfold, 40d. Ric. Norcliffe, Ric. ffletcher of Brighouse, 12d. each, for placing cattle on Rastrick Common.

1605. Thos. s. and h. John Smythe of Lightcliff quit-claimed to John Cowper of Deynehouse, the long and two little parocks. Rob. Smyth and Ric. Wade, 40d. each, not scouring the ditches at Hipp. Rob. Beley (40d.) drew blood from Ric. fflather (10d.)

Condition of Rastrick and Brighouse.

A Deed, dated June 11th, 1605, recites that, whereas John Thornhill and others, had petitioned Sir John Fortescue, Chanc. of the Duchy of Lancaster, showing that there had time immemorial been an antient Chapel within the township of Rastrick, called St. Matthew's Chapel, within which Divine Service had been celebrated, and also a school for the education of youth above 50 years ago, which chapel, for want of due maintenance for keeping a curate there, had for the greatest part of 50 years last past been profaned and converted into other uses, till it was reformed by the Stat. temps. Eliz. for reviving of things given to charitable uses; since which time the said John Thornhill and others, had bestowed great sums of money in repairing and enlarging the same, and maintaining divine service therein for a year last past; and that every Sunday and holiday a great number of people did resort thereto, and were likely so to do if divine service were continued, for that a greater part of the inhabitants of the said township were two miles distant from their "Parish Church of Eland," the ways foul in winter, and the causeways decayed for want of repairing, by reason whereof many who were willing to be present at divine service at Eland twice a day, were enforced in the afternoon to be absent; and many of the younger sort had taken occasion thereby to occupy themselves on Sundays and holidays in the afternoons at unlawful games; which abuses had been greatly reformed during the past year, and were likely to continue so, if divine service might be provided for. And for that the said township of Rastrick was very small, consisting of not above 24 families, and the whole township not containing above 12 oxgangs of land, and therefore unable to bear the charges of celebrating divine service or instructing youth in the said Chapel, and therefore humbly intreated his Honour to grant licence to enclose and improve from the waste and commons in the said township, some few acres of ground as might be least hurtful to the inhabitants there, and to convert the same to the use and benefit of those who should celebrate divine service, and keep a School in the said Chapel, for which grounds they were willing to pay yearly to His Majesty 4 pence of new rent for every acre. On perusal of which petition, and conference had with Sir John Saville, one of the Barons of the Court of Exchequer, who lived within 2 miles of the said Chapel and affirmed the contents of the said petition to be true, and that by means thereof the inhabitants of the Manor of Brighouse, who are more remote from the Church (of Eland) than the inhabitants of Rastrick, may likewise resort to the said Chapel.

1606. Thos. Hanson of Brighouse held land in Soyland. Ric. Sunderland, gent., took of the lord Randes in Nm., and a parcel formerly John Scolefeld's in Coley Lane, near Oldroid S., Copley Inge N., in tenure of Wm. Northend; 1 acre near Coley Chapel at Wynterslack E., Coley chapel yard and Coley and Halifax road S., Shelf N., also Falroyd, Towlerynge &c: paid 30s. ingress. Ric. Barrowclough of Halifax, fined 40d. for carrying away Halifax towne butts; Wm. Tillotson for shooting arrows at the pricke. Thomas fflather, Brighouse, fined 6s. for placing 6 oxen on Rastrick Common; also he, Ric. Norcliffe and Ric. Flather were fined 1s. each for placing their cattle on Rastrick Common. John Tayte of Hipp. (fined 8d.) for an affray at Clifton with John ffletcher, (fined 12d). John Royde and Lea his wife of Hipp. surr. 3½ rodes to Henry Preston of Ealand. Hen. fferror resided at Cromwelbottom.

1607. Rob. Brodeley of Clarehall in Cambridge, (s. and h. Robt. of Lane ends in Hipp., deceased,) Ric. Nicholl of Halifax and Anna his wife, widow of said Robt., and Eden Bairestowe of Wakefeld, spinster, surr. mess. at Lane ends, with barn, garden, Walloyne close, held by copyhold, and Croft under the Lathe, also Wollyses closes, Little Southedge close, and Wodclose, now held by John Horsfall, and a cottage held by John Carleton, to Ric. Brodeley of Hipp., ingress 7s. 3d. John Armytage of Kirklees, Esq., being dead, John A. Esq., his son and heir paid 6s. 8d. ob. heriot for 2 closes, $3\frac{1}{2}$ acres, called Hartsheade carrs, and 5 closes in Nm. Ric. fflather, Brighouse, 12d. for a horse placed on Rastrick common. Arthur Emson fined 10s. for breaking Hipp. fold three times. Wm. Thorpp, Sam. Wilson, Edw. Usherwod fined 1s. each for affrays at Hipperholm. Wm. Pollard 5s. for drawing blood from Abm. Brodeley.

1608. Thos. Pilkington lately of Nether Bradley, now of Stanley, and Wm. Ramsden of Longley, Esqs., surr. the fulling mill, called Brighouse Milne, ¼th of water corn mill, called Brighouse Milnes, with stagnas, goits, sects, services, running waters, in the tenure of John Thornhill of ffekisby, Esq., to the said J. T., who paid 53s. 3d. Judah Hopkinson of Rampton, Notts., clerk, and Agnes his wife surr. Otesroid, $11\frac{1}{2}$ ac., in Nm. to Ric. Hopkinson of Shipden Hall. Bryan and Robert Crowther, brothers, Jane wife of Brian, and Saml. s. Robt., took lands in Nm. John Ramsden of Hipp., s. Rob. R. of Royleshead, surr. Royleshead in Sowerby to Hen. Greenwod. Thos. Whitley and Wm. Stephenson 10d. each for affray at Hipp. John Hanson 12d. for gathering brackens on Rastrick common.

1609. Ric. Richardson of Tong (Bierley), surr. Pighells in Nm. to his son Ric. Ric. Brodeley drew blood from Wm. Speight at Hipp., fined 5s.

1610. Geo. ffairebancke of Lydyate surr. 3 acres to Mary Bancroft and Agnes Wilson his sisters; remainder to George s. Ric. Wilson. Saml. Saltonstall, Knt., of City of London, and Lady Elizth. his wife, (by Nic. Hanson of Ealand,) surr. lands &c. in Hipp. in the tenures of Isaak Brodeley, John Horsfall, Wm. Potterton. Wid. Barrowclough, John Whitley, Abm. Brighouse, Jonas Brighouse, and W. Speight, to Thos. Whitley: also John Northend's tenure to John Northend. Thos. Whitley of Synderhills took

MAP, 1610. [Lightcliffe should be across the stream, at Estfeld.]

waste land at Northedge lanehead, abutting on Bryanscoles, W., John Northend's lands, E. and S., Henry Preston's lands, N., and John Haldesworth's new house at Synderhills. A special enquiry was made

this year as to all the manorial tenancies. "A treue and p'fect rentall
of the names of all those coppieholders and ten'tes of and within the
graveshipp of Hipp'holme p'cell of the Lordeshipp and mannor of
Wakefelde which have compounded with his highness for the confirm-
acon of theire estates, and certeyntie of theire fines of and for all and
singuler theire coppiehoulders, mess., cottages, &c. *inter alia*, Saml.
Saltonstall of Huntock, gent., Preistley, late Edward Kentts, 7s. 9d.,
parcel in Lightcliffe, ob (½d.), Osborneroides late John Ryshworthe's
of Coley, Esquier, 18d., Sir Saml. Saltonstall, knighte, lands late
Oglethorpe's, 8s. Rob. Hemingway of Mythom for Bothamhouses,
Hawkynroid &c., 3s. 5d. Ric. Sunderland of Coley Hall, gent., his
father's lands at Sunderland, 13s., Rishworth's lands in Coley and
Hipp. 3s. 4d., Rob. Sowod's in Hipp. and Bryanscoles, 14d., Randes,
18d., Johnroidhouse, 11d., Boothestown 3s. 4d., Barnes 11d., parcels
in Nm. and Hipp. 3s. 11d. Isack Whitley for Eastefeld in Lightcliff
9d. Wm. Northend, Hipp., 21d. Ric. Brodelay, Lane ends 2s. 11d.
Thos. Hanson, Bryanscoles, 2s. 2d. John Thornhill, Esq., for mills
16s. 1d. Henry Preston, Hipp., 3d. John Roide, Hipp., 7d. Geo.
ffairbank, Lydyate, 11d. Wm. Feilde for Cawsey, &c., 12d. Saml.
Hoile, Hoilehouse, 2s. 5d., Soperhouse lands 8d., John Booth's close
7d., Bowlshey, 2s. John Armytage, Esq., coppieholds, 11d. Hen.
Cockcroft of Burleis, coppieholds in Hipp. 2s. Thos. Whitley, junr.
Synderhills, 22d, for Diconson's, Nm., 15d. Nich. Richardson for
Pighell, 3d. John Norclyff for Lydyate 6d., and many others in
Northowram, Shelf, &c.

In Rastrick, John Hanson, Woodhouse, 16s. 11d. Thos., John,
and Robt. sons of Thos. Hanson, decd. 17s. Thos. Hanson of Brig-
house 3s. 9d. Thos. Hanson of Totehill 5s. 1d. Edw. Hanson 5s.
Thos. and Nich. Hanson, 1d. Thos. Broke 7s. John Goodyeare 3s.
Gilbt. Hoile, 20d. Thos. Malynson 19d., Wm. M., 2s., John M., 2d.
Jas. Towleson 4d. John ffirth 7d. Thos. ffirth 10s. 7d. &c. Michael
Slater of Hipp. conveyed a mess. to John Cowper of Deanehouse and
Edwd. Slater in trust for Michl. s. said Michl. Jas. and John Tolson
fined 40d. each for drinking on the Lord's day.

1611. Henry fferror, of Ewood, Esq. being dead, John his brother
and heir, of London, gent., paid heriot for 2 coal mines in Sowerby
and one in Hipp. grave. Ric. Brodeley took 1 rod waste under Lathe
in Hipp. Jane wid. Rob. Boythes of Bothestown, now wife of George
Rawden, of Rawden, held Nm. lands. John Horsfall and John
Appleyard 10s. each for not scouring ditches and mending the road at
Croftend in Hipp. John Armytage of Kirklees, Esq., surr. 5 closes in
Nm. to Ric. Sunderland of Coley Hall. Saml. Saltonstall of Huntak,
Esq., conveyed to the use of Ric. his son and Grace d. Rob. Kaye of
Wodsome, intended wife of Ric., Wynteredge in tenure of John
Appleyard, Nether Wyntercloses, Knowlheys, &c. (1 bov., 9 ac. 3 rds.)
also Osburnroids, &c., and lands in Horbury to Ric. Beaumont of
Whitley Hall, Henry Savile of Methley, Knights, Wm. Ramsden of

Longley, and John Carvell of Nunmunckton, Esqs., in trust. Nich. Flather of Brighouse, 12d. for placing 3 oxen on Rastrick
common.

1612. John Thornhill of Fixbye, Esq.,
being dead, his brother and next heir, Thos.
T., Esq. of Fixbye, paid 48s. 3d. heriot for
usual leases of mills at Brighouse, at 16s.
1d. yearly rent. Mem. that Ric. Brodeley
of Hipp'holme shall permit and suffer one
current or course of water discendinge
downe the highwaye leadinge to Hallifax at

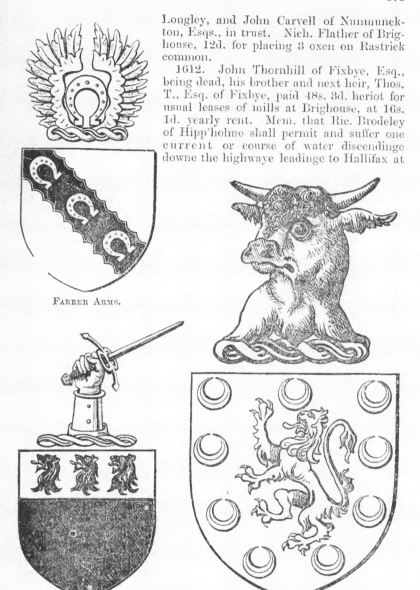

FARRER ARMS.

RICHARDSON (of Bierley) ARMS.

BEAUMONT ARMS.

Hipp. Townend to discende and run with the aunceyente course or current of water discendinge into the landes of Thomas Whitley formerly the landes of Sir Saml. Saltonstall as of righte it oughte to do upon payne of 10s. each tyme he diverts it into the road, and 10s. each tyme for damaging the road. Wm. Overall of Estwod in Rotherham, being dead, Rob. his son and heir paid heriot for 1 ac. 1 rd. at Lightcliffbroke, and Cliffhouse 1½ bovates, and 20s. for lands in Sowerby; his guardians during his minority being Wm. Routh of Wallswod, and Chas. Laughton, Aldwarck, gents. Thos. Whitley surr. mess., house, barn, backside, garden, fold, 6 closes—Brodecroft, 2 Westfeilds, Overnorthedge, 2 littleboylesales, to Edw. Walker for 10 years.

Court and Turn, Oct. 6. Jury, Henry Ramsden, Edw. Stancliffe, Wm. Drake, John Waterhouse, Rob. Sunderland, Thos. Hanson, Thos. Denton, Thos. Lockwood, Saml. Hoole, Thos. Woodhead, Edw. Molson, Geo. Haighe, Jas. Gleidhill, Ric. Soithill, Rob. Taylor and Edwd. Aneley. Arthur Elmesall fined 10s. for obstructing the running water at the end of his croft. Wm. Greave of Brighouse 10s. for obstructing the highway with his dung heap, (stercoraris suo). Michl. Thorpp and Wm. Walker for not coming to court at the constable's mandate, 2s. each. Nich. Flather, Brighouse, 1s. again for his oxen on Rastrick common. John Northend and Margt. his wife, of Hipp., surr. lands formerly Sir Saml. Saltonstall's, to Ric. a younger son of Thos. Whitley of Synderhill and Sarah his wife, a daughter of said John Northend. Thos. Hanson, Brighouse, surr. a new house in Soyland to Geo. ffirth for 20 years. John White of Hipp., and Eden his wife surr. land in Nm. to her brother John Hoile. Thos. Hanson fined 40d. for his cattle grazing on Rastrick common; he claimed a right on account of some Rastrick land.

1613. Danl. s. late Rob. Boothes, of Boothes-town, conveyed lands to his son Daniel. Edward Stancliffe conveyed his lands to sons and three grandsons named.

Edwd. Stancliffe, Scowte.

Michael, of York.   John.   Samuel.

Rob. Hemingway of Overbrea being dead, John his son and heir paid 9s. 10d. heriot. Halifax cloth-hall and corn-shop are mentioned.

Edward.   Ric.   John.

Surrender of lands in Sowerby by Henry Foxcroft and his sisters to Thos. Whitley of Synderhills.

Thomas ffoxcroft of Soyland ═ Alice, widow, in 1613.

Henry, of Kirkstall, a younger son, = Elizabeth.

Grace, = John Brighouse, of Brighouse.

Judith, = John Hoyle, of Burndmore.

T. W. of Synderhills let Eastfeilds, 2 closes, in Lightcliffe to John s. Rob. Hargreaves for ten years.

1614. Ric. Brodeley fined 20s. for watercourse diversion, and a special jury decided that the water from Richard's close called Paradice ought to pass through the ffenyes belonging to Thos. Whitley. Edwd. Waterhouse, Knt., s. Robt. W. of York, Esq., and Lady Abigail wife of Edw. surrender Nm. rents to Arthur Ingram of London, knight. Rob. Batt, of Newtontonye, Wilts, S. T. B., John Haldeworth of Blakehill, Nm., his sons Saml., and Jonas H. of Lightcliffe, clothier, take Blakehill, Howroyd, &c. in Nm., which were conveyed to Jonas Haldworth, of Lightcliffe. Thos. Whitley, Synderhills, surr. 8½ ac. in Nm. to his son John, and Miriam, d. John Blackwod, intended wife of John W. Hipp. village had to repair the highway from Place broke to Baliebrig on pain of 20s. John Haldesworth of Astey, gent., surr. 4 ac. in Hipp., paying 16d. rent to the lord, to Martyn Aykeroyde of Hipperholm, ffremason ; ingress 2s.

1615. John s. Rob. Hemingway of Ouerbrea being dead, his sisters and heiresses, Sibella, Edith, Phebe, and Martha paid heriot. Robt. Overall being dead, his three aunts, and his two cousins George Elwes and Ric. Rawson, paid heriot for

Wm. Overall	Frances	Elizth.	Winifred
	= Rob.	= Rob.	= Thos.
Rob. of Estwod,	Ash-	Elwes.	Rawson.
Rotherham.	more.	George.	Richard.

Lightcliffe and Sowerby lands. *Mem.* that Sep. 16 was the great flood in West Yorkshire, the Rivers Calder &c. overflown, stone bridges at Eland and Kighley and twenty wooden ones demolished. Rob. Hanson broke Hipp. pinfold four times, fined 13s. 4d. ; Arthur Elmsall had to pay 6s. 8d. for two like offences. A number of tenants in Dalton fined 1s. each for not bringing their draught horses at the road mending. Ric. Norcliffe and Nich. Flather of Brighouse for not ringing their pigs, fined 1s. each. Arthur Elmsall for diverting a watercourse fined 10s., and breaking Hipperholm pinfold, 3s. 4d.

1616. Wm. Northend of Coley, yeoman, surr. Ivinecarr or Grenewayclogh in Nm. to John N. of Nm.-fold for 20 years. John Hanson of Woodhouse, yeoman, and his younger brother Thos. H. of Brighouse, clothier, held lands. Ric. Wood of Coley, s. and h. John W., deceased, surr. mess., 6 acres in Ric. Broddell's tenure, and Ivencarr close in tenure of Wm. Northend of Hipp. to said W. N.

1617. Thos. Whitley, Synderhills, had to serve as Sowerby greave for his Soyland lands. Thos. Hirth of Boothroyd had removed to Kirkeheaton. Ric. Brodeley of the Lane ends, yeoman, surr. on the event of his death, Lane ends, two barns, a garden, close called Croft under the Lathe, Walloyne close, Wollyses closes (3), Little Southedge close, Woodclose, Claybutts, to Matthew B. of the City of London, his son and heir. This Matthew Broadley was the founder of HIPPERHOLME GRAMMAR SCHOOL. Under Halifax, Ric. Barrowcloghe hath not inclosed and railed the staires of his tavern at Loveles Lane, or street, fined 40d. Thos. Whitley of Synderhills, and Michael his younger son conveyed lands in Sowerby to Jas. Hoile.

1618. Before John Savile, knight. (Edw. Carye, knt., omitted.) On the death of Marmaduke Pereson, his widow and daughters claim 8 acres in Nm. in tenure of Wm. Field.

John Hanson, grocer, London, surrendered Rastrick Hall in the tenure of Robt. his brother, to said Robt., ingress 11s. 4d. Ric. Saltonstall of Huntwick, Knt., and Lady Grace his wife, surr. Preistley lands in tenure of Alice Mitchell, widow; Brokehouse, Oldroyd, &c. in Priestley, in tenure of Alice Stones, widow; lands in Preistley in tenure of Margt. widow of Robt. Fairebancke; Wynteredge with tentercroft and Wynters in tenure of John Appleyard, with a cataracta or waterweare from Copley broke (Coley mill), and ffurtherbrokehouse bothom in Preistley, to Ric. Sunderland: ingress 23s. 3d. Robt. Deane, of Eckesley, and his mother Isabella Saltonstall, widow, on the event of the death of Judith wife of Jasper Blythman, Esq., widow of Wm. Deane of Elland Hall, surr. lands in Nm. to John Crowther, M.A., rector of the church of Swillington.

Wm. Sympson, Northourum.

Alice   Agnes
⚭Marmaduke Pereson

Anna, co-heiress,   Margt.
= Christr. Cotes.   = John Warriner.

Wm. Dean ⚭ Isabel d. John Bairstow = Saltonstall, 2nd husband.

Robert, of Exley and   Wm. = Judith Hanson = (2) Jasper Blythman.
        Priestley.   bur. at Eland
    ⚭Ann ——   Mar. 7, 1633.

Gilbert,   Wm., Turkey Merchant, taken by Turks,*   5 daughters.
    lawyer.   afterwards by the Tartars.

Wm.   dr.   dr. = — Kirk.
    =Bishop
    Lake.   Robert.   dr. in London.

Deanhouse in Shelf, near Norwoodgreen, is so named from Simon del Dene's family, who bore for arms, Argent a fesse dancy, in chief three crescents gules.

Edwd. s. and h. Gilbt. and Margaret Hole of Brigroyd, Rastrick, paid 5s. heriot at his father's death. Wm. Northend of Coley, yeoman, surr. Ivencar (1½ ac.) in Nm. to Abm. Sunderland of the Middle Temple, London, Esq., s. of Ric. S. of Coley Hall, Esq., ingress 7s. 6d.; reconveyed the same to John Bentley.

1619.—Thos. Savile, Knt., chief seneseal. John Royds of Hipp., yeoman, surr. 2 acres at the Hilles, formerly his uncles'—John and Ralph R.,—to Andrew Gill of Lightcliffe, badger. John s. and h. Hugh Norcliff of Liddyate, deceased, surr. Lyddyate to Ric. Wilson of Lidyate, reversion to Sibill widow of Hugh, now wife of Wm. Ramsden,

*Hence the local expressions,—" He's a Turk"; " He's a Tartar."

COLEY MILL.

for her life. Thos. ffirth of Boothroyd, now of Brearley, yeoman,
surr. 4 closes, Rastrickfeild, Whiggingefeild, Over Brighowsefeild,
Nether Brighowsefeild. John Haldesworth of Astay, gent., surr.
mess., bovate, 9 acres in Hypromegrave to his younger sons Thos.
and Robert. John s. late Hugh Norcliffe quit claimed lands in
Warley to Henry Greenwood. Twenty-three persons fined 40d. each
at Halifax *Turn* for blood drawing. Ric. Scolefeld, Hipp., 2s. for not
attending when ordered by the constable. John Malynson of Hartshead surr. a house and ½ acre in Rastrick to Ric. Thorppe of Thorny-
allbrigges, clothier. Michael Brodeley of Norwoodgreen paid 40d. for
an affray. John and Leah Royd, of Hipp., conveyed 2 closes in W.
Speight's tenure, to Ric. Richardson of N. Bierley. (Grotesque faces
still adorn the capital letters.)

1620. Wm. Hoile of Rotherham, yeoman, and ffrances his wife,
widow of Rob. Ashmore, (see 1615,) surr. 1 ac. 1 rd. between Lightcliffe Brooke W., Ric. Wood's close N.; also ⅓ of mess. called Cliffhouse
and ⅓ of 1½ bovs., and rent of 8 acres in Sowerby to the use of himself
and wife. Wm. Richardson of N. Bierley surr. 2 closes and edifice in
Hipp. in Wm. Speight's tenure, of annual rent of 4d. to the King, to
to Sibille wife, and Ric. and Wm. sons of W. S. John Haldesworth
of Asday, gent., being dead, his son John paid heriot for lands in Nm.
and Hipperholme. John Thornhill of Rastrick and Jane his wife,
widow of John Ramsden, claimed lands. Thomas fflather of Brighouse, clothier, mentioned. John Dickson, of Lightcliffe, for the good
love, favour, and natural affection he had to Wm., Anna, Grace,
Maria, and Judith, children of Isaac Whitley of Lightcliffe and Maria
his wife, sister of said John, surrendered (by John Whitley of the
Sowwoodgreen in Hipp.,) six acres and buildings thereon in Sowerby
to Isaac, and Michael Whitley of Shelf, to be equally shared at his
death to said children. Rob. Rayner of Hartshead is dead, his son
Robt. paid heriot. Rob. Nettleton of Almondbury being dead his

four sisters paid heriot for lands in Holm grave,—*Jenetta* wife of ffrancis s. Matthew s. Roger Thewlis ; *Margaret* wife of John Horsfall of Heaton, s. and h. Wm. s. John Horsfall ; Thos. Pault's wife, and Robson's wife. Elizth. d. John and Margaret Horsfall *married* Peter Battie, and Ric. Battie of Knaresbro their son took some of the land.

Turn, Oct. 10. Jury, Henry Ramsden, gent., Wm. Whitley, Wm. Northend, Jasper Brighouse, John ffeild, John Mawde, Thos. Hanson of Totehill, Jas. Otes, Rob. Roper, Ric. Haldesworth, Saml. Appleyeard, John Hirst, Thos. Denton, Rob. Wood, Wm. Brookesbank, John Barraclough for not amending the highway and filling up a delf at Housedge (? Hovedge), 20d. John Nicholl of Linlands broke Rastrick fold twice, 6s. 8d. Saml. Hoile of Hoile House, Lightcliffe, conveyed (after his death) a bovate in Hipp., and Bowleshawe (6 ac.), in Nm., to his son and heir Saml., and to Priscilla d. John Cowper of Deanehouse, intended wife of Saml. junr. Rob. Hanson of Rastrick and Sarah his wife surr. Rastrick hall to Thomas H. of Rastrick his elder brother. Edw. s. and h. Gilbt. Hoile, of Brigroyd in Rastrick, decd., surr. 6 acres to Saml. Hoile of Briggroyd and Elizth. his wife, natural sister and heir of said Edw.

1621. John s. Hugh Norcliffe of Lightcliffe, and Sarah wid. and executor of Martin Aykeroyd, ffreemason, of Hipp., surr. lands to John Hall for 14 years. In Sowerby, Edward Holland, Esq., brother and heir of Ric. Holland of Denton, Esq., and Rob. Brearcliffe of Brearcliffe, Lane., yeoman, held lands. Edwd. Hanson of Netherwodhouse and Rob. H. of Rastrick surr. Briggroyd to Thos. H. of Brighouse, brother of John H. of Woodhouse (John's wife was named Jennet), with remainder to Thomas' children, Arthur, Ric., Judith, and remainder to his eldest son Thos.

John Hanson of Woodhouse, deceased ⊤ Jennet.

Agnes	Mary, decd.	Margaret, decd.	Katherine
= Ric. Law.	⊤Walter Stanhope,	⊤ThomasBrooke,jun.	d.un-mar.
	Horsforth.	Thomas, son and heir.	about
	John, son and heir.		1626.

John Hanson being dead, his four heiresses, two of whom being dead, their eldest sons took their place, paying heriot for Linlands, Netherwoodhouse, &c. Ric. Sunderland, Esq., Coley, claimed lands in Nm., Sunderland, &c., rented to Abm. Sowden, gent. of Middle Temple, London. John Hall broke Hipp. pinfold, 40d.; Ric. Brodeley not mending the pavement at Lane end grene, 10s.; John Midgley of Halifax drew blood from Wm. Ramsden of Lidyate, 6s. 8d. Arthur Elmesall the Hipp. constable, for not coming to the court in time, fined 6d.

1622. Jas. Wood of Hipp., and Isabella his wife surr. Westercroft in Nm. to Henry Northend, Nm. John Norcliffe of Lightcliffe and Edith his wife surr. lands in Nm. to Jonas Grenewood of Boothes. Isaac Whitley of Lightcliffe being dead, Wm. his son and heir paid 4s. 9d. heriot for Overmeasure, &c. in Sowerby, and great close in the

Eastfeild, Lightcliffe. Nich. Stancliffe of Hagstocks, Nm., took lands of Ric. his father, deceased, clerk, of Essington, son and h. of Jas. S. of Hagstocks. Thos. Hanson of Totehill being dead, his son Edwd. of Nether Woodhouse, paid 21s. 10d. heriot. John Hirthe and John Mallynson 1s. each, for playing at painted cards at Rastrick. Jenetta Hanson, wid., and her dau. Agnes Law, widow, fined 2s. for not ringing their pigs. Arthur Elmesall, Hipp., reported John Hargreaves, John Nicholls and Wm. Byns for not mending Soperhouselane, 40d. each; Simon ffairbanck and Hen. Scolefeld for the road between Lightcliffehill and Lidget Grene, 20d. each; and Simon ffairbanck, Gilbt. Brookesbank and Jasper Hoile, 40d. each, for not attending their days when the highways were being repaired. Nath. Sowwood and Sara his wife, lately of Lightcliffe now of N'owram, surr. 4 ac., (after Sowwood's death) in the tenure of John Longley, John Blagburn, and Andrew Gill, to John Haldisworthe of Hoile in Hipp'holme for 60 years, at a peppercorn (grain of pepper) rent at pentecost, if demanded. Thos. Hanson of Brighouse surr. land at Maydenstones, Soyland, to Margaret his wife for life, remainder to Ric. his youngest son; Netherwoodhouse and Heley wood and Inge to Thomas his son and heir, remainder to sons Arthur and Ric.; Okesgrene to son Ric.; and Middleynge and Hurst, Okesgrene, to son Arthur. Hugh Mallinson of Hipp., fined 40d. for not permitting the water at Bawdslosh to have its ancient course, to the damage of the highway. John Mallynson of Hartshead and Eliz. his wife, and Ric. Thorpp of Thorniall brigge in Brighouse, surr. a rode and edifice in Rastrick to Edmd. ffox of Totehill.

1623. Arthur, brother and px. heir of Thomas Hanson of Brighouse, paid 17s. 9d. heriot for Netherwoodhouse and Briggroyd. Ric. Sunderland, Esq., Edwd. Sowood and his son Nathl., and Thos. Whitley, formerly of Synderhills, held Earl Leicester's lands in Nm. formerly: enquiry report.

Court and Turn, Oct. 6. Thos. Richardson, Wm. Whitley, Michael Bairstow, Saml. Akroyd, and Abm. Wilkes fined 40d. each for breaking Hipp. pinfold. Wm. Judson, Jas. Dalton, Thos. Wood 6s. 8d. each for not filling up nor fencing delves at Norwoodgreen. Wm. Ambler of Hipp., clothier, and Sarah his wife surr. Netherynge, Nm. to Thos. second son of John Royd, Hipp. Halifax, Brighouse, and Kirkburton courts continued to be held on three succeeding days, but not always in same rotation. At Halifax, Thos. Watson had thrice taken water from the town well to the dyeworks (baphiam) of Henry Horsfall. Ric. Sunderland, Esq., Coley Hall, surr. two closes in Brianscoles, Nm., 2 acres in Saml. Etall's tenure, to Rob. Hemingway of Mithome. Henry Preston of Ealand surr. 3½ rds. in Hipp. to Henry Wilson of Ealand, *generis* of said H. P.

1624. Thos. Savile, Knight, head seneschal. Wm. Whitlee, junr., of Lightcliffe, s. and h. of Isaac, decd., surr. Greatclose in Eastfield, now in several closes, in tenures of Wm. Whitley, senr., and Rob. Whitley, to the use of John W. of Sawoodhouse, Hipp. Henry Hoile

L

of Worrall, brother and heir of Wm. H., of Rotherham, defunct, surr. after death of Francis wife of Wm. Carre, wid. of said Wm., her thirds of 1 ac. 1 rd. at Lightcliffebroke, Cliffhouse (1½ bov.), and Okenclough (8 ac.) in Sowerby, [Overall's estates formerly,] to Rob. and Elizth., son and dau. of late Rob. Ellwes of Wadworth, and to Rob. and Wm. sons of (Wm.?) Rawson of Brinsforth. Wee doe finde that there is three score graveshippes in graveshippe of Sowerby (ffortie in S., and twentie in Warley,) also that every helper is to pay to the head grave ffourepence for everie penny rent towards his service and charges as heretofore hath been accustomed. The list of 60 is then given. Rob. s. Michael Bentley, Halifax, being dead, his sister Hester, wife of Edmd. Brearcliffe, yeoman, paid 6s. heriot. John Bentley of Lightcliffe, s. and h. Rob. B. of Adderisgate, decd., and Hester wife Ed. Brearcliffe of Halifax, took Damhead in Nm. John Dickson, Lightcliffe, surr. 6 acres in Sourby to Isaac Whitley, Lightcliffe, and Michl. Whitley, Shelf. Ric. Sunderland of Coley Hall, Esq., surr. Carreynge in Preistley in tenure of Alice Mitchell, widow; Nearer brokehouse, Oldroyd, Knowlheys, in tenure of Alice Stones, widow; other Preistley lands formerly in Mgt. ffairebancke's tenure, now Rob. Field's, Prudence and Grace Fairbank's; also Winteredge, barn, garden, tentercroft, Wyntercloses (3), in tenure of John Appleyard; a waterweare to draw water from Copley brooke, and lands formerly Ric. Saltonstall's of Huntwik, Knight, east of Copleybroke, to Saml. Sunderland, gent., his younger son, and Anne, dau. Edw. Waterhouse, formerly of Preistley, deceased, intended wife of sd. Saml. Gilbt. Bridge fined 10s. for not mending the way between the Roger Spowte and Cliffhill foote, Hipp.; and John Baraclough for not cleansing the ditch, nor mending the way between his house and Rob. Rawnsley's house, 40d. Wm. Byns for placing a scabbed horse on the common, Hipperholme, 40d., and for not ringing nor yoking his pigs 40d. John Stocke's wife for breaking the lord's purc at Hipp'holme. Hugh Mallynson for drawing blood from Michael Pearson, 10s. Wm. Whitley, junr., now of Halifax, s. Isaac W. of Lightcliffe, decd., and Agnes wife of Wm. quit-claimed to John W. of Sowood house the great close in Eastfield; and Sowerby lands to Rob. Hargreaves of Lightcliff, chapman. John Wilson of Ealand and Sibella his wife, and Agnes Preston of Norland widow of Hen. P. of Ealand, surr. 3½ rods in Hipp. to Thos. Whitley of Synderhills. John Haldiworth of Hoile in Hipp., and Michael his son, took lands.

1625. John s. Edw. Northend, Nm., surr. Willroydhouse, Nm., to Wm. N. of Hipp. in trust. John Hargreaves, for encroaching on waste at Hipperholme Townegate, fined 39s.; Rob. Nowell, gent., and his wife, 39s., ditto. Affrays and blood drawing at Hipper. 5s. each,—John Norcliffe, John Watmough, Ric. Willie, John Best; and John Scolefield of Hipp. for one at Halifax, 10s.

1626. Wm. Rookes of Fixby, gent. Geo. Elwes surr. his share of Cliffhouse, &c., to his wife Alice. Nathl. s. Nathl. Sawood claimed Nether Hylelee, 4 acres, in Edw. Sawood's tenure. Rob. Nowell,

gent., broke Hipp. pinfold.   Rob. Hargreaves, Andrew Gill, Maria
Medley for not mending 'their ways' between Geo. Hargreaves' house
and Hellywellsike, reported.   Simon Fairbanke, Henry Scolfeld, Geo.
Jackson, Maria Medley, 5s. each, for road between Geo. Fairbank's
house and Lydgettgrene to Lydgett yate.   Ric. Pearson, Esq., and
Grace his wife, d. and co-h. of Edw. Waterhouse of Preistley, deceased,
surr. edifice and ¼ rod to Saml. younger son of Ric. Sunderland of
Coley Hall, Esq., which Saml. had married Anne, the other co-heiress.
Thos. Whitley surr. Eastfields, Lightcliffe, to Andrew Gill for 21
years.

    1627.   Michael Slater, Hipp., conveyed 2 acres in Hipp., to John
Cowper of Deanehouse and Edw. Slater of Wadehouse for use of
Michael s. said Michael, and Johanne d. Rob. Rawnsley, intended wife
of Mich. junr.   Jane wid. of Geo. Rawden of Horsforth, previously
widow of Rob. Boothe, took lands in Nm.   Brighouse *Vis. ffranci plegii
et Cur. Leta D.M. Regis cu' Turns tent. ibm* 2 Oct. (View of Frankpledge, court leet and turn.)   Jury, Saml. Hoile, senr., yeoman,
Arthur Hanson, Andrew Gill, Jas.Otes, John Sutcliffe, John Bairstowe,
Jere. Bairstow, Henry Nicoll, John ffirthe, Edmd. Dyson, Rob.
Aneley, John North.   John Whitley led water across the highway
between Thomas Sugden's lane end, and Belly Bridge against the
pain of last turn, fined 10s.   Saml. Akeroide broke Hipp. pinfold,
6s. 8d.   Robt. Nowell, gent., diverted a footway at Broadfeild head
and Sower Ynge topp, fined 20s.

    1628.   Before Thomas Viscount Savile, Baron of Castlebarre, chief
seneseall.   John Armytage, Esq., of Kirklees, Arthur Hanson of Brig-
house, and the rest of free tenants do homage.   Ric. Saltonstall of
Huntwick, knight, surr. ½ rod in Lightcliffe, north side of the *Street*,
leading from Halifax to John Rayner's house, to John Rayner of
Lightcliffe.   John Thorppe of Thornhill Brigge, was a juror.   Robt.
Tillotson and Mary his wife held Laverock hall lands in Sowerby, and
Jonas Tilson surrendered Crawelshawes there to John his son.   A
great trial of right of road was held at Brighouse, (written in English).
Beginning at Toothill Hall the road went by the Smallees, Lambcote,
Woodhouse clough, Over and Netherwood house, to Brigroyd and
Brighouse Brigge, and was an ancient highway: witnesses,—Thos.
Mallynson of Hartshead, husbandman, 4 score and 4 years old, born
and brought up at Totchill, lived within three miles of it all his life,
did lead hay with waynes, and did chop bowes of fruit trees and other
wood wch hee thought wd. trouble topp loads but was never challenged
for it, and went through Overwoodhouse fold and there were neither
gates nor stiles set there.   John Goodheire of Stainland, joyner, 4
score years old, lived at Rastrick most of his life, forelike testimony.

    Elias Watson of Overthwonge, clothier, 3 score and ten, born at
Brigeroid, and lived there till 26, &c.   John Oldroyd of Hanging-
heaton, clothier, 3 score and 14, lived at Netherwoodhouse seven years
in his youth, &c.   John Halme of thedge in Eland, clothier, 3 score
and 10, lived 8 years at Netherwoodhouse, &c.   Anthony Harrison,

Southowram, clothier, aged 59, lived at N'woodhouse and at Brighouse, servant to John Hanson twenty years ago, &c.

Thos. Whitley, Synderhills, surr. Crofte at backe of the house, Croftend, Bulfall, little Bulfall, Moreroids and Upper Northedge in Hipp. to Wm. Haldisworth for 20 years. John Jackson to amend the highway on pain of 12d. Saml. Akeroide fined 10s. for bad road between Hipp' wells and gatefold. Ric. Speght fined 10s. for drawing blood from Peter Thorpe, junr., of Sutcliffe Wood.

1629. Ric. Saltonstall of Huntwick, Knt., Henry Savile of Methley, Knt. and Bart., Ric. Beaumont of Whitley Hall, Knt. and Bart., and John Carvile of Nunmunckton, Esq., surr. Osbornroid, 6 acres, formerly John Rishworth's of Coley, Esq., now in Roger Bancrofte's tenure, to John Whitley of Sawoodhouse. John Thorppe, of Hipp., not coming to the turn by order of the constable, being one of the four men to serve, fined 12d. Saml. Akeroide fined 10s. for not mending the road between John Roid house and Northedge steele, and Hilsmire. John Wareinge* for affrays on W. Hopkinson, 10s., on Rob. Rawnsley, 5s. Michael Elmesall for taking partridges in Hipp. with a net and other illegal modes, fined 10s. Pains laid on Rastrick for overstocking the common: a horse was estimated at 40d. a week, a beast at 18d., a sheep 4d. A hogge or swine unringed at all times, and unyoked between May 1 and Sep. 29, 3d. a day. A draught (of horses) was estimated at 40d. per day, and those farmers having no draught were required to supply able persons when the roads were mended, &c., or pay 12d. a day. A day's work was such an amount as had to be given by boon labour in a day, and was at this time a fixed quantity. Those who gathered 'donge' on the wastes had to pay 12d. per burden. For breaking a hedge the fine was 12d. All tenants had to repair their hedges annually on pain of 40d. 10s. fine was imposed for scabbed horses placed on the common. Whosoever shall use any foote way betwixt Brighouse and Overwoodhouse where there is no set foote way shall pay 12d. Any not householders in our township having a horse on the common shall pay 40d. per week, for a cow 12d., sheep 4d. Whosoever keepeth any geese that shall trespass in the grasse or corne of his neighbours, fine 12d. No house to be let to a stranger without consent of the greater part of the inhabitants unless there be a bond of £20 to the churchwardens and overseers of the poor of the parish of Eland. No new house to be built unless there are four acres of common available for it.

1631. John Whitley had turned a horse of John Blagburn's and one of Thos. Kitchyn's into the land of Wm. Rookes, gent., Hipperholme, therefore fined £1. Court Baron of Thos. Leake, Esq., to the use of Henry, Earl of Holland, before Thos. Lord Savile, Baron of Pontefract. Ric. Wilson formerly of Liddyate being dead, his son and heir George, paid 2s. 10d. heriot for the east end of a messuage, called Liddyate, with fold, barn, greatynge, lathecroft, 2 acres, formerly Hugh Norcliffe's. Thos. Wood, Hipp., for not yoking nor ringing his

---

* Probably Waring Green gets its name from this family.

pigs, 40d.; for breaking the fence of Matthew Lome at Thornroyd, 2s. Thos. s & h. Thos. Whitley of Synderhills surr. a barn and threshingfloor, garden, fold, also three Westfeilds, Lower Northedge and the Hilles in Wm. Hird's tenure, to Wm. Hird for 21 years.

1632. Court Baron of Rob. Leeke and Wm. Swinsoe, gents., to the use of Gervase Clifton, Knt., and Bart. John Northend of Hipp., s & h. Ric. N. of Nm., surr. Pighells in Nm. to Edward N. of Nm., younger son of said Ric. John Jewett fined 40d. for affray at Hipp. with Wm. Haldworth, and Ric. Jowett fined 10s. for drawing blood from Jonas Wilson. Ric. Sunderland, Esq., Coley, surr. Horwithins, Nm., to John Priestley for 21 years. Matthew Mitchell of North-ouram, chapman, and Susanna his wife, held lands in Nm. see 1634. [He had married at Halifax, in 1616, Susan Butterfield, and their son Jonathan, whom they took with them to New England in 1635, when the boy was 11 years old, became a celebrated minister of religion, and is still referred as one of America's greatest worthies. Mather called him "Matchless Mitchell." He died at Cambridge, U.S.A., in 1668.]

1633. Rob. Elwish (Elwes), of Chesterfield, surr. Cliffhouse, 1½ bov., and 1 ac. 1rd. near Lightcliffebrooke to Rob. Hargreaves. Ric. Judson of Norwoodgrene received two tenants into one cottage, fined 20s. John Roides, Hipp., yeoman, and Leah his wife, surr. 3½ rods in Hipp., formerly his uncle's, in tenure of Agnes Clarkson alias Brooke, to Saml. Pollard, yeoman. *View of Frankpledge, Turn &c.* Saml. Hoile of Hove Edge, a juror. Rob. Hemingway of Mithom, yeoman, surr. 1½ ac. in Hipp., a house called Bothomhouse, a garden, p'rocke, three closes called Stanhoppe—Starrebancke, Wellcroft and Satlespring, and two closes in Bryanscholes to Jas. Mitchell, Nm., for 20 years.

1634. Court Baron of Gerv. Clifton, Kt. and Bt. Thos. Whitley of Sinderhills being dead, Jere. Oates and Anna wife of Jas. Oates junr., cousins and px. heirs, gave 41s. 3d. heriot for lands in Hipp., & Sowerby. Jane Northend of Southouram, wid. of Ric. N. of North-ouram, quitclaimed lands in Nm. to Matthew Mitchell of Nm., formerly of Southowram; see 1632. Thos. s. & h. Thos. Whitley, junr., deceased, of Synderhills, paid 41s. 3d. heriot for Thos. Whitley, senior's, property; Maria wife of Saml. Nelson, widow of Thos. Whitley, mother of said Thos. to have his custody. Mary wid. Francis Taylor of York, apothecary, surr. Skowte in Nm. to Michl. Whitley of Shelf. At the request of Thos. Thornhill, Thos. Brooke, Edwd. Hanson, Arthur Hanson of Brighouse, and Jas. Attye, a grant for 1000 years of parcel of land on Rastrick common was made in trust for the benefit and mainteynance of such preacher or minister for the tyme beinge as shall preach the word of God in the chappell of Rastricke com'only called Sct Mathew chappell from year to year, at 5s. 4d. yearly rent; and 4s. a month rent if there should be no minister. Twenty one acres assigned between Lower Coate, Clough and Roundhill; ingress £42. At Hipperholme, John Rookes and

Saml. Starke for shooting by engine and killing the game, fined **20s.** each. Ric. Hanson and Joseph Thorpp fined 10s. each for affray and blood-drawing. Ric. ffenix for affray and blood-drawing from Isaac Waterhouse, Timothy Thorpe, and Danl. Gibson 23s. 4d.; and Timothy Thorpp 3s. 4d., for ditto from Jennetta wife of Ric. ffenix. Thos. Wood of Hipp. for not ringing his pigs 4s., and 20s. for harbouring a runaway three days and three nights.

1635. Jeremy Otes, Oxford University (Braz-Nose Coll.), being dead, Jas. Oates junr., of Whynnyroyd, Nm., his brother and heir, paid 22s. 7d. heriot for lands formerly Thos. Whitley senr's., in Hipp. and Sowerby. Thos. Haldworth of Astay, gent., took lands in Hipp., in tenure of Saml. Bothomley, clothier. George Booth, clerk, and Robt. his son, clerk, and John Crowther, M.A., clerk, late vicar of Swillington, held lands in Nm. John Okel, vicar of Bradford, clerk, and Martha his wife, formerly wife of Ric. Batt of Spenn, gent., held lands in Nm. Wm. Hird broke Hipp. pinfold, fined 40d., and Nich. Batley, Timothy Gibson, Ric. Sunderland, Timothy Thorp, and Thos. Wood for affrays, 40d. to 10s. John Longley of Thornhillbrigge erected a cottage contra statute, fined £10. John Wilkinson and Henry Pearson, 20d. each, for fishing with a shove net.

1636. John Roide surr. lands in Hipp. to his youngest child Wm., and Martha and Hester his daughters were to be guardians of their brother. Ric. Sunderland of Coley Hall, Esq., being dead, Abm. his son, of High Sunderland, paid 17s. ingress. Saml. Hoyle, senr., Hoyle House, surr. Soperhouse in the tenure of John Hodgson, and Brownhill crofte, 3 rds., to Daniel H. of Hoyle House, his younger son. Saml. Watson of Rosedale, yeoman, surr. Horwithins, Nm., to his brother John W. of Scarbrough, yeoman.

Joshua Brooke paid heriot for lands of his deceased brother Thomas, late Hanson's. Robt. Asman (Aspinall) of Fixby mentioned. Rob. Aspinall was constable of Fixby next year.

John Hanson, Woodhouse, gent.

Margaret, a daughter.

⊤ Thos. Brooke, senr. of Newhouse, Hudd.

Thomas B. junr.   Joshua B. of Newhouse. s. and h.

Brighouse *View of Frankpledge.* Rich. Longbothome of Priestley, John Gleidhill, Lightcliffe, John Preston, Lightcliffe, Wm. Darwin, Halifax, Chas. Elliott, Hipp., John son of said Charles, fined 5s. each for making a way across the lands of Abm. Sunderland, Esq.

1637. Thos. Haldisworth of Astay, gent., surr. 4 closes in Hipp. and Nm. to John Lister of Overbrea. Saml. Nelson of Sinderhills, gent., and Mary his wife surr. lands in Nm. to Jas. Otes of Marsh, Nm., and Mary his wife. Wm. Royds of Hipp., and Beatrix his wife surr. 3 rods in Hipp., and the Hills, 2 acres, formerly Ralph Roides, uncle of John Roides, to Jas. Otes, junr., Whinnyroids. Alexr. Patricke, Hipp., for not mending the footway at his house and cawsey end. Abm. Sunderland of Sunderland surr. mess. at Preistley green, in the tenure of John Appleyard, to Samuel Appleyard his son ; and Winteredge to Ric. Appleyard, another son. Arthur Elmsall for not filling up a colepit on Norwoodgrene, fined 20s., and Ric. Judson 5s. John Turner, Hipp., fined 8s. for not ringing four pigs. Edwd. s. Rob. Hanson of Rastrick surr. 2 closes in R., called Towneynge and Overthreenookedclose in the tenure of Sarah his mother, to Wm. Thorpe of Sleadsike, yeoman.

1638. Nich. Smith of Hipp., yeoman, conveyd a plot (17 yds. by 15) and edifice in Hipp. to Saml. Sunderland of Coley Hall, gent. Saml. Hoyle of Hoyle House being dead, Saml. his son paid 13s. 3d. heriot for Bolleshawe (Nm.) and ½ bovate in Lightcliffe. John Okell of Bradford, clerk, Nathl. Booth of Popeley, yeoman, John s. and h. Tobie and Judith Booth of Boothestown, surr. Boothestown to Rob. Hall. Brighouse *V. Frankpledge, Court and Tourn*. Wm. Horton senr. gent. fined 39s. for diverting a watercourse at Houldroide (How-royd, Barkisland.)

1639. John, s. and h. Edw. Brearcliffe and Hester his wife, paid 7s. 6d. heriot for Nm. lands, his father being dead. John Whitley of Rooks took Sinderhills, in tenure of Judith Pannell. Michael Bentley of Siddallhall, yeoman, (formerly of Hipp.), his son Michael of Hipper-holme, yeoman, and the latter's son Michael, of Hipperholme, surr. Symcarr, Nm. to Elie Mawde of Warley, clothier. Michael s. Michael Slater of Hipp., and Jenet wife of Michael junr., dau. Rob. Rawnsley, surr. lands in tenures of Thos. Fielden and Michael Brodelay to Sarah wife of Thos. Richardson, dau. Michl. Slater, junr. Saml. Hoyle being dead, his widow Elizabeth, and Saml. the son, paid 5s. heriot for Brigroid, Rastrick. Thos. Rawson of Waddsworth, yeoman, and his sons Rob. and Wm., surr. Warlers and Allonroyds, in Lightcliffe, in Rob. Hargreave's tenure, to Thos. Sugden of Lightcliffe, yeoman ; and Cliffchill and Westheadley (Westheathley,) to Rob. Hargreaves.

1640. A John Rookes resided at Halifax. Saml. Sunderland of Coley Hall, gent., and Nichs. Smith of Nm., formerly of Hipp., yeoman, and Mary his wife, surr. the plot (17 by 15 yds.) and edifice in tenure of John Scott, Hipp., to Henry Wadsworth of Ovenden and J. Dene of Denholme, yeomen. Rob. Hemingway, Mitholme, and John his s. and h., surr. Nm. lands in tenure of Nathan Sharp to Jonas, younger son of sd. Rob.

1641. Grace Deane of Slead Hall, spinster, d. of late John Deane of Blakehill, Nm., surr. the auncient Oldhouse at Blakehill, barn, threshingfloor called Overbarn, &c., to Rob. Bairstowe of Nm. Judith wid. John Booth M.A., clerk, being dead, John his s. and h. of Lee-brigge, Nm. paid heriot 1s. PLAGUE. Mem. that respecting the inhabitants of the towns of Rastrick, Hipp'holm, ffekisby, Northou-ram, Shelf, Quernby, Clifton, Dalton, Hartshead, Stainland and Barkisland, the jury at Halifax report that the pest or plague is very prevalent within Hipp'holme and Shelfe. There was no court held at Brighouse in consequence in Oct., but on April 26th, the usual *View of Frankpledge, Court and Turn* were held, when the owners of lands between the houses of John Thorp and John Whitley were forbidden to cut the hedges next the highway on pain of 40d.

1642. John Kershaw was Hipperholme greave. Henry Hoile of Siglesthorne, clerk, surr. Nm. lands. Thos. Drake, rector of the par. church of Thornton-in-Craven, quit-claimed Highroyd, Nm., to Thos. Lister of Shibden Hall. Edward Emsall was constable of Shelf.

1643-4. Rolls missing. The battles of Atherton Moor and Marston Moor, and skirmishes at Bradford, Halifax, &c., may account for their omission or loss.

Touch Gun.

1645. Oct. 14. *Frankpledge &c.* No jury recorded; no constable mentioned. John B. of Southowram, s. & h. of Saml Bothomley of Preistley greene, paid 8s. 3d. heriot, his father being dead, for a house called Newhouse, garden, croft, Longyngclose, Hawroide close, Nether-churwellbothom, Lytlerydeing, and Overbanckes in Nm. Langdale Sunderland s. & h. Abm. S. of High S., deceased, and Elizbth wife of Langdale surr. Medleyhouse and 6 acres in tenure of Rob. ffearnsyde of Nm., to said Rob., his wife Grace, and son John. Timothy Thorpe

Capt. Langdale Sunderland, (Copied from the Oil-painting now in New Zealand.)

of Sinderhills and Mary his wife, widow of Thos. Whitley, junr., surr. Nm. lands to John Ryall of Midgley.

1646. Timothy Waddsworth, of Warley Hill, yeoman, took of the lord of the manor the minerals and colebedds in Hipperholme graveship at 15s., which John flarrer of York, Esq., formerly of Ewood, surrendered. Brighouse, View *Frankpledge &c.*, April 27. John Stocks of Norwoodgreene drew blood from Nathan Crowther of Nm. Langdale Sunderland of Rastrick, Esq., and Elizabeth his wife surr. Bermeshill, Nm. to Nathan Crowther of Nm.; and Brianscholes and Ivincarrs to Daniel Hemingway of Coley Hall, chapman, and Preistley greene in Saml. Bothomley's tenure to Henry Preistley of Preistley greene, the rents of Preistley green to be appropriated to his wife Eliz'bth Sunderland, dau. Thomas Thornhill of ffekisby.

1647. Daniel Hemingway of Coley Hall being dead, Danl. his s. & h. paid 7s. 6d. heriot for Bryanscholes in Nathan Sharpe's tenure, and Ivyncarrs. Arthur Hanson of Brighouse took of the lord a lathe at Brigroid, and Brigroidynge, Birkynge, & Heeleyynge, rented to Edwd. Mawde of Brighouse, yeoman. The names Hartshead-cum-Clifton occur joined, though two constables are chosen as usual. Jonas s. Rob. Hemingway of Mythome paid 9s. 9d. heriot for lands in Nm. and Hipperholme, his elder brother John being dead. Rob.

Hargreaves, Lightcliffe, surr. 6 closes in Lightcliffe, called Wharlers, Allonroides, to Thos. Sugden of Lightcliffe, yeoman. Langdale Sunderland of Coley Hall, Esq., re-conveyed High Sunderland and Coley to himself. John Whitley, of Rookes, surr. Osburnes, 6 acres, formerly John Rishworth's of Coley Hall, Esq., to Nathan W., a younger son; Oldroyd in Nm., 6 acres, to Joshua W. another younger son; the great close in Eastfield, Lightcliffe, to his sons Michael and John, with remainder to Matthew his oldest son.

COLEY HALL GATEWAY, BUILT THIS YEAR.

1648. Matthew Brodeley (founder of Hipp. Grammar School,) being dead, Isaac his brother and heir paid 9s. heriot for a messuage, garden, croft, underlathe, Walloyne, 3 closes called Wollyses, Litle Southedge close, Woodclose, cottage, Claybutts, &c. Timothy Thorpe of Sinderhills, yeoman, surr. lands in Stanley (Wakefield), to Wm. Thorpe of Sleadsike, yeoman. John Rayner being dead, Thos. his brother and heir paid heriot for a parcel north of a house in Lightcliffe in John Langcaster's tenure, north side of the highway leading from Halifax to Lightcliffe chapel, formerly Ric. Saltonstall's, knight. Brighouse *View of Frankpledge, Court and Tourn.* Jury, Ric. Ramsden, Thos. Sugden, Henry Preistley, Arthur ffourness, John Scolefield, Edw. ffox, Rob. Haigh, John Lumbe, John Northend, John Sunderland, John Meller, Rob. Hileleigh, John Dacres, Saml. Preistley, John ffirth. Saml. Grave of Thornhillbrigge fined 10s. for drawing blood from Henry Brighouse. John Brearcliffe of Halifax, apothecary, held Nm. lands.

1649. Saml., s. & h. Saml. Hoile of Hoile House, deceased, held ½ bovate and 6½ acres in Lightcliffe. Joshua s. & h. Jas. Otes of the Marshe, Nm., cousin of Thos. Whitley of Sinderhills, yeoman, surr. lands in Nm. and Sowerby, to Susanna wife of Simon ffairbancke, dau. said Thos. Whitley. Thos. Hanson being dead, John H. Rastrick, his son & heir, paid heriot 19s. 6d. Reported that Ambrose Cou'dall had erected a cottage on Norwoodgreene. Rob. Rishworth, yeoman, of Thornton, Bradford-dale, and Dorothy his wife, surr. Nm. lands to Joseph ffourness. Thos. Fairbanke of Flaxby in Craven, yeoman, s. & h. Simeon F. of Southowram by Susannah dau. Thos. Whitley of Sinderhills, surr. lands in Sowerby to Jas. Oates of Marsh, Nm. Saml. s. of late Saml. Hoile of Hoile House, Priscilla his mother, and Beatrix his wife surr. Bowleshaye, Nm. to Ric. Best of Landemere ; and Bancke, Comynge, and Halfakers in Lightcliffe to Abm. Lome, junr., yeoman, Brighouse.

1650. This is really, like the preceding, the roll for the following year mostly. English now begins to be the common language of these rolls. Three proclamations—" At this court it is certified that Ric. Sunderland, Esq., grandfather of Langdale S., Esq., held High Sunderland, Priestley &c., if any claim, let them come in and they shall be received. To this court cometh Langdale Sunderland of Acton, Esq., before the Rt. Hon. Ld. Vt. Savile, Earle of Sussex, High Steward of the Manor or Lordshipp of Wakefield, and taketh of the Lord of the Manor all those closes at Coley formerly John Rishworth's, Esq., yearly rent to the lord of 4s. 4d.; those formerly Edw. Kent's now in tenure of Ric. and Sam. Appleyard, Rob. Smith and Henry Priestley, yearly rent to the lord of 7s. 9d.; the Preistley lands formerly Edw. Waterhouse's in tenure of Wid. Deane and Wm. Walker, rent 6d.; also messuage in Hipp. formerly Rob. Sowood's, late in tenure of Jonas Rippon, now Jas. Brearley, rent 6d.: and several parcels purchased by Ric. S., grandfather of L. S., rent 12d ; &c., total rent 32s. 4d. ; fine for ingress £4 17 1 cb. (¼d). Joseph Bentley, Lightcliffe, clothier, surr. the Rydeinge in Lightcliffe to Henry Fletcher of Southowram, chapman.

1651. Brighouse *View of Frankpledge, with Court Leet and Turne* April 20. Hipper. Inhabitants there sworne say all is well. To this court cometh Isaack Brodcley and witnesseth on oath that Ric. Northend of Hipp'holme, yeoman, surr. Dec. 11., 1650, messuage, house &c. in Hipp. to Ric. Hargreaves and Mary Bairstow in trust for John & Susan, children of said Northend. Thos. Sugden, Light-cliffe, yeoman, surr. 3 Wharlers and 3 Allonroydes in Lightcliffe to Rob. Hargreaves' youngest son, Joseph; Nm. lands to his second son Rob. ; other Lightcliffe lands to Henry his fourth son. Nathl. Sowood had broken the pinfold at Hipp. Isaac second son of late Isaac Holdsworth of North Bierley, yeoman, took lands in Sowerby. Ric. Richardson, gent., Wm. Crowshawe, Edwd. Atkinson, Thos. Nayler did ride over the grounds of John Hoyle in Lightcliffe; fined 10s. each. Arthur Hanson of Brighouse did surrender lands at Woodhouse to Edwd. Hanson of Woodhouse, gent.

1652.   John Brashaw of Halifax hath killed a Bull unbayted, fined 40d.   Three persons at Heptonstall fined 40d. each for keeping a feast on the Sabbath day.   *Frankpledge, Court and Turn*, Jury, Thos. Sugden, John Hopkinson, Edwd. Brooke, John Hoyle, No'uram, John Hall, Saml. Hoyle, Saml. Armitage, Ric. Brookesbank, Edmd. Moorhouse, John ffirth, Thos. Priestley, Jas. ffourness, John Hoyle, Dalton.   Jere. Batley, of Hipp., did not yoke and ring his swine, 40d.

1653.   Mary wid. Danl. Hemingway paid 12d. for tuition (that is, leave to govern the affairs) of Daniel her son.   Samuel Sunderland of Harding, (Bingley), and Peter S. of Fairweathergreen, Allerton, for £300 paid by Timothy Wadsworth of Ewood, gent., surrendered lands in Nm.   Langdale S. of Acton and Elizth. his wife surr. Priestley to Henry and Jonathan Priestley, brothers.   Jas. Gleidhill and John Gibson fined 10s. for affray and drawing blood from Wm. Ainsworth, gent., and Joseph Firth, his man, Hipperholm.   Susan Whitley and Doro. Wilkinson did hearken Jeremy Batley's house; (eavesdroppers).   Ric. Thorpe, John Thorppe, John Wilson and Rob. Smith are appointed Ouerseers of the Highways for this present year.

Thomas Fairbank quit-   Simeon Fairbank, Southowram,
claimed lands in Soyland   ╤ Susan
to Jas. Oates of Marsh,   Thomas, of Flexbie in Craven, yeoman.
Nm.   ╤ Martha.

1654.   Langdale Sunderland, Esq., surr. Coley to Wm. Horton of Holeroid (Howroyd in Sowerby), and Wm. his son.   Joseph Bawmforth, leather sealer at Halifax, failed in his duties, in testing the leather.   Francis Priestley witnesseth to exchange of lands between Jonathan Priestley of Sowerby, clothier, and Henry P., of Halifax, yeoman, brothers, for lands at Priestley.

1655.   Ric. Appleyard of Winteredge, yeoman, took lands at Winteredge of the lord.   Wm. Horton, gent., being dead, his son Wm. took Coley and Hipp. lands.   Joseph, younger son of Rob. Hargreaves, decd., took Wharlers in Lightcliffe.   Thos. Whitley of Halifax, gent., surr. Northedge to Wm. Hird; little bulfall at Northedge to Jas. Phillips; Eastfield great close to Andrew Gill; each for 21 years.   Jeremy Bentley * of Eland, gent., taketh of the lord Netherwoodhouse.   Jas. Phillip fined 6s. 8d. for killing a hare; Ric. Hargreaves 3s. 4d. for not yoking and ringing his swine.   John Northend of Hipp. being dead, John his son and heir paid 6s. heriot for Nm. lands.   Certain legacies had to be paid at or in the south porch of the chappell of Coley.   Nathan Drake † of Carlton near Pontefract, yeoman, Feb. 6. 1655, surrendered ¼ rood called Godley, into the hands of the lord to thuse and behoof of John Hodgson‡ of

---

* M.P. for Halifax.   † See Drake's Diary of Pontefract Siege.   *Surtees Soc.*
‡ Capt. Hodgson of Coley and Cromwellbottom.

Southowrome, gent. Next follows a note on Hoofe Edge, but eighteen years have elapsed since these notes were taken, and I have not been since to finish the pleasant task, which I now leave for some future antiquary to complete. To Mr. Fairless Barber who urged me to commence this work, and to Mr. Stewart and Mr. Townend for favours then granted, the heartiest acknowledgments are due. The following is a reduced copy of the bill posted half-yearly and may serve to bring this chapter up to date.

———o———

MANOR OF WAKEFIELD.

Notice is hereby given

THAT THE

GREAT COURT LEET

Of our Sovereign Lady the Queen,

WITH

THE VIEW OF FRANKPLEDGE AND THE TOURN,

Will be holden at the ROYAL HOTEL, in

BRIGHOUSE

On TUESDAY, the 6th day of MAY next,

At TWELVE o'Clock at Noon, at which time and place all Persons inhabiting within the several Constabularies following, viz.--

Northowram, Shelf, Hipperholme-cum-Brighouse, Rastrick, Quarmby, Dalton, Fixby, Stainland, Barkisland, and Hartishead-cum-Clifton,

Are required to answer their Call or Essoign, or they will be amerced; and that at the same time and place will be holden the

GREAT COURT BARON

OF

SACKVILLE WALTER LANE FOX, Esquire,

Lord of the Manor of Wakefield,

Where all persons holding Freehold or Copyhold Estates within the said Manor, lying and being within any of the Constabularies or Townships above-mentioned, are required to answer their Call or Essoign,* or they will be amerced.

Wakefield, April 14th, 1873.   B. W. ALLEN, Printer, Wakefield.

———————

* Essoign means a justifiable excuse.

Here we would gladly have left the story of the great Courts held at Brighouse, for although their ancient glory had departed the form and name still remained; but before 1890 the half-yearly placards ceased to be posted, and small bills were sent to solicitors for suspension in their offices, and alas! the Brighouse Court was dropped out. The bill for 1892 announces that the Great Courts Baron and Courts Leet, *if held at all, which is not certain,* will be held as follows: Halifax, Monday, 25th April, and Monday, 10th October. Holmfirth, Wednesday, 27th April, and Wednesday, 12th October. Wakefield (Baron), 29th April, and 14th October. Wakefield (Leet), 30th April, and 15th October. The Constables and other Court Leet Officers are sworn in at the April Leets. Court days at Wakefield for copyhold business are held every three weeks. The words in italics tell the decadence as laconically as the Hebrew word Ichabod.

*[Frankpledge, mentioned on the last few pages, means freemen's surety. At fourteen years of age a freeborn male tenant had to get pledges for his fidelity, but afterwards the person's oath taken before the Sheriff was sufficient. Viewing the Frankpledge was examining the list of freemen.]

Sub-Manors.

FROM Saxon times it was customary to 'let off' berewicks or sub-manors, but these courts only controlled ordinary manorial business, and the inhabitants of the sub-manors had to attend the great manorial courts and especially the sheriff tourn.

RECTORIAL MANOR. The Priors of Lewes, Sussex, held Halifax Church and the rectorial manor, and regularly held the half-yearly manor court or halmote at Halifax. At the Dissolution of Monasteries this manor reverted to the crown, 1537, and was held for a very short time by Thomas, Lord Cromwell. It was leased to Robert Waterhouse by Henry VIII., and passed to his son John, grandson Robert, and great-grandson Sir Edward Waterhouse, who sold it to Arthur Ingram, Esq. To this manor Heporam, Shelf, Northowram and Ovenden contributed 6d. each, with tithes, fruits, sokes, mulctures, &c., in Heporam and many other places. One of the Ingrams became Lord Irwin, and the Ingrams of Temple Newsam own the manor. The lord insisted that corn should be ground at the Halifax mill, and one twentieth part of each stroke, or half-bushel, grown in the manor, and $\frac{1}{24}$th of hard corn, and $\frac{1}{30}$th of all other corn should be taken by the lord. The mulcture dish

INGRAM ARMS.

was to be regularly inspected at the half-yearly courts at the Mulcture Hall, near Halifax Church. Oats were to be dried at the lord's kiln at 4d. per horse load. The demands of this court were very galling to the Quakers down to modern times.

BRIGHOUSE MANOR. When this Berewick was formed, we have no traces, but in 1346 John, Earl of Warren, granted it to John de Eland, who granted it back to his father Sir John de Eland and his mother Alice and the heirs males of their bodies, with reversion to Philip Eland, Esquire. Dodsworth, the antiquary, whose MSS. are mostly at Oxford, but the one from which we are quoting is in the British Museum, No. 797, and written by his assistant Jennyns,) saw this Brighouse charter at Carlinghow, Batley, and it bore a seal of the arms of Eland, an escallop shell. Hanson, our Rastrick antiquary, one of whose note books is at Shibden Hall, also was at a loss to account for the origin of Brighouse manor. The Sir John Eland just mentioned was the knight who was murdered near Brookfoot, so we find a charter of 1363 records that John Savile of Eland, knight, and Isabel his wife, daughter of John de Eland, acknowledged the manors of Carlinghow and Brighowse to Thomas the son of John de Eland, knight, and to the heirs of his body, with remainder to the heirs of said Isabel. This Thomas is said to have been Isabel's half-brother. In 1373 Geffrey of Warburton, knt., and Alice his wife were plaintiffs to a fine, and John Sayvill of Eland, knt., and Isabel his wife, deforciants, of the same manors. The Elands of Carlinghow retained their interest in the manor of Brighouse, for Robert Ealand, Esq., held a court at Brighouse, June 28th, 34 Henry VIII. Marmaduke Ealand, gent,, son and heir apparent of said Robert, held one, Oct. 9, 29 Elizabeth. A pedigree of this Branch I have not yet seen, but in 1346 there was another charter wherein John s. John Eland, knt., had given the manor to John de Eland, knt., and Helen his wife. Was she a former wife? Alice is named above. At an Inquisition held at Pontefract 5 and 6 Philip and Mary, the Jurors say upon their oath that Henry Savile, knt., long before his death, was seized in his demesne as of fee in this manor and others, and that it was held of the Manor of Wakefield in free socage by fealty only. These fines were simply a method of transferring property.

Robert Clarel and Wm. de Kenerisworth gave to Hugh de Totehill and Joan his wife the Manor of Brighouses for their lives, and to John de Totehill their younger son after their decease, dated 1349. If this refers to our Brighouse, it shews that the Elands only got it as above in 1356. Sometime before March 5th, 1661, Sir John Armytage became possessed of Brighouse manor, for he held a court baron here on that date. The Armytages have continued to hold the court occasionally, till they disposed of the manorial rights to a Mr. Gill, from whom they passed by purchase to Mr. Kaye Aspinall in 1859, who named his house The Manor House instead of Quarry Mount. He held a court baron Nov. 20, 1861.

HIPPERHOLME MANOR. This manor was parcel of Wakefield manor down to Elizabeth's reign.* The Thornhills of Fixby somehow got this nominal manor, and held a court baron occasionally under Hipperholme Thorn. There would be more picturesqueness than dignity in this revival of an out-door hall-moot, for their power was almost *nil*. At one, held August 22nd, 1688, Sir John Armytage, Bart., and Joshua Horton, Esq., were amerced in 2s. 6d. each for non-appearance, and several others 1s. each. Another court was held Sep. 25, 1701. Watson states that the bailiff for Wakefield Manor collects yearly Earl Warren rents at Hipperholme, Fixby, &c., which some say were first paid for the use of candle-lights, but he properly considered them to be quit-rents. Hipperholme was free (2 Henry VIII) from paying toll, stallage, piccage, pannage and passage, being old demesne land in the Duchy of Lancaster.

FIXBY MANOR. Sampson de Wriglesford granted certain acres of woodland in Fekisby; and John de Wriglesford, in or before the reign†

---

* Harl. MS., 797, in the British Museum records Fines between Thos. Scargill, Esq., and Mary his wife, deforc., of three parts of the Manor of Hipperholme, &c., the right to Wm., Roger, and Richard, and the heirs of said Wm. 1434. Fine between Wm. Scargill, senr., Esq. and Elizabeth his wife of the same three parts to the same three persons, Wm., Roger and Richard.

† The Witnesses were Henry de Eland, Robert de Lyversedge, Robert de Hyperum, Henry s. Ric. de Eland, Robert his brother, Gamarli Flandrensis, Thomas and Richard his sons, Henry his brother, Jno. (Ivo) Talvas, Robert de Ardislow, Gilbert Grimbald, John Linthwayt, &c.

of Henry III, granted lands to Walter de Wriglesford, who granted a carucate or ploughland in Fekisby to Michael Bertwisell, and Henry son of Henry of Fekisby granted all his lands there and the marriage of the heir, to the same Michael, who by marrying Maud sister of the said John Wriglesford held Fekisby in demesne and service, homages, wards, &c., but had to give a pound of wax to St. Ellen's chantry, Almondbury. It afterwards came to William de Bellomonte, or Beaumont. A William Beaumont, knight, granted half the town of Fekisby, called South Fekisby, with wards, marriages, &c., to Thomas de Totehill and Wm. de Totehill his son. William of Thornhill (called Richard in mistake by Watson,) having married Margaret daughter and heiress of this Wm. de Totehill brought this moiety to the Thornhills, who got their name from their ancient homestead at Thornhill, near Dewsbury. The other half-manor was probably purchased, for it was found in 1577, by an Inquisition at Wakefield, that Brian Thornhill held Fekisby of the Queen, as Lady of Wakefield Manor, as the tenth part of a knight's fee, and that he claimed to have a manor in Fekisby. From him it passed in a direct line to the present owners. From Mr. Hanson's note books, we also learn that in 1294 and 1297 William Beaumont entered on lands in Fekisby which Robert de Hoderode held. In 1337 John s. Thomas de Shepley sued Wm. Totehill and Modesta wife of Thomas Totehill in a writ of right as cousin and heir of Robert de Hoderode for four messuages and three oxgangs, and two messuages and two oxgangs in Fekisby.

In 1292 John, Earl of Warren and Surrey, claimed free chace in Fekesby, Northourum, &c. In 1307 Beatrice d. Thomas de Fekesby gave 3s. 4d. relief for 3 acres on her father's death. In 1326 Thomas s. Wm. de Fekisby gave 3s. 4d. relief for two messuages and two bovates there. In 1333 Jone and Maud daughters of Richard de F. gave 2s. relief for messuage and eight acres. Wm. de Bellomonte gave to Thos. de Totehill the half of Fekisby, and James s. Hugh de Eland, knt., purchased six tofts in F., and sold them and others to Thomas de Totehill. Mr. Hanson was shewn in Jan. 1593, by Brian Thornhill, Esq., a deed sans date reciting that Thomas de Totehill (whose wife's name was Modesta) gave all his lands &c., in Fekisby, Rastrick, Hiperom and Lindley to his s. and heir Wm., with remainder to son John, with remainder in equal parts to his daughters who had married Sausermer, Hoyle, and Fleming of Bradley.

In 1343, William the son and heir having held the premises, Margaret his daughter and heir by reason of her nonage was ward under Earl Warren. In 1316 Thomas de Totehill recovered possession of a messuage and 9 acres in F. against Ric. d'Lisle (Insula) and Jone his wife and Alice d. Hugh de Fekisby, and against John s. Henry de F. The last named gave to Thomas de Totehill 1 rode and half, remainder to William and John sons of Thomas and to their sisters. Henry de Totehill's widow Avicia, and Maud and Beatrix his daughters released their lands in F. to Wm. de Totehill. Beatrix d. Thos. de Fekesby quit-claimed her lands in F. to Thos. de Totehill,

M

Modesta his wife and William his son. Wm. brother and heir of Robert de Meksborough gave to John s. Thos. de Totehill a mess. and half-bovate in F., with remainder to Wm. brother of said John, and to Beatrix and Isabel their sisters. Roger s. Wm. de Fekisby gave to John s. Dolphin de Bradelay 14 acres in F. and an acre in Fekisby fields. Elen d. Ric. de F. in her virginity gave lands to Thos. s. John s. Elen de F. John de Schepley released lands in F. to Sibil widow of Wm. de Totehill, 1340. In 1338 the King commanded William, son, and Modesta, widow of Thos. de Totehill that they give to John s. Thos. de Schepley six messuages and five bovates whereof Robt. de Hoderode cousin of John, whose heir he is, was seized. Agnes widow of John s. Henry de F. quit-claimed to Wm. de Totehill lands in F. Jone and Maud daughters of ¦Ric. de Fekisby, in virginity, gave lands in F. to Robt. s. Thos. del Wood of Fekisby. An indenture, 1361, between Wm. de Riley and Hugh s. Wm. Stevenson witnesseth that Wm. gave to Hugh all the land in Cliff, Bromcroft, Callercroft, and Withins in Fekisby and 5 acres at Totehill in Priestroodwood in exchange for Greenhill and 17 acres in Fekisby field. Jone widow of Henry de Stansfeld gave to John de Nottingham lands in Rastrick, Fekisby and Linley, 1430.

In 1479 it was found by Inquisition at Wakefield that Brian Thornhill held a messuage and four bovates in F. by knight's service. He died about that time, and Wm. s. John s. of said Brian, 16 years of age, was cousin (that is, grandson) and heir.

The Fekisbys had lands in Lindley cum Quarmby and Old Linley, for John s. Elen de F. gave to his daughter Eve lands held of Wm. de Werlewith (Wriglesford) and Thos. s. Elias de Lynley in Old Lynley. Witnesses, Hugh de Rastrick and Robt. de Bothomley. Henry s. Roger de Bradley gave to Henry s. John s. Elen de F. lands formerly held by Hugh s. Aldus in Linley—Witnesses, John de Eland, Henry de Rishworth, Wm. de Bradley, &c. (Mr. Hanson's Red Book.) Mr. Hanson saw a deed at Fixby in 1593, where feoffees gave the manor of Fekisby, and lands in Rastrick, Hiperom, and Lindley, to Margaret widow of Ric. de Thornhill for life, remainder to her son Wm., remainder to John Thornhill, son of Katherin her daughter. (This son would probably be legitimate as surnames were not fixed.)

TOOTHILL MANOR. This was held by Henry de la Weld, who enfeoffed William de Rylay with it in 1332, and the said William gave it to Ric. de Northland, chaplain, and John son of Eve, who conveyed it in trust to Henry de Savile and others. About 1360 it was the property of the Toothills of Toothill, from whom it passed by marriage to the Thornhills, like Fixby. Katherine Thornhill married John Leventhorpe of Leventhorpe, Bradford, having become possessed of the manor of Totehill. She and her husband reconveyed it to her brother Wm. Thornhill, 7 Henry VI. An interesting certificate is recorded by Watson of this reconveyance : " Forasmuche as it is meritory and needful to every Xptian man of every doubtful matter to bere record and wittnes of the truthe, that whereas John Leventhorpp was possessid and seisid of a mannor callid Totehill, with all their appurt. within the towneshippe of Rastrike, as in the right of Katerin his wieff, of the which mannor with all their appurt. beforesaid by thassent and consent of Katerin the wieff of the sayd John, mad a feoffment and graunt unto Wm. Leventhorpp son of said John and Katerin, with other, under the form and condicion that followes, that is for to say that the sayd William with other feoffers shold make a lawefull estate of the sayd mannor with all their appurt. to Wm. Thornhill, brother to the said Katerin and to the heirs of his body laghfully begotten, and that the children of the said John and Katerin to the said Wm. Thornhill and his heirs might more worshippfullye be receyvid and welcomid, I Sir Thomas Strenger, parish preiste of Eland, recordeth that the said Katerin disclosid hir will unto me att Schingildhall, that this said feoffment was made to the use and profitte of Wm. Thornhill, brother to the sayd Katerin in the form beforesaid : of the which will beforsaid to report and beare record the sayd Katerin gav me the sayd Thomas Strenger, fifteen pence. Sealled in the presents of John Gleidhill of Eland and Alice his wieff and many others." Wm. the son of John and Katherine Leventhorp of Sabrigeford in Hertfordshire, with the consent of his mother, quit-claimed this manor as above, 1429. From that time it has remained with the Thornhills of Fixby. The Toothills held lands in Shelf, Skircote, Ovenden, Rastrick, &c., which with any manorial rights that Rastrick ever had apart from Wakefield manor passed to Richard (otherwise William according to Hanson's notes,) Thornhill when he married Margaret d. and heiress of Wm. Toothill by Sibil d. and heiress of Thomas de Fekisby. The Duke of Leeds claimed the waste land at Bridge End when the chapel was built, but Rastryke, Hyprum, &c., are given as manors under Wakefield, 1 Ed. III. Cal. Rot. Ch., Lancaster.

Ric. de Toothill

Thomas, Matthew, lands in
 ᅟ=Modesta ᅵ Hipp..1314,1337.
Wm. ᅟ John
 ᅟ=Sibil, ᅵ
 ᅟ ᅵ d. ᅟ Hugh. He was Stew-
 ᅟ Thos. ᅟ ard for Hx. Manor
 ᅟ deFek- ᅟ in 1363, under the
 ᅟ isby. ᅟ Prior of Lewes.
 ᅟ ᅟ Thomas.
Margaret, married (Richard or)
 ᅟ ᅟ Wm. de Thornhill.
Toothill Arms: Or on a chevron
sable, three crescents argent; field
is given as argent on a monument
at Elland.

Askolf de Thornhill
 ᅵ
Jordan ᅟ For each of whom see
 ᅵ ᅟ fuller account in *Halifax*
Jordan ᅟ *Families and Worthies*,
 ᅵ ᅟ culled from Watson's
SirJohn *Halifax.* These pedigrees
 ᅵ ᅟ are given as a handy re-
Sir ᅟ ference to the family, but
Richard I prefer any statement
 ᅵ ᅟ in the foregoing rolls for
 ᅵ ᅟ accuracy.
Sir John=Beatrice
Sir Bryan
 ᅵ
Thomas=Margaret Lacy,
 ᅵ Cromwellbottom.

Richard (called Wm. in
Hanson's MS., but
Watson hasRichard)
⊤Margaret de Totehill
of Fekisby.

Wm.   John, Rector   Robert   Catherine = John
⊤Barbara Hopton.   of Thornhill.   Leventhorp
Brian
| *Arms of Thornhill*—Gules, two bars
John⊤Elizabeth Mirfield.   gemells, and a chief, argent. Sir Wm.
                     Fairfax gives, Gules, two bars, ermine.
William

John ⊤ Jennet, d. Nicholas Savile, Newhall, Elland.
b.1529
    John ⊤ Elizabeth Grice

       Brian = Jane Kaye.   John ⊤ Jennet d. Edmd. Marsh.
       d.1598
       s. p.   John, J.P.   Thomas, J.P.   Jane = Wm.Rookes,
                 died s.p.   ⊤Ann Triggot.   Royds Hall.

John,J.P.,Major Elizabeth = LangdaleSunderland, Margaret = SirJohn
of Agbrigg and   of Coley, Esq., Capt.   Armytage
Morley Regim't   in Royalist Army.   Bt.,
⊤Everilda Wentworth in 1650.   Kirklees.

Everilda = Thos. Horton, Esq.,   George, bap.   Frances, who printed
bap. at   Howroyd.   1655.   a Catechism.
Hartshead.   ⊤ Mary Wyvill

Brian   Thomas,   John   George succeeded to estates on his
       High Sheriff   brothers' deaths.
       1745.   ⊤ Sarah, d. John Barne.

Mary = Miles Barne.   Thomas, will 1790.   George   Sarah = SirJohn
                                            Blois.

The line of the Thornhills for the last hundred years may be learnt
from the following abstract of title to five cottages, Horsfall Buildings,
at the Well hill junction of Rastrick Common and Gooder Lane,
where my maternal relatives have resided a hundred years.

Thomas Thornhill, Esq., Fixby, made his will in April, 1790,
leaving his estates at Fixby, Rastrick, Lindley, Quarmby, Deighton,
and Calverley, in trust to his son Thomas Thornhill, to his nephew
Barne Barne and his brother-in-law (wife's brother) Wm. Lynne and
his brother George Thornhill. He died March 22, 1800. In 1835

HORSFALL BUILDINGS, RASTRICK COMMON.

Thomas his son married Clara Pierse, spinster, and had issue one child, Clara Thornhill, who was born May 20, 1836. For his second wife, Thomas Thornhill the son married Honoria Forester, spinster. On the 29th May, 1844, Mr. Thornhill the son died. His widow Honoria married Henry Hungerford Holdich Hungerford. In 1852 and 1854 Acts of Parliament were passed authorizing sale, leasing &c. of the Thornhill Estates. In 1855 Clara Thornhill of Fixby, spinster, in her 20th year, a ward in chancery, agreed to marriage settlements with Wm. Capel Clarke, who should assume the surname of Thornhill as the last and principal name and bear the coat of arms of Thornhill quartered. The marriage took place Nov. 20, 1855, and she attained the age of 21, in May, 1857. In July 1859, Mrs. Honoria Hungerford died at Pau, Basse Pyrences, and was buried at Dingley, Northants. Mr. and Mrs. Clarke Thornhill resided at Rushton Hall, Northants. They and Thomas Thornhill of Riddlesworth Hall, Suffolk, Esq., Dr. John Hodgson Ramsbotham, Leeds, Christr. White, gent., London, as Trustees, attest many Rastrick deeds of sale, or lease.

Hannah Worth, Enoch Bottom and John Denham held the Rastrick Common cottages on 99 years lease from 1857. John Denham of Huddersfield died in Nov. 1859, and Joel Denham, the heir, bought the cottages of Worth and Bottom and the freehold of all three parcels. He died in 1883. His widow Mary Ann, John D's. widow, afterwards Sarah Sykes, and John Wm. D., all of Huddersfield, gave them to Mr. Johnson Wilkinson her nephew, who sold them to me in 1892.

Kirklees Nunnery and Robin Hood.

KIRKLEES GATEHOUSE.

Though Kirklees is not within our bounds, its proximity and long association with Brighouse justify the following notice. Its owners have for a long time been lords of the sub-manor of Brighouse. Clifton upon Calder and Hartshead are both mentioned in Domesday Book, 1087. In Horteseved, Gerneber had two carucates of land to be taxed. There was woodland three quarentens square. In the time of King Edward the Confessor it was worth ten shillings ; now five shillings. Elsi held it of Ilbert de Lacy. In Cliftone, Eschelt had seven carucates, with woodland half-league long and three quarentens broad. Worth £3 in King Edward's time. Ilbert de Lacy has it *and it is waste*. These words re-echo the story of cruelty committed by the Conqueror in quelling the Yorkshire rebellion. The reader will be familiar with the names of many old Clifton and Hartshead families, as they were subject to the Court Leet at Brighouse, for the Warrens got the two places from the Lacies. The venerable Church at Hartshead, with its Norman remains, probably existed in Saxon times, like the Walton Cross close by. William le Flemyng or Wm. Flandrensis became possessed of the Manor of Clifton soon after 1100. Regnerus or Rayner le Fleming, his son, founded the St. Barnard or Cistercian Nunnery at Kirklees about 1155, and a William, Earl of Warren, confirmed the charter, and it was again confirmed by King Henry III in 1236. Dodsworth quotes the founder's deed thus—" To all the sons of holy mother the Church, Reiner son of Wm. Flemyng greeting,—Be it knowne to ye all that I

KIRKLEES GATEHOUSE.

Reiner Flemyng have given, granted and by this present charter confirmed in free, pure and perpetuall almes to God and to St. Mary and
to the Nonnes of Karkales the place in which they remayne to wit
Karkelay and Hednesley as the water of Kelder goes to the old myll,
&c." To this is affixed a brave seal with the donor on horseback.

NUNS' GRAVES, KIRKLEES.

Cistercian Nuns wore a white tunic or robe, a black scapular or head-dress, and a girdle. They led a very austere, silent, and diligent life, working in the fields as well as sewing and spinning. Elizabeth de Staynton is the first prioress on record. The Norman French inscription on her tombstone is illegible. Translated, it read, "Sweet Jesus of Nazareth, Son of God, have mercy on Elizabeth Stainton, Prioress of this House." Other prioresses have been—Margaret de Clayworth 1306, Alice de Screvyn 1307, Margaret Seyvill, Cecilia Hick, Joanna Stansfeld 1491, Margaret Tarlton 1499, Margaret Fletcher 1505, Cecilia Topcliffe 1527, Joan Kepax 1539. Dame Joan Kepast having surrendered the house in 1539, retired to Mirfield where she was buried in 1562. We have no means of compiling a list of the sisters, but when the Archbishop's rolls at York are printed or examined a long history of Kirklees and its supporters will be brought to light. Confirming this statement, I may add the following extract I came across under date 1491 :—"Confirmation of the election of Prioresse de Kirke-leghes on the death of lady Cecilie Hik, Dna Johanne Stansfeld Obediencia. In the name of God Amen I dame Johne Stansfeld chosyn and confirmed p'oresse of Kirkleghes of thordr of Saynte Barnarde of York shall be true and obedient to the moste reuerende fadir in God Thomas by the grace of God Archebisshop of Yorke primate of England and legate of the courte of Rome and to his Successors lawfullie entring a'd to their Officers and ministres in all manr of lawfull commandments so God me helpe and thies eu'ngelists." Amongst the Kirklees benefactors were Alan son of Peter of Culling-worth, Robert son of Gilbert of Barkeston,—the son of John son of Amandus of Shelf, Raimund de Medley, Robert son of Gilbert who gave annually a half 'skep' of frumenty, Sir John le Fleming who gave a serf named Alice, daughter of Wm. Mounger of Clifton, with all her belongings and her heirs, the witnesses to which deed, written soon after 1300 probably, were Henry s. Godwin de Clifton, &c. In 1374, Thomas de Malhum, Richard Brand, and Ric. de Calthorn, chaplains, had leave granted to convey to the Prioress and Convent of Kirkeleghes a messuage and 18 acres, &c., in Hertesheued and other lands. A full account of these may be found in Vol. 1., *Yorkshire Notes and Queries*. (Article by Mr. Chadwick.)

I do not find that any rents were paid out of any lands in Rastrick, Brighouse or Hipperholme. At the dissolution, "freely resigned" it says, but "forcibly evicted" was the spirit, John Priestley's widow was tenant of the Shelf lands, paying 13s. 4d. yearly to Kirklees. Thomas Savell of Clifton, gent., paid £114 to the King, Henry VIII, for Mirfield Rectory, &c., which had belonged to Kirklees, and he also rented the Priory grounds, but in 1545 the Kirklees estate, about 260 acres, was granted to John Tasburgh and Nicholas Savile for £987, and an annual acknowledgement of 13s. 4d. to the King. The Ramsdens of Longley obtained the priory possessions in Huddersfield, Hartshead, &c. Cuthbert son of Thomas Savile of Clifton, Wm. Ramsden of Longley and others were authorised to alienate Kirklees

to Thos. Gargrave, Esq., in 1547, who immediately conveyed it to
Thos. Pilkington of Bradley. Robt. Pilkington sold it in 1565 to John
Armitage of Farnley Tyas, yeoman. The Manor of Clifton descended
in 1307 to Reginald le Flemang on the death of Wm. his father.
John le Fleming being dead, Thomas his son did fealty, 1351, for
Clifton, rendering 20s. yearly and suit of Court every three weeks,
paying for relief 20s. In 1406 Thomas Fleming, Knight, was lord.
In 1420 Thomas F. did fealty for the manor. In 1523, Jone, wife of
John Constable of Clifton, Esq., obtained lands from Sir Walter
Calverley. Her daughters and coheiresses married as follows, Anne
to Anthony Thorald and Cecily to Wm. Reyner, who held Clifton, 38
Eliz. In 1632, Elizabeth and Jane, sisters of Sir Henry Savile, held
Clifton-upon-Calder, viz., Clifton Hall, two barns, 60 acres of land,
30 acres of meadow, 100 acres of pasture, 40 acres of wood, 100 acres
of common and moor. The Armytages became possessed of Clifton
mostly, by purchase. Hartshead owners have been Adam de Radcliffe,
who gave to his son Robert all his right in the town of Hertishest,
rendering a pair of white gloves yearly. Richard the son of this
Robert de Radcliffe sold his lands there to John s. Wm. Fleming,
1317, except land let to John Clerk, who regularly served on Brighouse
Jury. In 1333, Wm. de Aberford did fealty for tenements in Hertesheved purchased of Dionisia d. John le Clerk of Hertishead. Before
this date Wm. de Radcliffe gave all Herteshevet, to wit, 2 carucates
to his son Hugh, who had to pay a pound of pepper yearly as acknowledgement. Wm. s. John ffleming gave to Thomas son of said Wm. ff.
his Herteshevet lands, 1343. Robert Fleming, 1423, for 12s. yearly,
gave to Richard Brigg and Margery his wife land in Hartshead. In
1469, Wm. Fleming, Esq., conveyed Clifton Manor, after the death of
Thurstan Banaster who held it for life, to Henry and John Sothill,
Esquires, which lands were John Fleming's, Knight, father of Thomas
Fleming, Knt.

Three centuries ago, Dodsworth copied the lines :
" Clifton standes on Calder baneke And Harteshead on a hill,
　Kirkeleyes standes within the dale And many comes there til."
Another couplet has long been repeated, how long we cannot say—
　" Hartchit-cum-Clifton, Two cracked bells and a snipt un."
In Kirklees Park, near the Roman Camp and old Sand-pit, is the
grave of the renowned outlaw, Robin Hood. Some would have us
believe that no grave ever existed here, and indeed that Robin Hood
is a myth. It is the nature of some people to be sceptical. That
there was a Robin Hood and that he was buried at Kirklees, I am as
convinced as that Sir John Eland was slain at Lane Head or Brookfoot.
Not only does the earliest English literature give ample evidence, but
local tradition, and place names, reaching from Whitby to Todmorden,
and thence to Nottingham, support it. Into the story of Robin Hood
we cannot possibly enter, but must refer the reader to Ritson's " Robin
Hood Ballads," most of which have local colouring. Robin or Robert
was born at Loxley, near Sheffield, but whether he was son of William,

earl of Kyme, or of Waltheof, earl of Huntingdon, or of lower origin
must be left unsettled.

> "No man that cometh to this wood,
> To feast or dwell with Robin Hood,
> Shall call him earl, lord, knight or squire,
> He no such titles doth desire,
> But Robin Hood, plain Robin Hood,
> That honest yeoman, stout and good."

ROBIN HOOD'S GRAVE.

In our manorial notes we have seen how soon 'outlawry' was pro-
nounced for slight offences, and have come across many names to shew
that the characters in these ballads were based on actual inhabitants.
Sir Roger of Doncaster tried to poison Robin ; and if he was the Doncaster we have seen as steward of the manor, there was no wonder.
William of Goldsbrough's name I have often met with in old deeds.
Friar Tuck of Fountains, Much the Miller's son, Will Scarlet, Will
Studley, Gamwell the forester, Little John the Naylor, and George a
Green the Wakefield pinder are as true to life as any historical per-
sonage. Sherwood, Barnsdale, Kirklees, Brianschole and Sowerbyshire
woods afforded full harbourage for these outlaws. John de Kirkby,
the Royal Treasurer, in 1285, held an inquiry in the King's name
concerning the titles of manors, but met with resistance when he
demanded to know whence Earl Warren got his manorial rights.
Baring a rusty sword, the Earl replied, "By the sword our fathers
won their lands with the Conqueror, and by the sword we will keep

them." The story of the Elland feuds seventy years after this shews that an outlaw was a popular man, and was in little danger of betrayal. In 1288, Ralph, a forester of Sowerbyshire, was wounded so severely that his life was despaired of, and several men were arrested because, though witnesses of the event, they would not divulge the name of the man who wounded him. Long after Robin Hood's time we meet with notorious outlaws. The allusions to Lincoln and Kendal green cloths, and not to Halifax, which had not then become famous for its cloth as it soon afterwards did, are interesting side-lights in the story of ' the prince of robbers and gentlest of thieves.' No wonder that the Saxon descendants revered his name, when we remember the terrible havoc of Norman William, and the harsh game laws and cruel bondage before the days of the Black Death. Their brief holydays were brightened by the performance of Robin Hood plays by strolling players on village greens. Bishop Latimer, preaching before Edward VI., says, "I came to a place, and I sent word overnight that I would preach there in the morning for it was a holyday. I thought I should have found a great company, but when I came there the church door was fast locked. I tarried more than half an hour, and at last the key was found, but one of the people said, ' Sir, this is a busy day with us ; we cannot hear you. It is Robin Hood's day. The parish are gone abroad to gather for Robin Hood. I pray you hinder them not.' So I was obliged to give way to Robin Hood's men."

Robin Hood's day was May 1st, and we know what great rejoicings, that even the Puritanism of Oliver Heywood's time could not kill, took place around the village Maypoles, when the lads and lasses bedecked with boughs from the woods danced around the village May Queen. My great-grandmother told me what consternation was caused in Rastrick in her early days (c. 1785,) when the Brighousers had stolen their Maypole. Robin Hood enters into our general proverbs. "Many men talk of Robin Hood who never shot with his bow," that is, brag. "To sell Robin Hood pennyworths," is to sell at half value. "To overshoot Robin Hood," is to out-Herod Herod. As I shiver whilst writing these lines, I remember the force of the Brighouse saying, "Robin Hood feared nought but a thaw wind." Of course, I need not mention the Robin Hood and Little John Mills at Brighouse, nor the public-house near, where

> "If Robin Hood be not at home,
> Come take a glass (gingerbeer) with Little John."

This Little John was not the original Naylor, but John Walker.

In 1247, at the age of 87, the old veteran wended his way to his cousin, that is—relative, a nun, or the prioress of Kirklees to be ' blooded ' for pains he was suffering, which she did so effectually as to weaken him to that degree, (wilfully it seems), that he had only sufficient strength to summon Little John by a blast from his horn. From the upper window of the gatehouse he shot his arrow, to indicate the place of his burial. The building shewn in the picture can hardly be the edifice of 1247, however. His gravestone has not only had to be strongly railed to a great height, but bars were rivetted across the top to keep vandals away, who for various reasons, one being as a charm against toothache, desired fragments of the stone. Dr. Gale copied the epitaph on this stone nearly 150 years ago. The following is an exact copy of the wording taken from the stone in 1888 :—

> "Hear underneath dis laitl stean
> Laz robert earl of Huntingtun
> Ueer areir ver az hie sa genð
> an pipl kaulð im robin henð
> siek utlawz az hi an iz men
> vil england nivr si agen.
> obiit 24 Kal Decembris 1247."

These Arabic figures shew that the stone is not very ancient, but long centuries back Drayton sang of the Calder that—

> " She in her course on Kirkley cast her eye,
>   Where merry Robin Hood, that *honest* thief, doth lie ;"

and Braithwaite, in his Strappado for the Divell, 1615, speaks of the valorous George a Green, Pinder of Wakefield, thus—

> " How stoutly he behav'd himselfe and woulde
>   In spite of Robin bring his horse to th' fold.
>   His many Maygames, which were to be seene
>   Yeerely presented upon Wakefield greene,
>   Where lovely Jugge and lusty Tib would go
>   To see Tom Lively twine upon the toe ;
>   Hob, Lob, and Crowde the fiddler would be there,
>   And many more I will not speak of here."

We have often referred to the pinders, especially to the family that got that name from their office at Hipperholme, and the following lines from the ballad of George a Green will illustrate the character needed for that office. The ballad was printed before 1556.

> " In Wakefield there lives a jolly pinder,
>   In Wakefield all on a Green,
>   There is neither knight nor squire, said the pinder
>   Nor baron that is so bold
>   Dare make a trespas to the town of Wakefield
>   But his pledge goes to the pinfold."

The house near the stream, known as the gatehouse, is the only perfect relic of the priory remaining. The east and west gables are built of timber. From the survey made at the Dissolution we learn that there were very few glazed windows in the Nunnery. Some of the old oak was probably used in the present Hall which was built on higher ground shortly after the Armytage family purchased the estate. Visitors will be pleased to see two old coaches in the coach-house. These are about 200 years old, and the iron rims instead of being complete circles are fixed around the wheels in sections. The carriages were adapted for fording rivers. At the marriage celebration of the Prince of Wales, 1863, they formed a special feature of the Brighouse procession. The coachmen and others were dressed in imitation of

Robin Hood and his men.   "The Three Nuns" hostelry reminds the
Wakefield road traveller of
his proximity to the ancient
Nunnery, whilst the Dumb
Steeple, near Cooper Bridge
at the junction of the Huddersfield road, probably means
"Doomed Steeple," indicating that a doomed person
reaching this point was safe.
These places of sanctuary,
like the Cities of Refuge in
Bible history, were a public
benefit in lawless times, but
the civil authorities stamped
them out as much as possible,
and in 1548 they were totally
abolished. I ventured this
explanation of the name
"Dumb" some years ago,
and a local writer has since
accepted it as correct, but it
is not proven. At the beginning of this century the Steeple
was the scene of midnight
rendezvous for the Luddites.

DUMB STEEPLE.

Returning to Brighouse along
the Wakefield and Elland Turnpike Road, one of the old holy wells is
passed, now written Alegar, possibly Holycarr well. It is generally
pronounced 'Elliker.' This well used to be a very popular place of
resort for young people on Palm Sunday mornings, when bottles of
spanish-juice water were as numerous as the visitors.

Nor must we forget that half-mythical person the Hal or Fool of
Kirklees. Kings we know kept Fools, and our county-man Wallet
prided himself on being the Queen's Jester. The Rawsons of Bradford benevolently kept a half-witted hal, and Johnny Worrall of
Halifax was another. Our portrait has been passed down as that of
Johnny Worrall, and Mr. Eeroyd Smith (brother of two Brighouse
"Friends," now removed southwards,) affirms that it is wrongly
ascribed to Hal Pierson of Kirklees, except that they were much alike
in appearance as well as in office. Hal Pierson seems to have lived
at Kirklees Hall about 1730, but his memory is still kept alive when
any fool is described as "Warr ner t'Al o' Kurklas Ole," which being
interpreted means, "Worse than the Hal of Kirklees Hall." For
record of his tricks and sayings the reader may turn to Vol. I. of my
Yorkshire Folk-Lore.

A visit to quaint old Hartshead Church we reluctantly pass by, and
can but glance at Hiley, or Hilileighe, or Cross Hall, otherwise Clifton

Hall, the home of Percys, Stansfields, Saviles, Armytages, Hilileighs, in former days when its beauty had not faded away. Slight traces of its internal adornments in stained glass and plaster have remained to recent times.

HAL OF KIRKLEES.

This portrait was evidently drawn by Williams, the Halifax artist of last century, and probably taken from life, so that Johnny Worrall was likely to be the subject, rather than his friend at Kirklees.

But we cannot leave Kirklees without recording the barest outline pedigree of the family that has been so closely identified with it and Brighouse for three centuries.

Wm. Armytage ⊤ Katherine d. Henry Beaumont, Esq., Crossland.

John, Farnley Tyas, ⊤ Elizabeth Kaye, Lockwood.

John, d. 1624.

John, High Sheriff, d. 1650. Edward, of Barnsley⊤Elizth d.Ed.Hanson
John,of Barnsley,d.1664.

Francis,1st Bart. Elizth. = Sir John Savile.
= (1) Mary, d. Matthew Whitley, Shelf.
⊤(2) Elizbth. d. John Dransfield,Elland.

Sir John, b. at Hartshead, 1629, Francis, b. George, d. 1709.
High Sheriff, died 1676-7. 1631.

⊤Margaret,d.Thos.Thornhill, Sir Thomas, Samuel, bap. at Barnsley,
Esq., of Fixby. b.1673,became created Baronet 1738,
Bart.in1736,d. having succeeded to
SirThomas, b.1652, d.1694. s. p. 1737. Kirklees estate, d.
Sir John, b. 1653, d. 1732. Nine other 1747.
Sir George, b.1660; d.1736. children; the ⊤Ann Griffiths, bur. at
Madame Beatrice, b. 1664, sons leaving Hartshead, Nov. 27,
d. 1686-7. This young lady no issue. 1738.
kindly remembered the poor
of Hartshead - cum - Clifton, Sir John Sir George,⊤Anna Maria
and to this day, a certain slain in High Sheriff, d. Godfrey
number resort to the Hall on France, 1775, bur. at Wentworth,
St. Thomas' day, where, on 1758. Hartshead, Esq.
presenting two fresh eggs, aged 27. Jan. 29, 1783.
they each receive a quantity
of wheat for frumenty and Sir George, b. 1761⊤Mary, d. O.
6d. or 1s., as needs be. bur. at Hartshead, Bowles, Esq.
July 21, 1836.

John, d. 1836, May 31.
⊤ Mary, d. W. Assheton, Esq.

Sir George, born Aug. 3, 1819. Capt. Godfrey,
⊤Eliza Matilda Mary, d. Sir Joseph Radcliffe, Bart. &c.

George J., F.S.A., Chairman of L. & Y. Rail. Co.

Wills.

Having had a long spell at Wakefield Manor Rolls where I had the field quite to myself, but which will undoubtedly become the favourite exploring ground to future genealogists and antiquaries, I tried the wills at York by Mr. Fairless Barber's suggestion, as no one had searched them for the West Riding, except Dr. Sykes, and Genl. Plantagenet Harrison had spent some time amongst them, and Canon Raine had especially ploughed the field for the county families. Four volumes of Wills of chief families had been published by the Surtees Society, and since I finished my Bradford and Halifax extracts the Yorkshire Archæological Association has been induced to print the Index to the Wills. As the MS. index was far from perfect, from the first wills of 1389 to 1508 I copied from the books in which they are entered, each book being fairly a load for a wheelbarrow. From 1508, except 1514-1530 where the index was uncertain, I followed the index. Before 1490 the wills are mostly in Latin, and all bear traces of having been written by the priests.

1398. Wm. Bower, Halifax parish, administration granted.

1400. Henry Boye, Halifax parish, administration of goods granted.

1402, Oct. 5. Will proved of John del Burgh, Midgley, Halifax parish. In the name of God, Amen; he ordered his body to be buried in Halifax church; gave to the vicar his best beast and 40s., to the fabric 6s. 8d., for oblations at his funeral, 6s. 8d. To Thos. Burgh 33s. 4d. To John s. said Thos. 13s. 4d. To John Bothom 3s. 4d.; Margote de Bothom, 12d.; Wm. Otes, junr. 40d.; to celebrate mass for him 21 marks; for a window to be made in the chancel 10 marks; repairing the Library 10 marks; to the three chaplains 10s. To John Hudson 40d., Matilda Colyer 12d., Margaret Sprent 12d., John de Wroo 40d., Eva del Waddesworth 12d., Ralph of Halifax 12d., John de Berstawe 40d., John de Miggelay 40d., John de Kent 12d. To the House (Nunnery) of Kyrkleghes 13s. 4d. To the children of John de Lyndsay 5 marks, of Diote Drake 7 marks, Henry Gibson 6s. 8d., Alice de Brerelay and her sister 6s. 8d. Five marks for funeral expenses, 5 marks for the poor. To John Wyld's wife 3s. 4d. Rob. Carter and wife 12d. To Diote Drake, a cow, a patella, a coverlet. John de Lyndsey a cow. John Turnor's wife a cow. Hen. Batte's wife a cow. John Sladen's children, a cow. Wm. Dikson and John Dobson a cow. Ric. Thomas, senr., a cow. R. T. jun., a cow. John de Miggeley and Ric. his brother a cow. Rob. Wydhop wife a cow, &c. John and Wm. sons of Thos. Milner, two bullocks, John Milner senr., two oxen, John his son two oxen, Alice Ellisson wife two oxen, Janyn de Sowerby's son two oxen. Ric. de Miggeley aforesaid two oxen and 13s. 4d. Thos. Cappe one ox. He gives Isabella his wife 20 marks if she remain unwedded; otherwise the executors are to bestow it for good of his soul. To Jolina, an unmarried daughter, 2 marks if she marry according to the Executor's wishes. Bequests to

Margaret his daughter, and John his son. Robert de Prestlay and Margaret his wife, and Thos. brother of Margaret were closely related to him. Written July 12, 1402. John Kyng, vicar of Halifax, Thomas de Burgh, brother of testator, and Ric. de Miggelay were executors.

1402, March 14. Administration granted to Isabel widow of Henry Godlay, Halifax parish, and to Thomas his brother.

1402, Nov. 21. Gilbert Otes, Halifax, Wm. Otes executor.

1463, March 20, proved May following. Will of Wm. Haldesworth, senr., of Halifax parish; orders that his body be buried in Halifax church, and gives rents from Northouram lands to support the chapel of Blessed Virgin Mary. Mentions Johanna his wife, Ric. his son. Witnesses, John Brodelegh, chaplain, Rob. Egleslay (Exley), &c.

1499. Henry Kent of Wakefield took out administration of goods of Sir John Kent, vicar of Bristall.

1438. In dei nomine, amen, John Kynge, vicar of Halifax, May 14, 1438, gave his soul to the blessed Virgin Mary, and his body to be buried in John the Baptist church, Halifax. Bequeathed his best animal as mortuary gift. To Halifax church a book called ' pupilla.' Rob. Singleton, chaplain. This was the Hawking or Sportsman Vicar.

1459, 22 Aug. Administration to all the goods of John Rishworth of Coley, who died intestate, granted to John and Jas. his sons, and to Ric. Rokes.

1432. John Smyth of Bradford-dale, directed that his body be buried in Bradford churchyard; mentions Alice his wife, Wm. his son. Dated at Manyngham April 10th, proved May 7th.

1474, June 7. Written April 5th. John Lacy of Cromwellbotham, to be buried in Halifax church; gave to the vicar the best animal; 6s. 8d. for two torches to burn at the wake, 2s. for candles at his burial. To Rothwell church 6s. 8d., Methley church 6s. 8d., to priest at Elland 8s. &c. To Elizbth ffluntill 10 marks towards her marriage. Also to Jane d. Gilbt. Lacy 10 marks. John s. Ric. Lacy 40s. Geo. Kay 40s. Geo. Lacy 40s. John Rysshworth's sons and daughters, 40s. Brian Thornhill and his wife 40s. John Thornhill their son 40s. Granted an annual sum for a priest to celebrate for him, his wife, &c., in Halifax church. His son Richard, Gilbert Lacy, Persevall Amyas and John Rysshworth were executors. Witnesses, Rob. Ecclesay, Rob. Peke, Sir Thos. Oglethorp.

1470, Dec. 1. Ric. Bemond of Whitlay, mentions his sons Thomas, Ric., Wm., Robt., Christopher, and daughter Elizabeth.

1465. John Suthclyff, and 1467 Thos. Suthclyff died, both bur. at Heptonstall, St. Thos. of Canterbury church. The latter mentions his wife Johna, and sons Ric. and John.

1475. Administration to the goods of John Rissheworth of Hyppron, who died intestate, granted to Christr. R. March 4th.

1473. Will dated 1471 of Thos. Battes, Halifax parish; gifts to several churches. Mentions his wife Johan, brother Robt., sons Robt. and John, whom with Wm. Otes of Shepeden he made executors.

N

1478. Will dated Dec. 20, proved Jan. 20, next month, of Ric. Northend of Halifax parish, senior. Gave his body to Halifax churchyard, his soul to Almighty God, the Blessed Mary his mother, and All Saints. To Halifax vicar his best animal as mortuary. To the friars of St. Robt., Knaresbro' 4d., the minor friars Doncaster 4d., friars of St. D. de Toftes, York, 4d. To John Fox, clerk, 12d. Ric. Rode, clerk, 12d. Henry Greenall 12d. Wm. Presteley a russet cloak, Wm. Sharpp a green coloured cloak; Alice Wood a cow; Wm. Brodelee 6s. 8d. Rest to John the son, and executor. Witnesses— John Brestallw, John Lister and others.

1476. Henry Smyth, Manyngham. Ric. Gibson of Halifax parish was an executor. His children were—Persevall, Wm., George, Alice, Elizabeth.

1481. John Hawme of Eland directed that his body should be buried at Eland chapel. To John Prestlay his servant (famula) £4: rest to John Hawme, monk, his son. Witness, Robt. Gleydill, capellanus.

1477. Thos. Wilkinson, vicar of Halifax. Gifts to John W. of Eland, &c. Witnesses, John Sayvill of Sowtherom, gent., Edw. Lacy, John Barestowe.

1481. Rob. Waterhouse, Halifax, gave Thomas Horsfall a cloak, 12d. for a little bell at Halifax church. Johan his wife, John his son.

1402. John de Thornhill, rector of Thornhill, Will proved Sep. 5.

1476, March 12. Administration granted to Elizabeth widow of John Thornhill of fekysby, defunct.

1486. John Wolewrowe (see Hanson or Colier in the Rolls,) of Kirklethes, Will dated March 10th, proved 22nd. To be buried in the chapel at Herteshede. Gave 8d. for a mass at the chapel. To Cecilia Hyk, prioress of Kirklethes, 10s., the sisters there 40d., Cissota his sister 12d., for a little bell at K. 20d. Witnesses, Rob., Kepas, capell., George Raner, capell. de Herteshede.

1492. Richard Symmes, of Barnsley. Will proved Oct. 5. Mr. Ric. Symmes, vicar of Halifax, Gerard Lacy, executors; John Savile, knt., supervisor.

1492. Proved Oct. 6. Will of Gilbert Lacy of Halifax parish, desires to be buried at Halifax church. Johan his wife; Arthur his son. Witnesses, Brian Ballive, Wm. Redis, chaplains.

1494. Will written June 20; proved June 21, 1495. John Wilby, Halifax parish, compos mentis and sane memorie gave his soul to God, Blessed Mary and All Saints, body to be buried in the south of the church of St. John Baptist at Halifax. The best animal to Mr. Ric. Symmes, vicar, for mortuary. To Jas. Norclyff, gent., 26s. 8d. Mentions Johan his wife, John Wilby his bastard son. Thos. Gleydhill, chaplain, and Thos. Wilby his cousin executors. Witnesses, Wm. Rookes, John Stancliff, John Jepson, &c.

1496, Dec. 5. Admin. goods of Mr. Ric. Symmes, vicar of Halifax, to Wm. Symmes, Barnsley. The last named died Oct. 1501; Will proved Nov. 3rd.

1504, Aug. 12. Will proved of John Bonny, Hartshead. Buried at Hartshead. Son Christr., Rob. Auly, chaplain, and Thos. Bonny, executors.

1504. Robt. Otes, held cowroides near Gledeclif, Agnes his wife, Wm., Robt., Margaret, children. John and George, his brothers. Rob. Savile was one of the executors.

1507. Written Sep. 10, proved Oct. 30. John Mitchell, to be buried in Halifax churchyard. Agnes his wife, Rob., John, Jas., Richd., sons. Executors were Thos. Gleydhill, clerk, and Wm. Mychell. Witnesses, Gilbt. Cley, chaplain, Ric. Gleydhill, Wm. Wilkinson. "Proved before me Thos. Jenkynson, curate of Halifax." Jenkynson was afterwards vicar of Ilkley.

1507. Written Aug. 18, proved Oct 28. John Walker, Southworme (Southowram). To John Lacy, Esq., 46s. 8d. Witnesses, Edw. Kent. John Hanson.

1508, Dec. 15. Admin. goods, Rich. Fletcher of Brighouse, to Agnes his wife and to John Peresey of Hertshead.

1512, March 20. Will written of Alex. Fyrth. To be buried at Eland. Wife Isabel; sons Arthur, Wm., Umfry, John. Wills of Percival Firth, Eland parish, 1438, and Nich. F., Halifax parish, 1494 had been proved.

1509. Written Aug. 20, proved Dec. 14. Will of John Hanson, Sotherne (Southowram). Best beast to the vicar. Thomas his son two shoppes in Halifax. Ric., Rob., Geo., Edmd., Gilbt., Edward, his sons 40d. each. Richard to have the new milne. Sir Thos. Jenkynson, vicar of Ilkley, and Sir Thos. Gledehill, vicar of Connesburgh, Brian Otes and Edw. Kent, supervisors. Witnesses, Sir Thos. Jenkynson, John Milner, John Saltonstall, Ric. Hall, Christr. Waterhouse.

1513. John Hanson, elder, Elland parish (i.e. Rastrick). Mortuary gift as usual. To the bridge of Brighouse three trees, value 5s. To Elland church 4s. Executors, Kathrine his wife, John his son, and Thos. Baymont, Witnesses, John Bothomley, chaplain, (probably at Rastrick chapel), Henry flecher, Jas. Rawnsley, Jas. Hirst, Ric. Hanson.

1513. Richard Haldeworth made his wife Elizabeth, and John Waterhouse, executors. John Risshworth, Esq. was a witness. Wm. Haldesworth's will proved in 1468.

1509. Nicholas Bentlay, Hypperome, will proved April 26. Sir Wm. Bentlay, vicar of Hodersfeld, died 1466, without will.

1508. Edw. Best, Shipden died intestate ; Isabel his widow.

1515. John Boothes, Halifax parish. Gilbt. and Christr. sons.

1517. Ric. Fayrbank. Body to be buried at Heptonstall kirkyerde. Horse for mortuary gift. 40d. to his ffader at Kendall. 40d. to Sir Wm. Fairebank prest. to say a trentall of masses for his soull, and for another to be said at a chappel in "Kendall as I was borne, 5s." Alice his daughter, "and the chylde wh. Alys my wife gothe now great with iff itt please God to sende it to lyve." Witnesses, Wm. Farebank, prest, Henry Ferrer, Edwd. Fairebank, junr.

1517. Thos. Prestley, to be buried at Elland chapel. Margt. wife; John, Ellen, Margaret, children. 1536. Wm. P., bur. at Elland.

1517. Agnes wid. Robt. Brodeley; bequests to Thomas, Johan, Grace, Agnes their children. John Kent, Bradford, Edw. Kent, senr., and Thos. Brodeley, supervisors. Witnesses, John Barstow, chaplain, Ric. Eckylsley, Edw. Kent.

1518. Gilbt. Saltonstall, Shelffe, mentions his brother Edwd., and sons Edward, Ric. and Wm. Witnesses, Sir Wm. Alt, prest, John Saltonstall, Ric. Haldworth.

1518. John s. John Haldesworth gave his soul to God, our Lady, and All Saints in heaven. To Margaret wife of Rob. Boye, 3 con'letts, a blanket, 2 sheytts, a bedstok. To mending the ways about Halifax 40s. Ric. his brother, and many others, kindly remembered.

1518. Wm. Rooks (of Royds Hall) gave his soul "to God Almighty, our blessed Lady his moder and to all the holy company of hevyn, and my body to be buried in Bradford church;" gave the best beast after the custom of the country as a mortuary. To the high altar for tithes forgotten 20d. To Kirkwork of Bradford 6s. 8d. To chappel of (Cleck) Heton 7s. To Jennet Wylkynson his sister 9s. or a cowe. To Thos. Rooks, 13s. 4d., Gilberde Rooks 13s. 4d., Agnes Rooks 13s. 4d. His wife Anne, executrix. Sir John Tempest, Sir Thos. Strey, John Milner, Sir Thos. Eccope, preist, feofees for 8 years of lands in Shelf, &c. Witnesses, Ric. Rooks, Ric. Walker.

1521. Sep, 23., proved Dec. 3. John Turner, Brighouse, compos mentis, and sane memory, gave his soul to God Almighty, the Blessed Mary Virgin and All Saints, and his body to be buried in Elland churchyard. To the vicar of Elland he gave his best animal for mortuary. To the use of the said church 8s. Rest to Isabel his wife, and Wm. Beamont, executors. Witnesses. John Brokkysbank, curate, (of Rastrick, probably), Henry Flecher, John Wilton.

1521. John Brodle[y], mentions Alice his wife, John son, Jenet daughter.

1520. Rob. Deyne, mentions Agnes his wife, Wm. and Ric. sons.

1521. Jas. Symson appointed Jenet his wife, and Mr. Wm. Palden, maister of the Hospitall of Saynt John in Conventre, executors. Witnesses, John Waterhouse, Brian Otys, Henry Ferror.

1521. Alice Shepley, Hertshead, to be buried at St. Peter's, Herteshead. Her best whike goods (wick) for mortuary. John her son to be executor. Ric. her son to have 26s. 8d. at lawful age, and Edward, her son, 33s. 4d. Witnesses, Sir Robt. Aulay (the priest), Rob. Hanson, Laurence Hirst.

1523. Ric. Wilton, to be buried at Halifax; Johan his wife. Witnesses, John Mawde, W. Birton.

1526. Ric. Ambler gave 6s. 8d. to buy a book for Halifax church. Left Ambler Thorn to Alice his wife, Nich. and Robt. his brothers. Witnesses, Mr. Doctor Haldesworth, vicar, Sir John Birkhed parish priest, Sir Ric. Wilson, John Cockroft, Wm. and Rob. Ambler. Proved before Sir John Helewell, chaplain, Eland.

1526. John Hemyngway gave to Elene, wife of his son Ric. a close called Joneridynge; to John Hemyngway 4 stones of wool. Executor, his son James.

1526. John Mylner gave 5s. to byeing a masse buke to oure ladye altar in Halifax church. To Elizabeth Smith, his wife's daughter, a cowe. To John Smith, a pair of Walker Shires, 5 yards of blu clothe, and a cowe. John Wilkinson a blake calf. Wm. s. Rob. Milner to have rest of lease of Stoneroide mylne at 40d. yearly to Wm. s. Wm. Rayner, and give 16d. to Saint Antony light. Wm. his brother to have his Kendall Jaket. Gilbert Milner to have his Jake, Thos. Milner his salett and a paire of white hoise. Isabel his sister to have 40d.

1528. John Hemingway of Bray (Brea) forgave to his eldest son £4 6s. 8d. which the son owed him, and gave him 13 white carsies. To John Wis or Whys to remember me and pray for my sall, 40d. To Sir John Hemingway, and to Geo., his sons, £10 each. To Alice his daughter and her husband Edwd. Farebank a cowe, plough and yoke. To Jenet his daughter and her husband John Horton, a horse. Rest to Ric. his son. [It will be noticed that many of the yeomanry trained up a son to become priest.]

1529. John Thornhill, flixby, to be buried at Eland, Sir John Brokesbank, chaplain, a witness, and most probably he wrote the will.

1529. Brian Otes, elder, gave rents to Kirkwardens of Halifax 6s. 8d. yearly, for mending the hyeway between Halifax and Shibden broke. To Sir Gilbt. Clay and Sir John Brodlee preists, bequests. Also 6s. 8d. for a dirge in Halifax Church annually. To Alice widow of his uncle Chas. Otes, a blake gown. Elizth. his wife was executor. Witnesses, John Pek of Wakefeild, Esq., Sir Thos. Gledehill, Sir Rob. Skelton, Sir John Helewell, Sir Wm. Otes, preists.

1531. John Hirst of Gledholt mentions Edwd. and Thos. sons. Witnesses, Sir Peter Langfella, vicar of Huddersfeild, John Armitage of bridge.

1533. Thos. Northend, seke in bodie, hoole of mynd, directed the burial of his body to be in the middle Allay in Halifax Church, before the crucifix of our Lord. To the chapell of COLDLEY, 20d. to be putt to the most neddis thereof. To the freres at Thikhill (Tickhill) 10s., freres of Doncaster 10s., for xxx messes (masses) each. To Ric. his eldest son £3 6s. 8d. To Agnes wife of Rob. Vicars, a stone of wooll worth 5s. Isabel his wife, John his son, executors; rest equally to his children, Rob., Christr., Johan, Margaret, when of lawful age.

1533. John Bothomley, to be buried at Eland; Elizabeth wife; John, Jenett, Marion, children. Sir John Brook, priest, a witness.

1533. Ric. Whitley mentions John his brother, Elizth. and Isabel daughters. Margaret his wife, executrix. Proved before Sir John Helewell, Eland.

1535. John Haldesworth of Astey gave his sall to God Almighty, to his blessed moder and virgin our ladie Sancte Marie, and all holie

saintes in hevyn; his body to Halifax Church.   To Sir Christr. Haldesworth his son 20s. Wm. Brooke of Hipperon his son in law 20s.
Ric., Gilbt., Wm., sons, executors.   Witnesses, Edwd. Kent, John
alias Jenkyn Mawde.

1534.   Ric. Rokes of Rodshall. Body to SS. Peter and Paule
church at Bradford. My curate to pray for me after thacte of Parliament, 40d. &c. &c. To Heton chapell 40d. To Colay chapell 40d.
Rest, after benefactions to several priests, to William his son. Proved
Sep. 13, 1535.

1536. Proved May 15. William Blakburne's will. Appointed John
Smythe of Lyghtclyf, and John Roode of Hypperon supervisors.
Witnesses, Sir Wm. Saltonstall and Sir Edwd. Hoppay, priests.   To
the priests serving in the chapell called ESTFELDE CHAPELL (that is,
Lightcliffe,) 4s. per annum for twenty years from Bothum Ynge.
Mentions his wife Jenet, and children Jas., Edwd., Wm., Sibel and
Ann; and his brothers and sisters, Thos., Leonard, Alice, Margaret.

1536.   Rob. Auley, desired to be buried at Hartshead, gave 6s. 8d.
to churchwork; 20s. to prioress and convent of Kirkleghes, requesting
them to pray for his soul. To Ellen his sister a black gowne; sister
Agnes a marble gown; Elizabeth a black gown; Ric. Auley his godson
ten sheipe; Maistress Stansfeld a mare, a fillie, stagg, eight sheep,
a violet gowne, paire of linnen sheites, two pillows, two stone of woule,
a swarm of bees, and 20s. in money. To Sir John Trenchmyre a pair
of cloth hoise, Sir John Richardson ditto. Rest to his brother John,
and John's son, Gilbert.   Witnesses, Ric. Rayner, Rauf Blackburn,
Laur. Hyrste. Sir Robert had been priest at Hartshead.

1537. Edwd. Saltonstall mentions his sons Ric., Edwd., Wm., and
daughter Alice, wife of Henry Hoole.

1537. Ric. Best mentions Johan his wife, and Isabel daughter.
Witnesses, Sir Alexr. Emote (see "History of Haworth,") and Sir
Wm. Saltonstall, priests, and John Palden.

1537. John Holeroyde desired to be buried at Eland. Wm., Gilbt.,
Margaret, children. Witness, Sir John Brokesbank, preiste. Proved
before Sir John Helewell, capellanus, Eland.

1538. Wm. Holmes, glover, written 27 July, proved Sep. 26, ffurst
and principally I com'end my soull unto Christ Jhu my maker and
redemer in whom and by the merits of whois blissed passion is all
my hooll trust of clene remission of all my synnes, and my body to be
buried in Halifax Churchyard. This is one of the first wills written
in Protestant formula, and reminds us of that great event THE
REFORMATION.   To his sister Sebell Holmes, Sedbar, 13s. 4d.   Sebel
d. Ric. Brighous of Hypron 40s., said Robert 40s., Ric. Brighous,
Hypron, 40s. now in the hands of John Edylstones of Hypron.   To
Rob. Walker, Ovenden, my violett gown. To Sir Alex. Emott, preist,
one yrone chymney* now in the hands of Wm. Brodley by the water.
To said Ric. Brighous one Rowme in the 26th stall upon the sowthe

---

*Chimneys were movable commodities then; probably poor cottages were without
them.

sid of the middle Alley of Halifax Church. Bequest to Margaret d. Wm. Nicoll of Southowm. Rest to Jenet his wife. Witnesses, Rob. Brighouse, Wm. Kinge, John Palden, Rob. Walker.

1539. May 12, proved June 3. Henry Sharpe, N'ourum, gave his soull to God Almighty, Blessed Ladie Mary, and Holie company of Hevyn. To Jas. his son a longesettill and a great arke (chest). To Wm. and Agnes children of John Sharp two ewes. To his daughter, Wm. Cryer's wife, a whic; rest to Agnes his wife. Sir Alex. Emmote, curate of Halifax (formerly of Haworth), acted as surrogate for a large district, as Helewell of Eland had done before.

1540. June 30, proved Aug. 3. Wm. Brooke, Hyperon, gave his soul to God, Virgin Mary and All Saints, his body to have Christen burial in Halifax Churchyard. To his son Charles two bowes, a sword and a buckler. Rob. Otes his son-in-law, a cow and two calves. Geo. Ferneley, son-in-law, a bed value 13s. 4d. Agnes his wife to have her thirds. Rest to their 'childer,' Charles, Umfray, Ric., Jennet, Elizabeth, Agnes, equally.

1540. Ric. Bowtroide of Raystrike, pshe of Elande, soul in Catholic formula, body to be buried at Eland. Mentions Jenet his wife; children, Jas., Thos., Nicholas, Robt., Elizbth., Agnes. "Sir Thos. Ovington my gostlie father,* Mr. John Langton, Hugh Scolfelde clerke of the [Rastrick] Belfray Church," witnesses.

1541. Robert Hemingway mentions his wife Margaret, son John, daughter Margaret. Supervisors—John H., his father, and Wm. Haldesworth, his father-in-law. Witnesses, John Hemingway, of Breay, Thos. Waddington.

1541. John Smith of Lightcliffe mentions Jennet, wife; Wm., Rob., John, sons; Jennet, dr.

1542. Wm. Sonderland, Nm.; Alice his wife; Ric., Rob., sons; Alice, dr.

1542. Jan. 9, written Nov. 16, 1542. (The year ended in March then and long afterwards.) John Smyth of Lightcliff, sole and unmarried, of holl mynde, prfitt remembrance notwithstandinge the vexac'on of seknes do ordan and make my last will, giving my soul to Almighty God, bodie to the psh church yerde at Halifax. To Halifax Church 6s. 8d. Also I bequith to the nedes or repac'on of Estfelde Chapell 6s. 8d. To Sibell my basterde doughter £6 13s. 4d., Wm. bastarde sone 20s. Nich. Cook one of my lether cottes; John Kahyne one whitte cotte, John ffornes one whitt coite, Anne Kahyne one whitt cote, Thos. Coke my blake jackett without sleves, and my blake hatt. To evry childe to the whome I am godfather 4d. Thos. Smyth my sone and here all my meases, lands, tents. in township of Hipperome; all my waynes, carts, wheles, yokes, ploughs, harros, &c. and all tymber cutt or uncutt. To John Smyth my yonger sone, all lands &c. in Darbieshire for ever if the Kings Gracie Maiestie statuts will suffer the same. The said John Smyth to be my sole executor, with reversion of all my goods. On the day of my buriall to all neighbours and indigent poor resorting and comyng to the same fyve poundes sterling.

*Evidently curate of Rastrick.

I ordain and make my trustie frendes Richarde Roks of Idill and Robert
Smyth my brother supervisors, and assign to them governance of said
John Smyth my son and his goods during nonage, and give them 40d.
each. Thes witnesses John Hemyngwaye, Ric. Clif, Sir Jasper Hanson
(priest at Lightcliffe), Wm. Goodhall. Proved before Alex. Emmott,
Halifax.

1537, Jan. 3. Ric. Sunderlande of Hyc Sonderland, gifts to sons
Gilbert, William, Brian. Proved Jan. 10, 1543, before Sir Alex.
Emmott.

1544, May 2. Will proved of Richard Birkhede, giving his "soull
to God, verelie belevinge myself to be one of the chosen nombre that
shal be saved thrughe Christe." Elizabeth his wife, and towe eldest
sonnes Richarde and Martyne to have lands at Crofton, three younger
sons Thos., John and Robt., the lands in Halifax parish, provisions for
his daughters Anne, Sibell, Elizabeth, Isabell and Margaret. Overseers—Thomas Sauyell of Clifton, Mr. Ric. Pymonde of Wakefield,
Rob. Waterhouse, Halifax, Wm. Kynge, and John Best, preist, writer
hereof. Witnesses—Sir Wm. Saltonstall, priest, &c.

1545, June 26, proved July 30. Christofer Baroclougie of Hip-
crome, gave his soull to God Almightie, trustinge of clene remission
of my synnes thronghe the merits of Christs passion, and my bodie to
be buried in the churche yerde at Halifax. To Umfraye my sone, my
violette jackett, my grayc jackett and lether dublett, in full contenta-
con of his childes parte. Residue of all my goodes my detts paid, I
give and beqth vnto John, Isabell and Agnes, children. Ric. Roks of
Ydill and James Wodhede, supervisors. Witnesses, John Baroclough,
Jas. Knolls, Thos. Bowlande, John Wodhed, Edwd. Dobson. Proved
before Sir Alex. Emmote, curate, Halifax.

1545. John Palden, Halifax parish, made his brother Sir Ric. P.,
and John Milner of Pudsey supervisors of his will. Witnesses, Sir
Wm. Saltonstall, Ric. Milner.

1546, Nov. 23, proved March 1, next, Brian Stanclif of Lightclif,
seke in bodie notwithstanding holl of mynde and prfitte memorie loved
be god, do ordan &c. soull to Almighty God, his mother our ladie
sancte marie and to all the holie company of heaven, my bodie to be
buried in chyd. of St. John Bapt. Halifax, and to the vicar there I
give my mortuarie accordinge to the Kings gracie is acts. Grace my
dan. holl executrix, and give her all goods, cattalls and detts in whose
hands so ever except one third to my wife Isabell after the lawdable
custome of Englande. Witnesses, Nicholas Brodley, Edmunde Fare-
banke thelder, E. F. yonger, with others.

1546. Thos. Wodhead, Eland parish. Sir Ric. Northend preist,
witness.

1547. Proved May 5. John Homes, Norwodgrene, prishinge of
Hallifaxe, soull to God Almighty, St. Mary and All Saints in Hevyn,
body to Halifax Church. To Halifax Church repairs 40d. To brother
Ric. £6 13s. 4d. Ric. s. Raynold Hargreaves £3. Ellen his sister £2.
Ric. Hargreaves my brother-in-law 13s. 4d. Jas., Alice, Elizbth.,

children of said Ric. 6s. 8d. To Ric. Bene £6 13s. 4d. To my sister Jennet 6s. 8d. Sister Elizabeth 33s. 4d., Margt. Beu'laye (Beverley) £3 6s. 8d. To John Whitacres and Jennet his sister £2. Wm. Riley 6s. 8d. Sibell Hogge, 6s. 8d. To the ESTFELDE CHAPELL 8s. to be

LIGHTCLIFFE OLD CHURCH; built on the site of Eastfield Chapel.

one stok there. To brother Wm. £2. To the highwaie mendinge betwixte Kirkbie lone heade and plaice brige 13s. 4d. To Christr. Brodley's wife 6s. 8d. To Sir Jasper Hanson 40d. and to his mother 40d. To everyone of my god children 4d. John Wighall's wife of Yate 40d. John Crosley of Bingley 6s. 8d. George Myars 6s. 8d. Agnes my wel beloved wife the residue and one lease of Rokis Hall for terme of yeres that be not spent. Agnes my wife sooll executrix. John Broke my father-in-lawe, Wm. Beamonde, James Waterhouse and Henry Kent supervisors to see that noe man do her no wronge. Thes witnes Sir Jasper Hanson, Jas. Woodhede, Edwd. Dobson, Ric. Waterhouse, Robt. Beame, Wm. Riley. Probate by Sir Jasper Hanson curate there.

1549. Jas. Otes gave to Elizth. his wife, Jas. his son and heir, and Isabel dau., lands &c., langsettle, bedstocks. Witnesses, Sir Ric. Northende, preist, Ric. Brighouse, Brian and Ric. Otes.

1549, Feb. 10, written Dec. 24. Johana Thorpe of Lightclif, widdo, soul to Jesu Christe my maker and redemer in whome and by the merites of whose blessed passion is all my hooll trust to have clene remission and forgifnes of all my synes, and my bodie to be beried in the churche yerde of Halifax. I bequeath mortuary as usual. To John and Margaret my childer all my goods equally. I will that Margaret's part be put to John Wilton of Brighouse or as my frendes thinke the best. I make Wm. Thorpe and Edwd. Dobson supervisors.

Detts due to me from Jas. Haley, Halifax, £10 ; John Croder, Warley,
15s.; Ric. Northende of Hipperom 14s.; Ric. Heptonstall, Cliftonne, 6s.
8d.; Ric. Nailor of Scoles 7s.; John Holdesworth of Hoill 6s.; John
Barroclough of Houffege 4s.; Ric. Brodley of Thornyalls 20d.; Isabell
Fornes of Halifax, widdo, 13s. 4d.; Christopher Medley of Brighowse
7s.; John Michell of Halifax 20s.; Thos. Arondell of Shipden 12d.
Thies witnesses—Nicholas Appilyerde, Wm. Thorpe, Nicho. Brodeley,
John Thorpe, Edwd. Dobson, Wm. Baker.

1551. Wm. Rooks of Rods Haull, bequeaths lands at Reyvey in
the tenure of Bishop of St. Davids (Farrer, afterwards burnt at the
stake), lands in Wibsey, &c. to Johan his wife, and Wm. and Ric. his
sons, Anne and Elizbth. dau. Tristram Bollinge had married his
sister Anne. Sir Thos. Sharpe was to have his half-year's borde at
Royds Hall.

1551. Rob. Scoffeld, Lightcliffe, Augt. 20, gif and bequith my
saull to Jesu Christe oure God in whos blissed passion and by the
merites wherof is all my full trust to have cleane remission and for-
gyvenes of all my synes, and bodie to Halifax Church. Elizabeth my
welbelouyd wife to have her thirds. Rest to my six children, Anne,
Jane, Sibell, Isabell, Martyn and Henry. Supervisors, Ric. Brodley
and John Roods. Witnesses, Thos. Smythe, Gilbt. Hoole, Henry
Hemingway, Jaspar Hanson, clerke, writer hereof.

1551, Aug. 6, proved Dec. 9. John Walker of Lyghtlif, woullman,
(protestant form,) gave his wife her thirds of lands and goods. Son
John £10, the best horse, best panne, yron chymnaye. To John
Scholefelde my servant for his good service £8, and two of my horses
with all the geare, and £3 6s. 8d. of dett owing to me of Haine Hollyn-
prest. To John Walker now with me £5 at governance of John Roid
of Hipprom, and John Saltonstall my brother-in-law. To Edwd.
Schofeld 40d. Jennet d. Edwd. S. £1. Isabel his dr. 40d. Agnes
his dr. 2s. Wm. Grenefeld my servant 6s. 8d. Jenet, Agnes, Isabell
my daughters 42 marks when of lawful age. Witnesses, Thos. Smyth,
Ric. Dicconson, Ric. Otes, John Saltonstall, Jaspar Hanson clerk,
wryter hereof.

1551. Sibell Ryley of Heperem, widow. John Hogge my brother,
the best cowe. 20s. to the 6 childer of Christr. Ryley. Jennet Beamonde £1. Sir Jasper Hanson 2s. Sir Christr. Bentley 12d. George
Bollinge 2s. Rob. Kitchyn 12d. John Nicalls 12d. Henry Wilton's
wife, John Barroclough's wife, Agnes Rishton, Thos. Bollande, 6d.
each. Two godchilder 12d. each. Elizabeth Bolland one red coote.
Margaret Bridge my best petticote and 40d. Agnes Hogge the rest of
my best garments. Residue of goods to my father Ric. Hogge. Witnesses, Nic. Appleyerde, Edw. Dobson, James and John Woodhead.

1551. Sir Richard Blagburn lait chantry prest of Huddersfield,
now pensioner. Will proved, Mar. 16.

1552. Edmund Moldeson, Eland parish, gave 40d. to Jenkin
Royks, and 40d. to Raynald Teyller in peny or penyworth : rest to
Jenet his wife and Thos. his son.

1553. Rob. Hanson of Wodhouse in Eland Parish, in protestant form gives his soul, and his body to be buried in Eland Church garth near the rote of the old ewe tree near chancell doore. The Vicar of Halifax to have the usual mortuary. Whereas John Hanson of Huddersfeld, my nephew, owes me 26s.8d. for a parcel of land in Brighouse, late my deceased brother Thomas', I give it to the beldinge of one bridge standinge ouer the water of Calder betwixte Raistrike and Brighouse comonly called Brighouse bridge : 10s. at the commenct. of the buyldinge newe, 6s. 8d. when half-finished, and 10s. when just completed. To mendinge a waye called Lange doglayne betwixt Neyther Edge and Oldearthe close 6s. 8d. to be paid by Edwd. H. of Eland, my nephew. To mendinge of one waye in Brighouse, lienge betwixt the towne of Brighouse and Clifton bridge 6s. 8d., to be paid by my executors at such tyme as the inhabitants of Brighouse is or shal be mynded to make labor and coste themselues. To my brother John H., father of John H. of Huddersfield, I give an arke at Wodhouse. To John H. of Huddersfield a wyndle of rye. To John H. my cosyn, s. and h. of John H. of Huddersfield, one little chiste made of 5 or 6 bordes, ¼ yard long. To Edwd. H., Eland, a panne and windle of rye. To Ric. H. of Ovenden, my nephew, 6s. 8d. and windle of rye ; to his brothers Wm. 6s. 8d., Edward 6s. 8d. To Margt., Agnes, Anne, daus. of Thos. and Jennet Fraunce (which Jennet was sister of Ric., Wm., and Edward,) a cowe. Kathryne Malynson, another sister, a panne. To Thos., Wm., Jennet wife of Wm. Brooke, and Alice, children of Wm. Roger of Birstall and Margaret his wife, my sister, 26s. 8d. To my servant Elizabeth, sister of John H. of Huddersfield towe kie, one grete panne, one mashyne basyn, one brasse pott. On the 2nd Novr., and Good Friday after my deccase, three pecks of oitmell baked in brede to be given to power folks. Rest to Rob., Arthur, and Elizabeth, children of my brother John. Witnesses, Wm. Beamont, Brighouse, &c.

1553. John Hanson of Wodhouse in Rastricke, to be buried at Eland. Mentions his late wife Agnes, daughter Elizabeth, and son and heir, John H. of Huddersfield, to whom he gave a cupbord. His cousin (*i.e.* grandson) John s. and h. of said John H. of Hudd. towe sheepe. To John and Thos. sons of Edward H. of Eland my son 4 sheepe. Arthur H. my youngest son one sterk of one yere. Rob., Arthur, Elizth., my children, rest of the sheepe. Rest of goods to Edwd. H. of Eland, Thos. H. of Rastrick, and Rob., Arthur and Elizabeth, his sons and daughter. Witness, Hugh Gledhill, clerk, curate of Eland.

1555. May 16. Ric. Clyff, of Lightclif, seeke in body, (in protestant calvinistic form,) requires to be buried at Halifax. To Elizbth., Anne and Alice Ourall 40s. if they pay £8 to Margaret Ourall according to the will of their father, John Ourall. To Rob. Ourall a counter, yron chymney and a langsettle. (These things were luxuries at that time.) To Margaret Hemingwaye my servant 10s., and all my part of meane sheepe now in thandes of Rychard Heymyngwaye her

faither. I give to Margaret Ourall all my purchest londes, &c. in
Sowerby, and Ric. Bentley and Edwd. Hoille my supervisors to have
charge of Margaret Ou'all till she is 18; remainder to her systers,
Elizth., Anne, Alys. Witnesses, Edwd. Thorpe, Rob. Smyth, Edmd.
Fairbank.

1554. Ric. Hanson of Wolrawe, in protestant form, to be buried
at Hertshead, near my late father Rob. H. Alice my wife to have the
fermhold; and Thos. my youngest son the reversion of it. To my
dau. Elizabeth, wife of John Brouke of Dighton, a black cowe caulyd
Cuttocke for her canonical childes part. Robt. my eldest son to have
a pece of cloth and 20s. Gift to my nephew John H. of Ovenden.
Supervisors, Thos. and Rob. Smyth of Lightcliffe and John Hanson
of Huddersfield. Witnesses, Jasper Hanson, clerk; Rob. Hanson of
Woodhouse.

1555. Sep. 12. Richarde Brighouse of Hipperhome, thelder, (in
protestant form.) To John one of my younger sons, a mess. called
Greaffhouse in Lepton, and Roley lately bought of Robt. Beaumont
gent., with remainder to Ric., Rob., Edwd., Martyn, and Jaspar my
sons. To Edward also lands at Nether Whytley in Thornyll and
Heaton, lately bought of said Rob. Beaumonte. To Martyn and Jaspar
my youngest sons Norcliff in Shipdeyne, Southouram, and Nether
Rokkes, (in occupation of Edwd. Dobson and Nic. Appleyerd, late
bought of Anthony Rokes of Teilhowse Graunge, gent.); Styecalf and
Bothumhead in the lordshippe of Brighouse to his other sons. To
Isabel, daughter, wife of Brian Hardie 20s. yearly. Jenet, daughter,
wife of Wm. Pikkerd of Shipley, 20 marks; Sybill Brighouse, daughter,
40 marks of usual money of England or good pennyworthes. To his
grandchildren Grace, Isabel, Sybell, Agnes, daughters of Ric. Northend 20 marks to be shared equally. Rest to Agnes, wife, and Rob.,
Martyn and Jaspar sons. Witnesses, Wm. Haldysworth of Hipperholm, Christr. Northend, John Oytts, Ric. Rawson of Hipp'holme,
Brian Hardie, John Hanson. Proved July, 1556.

1556. Johna last wife of Ric. Gybson of Northourum (protestant
form.) To John Boys, Rob. Boys, Ric. Gybson, Edwd. Gybson and
Arthur Gybson my sons equally; and all that came to me by the
death of my brother Rob. Haldsworth, Vicar of Halifax.

1556. Nicholas Appleyard of Rooks, (in Catholic formula), directed
his burial to be at Halifax. Alys his wife to hold the fermhold.
Nicholas, John, Ric., Clare, Sybell, his children.

1557. Edward Mawde, Lightcliff, gave to Agnes his mother £13
6s. 8d. The lands freehold and copyhold to Anne his daughter.
Edwd. and Rob. Smyth 6s. 8d. George Haldsworth's wife 40d. Rob.
Hall my brother-in-law my best vyolett cote. Ric. Northend of Shipden
head to have charge of my daughter, along with Isabel my wife, his
sister. Rob. Smyth my brother-in-law, Ric. Mawde my brother,
supervisors. Witnesses, Rob. Bridgehouse, Christr. Snell, Thos.
Holtbye.

1557. Ric. Brodeley of Hipperome (in protestant formula) bequeaths his father's lands in Bradford-dale to his son Ric., Hipperome lands to his son Edward. Isabel his wife to have her thirds. Annuities to Elizabeth, Isabel, Sebell, Grace, Alys, daughters.

1558. Written July 11, 1556, (in Catholic formula), Wm. Beamont of Brighouse, to be buried at chapel of our Lady St. Mary at Elland. To the Hye Alter in said chapell for tithes forgotten, 12d. Joanna his wife remainder of lease of Peter Beaumont in Morley. Sons, John and Leonard. Witnesses, Thos. Wilson, clerk, vicar of Myrfeld, Sir John Trenthmeyer, preist, Thos. Beaumont, Lucke Longley. Proved before Sir Wm. Saltonstall, curate of Halifax.

1559. Wm. Clyff, younger, Halifax parish, to Wm. his father 40s., syster Alice 10s., syster Elizbth. 6s. 8d., Henry her son 6s. 8d., Sir Wm. Saltonstall, preist, 6s. 8d., Jenet sister of Sir Wm. 6s. 8d., her daughter Alice 6s. 8d. To Ric. my eldest son one copbord, counter, great arke, yron chymney, fether bedde, bolster, mattres. Similar bequests to his other children Edward, Anna, Elizabeth, Effame, Sybil, Margaret. His wife Alice to have her thirds. Bequest to " Mr. Richard Clyff my brother." Witnesses, Mr. Boyes prson of Gyseley, John Cockeroft, Wm. Saltonstall curet at Halifax. Proved before Mr. John Herryson, vicar of Halifax.

1559. Nycholas Scofelde of Lightclyff, hamlet of Hipprom, seke in body, of hooll mynde blessed be God but fearinge and mystristynge the incertentye of this caduke and tranestori' worlde maketh this my last will as ensuythe (protestant form) and body to be buried in Halifax churchyard not doutynge the same bodye shall aryse agayne at the genrall resurreccon a body incorruptable. To Isabel my wife and the child she is now wtall, lands in Hip'home townshipp and two parcels called Crymell and the Shais, and ¼ rode in Brighouses, holdynge by copye of Court Rooll of Maister Robert Eland, Esqr. Witnesses, Wm. Dobson of Soureby, Rob. Croslay of Lyghtcliff, Edmd. Fayrbank thelder, Lightcliffe.

1560. John Haldworth, clothier, gives Agnes his wife her thirds. Alice a bastard dau. beddings and 20 nobles. John his son, and Elizabeth his daughter by a fyrster wife to have the rest, except bequests to his sister Jennet, wife of Roger Jackson; Jennet and Jaune drs. of his brother Thos.; Agnes d. of brother Richard; Eve d. brother James; and to the youngest daughter of his brother Gylbert H. of Lightcliffe.

1560. Ric. Sunderland of Shelf gave 26s. 8d. to his brother Robt. for pore people; and two day warke of rie to his sister Alice, wife of Edward Longbothom. Residue to his brother Robert.

1560. Rob. Brodeley, Hipphohne, gave a quarter of rye to poore neighbours of Hipp'ome. After the death of his father Richard, the mess., 8½ acres of copihold; 2½ acres of Charlesland in Hipp'ome and Brighouse to go to Rob. his eldest son. To his daughters Isabell and Sybell 4 marks rent yearly. Rest to his wife Margaret, and Wm. his younger son.

1562.   Thomas Smyth of Lyghtclyff, gave to Margaret his wife the third of the freehold and copyhold in Hipp', Lyghtclyf, Brighouse, and Clyfton.   To my bastard sone Wm. Smyth £6 13s. 4d. when 21 years old.   To John and Thomas my sonnes, when John reaches 21, the lands held of the Queyns Maiestie and of Maistre Ellande, Esquyer. To John all my heirlomes in my mansion howse (Smith-house) in Lyghtclyfe as I founde thear. John Waterhouse and George Boythe supervisors.

SMITH-HOUSE.

Witnesses, Rob. Waterhouse younger, Rob. Bothes younger, Rob. Brighouse and John Cosynn.

1563.—Alice Hanson, wid. Ric. H., Wolrawe, mentions her son Thomas, and dau. Elizabeth wife of John Brouke.

1565.—Margaret Scoffeld, widow, of Whitwood, Hartshead parish, bequests to Isabel dr., Wm. son.   Witnesses, Wm. Kyrshay, Wm. Mylner, Thos. Leu'sege, Jas. Hayghe, John Hall minister at Lightclif chapel.

1565.—Christr. Northend, Hipp'ome, gave £11 to his bastard son Mychel, remainder to his son John.   Gilbert Saltonstall and Ric. Northend bro. of said Christr., to have charge of Michael.

1566.—Ric. Northend, clerk, Dewsbury, gives his possessions to his brothers Robt., Henry, and John.

1567.—Henry Savyll of Bradley in Eland, gave his copyhold lands in Brynscoles and Bolsha to Thos. his son.

1567.—Rob. Hanson of Wollerawe gave 12d. to the poore man's box at Harteshead, rest to Janet his wife, and children Ric., Sybell and Elizabeth, and one then unborn.

1568.   Rob. Sunderland, Shelf, gave Shelf lands lately purchased of Thos. Sayvile of Clifton, gent., to Ric. his second son ; and lands in Nm. to his youngest sons, Wm. and Edward, and to Alice, Agnes, and Margaret his daughters.

1568.   Wm. Hoyll, Lyghtclyf, thelder, sick in bodye of hole mynd and prfytt memorie thanks and prayse be gyven vnto God.   I gyve and bqueathe myself, my soull and bodye fully and holly into the hands of God Almightie my Maker and Redemer, and body to his onely sonne our Savioure Jesus Christ, trusting by his death and passion to have cleane remyssion and full pardon of all synnes, and my body to be buried in Halifax churchyard. Isabel my wief her thirds, and half the fermhold for rest of the term, and the other half to Wm. my son, being obedient to his mother. To Wm. all the lands, he paying 4 marks a year till it amounts to 20 marks, to the executors. Wm. Whytley my sone-in-law and Janet his wief one paire of lomes and one chymney and 13s. 4d. money. To Thos. Emsonne and Margaret his wief 40s. which amount he oweth to me. John my younger son, and Isabel my daughter to be executors. To Robt. Haldworth of Lightcliff, my best pair of hose save one, and my satyn cott (coat). John Ledall 4d. Edward my brother and Wm. Mitchell my brother-in-law, supervisors. With my proper hand, seal and mark. Witnesses, John Smyth, Edwd. Hoyll, Rob. Hoyll, Rob. Smyth, Wm. Mitchell, Gilbt. Hoyle.

1569. Wm. Haldsworth, Halifax parish, to Jennet H. my brother's daughter a read cowe. Wife of John Gybsonne my cosyn the black hawked cowe. Rob. Brighouse's wyfe the greater new chiste. Thos. Royde wyfe the lesser. Edwd. Stocks wyfe two metts of rye. John Thorp one mett of rye. Wm. Haldisworth a stroke of rye. Henry Greenwood, another stroke. John Brodeley of Winteredge one mette of rye. John Haldworth of Hoill my brother, supervisor. Witnesses, George Fairbank, John Northend, Thomas Standeyven, clerke, Edwd. Brighouse.

1570. Robt. Haldisworth of Hip'holme, gives to Agnes my sister, wife of John Gybson of Brookfoot, 10s. Lands to Hugh, my brother, for life. Bequest to John H. of Astay, another brother. Her feoffment to Elizabeth his wife. Bequest to his mother. John Hobkinson his father-in-law to be supervisor.

1570. John Haldsworth of Astey, leaves Astey to Robt. his son and heir, and Hipp'home farm to John, Hugh, Ric., Jane, Margrt. his other children.

1569. Ellen Hemyngway of Dovehouse, widow of John H., mother of Thos., Roger and Edwd. Waddyngton, younger sons, £20 bequest.

1569. Ric. Northend, Hiporn, seike in bodie, of good and prfite rememberaunce, prased be God, trusting for remission of synnes to Christ's passion, &c. To Agnes, wyf, her third part, and ane amberye and one great arke standinge in the seller. Rest to the children, Martyn, Mychael, Andrew, Isabell, Sibell, Agnes, Grace, Alice.

1572. John Tayte, Thornhill brigge, Eland parish, to Margaret my welbeloved wyf one half the possessions. To Jane Tayte my syster 40s. Poor of Halifax parish 40s. Brother Henry 40s. Thos. Crowder my servant 40s. Sybbell Tayte my sister 26s. 8d. Wm. Tayte my bastarde sonne or his mother Isabell Hall 20s. Henry my nevye 20s. Alice Crowder my maid servant 20s. Rest to Wm. bastarde sonne. Ric. Thomas alias Hawkstones 10s. Thos. Thornhill of Brighouse, Jas. Watehouse of Preestley, supervisors.

1573. Rob. Hoyle, lightclyff, of good &c. (protestant formula.) To Margaret, dau., a browne cowe and quye. Jennet, dau., a cowe and 8s. Anne, dau., cowe and an yron chymney. John, son, a black quye with a whithead, a chimney and a paire of lombes. Rest to wife Jennet, and said children. Gibt. and Wm. Hoyle, supervisors.

1573. In the name of the Father, the Sone and the Holy Ghoste, so be it, I, Richde Sunderlande of Highe Sunderlande, &c., &c., one of those elect and chosen persons wch ar to be saved, &c., give £3 6s. 8d. for clothing to poor of Northourum, ditto to Haworthe poor, . . To Richard my yonger sone one capitall messuage called Coldeley Hall, *als.* Coley hall, with houses, barns, stables, oxhouses, dovehouses, kilns, waynehouse, orchardes, tofts, crofts, closes called Edwardroide, Lane close, Winters, Harryroide, moorroid, hye trefelde, Northroid, Marldefeld, Olderoid, Tolleringe; Water mylne with the dame, gotes and courses of water, Lathecroft, and rights over Oxheys to travel to and from one water corne mylne, as I had from John Rishworth, Esq., Alexr. R. gent, his son and heir, and Beatrix wife of said Alex.; and lands in the tenure of John Thorpe which I bought of Rob. Sowwod and Isabel his wife, and also the windmill in Shelf; and such stalles, seates and clossetts whatsoeuer in Halifax church and Coley Chappell as I had with said properties; with remainder if said Ric. the son die without issue, to Abraham my eldest son, and to my daughters, Janet wife of John Hemingway, Agnes wife of Gilbt. Deyne, Mary, Grace, and Sarah. Bequests to his brother Edwd. S. of Halifax and Ed.'s children Ric., Edwd., Thomas, Mary, Grace. To John Beamont of Halifax, sone of John B. of Briggehouse, deceased, £16 13s. 4d. in custodie for said children of Edw. S. John Rishworth of N'owram, John Woode, Hipprome, and others, supervisors.

1574. Grace d. Ric. Sunderland of High Sunderland, gave £10 to John Rishworth of Bowthes for her sister; 10s. to the wife of John Rishworth of Lanehead, Haworth.

1573. Margaret Walker, Lyghtclif, gave to Isabel her daughter a fether bedd, foure pillowes, pair of shetts, two cou'letts, two blanketts, a mattress, and all 'myne apparell.' To her daughter Jenet wife of Arthur Patchett £6 13s. 4d. To John, Saml. and Mary, children of John Hoyle, £8. Gilbt. Saltonstall, executor.

1574. Edward Hole of Hole House, trusting in the merits of Jesus Christ for salvation; body to be buried at Halifax. To Hipperhome poor 40d. To Ric. my younger son, lands in Allerton, Bradford-dale, and a paire of lomes, an arke called a dustarke, and a pair of bedstocks. Gilbt. my brother and Rob. Thorp custodians of Oldfield, and lands at Leebridge, Halifax, for Henry, my younger son. To Margaret my daughter, wife of John Malynson, £6. Jennet dau. £6. John, son and heir, all waynes, plowes, yokes, harwyes, tenter, sideborde in gomehouse, one bourde lying of the Randletrees, a long forme £3 he owes me, and 30s. Jespar my younger son £18. Mary Aldersley my grand dau. one speldid cowe called flowereld. Gilbt. my brother my best felt hatte. Rest to Henry my son and executor.

1574. Mary d. Ric. Sunderland of H. Sunderland gave to Abm. s. Henry Rishworth 2s. Mary d. Wm. Tyllotson 2s. Edwd. S., my uncle, £6. Bettrysse his wife my aunt £4. To Wm. Tyllotson, clerke, and scholemayster to my brethren, in consideration of his good will towards my brethren, £10. Rob. s. John Rishworth 40d. John R's. wyfe, of Laynehead, Haworth, 20s. Christr. R., wolman £10. (Also numerous other gifts.) To John Woodde of Coolay, wolman, £4. To sister Jennet, John Rishworth's wife, a mattress, two blanketts, paire of shetes, two coverletts, two rodds, one reade gathered pettycote, a pair of black sleves, and one rayment of lynnen. To Jennett their daughter a reade pettycote. To John Wodde of Coley, 16 pettycotes, one wyndoclothe, ten sacks, two mattress cloths, and woll to stuffe one of the mattresses, all in the custodie of John Hemingway. To John Wodde's wife a felt hatt. John Rishworth of Boothestown, wolman, John Woodde, Coley, wolman, Abraham Sunderland her brother, &c., executors. Wm. Tylson, clerk, a witness. (Tylson and Tillotson meant the same name, and I believe Archbp. Tillotson and Bishop Tilson can be shewn to be of the same family.)

1575. John Horsfall of Woodhouse, Huddersfield, left the farmhold to his son John. Gifts to his other son George, his daughter Elizabeth wife of Thomas Broke. Gave 40d. to Huddersfield brigg, and 40d. to Cowper brigg for repairs. To Alice and Isabel d. John Horsfall of Fieldhouse two spurre rialles of gold. To John H. of Quarmby, my best shirte. To James H., my brother, the best jackett.

1575. Wm. Clay of Norland, mentions his father Thos., wife Margaret, and two sons, Thos. and Chas. Witness—Jas. Metcalfe, minister.

1577. Henry Clay, Greteland, mentions his uncle Thos. C., wife Jane, brothers John, Ric. and Thos.

1575. Wm. Thorppe, Brighouse, to be buried at Elland; holie church to have her dutie. Sibell his wife to have ½ messuage-houses in Brighouse and elsewhere in Hipperholme-cum-Brighouse during her widowhood, but only ⅓rd if she married. Rest to Ric., Adam, Sibill, their children, giving specially to Ric. pair of best lombes, and best walkersheres. Rob., testator's brother, and Henry Tayler his brother-in-law, supervisors. Witnesses—John Wilton, Rob. Thorppe, Richard Hoile, Thos. Brighouse, Addam Wilton, Geo. Dickessone, John Hansonne.

1575. Thos. Woodde, Hipp'om, mylner, to be buried at Halifax. Elizabeth his wife her thirds. George his brother, the best shirte, two paire of hosse, two tunic cotes,—one worset, another lether, two jackes or cotts, a felt hatte, girdell, and daggere. Thos. s. Gilbt. Barrocloughe 12d. Saml. s. Thos. B. 12d. Rob., John, Betteris, Margaret, his children, £9 each when of age, at the (over)sight of John Woodd of Coolaye and John Barrocloughe of Lightcliffe. Witnesses, Jas. Watterhouse, Prstlay, John Wood, Ric. Kente.

1575. Wm. Fourness, Shelf. Witness, Wm. Tilson, clerk, (?Coley Chapel.)

o

COLEY HALL.

1575. John Horsfield (Horsfall), Woodhouse, to Mr. John Blithe of Quarmby, Esquire, my maister, 13s. 4d. George my brother, and Geo. son of said brother, to have farmhold. John Broke, of Grenehouse, to have a dagger.

1576. John Wood, Collay, wolman, gave Ric. his brother the best coote and a dagger. Barthol. Wood some hose. Jenet, testator's wife, Marie dau., and child unborn to have the rest. Thos. Hall of Shibden was his brother-in-law.

1576. Richd. Bomforth, Lyghelyfe; Agnes wife; Geo., Henry, Ric., Anne. and Mary, children.

1576. John Smyth of Smythows was a supervisor of Thos. Bairestow's will, Shelf.

1576. Jas. Watterhouse, P'stlay, gave his body to Halifax church abyding the comyng of the Lord Jesus Christ. Mortuary to the Vicar. To the poor inhabiting about me, and to repair of highways 10s. Anne my wife her thirds. Robt., Michl., John, Thos., Mary, Grace, Margaret, children. To Thomas for his education and preferment one acre at Snakhill in Rastrick in the tenure of Ric. Rawnslawe, I late had by deed from Rt. Wrpfull Sir Thos. Gargrave, Knt., and Henry Savill, Esq. Supervisors, Rob. Baildon of Baildon, gent., Rob. Rayner of Ricroft, John Ramsden of Bowers. Bequest to Gibsons of Lambcote, Bradley.

1580. Jennet Saltonstall, wid., buried at Eland. Elizth. Margt., Edmd., Ric., John, her children. Ric. Hoole junr., overseer of will.

1582. John Lacy of Leventhorpe, Bradford, Esquire, (of Cromwellbottom family). Gifts to his children and grandchildren, shewn on the pedigree, but not necessarily in order of age.

John Lacy

Richard, John, Nicholas, Wm., Dorothy, wid., Elizbth,
=Waterhouse =Walter
Ellen | Hartley
John, Ann, Ellen. Mary

Rosamond, Ellen, Francys, Margaret,
=Thos. =Walter =Walter =Jas.
| Wood Paslew Paslew, Stansfeld.
or ?Thos. (on death
Leigh. of her
sister?)

To John, son of Richard, he gave the armourie, a corslet, two plate corslets with sleves, two bills or lead mules, one speare, one bowe, sheaffe of arrowes, a calever, and a chest with three locks with all the evydences in yt, and Ric. and John Lacy and Martyn Birkhead, Esq., were each to have a key, and all be present when it was opened. To his cousin John Lacye of Brearley, Esq., he gave a fishinge nett. To Walter Tempest a gelding called grayface.

1582. Written 1577. Nicholas Appleyarde, Lyghclyff, gives his brothers John and Thos., and brother-in-law John Gleydell, 16s. each, rest to his wife Margaret. John Hodgson, of Wakefield, owed him 10s.

1583. Ric. Stevenson of Brighous, body to be buried at Ealand, among the bodies of the faithful. To Jannet his wife ½. For repair of Thorniall brige 12d. Thos. Hanson of Rastrick, and John Gibson of Lambcote, supervisors. Witnesses, Thos. Brighouse, John Hanson elder, John Wilson, Henry Haighe.

1585. Isabell youngest dr. John Walker, late decd., of Lyghtclyffe, gave to Saml. yonger son of John Hoyll all her lands in Townfield of Wharnbie (Quarmby), and in North Crosland. To Mary dr. said John Hoyll the household goods (except a bed), the best cassocke, best petticote, and best hatt. To Janet Scolfeld servant to said John Hoyll, a bedd, mattres, two cou'letts, two blanketts, pair of sheetts, and 30s. in Gilbt. Saltonstall's hands. To Danyell Hoyll my basse begotten sonne, the third of the property; remainder to syster Janet's children. Witnesses, Wm. Hanson, John Broke, Janet Scolfeld, John Hoyll wryter hereof.

1586. Abraham Sunderland of H. Sunderland, £100 for Sarah his sister, in charge of Ric. his brother, Wm. Haldsworth, S'ouram, John Rishworth, and my curate or any three of them. To John Rishworth, Shipden, my tenant, £10. Christr. Rishworth, Haworth, £1. Henry R's. wife £1. Ric. R. gent., the debt due from him relinquished. Lands in Bingley, Keighley, &c., to Ric. Sunderland, his brother.

1586. John Lacy of Brearley, Esq., to John his son and heir.

1586. Ric. Northend, Hipp'ome, yeoman, body to Halifax church-yard believing it shall aryse again. To Thos. and Anne, younger children, £4 yearly, on the death of his wife Agnes. Wm. the eldest son, committed to the care of Rob. Brighouse, Hipp'ome, my neighbour and verie frende.

1587. Edwd. Brodley, Hipp'ome, mentions his wife Alice, and children Isaac, Ric., Michael, and Sarah.

1587. Wm. Medley made his wife Margaret executrix. Witnesses, Edward Rawlence, Min'ster of Coley, John Haldsworth, John Appleyard.

1587. Rob. Waterhouse, Preistley, gave the estates at Brighouse and Preistley in trust to his brother-in-law, Wm. Hoyle. Mentions his son and heir Edward, daughter Anne, and a child unborn. To John Beaumont all his apparell. Wm. Liversiche 5s., Sibell Sharpe 5s., Michael Fouldes 12d. Executors, his wife Isabel, John and Thos., his brothers. Witnesses, Edward Rawlence, minister of Coiley, &c.

1588. Agnes Gibson, Upper Brookfoot. To Mary d. John Gibson a morter and pestell. To John Hamond, clerk, my bordeman, (curate at St. Ann's, S'owram), the best mattress, courlet, boulster, and a pewther pott. Ric. G. her son, executor.

1587. Petronell Prestley, Hepp'holme, widdowe. To five youngest children, Wm., Henry, Saml., Alice, Angelice, five marks each, to be paid by Rob. Hemingway of Ouerbrea as each became 21. To Rob. Hemingway 20 nobles. Grace and Jane, daughters, to have leasehold for two years. Rest to Edward, son. Witnesses, Rob. Lillie, Hugh Ramsden, and me Rob. Horton.

1590. Wm. Walker of Okenshawe, son of Robt. who had lands in Hipp. in right of Susan his wife. Mentions wife Jane, and children John, George, Roger, Jane and Ellen.

1589. Jo. Snype, Lighcliffe, shared his estate equally between his wife and child. John Kighley owed him 43s., Thos. Walker 33s. 4d., John Bawmforth, Wicke, 33s. 4d. His debts were to John Shackleton elder, 10s., Edwd. Bates 3s. 4d., Nich. Peele, Liversedge, 3s. 10d. Witnesses, John and Edward Barockelewe, Thos. Huylle.

1590. "In the Name of the Father, Son and Holy Ghost, I Robt. Thorppe, Thorneyall brigges, cornedriver, one of the number of the elect, &c.," give to "Anne my lovinge wief, her third. Ric., Mary, Susan, three youngest children, £10, and Susan to have also a quie. To Ann, eldest daughter, and her expected husband Thos. Child, the lands in Brigghouse for three years, and £6 13s. 4d., and her apparell. Rest to John, Rob., Michael, Ric., Mary and Susan ; Thornhill Briggs land to John ; Slead Sike lands in tenure of Ric. Hole to Robert ; lands in tenure of Isaac Longbothom to Michael. If my eldest sons marry during my wife's widowhood she shall lett them have housing." Witnesses, Wm. T., John T., Ric. Hole, John Hanson, junr.

1590. Martyn Birkhead of Wakefield, Esq., lands in Southowram to his wife Mary for life ; Harden Grange to son Daniel ; Nathaniel, the eldest son, to have the best geldinge, armour, weapons, the great boke of Fitzherbert's Abridgement of the Lawe, lands in Haworth, &c.

1590. Robt. Ealand of Carlinghowe, Esq., provided for Thomas, Alice and Cicely, younger children. Marmaduke, son and heir, to have bedstead, square table in the parlour, long table, counter, long-settle in the hall, &c. Gyles Fenaye, son-in-law, a purple clooke. Thos. Norclyf, gent., son-in-law, the great gold ringe with signit.

1590. Ric. Brokesbank of Barnes, Nm., gave Calderfall in Hipp., bought of Mr. Alex. Rishworth, deceased, to his son Abraham ; £100 to daughter Agnes, rest to Edwd., Gilbt. and Abraham, sons.

1589. John Hemingewaye, Lighclif. To Thos. Rainer my bro.-in-law 10s. Isabel White my god-daughter a rede petticote, Henry H. my best cloke. Thomas H. my godson, best jacket. Rob fairbank, brother-in-law, best dublet. Mary Bawmfurth, my servant, a lined cote. Elizbth. H., my servant, lined felt hatt. Margaret Lister a rede frise petticote. Rest of my wyves apparel and 6 pillow beres to my mother-in-lawe, to bro. Ric. wief, and bro. Thos. wief. Remainder to John, Edward, Thomas, sons. Brothers Ric., Edwd. and Thos. executors. Edwd. Fairbank my father-in-law to have care of my son Thomas till 15.

1590. John Colen, Norwoodgrene, mentions Jenet wife, and if Laurence my son happen to gett anie coles within my grounde, my son Edward shall share half.

1591. Feb. 29. In Name of God, Amen. I, William Hoill of Sleadhall, co. York, of prft memory, believing there is nothing more certain then death and uncertain then life, give my soul to God Almighty, trusting in the bloudshedding of Jesus Christ my alone Saviour, and my body to be buried at Halifax Church. To Henry my second son half acre called Thristwells of the nature of freehold in Sutclyff wood. To Danyell, 3rd son, 9 acres in Sutcliffe Wood in tenure of Roger Waddington. To Michael, youngest son, 7 acres and edifices in Shelf in tenure of Rob. Otes, and Longroid in Southoram. To Edward, eldest son, £13 13s. 4d. and one cubbard, one stand bedd in the chamber. Also to Henry £20 in money, Danl. £30, Michl. £30, Sarah, daughter, £66 : rest to wyfe Isabell, the executrix. John Hoile of Hoile House, gardner (guardian) of Henry; Ric. Rayner of Priestley, gardner of Danl. Supervisors, John Hoile my brother, John Hoile of Hoile House, Henry Hoile of Harthorne, Ric. Rayner of Preistley. Each godchild to have 12d. Proved 1592.

1592. Thos. Stancliffe, Hipperome. Isabel, wyfe, Michael, son ; my friend Ric. Thorp, Elland parish, to have tuition of Michael. To Thos. Northend, my sister's son, 12d. Agnes Whitwham my maid, 2s. 6d. Godchildren 12d. each. Witness, John Northend.

1592. Thos. Watterhouse, Preistlay, gave to the children of Ric. Kente, deceased, of Preistley, viz., Anne, Jeremye, Grace, Mary, Sarah and Isabel, and to the children of Thomas Walker of Preistley, viz. Robt., Ann, Valentyne, Mary, and Ales, the rents I had of my mother Anne Waterhouse for six years, the lands at Whytwood sold by Robt. Waterhouse in Brighouse, the lands in the occupation of John Mitchell, in Preistley, and Ric. Scholefeld's wyfe's rent in Lyghtlyf, to share equally among them, by John Waterhouse of Norwoodgreen. Thos. Hall, supervisor.

1592. John Hodgson, N'ouram ; Mary wife ; John, Daniel, sons ; child unborn. John Firth brother-in-law. Jane Paslew, Doncaster, to have 20s.

1592. Thos. Hanson, Rastrick ; Jenet wife ; Elizabeth and Judith drs. by first wife. Roger, son and heir. To Thomas, a younger son, he gave lands &c. and a pair of walker sheires. John and Robert, sons, to be under tuition of Thomas H. of Brighouse. Gift to John son of his brother John. Supervisors, John and Edward H., his brothers.

1592. Christr. Sharde, Lightclyff. Alice wife ; Thomas, Anne and Mary their child's parts. John Smyth of Lyghtcliff, my landlord, and Ric. Frith my brother-in-law, supervisors.

1593. John Hemyngway of ye Mithom, to Jonas, younger son, Sharp coite in N'owram ; Robt. eldest son, the rest. To Anne, daughter, bedding, silver spoones, &c. Susan d. of son Robt., a branded calfe. To the two daughters of Richard Northend, my brother-in-law, two pillow-beares and 5 marks each. To four children of my brother George Haldesworth, deceased, 10s. each. To John Hemyngway of Newarke, my cosen, £2. Annabel d. Leonard Crowther 6s. 8d. Thos.

Hemingway's wife, Halifax, 6s. 8d. Brian Otes 3s. 4d. Rest to my four daughters, Lucy Barraclough, Alice Oldfield, Mary Haldsworth, and Anne Hemingway. Ric. Sunderland of the High Sunderland and Wm. Haldsworth my brothers, overseers.

1593. Isabell wid. Bryan Hardie, Clayton, gave to Isabel d. Rob. Brighouse of Hipperholme, my brother, £2. To Anne d. Edwd. Brighouse, gent., Hipp., £2. To Jane Drake, N'owram, my new petticoate, my best hatt save two, one patlett and one smock, one apron, one paire of hose, and a paire of shooes. To Edw. Brighouse of Hipp., gent., £3. To John Midgley of Headley, 6s. Robt. Rakes (?Rooks) 5s. Ric. Boothe's wife, my best hatt but one, and to Mary his daughter, 10s. To poor of Halifax parish and town 10s., Bradford parish poor 10s. To Alice Lacie my bed with its furniture. To Alice and Bridgett Lacie, my daughter's children. the rest, except to my sister Alice wife of Robt. Brighouse, Hipp., my black hawked whye, and to my brother Martyn [Brighouse] one little spelded whie, (calf.)

1594. Edward Thorppe of Sutclyff wood, sycke in body, &c. mentions Elizabeth his wife and three children Peter, Saml., Grace.

1594. Written 1592. Ric. Hole, Lightcliffe, yeoman, To John his younger son, and Anne, Mary, Grace, daughters, mess., lands &c., in Ollerton, Bradford-dale, for twelve years. Edward, eldest son, one range. Janet, wife, executrix. Supervisors, John Hole of Holehouse my brother, and John Warburton *alias* Chadwick. Witnesses, Chr. Wooller, writer, and others. (? if C. W. was Curate of Lightcliffe.)

1594. Thos. Broadley, Lightcliffe, gave to his wife Susan her third part. To his children, Edwd., Michael, and Susan, 2s. 3d. each., Edward to be in charge of Nicholas Broadley of Slead Hall during nonage.

1595, March 23. Sarah dau. William Hoole, deceased, of Slaid Hall, declared her will as followeth. fyrst shee did give hir soule into the handes of Allmightye God, believinge assuredlie to have forgiveness of her sinnes by Jesu Christe, and her bodie to be buried in the church or churchyard of Hallifaxe, hoping with the faythfull to have joyfull resurrection. And for the giveinge and disposing of her felial and chyldes porcion and all other hir goodes she did give them : unto Issabel her mother £12, Edward, Henry, Daniel, and Michael Hoole brothers, £12 each. to Sarah Wilson 16s., and appointed her mother sole executrix. Witnesses, Henry Hoole, Halifax, Nicholas Broadley, Laur. Pickard.

Wm. Hoyle, clothier, Lightcliffe, purchased Sleadhall, 1571, d. 1592.
╤ Isabel d. John Beaumont. Halifax.

Edward, d. 1596.	Henry, became Rector of Gisburn, sold Slead Hall to John Thorpe.	Daniel.	Michael.	Sarah, d. 1595-6.

1595. Jasper Brighouse of Bradford, yeoman, mentions his lands in Southowram, Hipprholm, Bradford, Horton, Shipley. To Wm. Hallstead, schoolmaster of Bradford. £53 6s. 8d. to redeem lease of lands in Horton and Shipley. To Isabel and Susan, daughters, £40 each. Tempest the eldest son to have lands in Bradford bought of James and John Dolliffe. Robt. and Ralph, two younger sons, also provided for. To Elizbth. B. my sister 6s. 8d., Elizbth. B. my neece £1. Jane Leigh 40d. Alice Hopkinson 16d. Rest to Isabel and Susan drs. of Mr. Martin Brighouse my nephew. Supervisors, Christr. Taler, vicar of Bradford, Wm. Webster, vicar of Calverley, Thomas Taler, Bradford. Proved before Wm. Webster, clerk; in 1597.

1596. John Scolefeild, of Coley, yeoman; Jennett, wife. John Wood and his wife Susan, my daughter, to have Siddall hall and lands. My wife the Coley properties for life, and the iron range, and cubbord are to be heirlowmes in the house. To John Wood the best chiste in the prlor, and one bedd with its furniture in the prlor. Wm. Osgrabie, marchant, of Kingston-upon-Hull owes me £20; I give the same to Saml. s. of my brother Robert, and a pair of loomes, and its furniture, a press, a pair of walker sheeres, a shereberd, a halfe of my handells. To Mary d. Michl. Hall a black hawked whye to be kept by my wife till she come to her noite. To my brother George, £2 due to me for a carsey clothe. To Henry, my brother, a paire of loomes at Wm. Broddell's house. To Wm., my brother, 10s. To John, son of my late brother John 10s. To Easter, Wm., Robt., Sarah, Prudence, and Richard, brothers and sisters of above Saml., £1 each out of his £20. Rob. and Nichs., my brothers, 6s. 8d. each. Ric. Sunderland of Coley Hall, gent., and Rob. my brother, supervisors. Witnesses, Ric. Sunderland, W. Tillotson, Thos. Hall.

1596. Edwd. Hoyle, Slead Hall, directed that his body be interred at Halifax. To my two younger brothers Daniel and Michael the profits of all my lands, to take up the rents from their uncle Henry Hoyle of Halifax, for five years, then to return to my brother Henry, with remainder to Daniel. Saml. Otes oweth me £5 13s. 4d., Abraham Baraclough £1, Edmund Haigh 17s., John Kepe, Harstead in Essex, £2, Nich. Broadley £10, Jas. Cooper 30s., Paul Person £1, Rob. Sunyard £3 5s., Saml. Auldersley, 23s. 4d., to be paid on his marriage; Thos. Smith £2, Edw. Hoyle £3 10s. 6d., Nicholas Broadley 16s. wanting 4d., Ric. Person 40d.

1597. John Holdsworth of the Hoyle, gave to Saml. and Susan his children £4 yearly rent from lands in Hipp., and Shelfe. John son and heir provided for. Half rest to Wm. and Saray Holdsworth, my base children. John Holdsworth of Astaid, Jas. Maude my brother-in-law, and Thos. Whitley thelder, supervisors.

1597. John Hoyle of Hoyle House, gave to Elizbth., wife, the seeled bed in the new chamber with fether bed, bolster, mattress, &c., rents of lands in Bradford-dale in the tenure of Ric. Hopkinson, Allerton. To poor of Lightcliffe 10s. To son Saml., the bed whereon I lye in the prlour, and a cubboard and sawen boards. To Margaret Aldersley my servant £10, and her brother Saml. £1. To Mary my dr., wife of John Foxcroft of Batley, and her children, £66 13s. 4d. Rest to Saml. my son. Witnesses, Martin Pyckson, Michael Smith, Edwd. Hoyle.

1597. Thos. Hole, of Lightcliff. I owe Gilbt. Saltonstall 46s. 6d. for three stone of wooll at 15s.6d., Elizabeth, wife; Mary, daughter. John the younger son to have his share when 14 yrs. of age. John and Gilbt. Hole to be overseers.

1597. John Waterhouse of Norwoodgreen, yeoman; to John, son, a table, three stande bedds, two cupbords, one great arke, three iron rainges, paying to my daughters Susan, Sarah and Anne £10, when he is 21 or married. John Cowper of Dean House, my brother-in-law, to have charge, with Isaac Waterhouse of Woodhouse, and John Brooke of Rookes, my brother-in-law. The Carr in N. Bierley, in tenure of Wm. Wood, to be purchased for £146.

1598. Gilbert Saltonstall, Rooks, gent., gave to Halifax Church £1., Halifax poor £1. Hipperholme poor £1 yearly for ten years to be delivered at my house at Rooks yearly every Christmas eve. Wragbye poor 10s. To Isabel my wife £10. Mary Savile my dr. £10. To repair of the chapell of Hipp'holme otherwise called the *Eastfeild Chapel* or Lightliffe chappel £1. Residue to Saml. somne and executor. Wm. Ramsden of Longley and my brother-in-law Saml. Ashton of Bisset, supervisors. Witnesses, Saml. Ashton, Matthew (H)eather, Thos. Greene, Thos. Walker. Proved 9 Jan. 1598-9.

1599. John Hanson thelder of Woodhouse, mentions "Margaret my wife." Give 10s. to preacher at my burial. Thomas H. of Brighouse, my second son, to have lands in Greetland, Ealand, Brighouse and Clifton, and a close of one rood between the two roads—Brighouse to Hipp., and Thornall bridge to Hipp. To Nicholas my youngest son and Mary his wife, and Robt. their son, the lands in Batley, Woodsome, Hipperhome, Brighouse and Eland as stated. Judith my youngest child, now wife of Wm. Deyne, the mess., &c. in Worsbro', with remainder to Nicholas my son. Mentions his late brother-in-law, Robt. Wade. To poor of Rastrick and Brighouse 10s. To repair of layne betwixt Brighouse and Clifton Bridge 6s. 8d. To Thomas my son my best cloak, jacket, jirkin, dublett, hoose, shoes, shirts, and two silver spoons. To the five children of son Thomas,—26s. 8d. to the eldest Thomas, £2 each to Arthur, Ric. and Joseph, and 4 marks to Judith. To Agnes, Mary, Margaret and Katherine, daughters of my eldest son John £2 each. To mending Brighouse brigge £1. To Margaret wife of son Thomas a peice of gold of 15s. To Doro. Farrer my dau.-in-law and servant £5, and to rest of my wive's children by her former husband Edwd. Farrer, £5. To John and Robt. youngest sons of my late brother Thomas 13s. 4d. each. To John and Edwd. sons of late brother Arthur, 13s. 4d. each. To Judith my daughter a gold peice of 15s., and to her husband Wm. Deyne, peice of gould of 20s., an yron bound wayne, a plowe with share and calter, and a spelded oxe at Swillington or Thorpe. To Mary wife of my son Nicholas, gould peice of 15s., and 40s. to her daughter Dorothy. To Robt. son of Nicholas the first book of Acts and Monuments of the Church. To John, eldest son, a sword, dagger, book of Statutes Rastall translation, my book called Supplimentu Cromcaru', my bible in latyne of Jeromes translation, and wch of all my prsident books he will chuse, &c. To Jennet wife of my son John a gould peice of 15s. To Thomas my son Langueth cronicles and Breviarie of health by Dr. Board. (See 1613.)

1599. Edward Brighouse of Hippholme, late of Bingley, thelder, gives to Rob. Barraclough £10, Edward Brighouse junr. gent., £30, Edward Hoyle £10, Christr. Fotherbie 4 marks, Jesper Brighouse £1, Isabel Sager six strokes of wheat, George Thornton a paire of breeches, dublett, nether stockes and a pair of socks, George Rowland a paire of fusten breeches, George Rowland's wife 2s., Jesper Pickard £8, Wm. Pickard £8 and the chiste that lockes with a cheane at bothe ends, and a cloke. To Mary Gill 3s., Raphe Brighouse 3s., Margaret Kighley a velvet hatt and £4, Abraham Brighouse £1. Rest to my brother Robert, the executor.

1600. Edmund Watson, of Lightcliff, clothier, mentions his wife Margaret; Elizabeth, Grace, Rose, Edmund and Michael, children.

1609. Margaret wid. John Hanson, Woodhouse. To Judith dr. of my son John Ferror £2. John Ferror £10. Rob. Ferror £10. Rob. son of Nich. Hanson £2. Dorothy dr. Nich. £1. Daughter Mary wife of Nicholas Hanson £10. To daughter Dorothy and her husband £10. To dr. Judith and Wm. Deane her husband £10. Daughter Susan and her husband Robt. Whittel £10. Her sons Henry, Robt. and John had been provided for. Anthony Wade of Kings Cross, her cousin.

1613. Nicholas Hanson, Ealand, servant and clerk to Rt. Worpful. Sir John Savile, Baron of the Exchequer, directs his burial at Ealand near his late father John H. of Woodhouse, and his auncestors, gives his lands in Eland and Huddersfield to his only son Robt. and only daughter, Dorothy, wife of John Farrer; the son then a Fellow of Magdalen College, Oxon, who by excess of study or something else had been melancholy but now amended: my daughter married to my great comfort, and having issue a son and a daughter both chargeable to me. To John Farrer the son-in-law and to the grandson John F. was given the cottage, &c. in Brighouse. To Mr. Sunderland, preacher at Elland, 20s. for the poor. To my brother John a new sattan dublet which was my late master's. Books to my brother Thomas and Arthur his son; sister Judith Deane; and cozen Thomas H. of Brighouse. Half of the books in his study to his son Robt. Hanson, and the other half (except his precedent books) to his son-in-law John Farrer; to the chapel of St. Matthew of Rastrick, he gives a book containing a *Hundred Sermons on the Apocalypse:* to his brother John Hanson, a manuscript *Bracton* in parchment. He had the *Acts and Monuments,* in two volumes, and the *Christian Warfare,* of which he makes special bequests. To his cousin Thomas Hanson of Brighouse, "such several books for song and scholarship as he and his brothers did chuse out of my books, which song-books cost me money." To his cousin Edward Hanson he gives four of his own precedent books; to his brother William Dean the book of *Resolution of a Christian.* His physic books he had already delivered to his friend John Mitchel, and some other scholar books were some time his. To Joseph Wilson another precedent book, "a special good one, written." He had already given a book to his brother John Farrer, teaching to *Learn to Live and Die Well;* and finally his *FitzHerbert's* Natura Brevium and some other law books he bequeaths to his cousin Mr. John Savile, the attorney.

1612. Alice Brighouse of Hipperholm, widow, gave £6 to son Jesper, a cow and beef flicke to son Abraham, a cow to Edward Gill's wife, clothing to daughter, Ann Haldsworth; rest to Jonas, son.

1614. Edwd. Saltonstall mentions his mother Jane, brothers John and Saml., sisters Anne and Judith.

1622. Mary Saltonstall of Huntwick, dr. of Saml. S., Esq., of Hull, gives her properties to her brother Sir Ric. Saltonstall, knt.

1619. John Blithman of New Laithe, Esq., Ruston parish, makes his brother Jasper supervisor of his will.

1632. Jasper Blythman, of Eland Hall, Esq., gave his brother Wm. the best horse, armour, apparel. To sister Mary wife of Stephen Skipwith £70. The goods brought to Eland Hall, plate, &c., to cozen Wm. Savill of Copley, now of Halifax, Esq. To governors of Halifax Grammar School £10; Halifax Workhouse £10. To poore at my funerall £5. To Gilbert Deane's four children by Elizabeth my late neice £200, to be paid by my loving cozen John Farrer, Esq., and James Murgatroyd, gent. To Edward Hanson, Netherwoodhouse, the writer hereof, £2. Judith my wife the rest. Cozen Sir John Ramsden of Longley, knt., supervisor. Proved 1633.

1632. John Hanson of Roidshall mentions his wife Isabell, daughter Elizabeth wife of Christr. Scott, his eldest son John; and made his two cousins, Edwd. H. of Netherwoodhouse and Arthur H. of Brighouse, supervisors.

1661. Arthur Hanson, Brighouse, gave to his sister Judith Swift the Parocke in Brighouse for her life, yielding to his son Thomas 6d., half-yearly. To Thomas and Richard his sons, and Judith his daughter, wife of Thomas Taylor,* he gave nine acres of common on Rastrick common near Roundhill for 950 years unexpired. To Thomas his son also a messuage in Bothomley in Barkisland for 18 years, paying yearly 5s. to Joseph his brother. To Thos. Taylor, grandchild, a cupboard and one table in the parlor of his father's house.

1662. Joshua Hanson of Briggroyd, Rastrick, yeoman, gave Briggroyd near the Calder in trust to Jeremy Bentley, Eland, gent., and Ric. Rawson, Tong, yeoman, for Dorothy his daughter, Jeremy his son and heir, and Anne his wife; £20 each to Thomas, Richard, John and Malon sons of his brother Richard.† £10 each to Thomas, Tabitha, Edward, Love, children of Thomas Taylor* of Brighouse, gent., and of Judeth his wife, sister of testator.

1674. Wm. Hanson, Brighouse, clothier, gave to his daughter Judith 10s. out of the housing at Brighouse lanehead; the best pair of loomes at Lanehead to his son John. Rest to his children, John, Wm., Susan, Judith, and wife Anne.

---

* This was Captain Thomas Taylor, Quaker.   † Richard Hanson was a Quaker.

1662. Jonathan Priestley of Sowerby, clothier, believing in the resurrection of the body, &c. gave to his nephew Jonathan Priestley of Priestley Green, the copyhold lands in his tenure, paying yearly 18d. to the lord of the manor, and also Haworth field in Sowerby, subject to annual payment of £4 to Thomas and Francis sons of Henry P., testator's deceased brother. To Francis his brother, Grace Wood his sister, £10 each ; Joseph P. of Goodgreave his cousin £2. Thomas, cousin, £2. Mary Nicholson, Warley, cousin, £2. To John, Joseph, Israel and Timothy sons of Joseph P. of Goodgreave £20 each. Jonathan P. of Priestley Green, executor. Signed I. P. his mark.

1672. Alexander Bate, of Cromwellbothom, Southowram, clerke, [curate of Lightcliffe,] give my soul to Almighty God. I give to Alex. my second son two messuages at Parkyate, Southowram. To Daniel, youngest son, messuage and five cottages. Wm., eldest son, Siddall Hall, Sm., and Giles house in Lightcliffe, now in my own

GILES HOUSE.

occupation, and all my lands in Cheshire to descend to my eldest son. To Mary my wife, the executrix, Yate-house and Linlands in Southowram. Witnesses, James Pearson and Joseph Lister.

Thus we may proceed indefinitely, and indeed ought to have enlarged on those already given, but space forbids. The wills of Gamaliel Marsden, clerk, of West Ardsley, 1681, son of a curate of Coley, and brother of three other clergymen, who like himself were ejected by the Act of Uniformity; Henry Brighouse of Brighouse, 1682, who built Bonegate House, and from whom the Ledgards are maternally descended ; Robert Gibson of Slead Hall, 1692 ; and scores more of interest must be omitted.

Robert Gibson, clothier, purchased Slead Hall, died 1692.
= Rhenetta

Michael, bequest of bread   Edward.   Mary,   Dorothy = Hall
to poor of Hove Edge,
d. 1738, aged 72.   Mary.
= (1) Elizbth, d. 1713. = (2) widow of Rev. Mr. Dade, Otley.

Robert,   George,d.1746,   Wm.,M.D.,   John,   Elizabeth,d.1770,   Ann,
d.1746.   = (1)——, (2)   Prof.   d.   =AbrahamFirth,   d.
= ——   Mary d. Thos.   Anat.,   s.p.   Clough-house,   s.p.
s.p.   Thompson,   unmar.   Huddersfield,
      Staincliffe, s.p.   d. 1769.

Abraham   William,   Elizabeth,   Sarah,   Ann,   Mary,   Catherine,
Firth,   d. 1771.   =Thos.Macaulay,M.D.,
d. s.p.   Thormanby, d. 1801.

Abraham Firth Macaulay, of Slead Hall,   Ann,
=   physician, d. 1823, aged 48.   = Richd. Ashworth;
                                 Manchester.

Henry,   Wm.,   George,   Thomas,   Charles,   Edwin,   Arthur.

Days of Romance.

WE have laboured thus far to remove the darkness from the Dark Ages, and the reader may be struck with one thing, the glamour of romance and unreality has to give place to a matter-of-fact life very little different from that of the public life of to-day. Wars and rumours of wars did not materially affect the common life; the Kings and Esquires were the great sufferers, as they deserved to be, though the rank and file fell out of the poorest.

BALLAD SINGER.

We have, however, had glimpses of wars, plagues, fairs, banditti, tragedies, gibbettings, &c., that afford the novelist and romancer full scope to make the old glamour and tournaments return, and perhaps some local Scott may arise, with wizard wand, to revivify the scenes. I prefer to discover first the real state of society, without forgetting the jolly feasts and holy-days that helped to brighten the existence of the poor down-trodden, yet on the whole, well-fed peasants. They had forgotten the happy days of Saxon freedom, but not the intuitive desire for self-government and improvement, and the decay of feudalism, the introduction of manufactures, the prosperity of the yeomanry class and other accessories, especially a widening of thought in religious matters, and enlarged educational facilities, and the spread of literature by the printing press, were rapidly raising the masses to be an acknowledged power in the land. Though it was impossible for a Robin Hood gang now to exist, or for pitched local battles to be fought, outlaws of the Nevison type, and village antipathies continued long after this time. Nevison had haunts about Hove Edge, Brighousers stole the Rastrick Maypole ; and one township often had sod, or clog fights with the next township. Hals were kept at great houses ; pipers and crowders, or fiddlers, led a wandering minstrel life, and ballad singers like the one given here, as drawn by Williams of Halifax, last century, existed to modern times. The vendor of last dying speeches found his trade gone when newspapers came into vogue. We still find the degenerate song-vendor at some markets and fairs, but Sunday School hymns and improved tastes have worked marvellous results. One would have been pleased if the dying speeches of the Halifax Gibbet culprits had been thus printed and sold. The ballad of the Elland Trag-edies is the best local one preserved to us. To learn how the populace spent their leisure hours, we must study the folk-lore of the district, but have only space here to indicate a few topics.

DYING SPEECHES.

The days of fox, brock, or badger, otter, and foomard or wild cat hunting were not over, for the parsons of Rastrick and Southowram and other churches were great encouragers. Bull-baiting and cock-fighting were constant sources of 'recreation'; and archery, football, and other games supplied the place of the reading and rational amusements of this day (barring the outrageous football mania of the past twenty years). Rushbearing had gone out of fashion before George III died, save one or two recent imitations. The singular thing is that Brighouse, though having no church then, kept this annual feast on the second Thursday in August, whilst Rastrick and Hipperholme had no feast. The bodies and bones of malefactors (real or supposed) dangled in chains from poles on Beacon Hill and numerous other conspicuous places down to the end of George III'rds reign, many of the culprits for sheep-stealing or coining. No wonder the benighted traveller shook in his shoes, as the wind weirdly whistled against the hideous obstacle, or as he heard the dreaded tramp of the highwayman. No wonder that hobgoblins, guy-trashes, bloody-tongues, padfoots, boggards, witches, gabble-ratches and headless horses (page 63) scoured the country on dark nights, and did their baneful deeds, in the imagination of the ignorant multitude. We do wonder that such silly notions are allowed to dominate some minds even to-day. Wizards made good livelihoods (especially a famous one at Southowram about 1790,) by fortune-telling, and restoring lost property. These are only a few of the great topics of conversation and belief in the days before ele-mentary education was enacted; and they governed the minds of learned lawyers, doctors, and clergymen too, down to John Wesley's day. Oliver Heywood, of Coley, who died in 1702, gives numerous insights of social life in these parts, about dreadful comets, &c., and to the four volumes I have printed from his "Diaries," and to the "Register" volume, I must refer the reader for further information.

Civil and Religious Strife, 1600-1700.

We have not space in this volume to enter upon the great conflicts, civil and religious, that distracted the seventeenth century, for to do justice to the Religious, Social, Educational, and Family History of the district a volume as large as the present one is required. Two men on either side in the Civil War were locally conspicuous. No memoir of Capt. Langdale Sunderland, of Coley Hall, of Fixby, and afterwards of Acton, has been compiled, though he was one of the staunchest Royalists under Lord Langdale, his kinsman, and a great sufferer when the fines were imposed under the Commonwealth. After diligent enquiries we found that some of his descendants are living at Ulverstone, and in New Zealand, and from them we have secured the portrait of the Captain, copied from an old painting at the Antipodes. Capt. Drake, of Shibdendale, has preserved to us an account of the Pontefract sieges, which has been printed by the Surtees Society. Capt. Thomas Taylor was a Parliamentarian officer, who married Arthur Hanson's daughter, of Brighouse Park, and eventually settled at the old Hanson home in the centre of Brighouse, and became like his brother-in-law, a follower of George Fox, the Quaker. Of his soldier life we know nothing, but of his religious life many events are recorded. He was buried in his garden in the centre of Brighouse, "standing upright," says Oliver Heywood, in his *Diaries*, and the gravestones were discovered some years ago, and removed by Thomas Dearnally to his residence in Brighouse Fields. Capt. John Hodgson's Autobiography was preserved in MS., and printed in Scotland (by Ritson or Sir Walter Scott,) in 1806, and re-edited, with notes, by J. Horsfall Turner in 1882.*

Many other local families took active sides in this civil strife, when great events followed in quick succession. Regiments were frequently seen passing our lanes, sometimes they were quartered in our villages; church services at Coley, Bradford, &c., were abruptly terminated; skirmishes at Kirklees, &c., and hurried burials in and out of church-yards not uncommon. Great national events followed in the train. Charles I. placed his head on the block, Cromwell rose to supremacy, Parliament struggled to preserve its balance between Monarchy and Presidential Autocracy, the second Charles scrambled into an oak tree to save his life, but received an ovationary welcome as King, May 29th, 1660, soon after the death of the mighty Cromwell. Sir John Armytage, of Kirklees, and John Peebles, Esq., J.P., the West Riding Magistrates' clerk, (who, though the son of an incumbent of Lightcliffe, we must confess deserved in some measure the popular epithet—The Devil of Dewsbury,) were conspicuous in retorting on the Parliamentarians, now that the sun shone on the Royalist side of the hedge. From this time the strife took more a religious than a civil aspect. The bulk of the Royalists were of the Established

---

* Autobiography of Capt. John Hodgson, of Coley, (and of Godley, Cromwellbottom, &c.)

P

Church party, and the Republicans and Puritans formed the Dissenters. Stringent laws against the latter, imposing civil disabilities,
widened the breach, but into ecclesiastical history we may not now
enter. This was the period when scholars were admonished to keep
diaries of events, and by this means, in the absence of newspapers,
we have preserved for us, along with parish registers, the family,

OLIVER HEYWOOD.

social, religious and local history of the period. Oliver Heywood's
Diaries are mostly in existence now, several of them having come
into my possession.

Heywood's friend and executor—Jonathan Priestley, of Winteredge, wrote his family history, which has been printed by the Surtees
Society. We are thus exceptionally supplied with local history for
this district, and we know more of the details of the period from
1650-1700 than of the following fifty years. Bible names were very
popular amongst the Puritans, and they invented doctrinal names
to give to their children in baptism, as Faith Priestley, What-god-
will Lister, &c. George Fox, the Quaker, frequently visited Capt.
Taylor's house, and preached to unruly mobs in the park, where the
Town's Office and Bank now stand. Brighouse Monthly Meeting,

which has now jurisdiction amongst the Society of Friends over most of the West Riding, owes its origin to these visits. Capt. Taylor had two relatives who became Quaker champions, and who, like himself and Heywood, and scores more of local dissenters, suffered imprisonment in York Castle for conscience' sake. These were the Rev. Thomas Taylor of Skipton, and the Rev. Christopher Taylor, incumbent of St. Ann's, Southowram, brothers, who joined Fox and forsook their livings and titles; Rev. was not used by clergymen then, but these two ignored plain Mr. Of their sufferings there is not space now to write, for the family history of the Friends would occupy much room; we must follow the civil and commercial chapters for the rest of this volume. An old malt-kiln used by the Taylors and Greens when there was a large malt trade in the district, stood on the actual site of the Town's office. During the brief Commonwealth, Halifax and Leeds had the privilege of sending a member each to Parliament. Mr. Jeremy Bentley, the first and only Halifax M.P. before the great Reform Bill, resided at Nether Woodhouse in 1655, and Mr. Adam Baynes sat for Leeds.

BRIGHOUSE MALT-KILN.

Assessments, 1590-1699.

Lists of names are not attractive reading, but they may be turned to great use. They shew when families settle in a place, and negatively when others leave, also the social status and material improvements; and the gradual growth of population and the introduction of industries. Pedigree making is a very minor but interesting advantage assisted by these lists.

We have been able to gauge the population in 1379, and of Rastrick in 1605 (p. 168,) when there were only 24 families in the township. The following lists shew the importance of the district as compared with neighbouring townships, and also give the names of every family residing here.

1590. The names of ye inhabitants of ye chappelrie of Lightcliffe, assessed by John Smyth, John Thorpe, Nicholas Thornill and John Boothe :—

	s.	d.		s.	d.
Mr. Samll Saltonstall ...	xiij	iiij	Ric. flirthe		xvj
Samuell Hoyle	vj	viij	Rowlande Gibsone	ij	viij
Thomas Thorpe and his sonne	vj		John Brooke		xvj
John Smythe	vj	viij	ffrancis Brooke		xij
Ric.Raynr & Edwarde Watrhouse	vj	viij	Hugh Ramsden ...		xvj
William Whitley ...	iij	iiij	nxor Wilfrey Peele		xij
John ffairbank	iij	iiij	Gilbert Brigge	iij	iiij
George ffairbank ...	iij	iiij	Robert Kitchen		xij
Hugh Norclyffe	iij	iiij	James Rawnesley ...	ij	iiij
John Bynnes	iij	iiij	nxor John Thorpe, of Sutcliffe		xij
John Boothes	v		Isaack Whitley ...		xij
John Bancroft	iij	iiij	Richard Gill		xvj
John Barraclough, elder ...	ij	vj	John Thorpe of thornill brigge	ij	
Ric. Hanson	ij	vj	Ric. Thorpe	ij	
Edward Hoyle	ij	vj	Charles Elliot		viij
John Barraclough, younger	ij	vj	John Michell		vj
Robert ffairbank	ij	iiij	John Medley		xvj
William Thorpe ...	ij		Robert Holdsworth ...		xij
Nicholas Thornill	ij	iiij	Henry Scholfield		xx
John Hollan [? Bollan] ...	iij	iiij	George Bawmforth ...		xij
William Barraclough ...	ij	iiij	Thomas Relphe		xij
Robert Judgson ...	ij		Abraham Heminwaye ...		xij
Lawrence Cowlinge		xx	Richard Stocke		vj
nxor Ric. Bollan ...		xvj	Humphrey Scolfield ...		xij
Edmond Watson		xx	nxor Wadingtone		iiij
Robert Stocke ...	ij	iiij	Richard Wade		viij
Andrew Marshall		xx	George Walker		iiij
John Petlington ...		xvij	Ric. haghe and frater ...		viij
nxor Thomas Hoyle ...	ij		Robert Smythe		iiij
nxor Edw. Dawes ...		xij	John Barraclough, Smyth		viij
Robert Hargreaves	ij		Ric. Barraclough, girdr ...		iiij
John Whitley		xij	Edward Judgson		iiij
Andrew Gill		xij	Peter Thorpe		iiij
John Jackson		xij	Gilbert Smythe		vj
Isaach Longbotham ...		xij			

This assessment, from the character of the writing and the persons mentioned, must have been made in or about the year 1590. Probably it was made for the repair of Lightcliffe Chapel. The sum £7 3s. 11d.

is a considerable amount when we consider the value of money three centuries ago.

1604.   Subsidy Roll, Hipp.   All in land at 2/8 in the £.

Ric. Sunderland ... ... viii l.	John Brighouse ... ... xx s.	
Saml. Hoyle ... ... v l.	Wm. Northend ... ... xx s.	
Edwd. Waterhouse ... ... iij.	Ric. Thorp ... ... xx s.	
Robt. Hemmyngway ... ... 1 s.	Michael Sclater ... ... xx s.	
Dorothea Smyth ... ... xxv s.	John Barraclough ... ... xx s.	
Thos. Smyth ... ... xxv s.	Thos. Whitley ... xxiij s. iiij d.	
Thos. Thorp ... ... xl s.	John Horsfall ... ... xx s.	
John Roydes ... ... xl s.	Thos. Hanson ... ...xxvi s. viij d.	
Riens Bradley ... ... xx s.	Jacobus Rawnsley in goods iij li ... v s.	
Johes ffairebanck ... ... xx s.	Sma. Vill. est iiij li. xix s. viij d. ob.	

1610.   Subsidy Roll, Hipperholm.

	£ s.		£ s.		£ s.
Rich. Sunderland	9	Thos. Thorpe	2	Richd. Thorpe	1
Saml. Hoyle	5	John Royde	2	Mich. Slaiter	1
Edw. Waterhouse	3	Richd. Broadley	1	Jno. Barrowclough	1
Rob. Hemingway	2 10	John Fairbank	1	Joh Horsfield	1
Dorothy Smith	1 5	John Brighouse	1	Thos. Rawson	1
Thos. Smith	1 5	Will Northend	1	Jas. Rawnsley	1

1664.   Subsidy Roll, Hipperholm.

	£		£		£
Stephen Ellis	2	Joshua Whitley	1	Wm. Greenwood	1
Richd. Langley	2	John Hodgson	1	Wm. Thorp	1
*Nathan Whitley	1	Jeremiah Field	1	*John Taylor	1
Henry Brighouse	1	Thos. Hanson	1	*Joshua Waterhouse ⎫	
James Mitchell	1	Joseph Wright	1	Widow Waterhouse ⎬ 2
	* Signifies goods.			Widow Spinke ⎭	

The County Assessment for 1584 is before me, and shews the valuation of each township :

Barsland	iij s.	Hipprholme cu'		Skircote cu' Shelf	ij s.
Bradford	vj s.	Bryghouse	vj s.	Southouram	v s
Clifton	ij s.	Hallifax	v s.	Wharnebie	v s.
Hartshead	ij s.	Mirfeld	vj s.	Wike	iij s.
Eland cu' Gretland	iiij s.	Northowram	v s.	Wakefeld	xv s.
Huddersfeld	vj s.	Rastrick cu' ffixebie	iij s.		

Land Tax, 1692, at 4/- per pound.

		£ s. d.		£ s. d.
In Agbrigge, Reall Estate.	£ s. d.			
Huthersfield	...	181 8 0	Hartishead-cum-Clifton ...	82 2 0
Mirfield	...	154 3 0	Hipprholme cu' Brighouse	117 12 0
Quarmby...	...	222 6 0	Hallifax	350 17 9
Wakefield	...	349 11 0	Northourame	337 16 0
In Morley Wapentake.			Raistrick-cum-Fekisby ...	68 12 8
Bradford	...	200 1 0	Southourame	206 3 4
Ealand-cum-Greetland...		153 10 8	Wike	46 18 8

Complaints about Rates and Values of Lands, and the way of assessing in Morley Division, 1699.

CLIFTON—	Yearly Rent.	Assess.
John Pilling of Sir John Armitage ...	£62	
Joseph Priestley, Sir John's Tenant ...	£25	16s. 4d.
John Rawusley, Sir John's Tenant ...	£30	29s. 1d.
Widdow Reyner for Hileleigh land, & for Rapers ...	£16	31s. 4d.
HIPPERHOLME—		
Joseph Eckles, Coley Hall, of Mr. Horton, about ...	£50	£4 5s. 6d.
Thomas Whitley of Mitholm, about ...	£10	18s.
Richard Kirshawe of Chas. Best, about	£2 10s.	3s.

	Yearly Rent.	Assess.
Francis Brook, Rishworth farm, of Mr. Horton	£8	10s. 6d.
Same for Shutt of Mr. Horton ...	£8	9s.
Henry Burn farms about	£3	3s.
Joseph Crowther for John Sharps about	£12	15s.
Broad Oake, about	£4 or £5	4s.
Joseph Eccles of Mr. Horton (dear) ...	£60	4/5/6.
Richd. Speight ...	£4	3s.
Joseph Holmes ...	£30	27s.
SHELF—		
Mr. Clifford's lands about	£7	16s.

An Assessment made for [ye] present [Overseers] this 7th November, 1692, for 8 months towards ye Relief of ye poore of Hippholme cu' Brigghouse by us whose names are underwritten.

HIPP'HOLME QUARTER.

	£ s. d.		£ s. d.
Mr. Will. Horton for Coley hall or ye occupiers ...	01 08 00	Richard Hudson	00 02 06
Mr.Edward Langley for Hippholme & Whitley land ...	00 10 06	Richard Speight	00 01 00
Samuell Saltonstall... ...	00 08 00	ye occupiers of quarrell hall and ye land	00 01 00
Ioshua Wright	00 08 00	Ioseph Shuckesmith for moses farme	00 04 00
Thomas Kitson	00 07 00	Michaell Ingham	00 07 06
Iohn Holroide	00 05 06	Izaeke Mann For Empson Farme	00 03 00
& for four closes at Broadoak	00 01 06	Ieremiah Whiteley	00 00 06
Ioseph Brooke	00 06 00	Robert Smith	00 01 06
Stephen Hird	00 05 00	Iohn Iackson For Hazlegreane	00 01 06
Ionas Coates	00 07 00		
& for Mr. Lister land ...	00 01 06	Mr. Thorpe	00 02 00
George Stockes	00 03 00	Ioshua Whitley	00 05 00
Ionathan Priestley	00 08 00	Abraham Broadley	00 00 06
Iohn Waddington	00 02 00	Francis Brooke for old Rishworth Farme	00 04 00
Mr. Oates for Finnis ...	00 07 00		
Anthony Whitley For Mitham	00 06 00	Andrew Hartley	00 01 00
George Ramsden for Lane ends	00 02 06	Ephraim Moore	00 01 00
Abraham Walker for ye other pt.	00 01 06	Daniell Empson	00 01 00
			07 15 00

NORWOOD GREEN QUARTER.

	£ s. d.		£ s. d.
Mr. Edward Langley for Priestley	00 10 00	for Eastfield	00 02 00
& for Mr. Ellis land ...	00 05 00	For Iackson Inge... ...	00 00 06
For Turner Farme ...	00 04 00	For Nickall Roide & Goft close	00 04 00
For claypitts	00 05 00		

NORWOOD GREEN QUARTER.

	£ s. d.		£ s. d.
Ab: Langley for Kitchinge closes & carr Inge	00 03 00	& For pt. of Gill Farme ...	00 03 00
For Gill Farme Tho: Wiley hath it	00 03 00	& For Izacke Kirshaw Farme	00 03 06
& For two closes at Hon-edge	00 00 06	Widdow Holdsworth or ye occupiers	00 02 00
Mr. Francis Priestley ...	00 08 00	Richard Robinson ...	00 01 06
Francis Brooke for ye shutt	00 03 00	Robert Willson ...	00 03 00
William Ramsden	00 08 00	Richard Robinson for Sharpes	00 00 06
Richard Riddlesden for pt. of Rooks	00 13 00	William Whitaker For Brook-esbanke land	00 01 00
Samuell Stanhope for ye other pt.	00 13 00	Iames Gill for Mitchills ...	00 02 06
Ionas Heaton	00 07 06	Ieremiah Empson	00 03 00
Thomas Shucksmith ...	00 03 00	————Tetlaw	00 05 00
Iohn Bland For Marshall Farme	00 02 06	————Brookesbanke ...	00 01 00
Ieremiah Robinson	00 04 00	————wh—lin	00 02 00
		... ...	00 01 00
			06 08 00

LIGHTCLIFFE QUARTER.

	£ s. d.		£ s. d.
Ioseph Firth	00 02 06	Iames Brearley	00 02 00
Michaell Ramsden	00 04 00	Henry Gill for pt. of Smith house	00 10 00
Iohn Robbards	00 01 00	Mrs. Brooke for ye other pt.	00 04 00
& For Boolefalls	00 02 00	Mr. Kirshaw	00 08 00
William Hirst For Shuck-smith Farme	00 02 06	Ab: Langley For wharlers ...	00 01 00
Samuel Smith	00 04 06	Abraham Walker For Crow-nest	00 11 00
Widdow Sowood & for Fayre-banke land	00 04 00	Edward Gibson For Nubie Farme	00 02 00
Widdow Houlmes	00 04 00	Mr. Lister for yew trees ...	00 18 00
Ab: Law for Upper cliffe hill	00 07 00	Iohn Sewnior For George Ramsdens	00 03 06
William Mann for Lower cliffe hill	00 05 00	& For Tazimonds ...	00 01 06
Gilbert Sturdy	00 09 00	Thomas Ray	00 12 06
Timothy Roper for John Gills & for peer trees	00 02 00 / 00 06 00	& For wood Close & Iennet Stubbinge	00 01 00
Iohn Whitaker	00 02 06	Iames Hauworth mason ...	00 03 00
Ieremiah Battley ...	00 02 00	Iohn Frost where Joshua Smith lived	00 08 00
and for pt. of Till carr ...	00 02 00	& for Tillcarr	00 02 00
Gilbert Sturdy Botham hall	00 03 00	Iohn Frost for Daniell Hoyle land	00 05 00
Thomas Grive for Daniell Walkers	00 09 00		08 15 00
& for A litill close Bo: of Tho: Sugden	00 00 06		
Ioshua Crowther	00 08 00		
Henry Brooke	00 02 00		

HOUEDGE QUARTER.

	£ s. d.		£ s. d.
Mr. Michaell Gibson ...	00 08 06	Iohn Bannforth	00 01 00
Thomas Sugden	00 02 06	Edward Gibson for Armsteads	00 01 00
Ab: Walker for Richard Flathers	00 05 00	Ioseph Wright	00 07 00
Ioseph Crowther for Sharpes	00 05 00	Iohn Thorpe & for pt. of Iacksons	00 06 00
Iohn Sharpe For Broade Oake	00 01 06	Mr. Mitchell for ye other pt.	00 01 00
Abraham Mallinson	00 06 00	Iohn Walker for two closes at Houedge or Oake ...	00 01 00
Henry Burne	00 02 00		

HOUEDGE QUARTER.

	£ s. d.		£ s. d.
Iames Leake & for Meggroide & springe	00 04 06	Iohn Lightowlers or ye occupiers	00 02 00
Iohn Lum for Springs ...	00 01 06	Iohn Hanson & For meanroide	00 04 00
Ioshua Holdsworth	00 06 06		
Ioseph Priestley	00 03 06		
			03 09 06

1692.

BRIGHOUSE QUARTER.

	£ s. d.		£ s. d.
Madam Thornell or her heares	01 00 00	Josias Whiteley for Clay farme	00 04 06
Wido: Brighouse	00 18 00	Mr. Linley for Brooke foote or occupiers	00 03 00
Mr. Michill	00 12 00	Henrie flather	00 02 00
Joseph Lister, Thornill Briggs	00 09 00	Mr. Walker or occupiers ...	00 01 00
Joseph Lister Sir Thomas Land	00 03 00	Joseph Rayner	00 04 00
Joseph Lister for fining millu or occupiers	00 02 06		05 16 00
Richard fflather	00 01 00	JOSHUA WHITLEY JEREMY HUDSON	
Joseph Crowther, Latte Mathew Scorfeild or occupiers	00 02 00	ABRAHAM LANGLEY THOMAS KITSON SAMUELL STANHOPE JONAS HEATON	
Timithie Scorfeild or occupiers	00 00 06	COLLECTORS OF ROYAL AIDE FOR THE TOWNSHIP.	
Jams Grime for Tho: Taylers	00 05 00	1661 Wm. Thorpe, Samll. Bentley	
Edmand Waterhouse for pound	00 03 00	1665 Thomas Hanson	
Abr: Lum	00 15 00	1666 Wm. Ffletcher, Thos. Tailor	
Widdo Hoole for bonegate...	00 10 06	1667 John Kershaw, Jeremy ffeild	
		1668 Wm. Wilton	

Septr. 17, 1666, William ffletsher's account given before us whose names are subscribed, he being collector for the Royall aide and his majesties present, further say by these remaining in his hand the which money he hath payd to the Constable, witnesse our hands

Richard apleyeard, Nathan Crosley, John Kirshaw, William Wilton, James Phillips

1668 Royal aide collected and our money for Duke of York.

The Reigns of the Georges, 1714-1827.

SMITH HOUSE.

There is enough material for a large local history in events of these four reigns, so we must content ourselves in this volume with merely indicating a few topics. In 1738 a remarkable religious revival

SMITH HOUSE PORCH.

culminated in the West Riding, under the Rev. Benjamin Ingham, of Osset, who married a Lady Hastings, into Ingham's Societies. This led to the frequent visits to Smith House of that venerable man John Wesley. The Holmes family owned the place then, and when a difference arose between the Moravians and the Methodists, Mrs. Holmes took sides with the latter. Meantime, a number of Germans or Moravians had been invited into Yorkshire to take charge of Ingham's Societies, and they had settled at Smith House, in the high three-storey building erected for them by Mr. Holmes, whilst an overflow

GERMAN HOUSE, LIGHTCLIFFE.

GERMAN HOUSE.

was told off to German House, then called Newhouse. A large school was held at Smith House, and if Mrs. Holmes, whose husband had recently died, had remained with the Moravians, it is probable that the Settlement, now at Fulneck, would have remained in Lightcliffe. The history of the Moravians reads like a romance, but must be left out for a special ecclesiastical volume; as must the stories of Rastrick, Coley and Lightcliffe Churches. We must not forget that to this date and to these events the present century is vastly indebted. The introduction of local preachers, beyond any religious influence, has promoted an independence of thought and expression that has materially advanced the present condition of social progress, whilst the religious instinct preserved the masses from unrighteous deeds. It would be well if the same considerateness, integrity, and charity were fostered to-day; and then masters and men, capital and labour, would be inseparable factors in social prosperity, and loss and jarring would cease.

In 1745, Joshua Guest, a native of Spout House in Lightcliffe, had reached the position of Lieutenant General of Dragoons, and, though

SPOUT HOUSE.

an octogenarian, ably defended Edinburgh Castle against the Young Pretender. The old General died the same year, and he was buried amongst the nation's great men in Westminster Abbey, where a monument and bust still testify to his worth. Sir John Ligonier, a great soldier from Hanover, was also conspicuous in the wars of that time, and his nephew married Penelope, daughter of Baron Rivers, Earl Chatham's relative. This was an unfortunate marriage, and the story of Penelope Pitt, from the pen of an Emily Brontë, would abound with romantic interest. I have copy of "An Act to dissolve the Marriage of Edward, Viscount Ligonier with Penelope, daughter of George Pitt, 1772," after six years' wedded life, for adultery with Count Vittorio Amadeo Alfieri. The husband fought a duel with Alfieri on this account. A pamphlet of 78 pages respecting the trial was issued in 1771.

| Jean Louis (John) Ligonier fled from France in 1697 with his brother. Fought with Lord Marlborough ; became Viscount. d. 1770. | Francois Ligonier d. at Falkirk in 1745 of fatigue. Edward, 2nd Viscount, d. 1782. |

Lady Ligonier was frail and beautiful. Forty years ago, fond grandmothers pronounced their grandchildren as bonny as Lady *Legoneer*, but who she was few remembered. I hunted out a few particulars about the 'grand lady,' and found an oil-painting at Mr. Thompson's, Chapel-le-Brier, depicting a hunting scene, amongst the riders being Mr. Thompson, who owned lands at Sutcliffe Wood, Mr. Aked, the Southowram parson, who shared the usual parsonic sport of that time, and Lady Ligonier. Parson Aked is just clearing a gate in splendid

SUTCLIFFE WOOD

style. What brought her ladyship to reside at Newhouse (not the New house just mentioned as German House, but the one opposite Lightcliffe New Church), I could never learn, or what became of her eventually, except that the peerages say she married a Captain Smith in 1784. Her paramour at Lightcliffe was a local man named Wright, I believe.

In order to encourage the woollen trade, the bodies of deceased persons had to be buried after 1678, in woollen dresses, or a penalty was imposed, and the undertaker had to sign a certificate stating conformity to the Act. The certificate bore the grim, unconsoling figure of a skeleton. The constables had many unpleasant duties during the war in obtaining soldiers. I have by me a list of the inhabitants of Rastrick, July 2, 1759, of males between 18 and 50, liable to be called out as soldiers. They are numbered 1 to 117 as they were written down from house to house :—John Bentley, John Garside, Wm. Goodhear, Wm., John, and James Walker, George Bentley, Wm. and Joshua Dawson, Michael Garside, Joshua and Joseph Collens, Ealy and Danel Dyson, Thos. Mitchell, James and John Hodge, Solomon Pitchfort, Michill Knowls, John Rangley, Wm. Aspinall, Wm. Parke, John Brook, John Apleyard, Jonathan (? Apleyard), John Whitwham, Joseph and Wm. (of Nunery) Aspinall, John Brigg, James Sykes, John Wadsworth, George Aspinal, Jas. Shaw, Joseph Brook, John Sunderland, Saml. Garfitt, Wm. Helm, Charles Smith, Joseph Stockill, Abrm. Marsdin, John Milner, John Marshall, Wm. Baritt, Benjamin Mallinson, Joseph Tiffoney, fox John Brook, law John Brook, owld John Brook, Joseph Blagburn, Saml. Sharp, Ried. Denham, Thos. and John Richardson, Joseph Firth, Joseph and John Goodhear, Joshua and Abraham Richardson, Joshua Farrer, Joseph, James, and Benjamin Horsfall, Joshua Bothomley, Wm. Clugh, Thos. Robards, Henery Rotherey, Mathew Fisher, Jonas Stot, John Blagburn, John Brigg, John Tiffeney, John Morton, Wm. Green, James Evison, Thomas Thornton, John Bothomley, Thomas Thornton of Woodhouse, Thos. Stake, John Hirst, Benjn. Morton, Abram Scholfield, James Denham, John Firth, John Bell, John Rushforth, James and Wm. Bothomley, Jonathan Denham, Ried. Boothroyd, Thos. Evison, Michl. Firth, Thomas Greenwood, Saml. Wilkinson, Edmund Cooper, John Preston, James Pearson, Joseph Marshel, Wm. Robson, frnses Horn, John Dorans, John Richardson, John Smith, Jonas Preston crossed off, John Singleton, Joshua Irdale, Wm. Rodes, John Stake, John Mallinson, Isaac Stocks, John Jackson,

Aabrm Mallinson, Joseph Lockwood, Jas. Holt, John Freeman, Thos. Fox, Joseph Thornton, Joseph Boothroyd, John Wood.

If space admitted, the descendants of many of these families could be inserted in pedigree form, but we must content ourselves with a few notes. Abraham Marsden was of the same family as John Marsden who was lotted or pressed for a soldier in Wellington's time, and fought in many engagements. His son, Mr. Henry Rowland Marsden, became Mayor of Leeds, and a large monument to his memory in one of the streets there is but one of the memorials to his worth. They intermarried with the Pitchforths. The Marsdens sprang from the village of Marsden, Colne valley. John Marsden was a farmer and publican in 1750 at Bridge End, like his father before him. Richard, son of John, married Grace Pitchforth and followed the same trades, and it was this man's son who was pressed in the army in 1812, when 22 years of age. He served twenty years and was then discharged with one year's pay (!), having fought in twelve engagements, and was several times wounded. He resided with Mr. Marsden when I got this information from his Worship, having reached the age of 85 on Feb. 14, 1875. The motto on the family arms is a capital pun—Mars Denique Victor est.

The customs of pressing and lotting for soldiers broke up many families, and spread the local surnames, along with the tide of emigration, over the British Empire and America; whilst the bondage of ' settlements' would have kept the old families at the old homesteads. The poor-law settlements were prolific of law-suits of one township against another. Every township's box contains bundles of papers of settlements, town apprenticeships, and bastardy cases. Here is one of the settlements. John Rushforth, of Fixby, having married Sarah Cooper of Rastrick, bought a little plot on Rastrick Castle Hill, desired to remove there in June, 1757, but could not do so until John Rakestraw, churchwarden, Wm. Drake, overseer, Joshua Holroyd, Joseph Fryer, and Samuel Mitchell, witnesses, had testified on oath before Saml. Lister and Wm. Lamplugh, Justices of the Peace, that Fixby township would be responsible if Rushforth, his wife, and child Susannah, became chargeable to the poor. He became, however, a good townsman, and his descendant, the writer, here gives his pedigree.

Thomas Rushforth, of Mirfield, d. 1648.
═Sarah Hall at Mirfield, April 1625 ; she married (2)
Thomas Wooen, senr., 1652.

| Thomas, b. 1626, d. 1631. | Henry, b. 1630. | Thomas, b. 1631, d. 1681, Mirfield. ═Sarah Wowen, 1661, d. 1681. | Sarah. b. 1634, mar. Wm. Hubank, 1657. Ann, b. 1637. George, b. 1639, d. 1668, leaving an infant son Jeremy. |

Robert,	Susanna,	Thomas,	Wm. 1668,	John, 1673,
b.1661,	b. 1663,	b. 1666,	George 1671,	=Elizth.Ellay
d.1681.	= in 1688	d. 1712.	d. 1704,	
	at Mirfield,	= (1)Elizth.	Sarah b. & d.	Robert, 1697
	Matthew	Blackburn,	1675,	Sarah, 1699
	Glover, of	1692,d.1695	Joseph 1676,	Susan\a 1707
	Allerthorpe.	=(2)Mary	d. 1679,	Joshua, 1710
		Firth,1698,	Joseph b.1680.	Elizth.1713
		d. 1725.		Ann(d.1728).

Thomas b. 1693,	Paul b. Oct.	Aquila	Joseph 1705,
d. 1694	1701,	=Elizth.	d. 1716
Thomas b. 1695,	=at Mirfield,	Gledhill	Martha
d. 1726	Mercy Saxton,	in 1734	1710
Daniel, b. 1699=( )	14 May,1727		
		Job b.1738	

Susanna b. 1722	Joseph b. 1728,	descendants now at
Joseph, 1724	ancestor of	Huddersfield.
Thomas, 1727	families at Horbury,	
Ruth, 1729	Dewsbury, Kendal, &c.	
Mary, 1732	George b. 1730	
Wm. 1735	John b. Nov. 1, 1732*	
Daniel, 1737.	Martha b. 1734	
(Descendants still	William	
about Mirfield.)	Rachel mar. Mark Phillips, Ossett.	
	Mary ,, Richd. North, Almondbury.	
	Susanna ,, Bartle Beaumont, Lindley.	
	Mercy ,, Benj. Bottomley, Lindley.	

* John Rushforth removed to Fixby (as did his father Paul, who died at Huddersfield Feb. 18, 1785, aged 81 (? 84), buried at Elland, with his wife Mercy Saxton, who died at Fixby 9 Sep. 1771, aged 67, see gravestone), and married Sarah d. John Cooper, sister of Edmund Cooper, both of whom served the town of Rastrick as Wardens, Overseers, Constables, &c. John and Sarah R. were married at Elland August 14, 1755. She died 9 July, 1800, aged 65. He made his will in 1806, proved 29 Sep., 1808, having died July 19th, aged 75. Gravestone at Elland. He was a millwright, and repaired the mills far and wide, as did some of his descendants, whose stories of midnight tramps on lonely moors, when chains dangled from the decayed bodies of gibbeted men, have been told to their children's children. As the children of John and Sarah Rushforth became allied by marriage to half the Rastrick population, the following sketch may be of interest, and shew what may be done in any one family history.

Their children were = |

Susannah, b. 1756,	John, b. June 19,	Stephen, bap. (at Ras-
Feb. 23, 5 p.m.	1759, see A.	trick like the rest,)
(Astrology was then	George Cooper, b.	1768. C.
believed in.)	April 17, 1762,	Sarah b. Palm Sunday,
=James Smith,	1 a.m., born under a	April 12, 1767. D.
Globe Inn, Rk.	lucky star, I expect;	Mercy, E.
	for he was my gt. gt.	
	grandfather. B.	

Charles   John   Edna = "Butcher"
Elijah   Rachel mar. Frank Avison ;   Pollard,
James   Allan A. butcher, Bridge   Brighouse
Stephen   End, was their son.

A. John, b. 1759, bur. at Elland, 8 Jan. 1793,
  = (1) Mary Holroyd who died 1782, aged 23.
  =F (2) Sarah Rhodes

John, b. Oct. 27, 1787,	Mary, d. Aug. 1822, aged 34	Paul Rhodes
d. Sep. 27, 1857	=Marmaduke Oldfield.	d. 1792
=Sarah Armitage, d.	Paul, innkeeper, Toothill,	inft.
26 Mch. 1856,	d. at Halifax, Feb. 1862,	Sarah,
aged 65.	aged 70. No issue.	bur. at
	=Betty Brierley	Elland

Hannah b. 17 Nov.   Allen   in 1800.
1811, 4-30 a.m.

Paul, Brighouse Lane Head, tailor, b. May 17, 1813. 1-30 a.m.
 Twice married.

Mary b. 26 Ap. 1815, 4-30 a.m., d. 1831.

John, Woodhouse, b. 8 Jan. 1817, 6-30 a.m.
 = Letitia Rayner.   Descendants living.

 B. George Cooper R., b. 17 Apr. 1762, 1 a.m., mar. when 18, bur.
   at Rastrick, 1844.

    =F(1) Susannah, sister of John and Thos. Richardson of
    Salforth, Bridge-end. She was born 21 Jan. 1762, d. 22
    Mch. 1792, buried at Elland. Living at Durham at the
    time of her marriage.

     =F(2) Mary, his cousin, (dau. of Joseph R., Horbury,)
     b. June 11, 1767, d. 13 Feb. 1799. Marr. at Wake-
     field Church, she then living at Lupset Hall. Her
     brother Aquila (Ack') of Kendal was an ingenious
     mechanic, musical composer, rhymester, whose
     descendants are numerous at Kendal, died at his
     daughter's, at Priestley Green, and is buried at
     Coley. His daughter Betty had married Wm.
     Greenwood, a noted Joannaite or Southcottian.

  1-5.   6-8.

1. Mary, b. 14 March, 1781, married Abraham Horsfall, Common.
2. A daughter, still-born, April, 1783.
3. Jonas Cooper, d. April, 1792.
4. Rhoda, b. 28 April, 1784, mar. John Pearson, whose nine children have numerous descendants in Rastrick, &c.
5. Sarah, b. 24 May, 1787, married Matthias Shaw, whose three sons—Matthias, John, William, were well known as musicians in Rastrick. Music was very much cultivated in this district from 1770 to 1850, both vocal and instrumental.
6. Susannah, b. Nov. 13, 1793, mar. John Cartwright of Holmfirth, whose descendants there, and at Rastrick and Idle are numerous.
7. Elizabeth, b. May 8, 1795, mar. Thomas Gooder of Anchor Pit, and their descendants are about Accrington and Preston.
8. Rachel, b. Sep. 6, 1798, married Benj. Noble. One of their sons still lives in his grandfather's house at Castle Hill.

C. Stephen R., millwright, b. 1768, d. 1850, bur. at Rastrick. His children were Edmund, d. 1869, aged 72, unmarried; Stephen who married Sarah Williams, and had four sons and a daughter, the latter the wife of Dr. Gamble, Elland; Jonas, a millwright at Leeds; Sarah; Susanna, wife of Henry Thompson, Leeds; Rachel, wife of James Taylor, Leeds; Ellen, wife of Wm. Hodgeon, Lightcliffe.

D. Sarah R., b. 1767, married Job Aspinall, butcher, Brighouse; whose son William, of Black Bull, married the sister of Mr. John Aspinall of Quarry Mount. Sarah's other children were John, (Common), Job, Simeon, (Manchester), Mark, Sarah wife of T. Firth, Lillands Lane.

E. Mercy Rushforth married Richard Rushfirth. These names and Rushworth and Rishworth have evidently had a common origin in these parts. Mercy's children were George, of Grimescar, (whose daughter Betty was wife of Joseph Crowther, Fixby, surveyor), Sarah, Nancy wife of Joseph Hepworth of Paddock, and the oldest was Mally, whose memory was most marvellous, for she could narrate family alliances and ancestries, and old traditions, by the hour together. She was twice married, (1) Richard Noble, (2) John Firth. Her daughter, Sarah, wife of John Raine, lived many years in Jamaica, but returned to Wakefield. James Richard Firth, another of Mally's children, has served Rastrick well on its Local Board.

Brief as this notice of a Rastrick family is, it may shew any reader who expects to find his own record in these pages that volumes would be required to do justice to many old families in the district we cover.

Crossing the Calder again, the following Assessment may be given as indicating all the houses, owners, and values in 1769. This list I copied many years ago when the town's books were kept at Harley Head, near Hove Edge. It is now in Mr. George Hepworth's keeping. What has become of the rest of the numerous books preserved there I do not know, but town's officials should make a point to secure them for the use of the future Town Clerk. There is no need to print the rate opposite each name, as it may be easily reckoned.

Q

"Assessment upon the Inhabitants of Hipperholme-cum-Brighouse, for the use of Jno. Oates, present Overseer of the Poor, at ye rate of ninepence per pound.

Jo. Jenkinson, Deputy Overseer and Collector, 15th Feb., 1769.

HIPPERHOLME QUARTER.

£			£		
20	Madam Horton (yields 15s. rate.)		3	Late Stephen Marsden	
34	John Shaw		1	Crossland Cottages	
9	John Mann		18	Richd. Pollard	
17	Thomas Rushforth		7	Hen. Flather	
6	John Stocks		23	Late Stancliffe	
18	John Thornton		11	Thomas Willans	
20	Saml. Thornton		1	Do.	School land
51½	Late Mr. Whittworth		3½	Mrs. Harrison	
8	Thomas Mann		2	Do.	Cottages
10	Mrs. Walsh		0½	Do.	for Wood
2½	John Hobson		14	Mrs. Simpson	
1	Widw. Jackson		4	Do.	for Speights
8	James Willans		2	Do.	New Houses
8	Fran. Nicholls		10½	Do.	for Roberts farm
10½	Thomas Asquith		16	Also late Mr. Jno. Simpson	
10	Jo. Asquith		1	Widow Shaw	
3	Mr. Walker, Wood End		1½	Widow Beaumont	
3	Esqr. Thornhill, Wood Side		12	Timothy Pullman	
1	Thos. Law, Wood Bottom		1½	Elkanah Slater, new houses	
13	Benj. Howorth		3	Dan. Sharpe	
0½	Do.	for Wood	9	Saml. Hardcastle	
2	Wm. Snowden		5	Do.	Lane ends
12	Widw. Blakeborough		0½	Do.	for Wood
11	Mr. James Chadwick		10½	Jereh. Carter	
1	Mrs. Waterhouse		1	Fran. Whalleys	
6	John Waterworth		2½	Wm. Rushworth	
2	Late Jo. Greene		0½	Wm. Mann, Synderhills	

LIGHTCLIFFE QUARTER.

£			£		
27½	Mr. Walker, Crow Nest, Pt. of Hill Top, Seven Cottages, and Simon Rhoyds		1	Do.	also James Mann Cott.
			1½	James Hargreaves	
			21	Joh. Hopkins	
15	Mr. Walker, Cliff Hill		7½	John Ramsden	
12	Do.	Lower Cliff Hill	3	Do.	Fair Banks
5	Do.	Paddocks and Flashes	1½	Widow Watson	
4	Do.	Dodges	1	Late Peter Atkinson	
7	James Miller and Howcarr		20	Mr. Wm. Stead	
14	John Rushworth		6	Thomas Woodhead	
8	Do.	for Hill Top	22	Mrs. Garside	
1½	Do.	Cottages	22	Do.	Kitching Closes
1½	Wm. Holland, Hive Croft		3	Do.	for School-land
8	Edward Mallinson		10	Wm. Brook	
12	Wm. Pearson		1	Do.	Pt. of late Banks farm
6	Richd. Hartley		4½	Little Smith House	
15	Wm. Swaine		2½	Mrs. Wainhouse	
8	Do.	Till Carr	29½	James Gleadhill	
12½	Abrm. Hemingway		2½	Do.	Cottages
23	Jon. Anderton		4	Mrs. Holmes	
12	Wm. Townend		1	Do.	Turnpike House
19	Thomas Mann				

HOVE EDGE QUARTER.

£			£		
26	Mrs. Firth, Slead Hall		4½	Mrs. Firth, for Springs	
5¼	Do.	for Cawles	2	Do.	for Wood

HOVE EDGE QUARTER.

£
24 Widow Waddington
8½ Abrm. Mallinson, Hill Top
20 Mr. Luke Howorth
14 Mr. Abrm. Mallinson
5 Mr. Saml. Howorth
6 Jo. Booth
2 Wm. Tate
9 Wm. Greenwood
4 Do. all the Cottages
9½ Hugh Mallinson
4 Isaac Naylor
2½ Late Widow Scholefield
8½ Wm. Holland
1½ Mary Flathor
2 John Pilling Cottages
1 Widow Longbottom

£
11½ John Flather
1½ Do. his House
7 Geo. Wilkinson
6¼ John Wilkinson
6¼ Josh. Hall
4 Do. Pt. of late Banks farm
12 John Sharpe
15 James Greene
13 Josh. Hemingway
1 Saml. Sharpe
10 Crispin Wilkinson
14 Jo. Ogden
2 Mr. James Dyson's Wood
0¼ Late Mr. Saml. Lister's Wood
0¼ Crossland Wood

BRIGGHOUSE QUARTER.

30 Esqr. Thornhill's Mills
38 Mr. James Stocks
10 Do. Waring Greene
2 Do. for Mrs. Ledger Cott.
1 Do. for Whitefields
1½ Late Firth's and Crowther's
25 Mr. Peter Day
4 Do. Malt Kiln
20 Mr. Saml. Nicholls
5 Mr. Eli Clegg [now White Swan.]
12¼ Mr. Jno. Pitchforth and Brooke
4 Jno. Hayley
8 Mr. Luke Howorth Houses [Beth.S.]
14 Mr. Wm. Raddcliffe
6¼ Mr. Jonas Crowther

3 Mr. Jonas Crowther his House
2½ Sir Geo. Armytage Cott.
4 Nicholas Botheroyd
16 Mr. Char. Sheffield
10 Wm. Wood
2½ Jno. Sowden [Thornhill Briggs.]
2½ Thomas Cooper
21 Jno. Binns
1 Do. Mr. Newstead wood
1½ Elkanah Hoyl House [Bridge End.]
2 Navigation Warehouse [Anchor.]
4 Jonas Fox
7½ Jno. Law
37 Mr. Jno. Gill
4½ Esqr. Ramsden Wood

NORWOOD GREEN QUARTER.

22 Jonas Wright
9½ Wm. Swaine
20½ Jo. Bolland
6½ Widow Shaw
18 Wm. Tettley
7½ Wm. Keighley
8 Jo. Heppworth
9 Late Jonas Holmes
0¼ Do. for wood
7½ Jno. Rhoyds
6 John Flather
4½ Jo. Ellis
1 Greenwood Cott.
1½ Furnace [Furness'] Cott.
5½ Saml. Mowbray
2½ Tim. Stocks
8 Luke Brown
6 Wm. Wigglesworth
4½ Jere. Empsall
1½ Late Jno. Terry
7 Richd. Oates
0¾ Do. for Wood
6 Jno. Oates

5 Wm. Ellis
1 Do. a Cottage
2½ Late Jo. Holmes
1 Sir G. Armytage Cott.
1 Jo. Oates Cott.
15 Jno. Brown
1½ Mr. Riddlesden wood
1 Mr. Geo. Taylor wood

Total Sum of Rate, £58 19s.

We whose names are here unto subscribed agree to this Assesst. As witts. our hands this 15th of Febry. /69,

JAMES GLEDHILL, JOSHUA HEMINGWAY, THOS. MANN.

West Riding Court of Yorkshire.—

Allowed and confirmed by us, two of His Majesty's Justices of the Peace for the said Riding, the 16th day of February, 1769. EDWD. LEEDES,* SAM. LISTER.

*Edward Rookes of Royds Hall on his marriage with the daughter of Robert Leedes, abandoned his paternal surname. He died in 1788 by his own hand, being in financial difficulties. The Lew Moor Co. got his estates.

QUEEN ANNE'S SQUARE.

The great local event of last century was the making of the Calder and Hebble Navigation Canal, the Act for which was passed March 5th, 1768.

From this date, or soon after, when the Navigation Warehouse near the Anchor Inn ⸱ was erected, may be placed the commencement of the commercial prosperity of Brighouse. The Anchor Inn was founded to supply the boatmen's real or supposed needs. The present building is modern, but the character of the old one may be known from the adjoining cottages, sometimes called Queen Anne's Square, but they are much older than her reign. Soldiers were picketed here in the Civil War time, and one of the chimneys consisting of four slates leaning together is worthy of inspection. The south aspect of the block is known as Daisy Croft, but the croft and its daisies have long since disappeared.

DAISY CROFT.

In 1839 an unskilled inhabitant drew from memory Brighouse as known in 1799, and as it is as perfect as we can get it, though the Triangle near the Town's Office, and opposite Captain Taylor's house, now the Conservative Club, is drawn too large, we perpetuate a reduced copy to contrast with the plan of the same locality in 1893. This latter plan leaves out, it should be stated, the populous suburbs

OLD WESLEYAN CHAPEL, 1795.

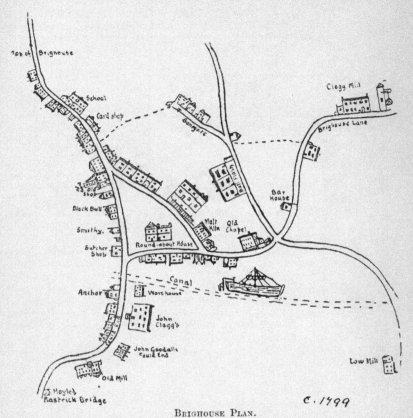

BRIGHOUSE PLAN.

c. 1799

of recent growth at Thornhill Briggs, Waring Green, and Lane Head.
Bethel Street and Police Street were known as Brighouse Lane which
was the main line from Elland to Wakefield, Dewsbury, &c. The
New Connexion Chapel gave its name to the first section, though the
original Methodist Chapel stood in the same lane, where the Park
Church (U. Methodist Free Church) now stands. This original chapel
became known throughout Methodist England on account of the dispute between the Kilhamites and the "Old Body." As the Friends
and Independents both worshipped on the Rastrick side of the Calder,
it was the oldest place of worship in Brighouse. At the "Top of
Brighouse," which expression shews how little Brighouse was, stood
Mrs. Bedford's School, which was established in 1741. Mary, widow
of John Bedford, of Thornhill Briggs, Esquire, by her will dated Dec.
13, 1735, directed that if the inhabitants of Brighouse did erect a
charity school there with good freestone and timber, within twelve

JOHN BURGESS, ESQ.

BEDFORD'S SCHOOL.

months of her decease, then her executors should appropriate £200 towards the education and maintenance there of ten poor children,

LEDGARD ARMS.

(five boys and five girls), and they should elect a Schoolmaster of sober life. The inhabitants erected a school, the subscription list being headed by Sir Samuel Armytage, 5 guineas : Mr. Radcliffe (ancestor of the Smith-house Radcliffes,) 3 guineas; Mrs. Gill (descendant of the Henry Brighouse who built Bonegate House, and mother of the Mrs. Ledgard who afterwards inherited Bonegate estate), 2 guineas; and fourteen guinea-subscribers, and others of smaller amount. The story of the defaced inscription, the loss of the endowment, and eventually of the school-house itself must be left over at present.

To Rastrick and Hipperholme Grammar Schools, justice cannot be done in the short space left for this volume. On April 13th, 1798, Rastrick Church was consecrated after re-erection, and interments now took place there instead of carrying the dead to Elland. One of the first burials was that of the old respected incumbent, the last of the old type of parsons whose character may be judged in some measure by the following notes kindly forwarded to me by the Rev. C. B. Norcliffe, M.A., Langton Hall, the representative of the Norcliffes, of Norcliffe in Shibden-dale, and other county families. Years ago I printed the name of Mercy Lacey in the local papers as the last instance, so far as I could learn, of public penance at Rastrick. I had then no idea the tradition was so old as these notes shew. It ought to be said that Mr. Braithwaite lived to be highly respected in after years. Many other interesting particulars must be retained for an ecclesiastical volume, but this extract from the Archdeacon's Visitations will give a little light on the Days of the Georges.

"1766. Rastrick. The Rev. George Braithwaite, Clerk, Curate, for neglecting to perform Divine Service in the said Chapel on Sundays and Holy Days, and particularly on Sunday the 15th day of June last past.

For being guilty of great profaneness and immorality in Drinking to excess and being Drunk within the said Chapelry of Rastrick.

For gaming and playing at Cards att public houses within the same and att other houses within the said Archdeaconry of York.

For committing the crime of fornication with Mercy Lacey of Rastrick aforesaid, single woman, [and begetting on her body one male bastard child,] and in general for acting and behaving in several instances so as he ought not to have done, and for omitting to act and behave in others as was his duty to do, as a Clergyman of the Church of England, and as Curate or Minister of Rastrick aforesaid.

1769. Rastrick. Mercy Lacey for Fornication with the Rev. George Braithwaite. Performed Penance."

The Kirklees Sale, by which Commercial Street district was thrown open for building, and other plots disposed of, took place in 1816, and from that date Brighouse has gone by gradual leaps to its present population.

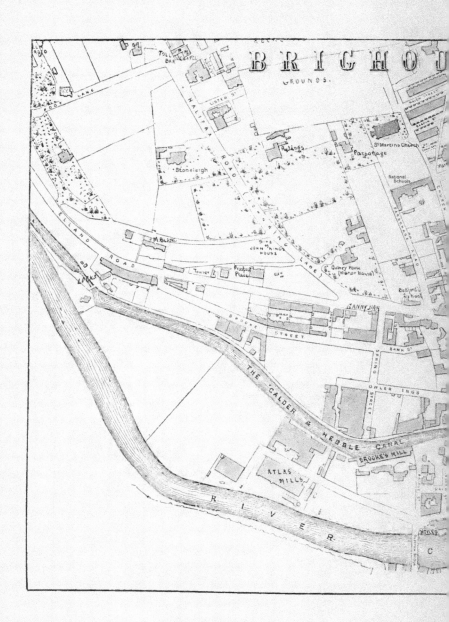

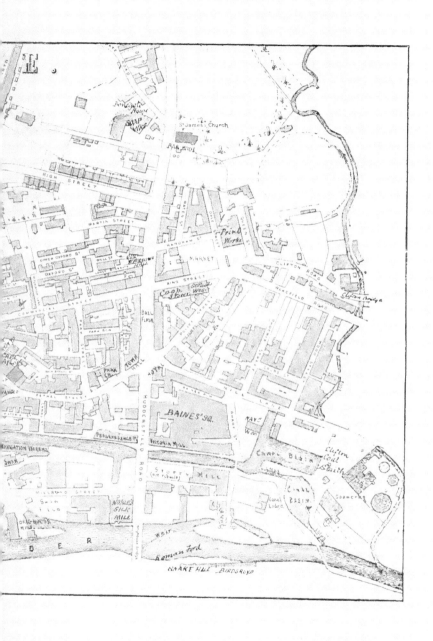

Modern Brighouse.

CALDER BRIDGE AND LOW MILL.

The story of the modern development of Brighouse and Rastrick, of its notable families, worthies, and industrial pioneers, shall be briefly told in this volume, more by pictorial efforts than by statistical accounts.

Bradford and Huddersfield Road necessitated the building of a second bridge across the Calder (about 1824-5,) between the two ancient Brighouse Mills—the corn mill and the fulling mill, and additional building land was thus available. The construction of the Elland and Obelisk (Dumb Steeple) Road took place about 1815, and building land was opened out along Brighouse Wood, and there the Towser, or prison, was erected. The Brighouse and Denholme-gate Road improved the ancient lane, afterwards known as John King lane, to Lane Head, Slead Syke, Hove Edge, &c. This was about 1826. The greatest stimulus of all was the construction of the Manchester and Leeds (or Normanton) Railway. No part of this line touched Brighouse, yet the directors gave the station the name of "Brighouse and Bradford," afterwards "Brighouse," and only recently "Brighouse and Rastrick" station. After five years Parliamentary agitation, the Bill for the construction of this line received the Royal assent, July 4, 1836; altered in 1837; ground being first broken in August, when Her Majesty had reigned three months. The Brighouse section, from Hebden Bridge to Normanton, was opened Oct. 5, 1840, and on the completion of Summit Tunnel, the whole line was opened March 1st, 1841. Leeds was 26 miles away, by rail, from Brighouse; Manchester 34. "Brighouse and Bradford Station" was on the sign-board, and coaches ran regularly from Bradford and Huddersfield to meet the trains.

BRIGHOUSE AND BRADFORD STATION, 1841.

JOHN BOTTOMLEY, ESQ.

RASTRICK RAILWAY EMBANKMENT, 1841.

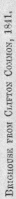

BRIGHOUSE FROM CLIFTON COMMON, 1841.

I have two coach tickets, white for outside, blue for inside :

OMNIBUS
FROM BRIGHOUSE
TO BRADFORD.

T. B. Hodgson.

Nov., 1842.

In 1845, John Hawkshaw produced plans of Railways, (a) Leeds *via* Fulneck, Bierley, to Low Moor ; (b) Bradford to Halifax *via* Low Moor, Pickle Bridge. Lightcliffe and Hipperhohne. (This was not opened till August 7, 1850) ; (c) Pickle Bridge *via* Bailiffe Bridge and Clifton Road (postponed till recent years) ; (d) Low Moor to Heckmondwike ; (e) Dewsbury, Batley, Holden Clough and Wortley ; (f) Cooper Bridge to Huddersfield. In the construction of the Lightcliffe line, the Bottom Hall valley required bridging by the beautiful arches shewn in the illustration. The Bottom Hall has a long history of its own, having been the Township Workhouse for a century, and here the ancient fathers met to legislate for the town before they opened a town's office at Harley Head.

Bottom Hall.

Taking up the leading family names of modern times in alphabetical order, we can but barely indicate the influence of the chief individuals on the prosperity of the district, some as founders of industries, others as serving the public on Boards of Health, &c., others for their professional eminence, and some as authors. Fuller justice to family records will claim amplified recognition in another volume. George J. Armytage, Esq., F.S.A., though not a resident, must not be left out on account of the family relationship with the Brighouse Manor. His eminence as a genealogist and antiquary, as editor of the Harleian Society Volumes, &c., and his qualifications as Chairman of the

Lancashire and Yorkshire Railway Company are widely known and appreciated. Lady Armytage is doubly interested in Brighouse for a branch of the ancient family of RADCLIFFE resided at Brighouse and Smith House for more than a century. Both the Armytages and Radcliffes were benefactors to Mrs. Bedford's School, "Top of Brighouse." The Lightcliffe Armytages, Cardmakers, were influential there all the reigns of George III. and his sons. They resided at

WICKHAM ARMS.

SIR HENRY W. RIPLEY.

Holme House, afterwards tenanted by Mr. Lamplugh Wickham, and subsequently by Mr. (afterwards Sir) Henry W. Ripley.

Mr. Peter ALLATT, who died in 1890, aged 81, was a well known inhabitant of Rastrick, and carried on business first as fellmonger and afterwards as wool merchant. Mr. Benjamin ATKINSON's druggist shop always calls to my mind pleasant memories of the kind, Christian gentleman, who died in 1871, aged 57, whilst his professional brother,

LILLANDS FARM.

J. G. BOTTOMLEY, ESQ.

Mr. Cardwell, was equally esteemed. Several pages would be required to note the influence of the ASPINALLS on the stone trade. John Aspinall, of Salford, Bridge End, died March 3, 1849, aged 76. Mary, his wife, Sep., 1847, aged 75. William Aspinall, Brighouse, died 1854, aged 67. John Aspinall, of Quarry Mount, died 1855, aged 52. His heir, Kaye Aspinall, Esq., on acquiring the Manor, named the mansion Manor House. He died April 24, 1872, aged 54. Thomas Aspinall, of Manor House, died in 1888, aged 43. The Southowram Aspinalls, now represented by the Rev. G. E. Aspinall, M.A., J.P., are descendants of Abel Aspinall, senior, of Rastrick, the father Abel, Jonathan, John, Cain, and Sarah, whose descendants flourish amongst us. The last named married Mr. William Helm, of the Helms of Lillands, identified with the woollen industry. Mr. Jonas BROUGHTON was father John, Benjamin, Arthur, Jonas, Thomas, Robert and Emma. John, the eldest son, became a cardmaker, as did his sons, but only one grandson now follows in the line. We are pleased to preserve his portrait as he appeared shortly before his death, though the negative is a poor one to start with. His grandson, Mr. Goldthorp Broughton, has kindly supplied it. The old gentleman died in 1864, aged 88. His children were Robert Heward, d. 1879, aged 80; Edward Heward, d. 1883, aged 81; Charles Heward, d. 1875, aged 68; Lauretta, wife of Job Fawcett, d. 1863, aged 59; Rhoda, wife of Wm. Gomersall, of Gomersall, (Vice-Consul at Genoa,) d. 1889, aged 78; and Lucy, wife of Wm. Marsden, grocer, d. 1891, aged 76.

MR. JOHN BROUGHTON.

Mr. Henry BYRNE, of Slead Hall, died Jan. 3, 1879, aged 76. Elizabeth Byrne, Jan. 12, 1852, aged 47. Mary Byrne, Sep. 5, 1875, aged 85. Mr. Samuel Henry Byrne, the son, has recently been added to the 'great majority.' His excellent character and business qualifications as partner in the firm of Ramsden, Camm & Co., wire-drawers, &c., cannot be too highly eulogized. Mr. William BROADBENT, who died in Nov., 1876, aged 66, served Brighouse officially in many ways, but his wife was equally known as a kindly dispenser of drugs. "Sarah druggist," as she was familiarly known, died in April, 1873, aged 66, but her wholesome advice is still handed down. Thomas and Benjamin BLACKBURN were brothers, who carried on business as cloth manufacturers at Holbeck. Thomas was a Cloth Hall Trustee at Leeds. His son Thomas settled at Popplewell, Scholes, near Cleckheaton, in 1820, as woollen yarn manufacturer, but after some years removed to the old water mill at Clifton Bridge. The second Thomas died in 1849, aged 70. His son Thomas commenced cotton spinning at Hightown about 1835. Soon after, he removed to Victoria Mill, Brighouse, and about 1841, he built the Phœnix Mill. He also erected the Atlas and Broadholme Cotton Mills, thus affording employment for many hundreds of people. The third Thomas died April 20th, 1879, aged 70. His brother Joseph died in 1890, aged 82. They were no relatives of Mr. Mark Blackburn, of Clifton, owner of the Granny Hall estate, whose property went to Mr. Joseph Rayner, of Slead House, Town Clerk of Liverpool, nor of the well-known Daniel Blackburn, who died in 1883, aged 76. Mr. Thomas Burgess died 1858, aged 76, and Sarah, his wife, 1858, aged 78. Their son John, founder of the extensive dyeworks at Birds Royd, died in Dec., 1869, aged 61. His wife, Letticia, representative of the old family of Morton, died in 1875, aged 60. Mr. John Burgess was of a scientific and literary turn as shewn by the fine library he acquired, which was dispersed on the death of his only son Thomas, in 1873. The latter had married a Miss Crossley, whose father had the adjoining extensive dyeworks. For the portrait of Mr. John Burgess, we are indebted to the courtesy of his daughter, Mrs. Maile, now residing in Essex. Mr. Thomas Bradbury, a moving spirit in Rastrick political and social life, and like Mr. Burgess, a devoted antiquary, died in 1870, aged 49.

No Brighouse gentleman was esteemed more highly for genuine uprightness and kindliness of heart than Mr. John Bottomley, the maltster, whose portrait we are delighted to perpetuate by favour of his equally respected son, whom Brighouse has delighted to honour for many years, and whose long services on the Local Board and in every public capacity, besides being the head of the old firm of manufacturing chemists at Brookfoot, prompted us to apply somewhat exactingly for his portrait to accompany these lines, and we are pleased to add his residence, Stoneleigh, as a specimen of the mansions that have sprung up in Victoria's reign. Mr. John Carr Bottomley's father (John,) died in 1862, aged 71, his mother Ursula, in 1861, aged 64.

Mr. John Brooke, senior, of the Rydings, a beautiful mansion near Manor House, and Stoneleigh, was long a well-known and beloved inhabitant of Brighouse. He removed his business place, as a corn miller, from Brookfoot, in 1826, to the newly-erected "Brooke's Mill," in Badger Lane, near Bridge End. He was a fine type of the old Squire, and many old inhabitants will rejoice to see his portrait. He died March 26, 1855, aged 71, and his widow, Mary, Oct. 12, 1867, aged 86. The poor lost great friends at their decease. Their son, John Brooke, Junr., Esquire, died in 1870, May 17th, aged 51. He had married the daughter of George Higham, Esq., solicitor, of Brighouse, whose professional eminence was acknowledged throughout the West Riding, especially in connection with Railway and public matters. Messrs. Chambers succeeded to the business. The genial kindliness of the Brookes superabounded in the only child of Mr. John, junior, the late Rev. John Brooke, M.A., whose remains were recently brought from his distant vicarage to rest in Brighouse churchyard.

STONELEIGH.

HIGHAM ARMS.

(See Higham family, page 288.)

BAINES family, of Shelf, is an offshoot—like the Baines' of Leeds, and the Mr. Baynes, M.P. for Leeds two centuries ago,—of an old family that settled mainly in Nidderdale and Ripon. They bore for arms, Sa. two shank bones in cross, ar., that in pale surmounting the one in fesse. Crest, a bone and palm branch in saltire ppr., whilst the Baines' of Bell Hall had for crest, a cubit arm erect, holding in the hand a shank bone in bend sinister argent. The bones form a pun on the Scotch name. The Nidderdale family according to Debrett (1808,) had been settled at Middlesmoor from before 1484, being then exiles from Scotland. The Baines clan were descended from Donald Bane, King of Scotland in 1093. See *Ripon Millenary*. The Shelf branch intermarried with the Mortimers and Nicholls, of Field head, as shewn by the monument in Coley Churchyard, from 1742, and there were buried Mr. John Baines of Brighouse, who died March 24, 1867, aged 73 ; Elizabeth, his wife, died April 8th, 1864, aged 71 : and their son, Samuel Baines, late of Brighouse, Fellow of the Geological Society, who died July 25, 1866, in his 52nd year. The monument was erected by his sister, Sophia Kershaw, of Crow Nest Park, in testimony of his worth and of a sister's love. The vast mills and adjuncts known as Baines' Square, in Brighouse, will justly perpetuate the memory of Mr. John and Mr. Samuel Baines, the former more as an on-looker and adviser, as commercial pioneers, who carried the fame of Brighouse manufactures to the markets of Lancashire and West Yorkshire. Mr. Samuel Baines had also a just reputation as a geologist and scientist. He is referred to as such in James' *Bradford*, and I treasure his memory personally because he annually gave prizes at the Brighouse Mechanics' Institute, of which he was President, and I carried away the first prize for mathematics in 1857. By over-trusting a manufacturer, in Derby (I think), he suffered a great loss, and his fine scientific library of 4000 volumes, with shells, birds, philosophical apparatus, fell to the hammer at Holroyd House, Priestley Green, April 19-22, 1865. Catalogue, 39 pages. To Mrs. Kershaw's concession, the future inhabitants are indebted for the portraits of these two Brighouse worthies.

R.

Mr. Joseph BARBER died March 19, 1862, aged 57. He was an attorney-at-law, of wide repute, and highly esteemed. His family alliances included most of the local gentry, but we are proudest of the attainments of some of his numerous family.

JUDGE BARBER. Mr. William Barber was the eldest son of Mr. Joseph Barber, solicitor, and was born at Castle Hill, Rastrick, Nov. 12, 1833. He was educated at St. Peter's, York, and Worcester College, Oxford. In 1859, he married Elizabeth, daughter of Mr. Henry Birch, and niece of the Rev. Joseph Birch. In 1862, he was called to the bar at Lincoln's Inn. In 1882, he was appointed one of Her Majesty's Counsel. For several years he was Professor of Real and Personal Property to the Council of Legal Education. In 1889, he was appointed Judge of the Derbyshire County Court, in consequence of which he removed from Pinner to Ashover. Ill-health compelled him to resign his judicial position in 1891. His death occurred at Ashover, March 29, 1892. He was President of the Jurisprudence Section, at the Social Science Congress, Huddersfield Meeting. In 1889, he was appointed a Magistrate for Derbyshire. His edition of Dart's *Vendors and Purchasers* is held in high esteem. As a Philanthropist and Temperance Reformer he was greatly appreciated. Sometime about 1855 he gave a lecture on the history of Brighouse, and the writer dates his first impulses as an antiquary from that time. A beautiful steel plate portrait of Judge Barber has just been issued to subscribers.

The VEN. ARCHDEACON BARBER, Chester, is another of the eminent sons of Mr. Joseph Barber, and as he still lives we are glad to content ourselves with such brief records of his useful life as the Clerical Directories afford, and specially pleased to preserve his portrait for our future townsmen.

Mr. FAIRLESS BARBER, F.S.A., F.R.H.S., deserves at the writer's hands the highest eulogium, as the reader will see by acknowledgments frequently given in these pages. The pleasant hours spent with him in Church Lane and at Castle Hill, and antiquarian rambles occasionally, have an undying interest. We have

MR. FAIRLESS BARBER, F.S.A.

JOHN BROOKE, SENR., ESQ.

to be content to retain the copy of the only portrait preserved of him, and to point to the Yorkshire Archæological Association, and especially to the Journal that he edited for it, as memorials of our townsman. Mr. Fairless was the second son, and born at Castle Hill, Jan. 11, 1835. He was educated at St. Peter's, York, and was a born antiquary. His tall figure was always conspicuous at the excursions of the Royal Archæological, and similar societies. As a local man he laboured with the best in promoting the best interests of the place and people. His enthusiastic labours, legal, literary, and philanthropic, shortened his days. His correspondence was almost world-wide ; Sir Gilbert Scott and others sought his advice on archæological matters. He was a welcome lecturer, and our newspaper files will testify to his abundant labours in connection with the Brighouse Mechanics' Institution, Penny Savings' Bank, Church matters, Parliamentary Elections as Returning Officer, Local Gas, Water, and similar Companies, &c. He was a staunch Conservative and Churchman, but never obtrusive or dogmatic. He was the embodiment of gentlemanliness. He died March 3, 1881, and was buried at Pinner, near London. A fitting notice appeared in the pages of the Yorkshire Archæological Journal, but no portrait. Some of his articles to that and other Journals were reprinted in pamphlet form.

MR. HENRY JOCELYN BARBER.

Mr. HENRY JOCELYN BARBER, another son, was born at Brighouse in 1846, and was also educated at York. He entered the profession of the Law on leaving school, and is well known in Halifax and Brighouse circles in that profession, but to most West Riding people he is best known as the Founder of the West Yorkshire Fire Brigade Friendly Society. When about 18 he became chief officer of the Brighouse Brigade, which post he held for twenty years. His exposures at different conflagrations, through water and frost as well as fire, have almost crippled him, but still his interest in the work is unflagging. In 1873, he published a pamphlet on "Salvage Corps," and in 1883 one on "Fire Inquests." His address at the Barnsley meeting, 1885, has also been printed. At Sheffield, in 1886, an illuminated address was presented to him. He possesses the antiquarian tastes of his brothers, is well versed in numismatology, bibliography, and the fine arts; and strongly favours the study of natural history. To his prompting, the issue of this volume must be largely attributed; to the memory of his brother Fairless it ought to be inscribed. The portrait is from a photograph by Davis and Sons, Halifax, and appeared in *Fire and Water*, June, 1890.

In the literary history we might perhaps claim that the great early astronomer and geometrician, John de SACROBOSCO, was a native of the holy wood of Fixby and Rastrick. Scotland and other places have tried to claim him, but Halifax parish has a very old traditionary right. Perhaps our first genuinely proved author was the Rev. Wm. AINSWORTH, curate of Lightcliffe. I have his long poem "The Marrow of the Bible," a very scarce and costly volume; and after thirty years search, I bought at Mr. Crossley's sale, Manchester, who had been forty years searching for one, the "Triplex Memoriale," three quaint sermons by Ainsworth. This volume I reprinted. The dear old name of the Rev. Joseph BIRCH must only be referred to here as author of several sermons; amongst them—"Consistency of Conduct Required from Believers—A Farewell Sermon in the New Parish Church of Brighouse, Oct. 26, 1862, by Joseph Birch, M.A., late Perpetual Curate." Printed by request. Brighouse, J. and A. Rushworth, 1862, pp. 19. "New Parish of Brighouse, Congregational Collections, 1842-62:" By Joseph Birch, late Pastor. Brighouse, J. and A. Rushworth, Commercial Buildings, 1862, pp. 12. In 1842 there was no legal district, being in Rastrick Chapelry. In 1856 Brighouse became a separate parish. Mr. Birch established the Brighouse Clothing Society in 1843, the first of several philanthropic movements he started. The average Church Collections for those years was £85. In 1854 the sum of £10 was raised for Soldiers' Wives in the Russian War, and in 1857, £13 towards the Indian Mutiny Relief Fund.

The pedigree of the BRIGHOUSES of Brighouse is not quite completed, nor that of the ELLANDS of Carlinghow. An important branch of the Brighouses flourished in Lincolnshire in the reign of Elizabeth.

Thomas Brighouse, of Brighouse, and Martin Brighouse, of Glentworth, gents., were parties in a deed of freehold land in Brighouse,

JOHN BROOKE, JUNR., ESQ.

9 Eliz. Col. John Morris's mother was a daughter of Brighouse of Newark. Col. Morris's son became Town Clerk of Leeds. John Brighouse of Brighouse held property here in 1607, but the most flourishing local branch was that referred to in the preceding pages. Richard Brighouse, of Bolling, Esquire, has the following registers of baptisms in Bradford Church,—Tempest, Jan. 24, 1618; John, March 19, 1619, died July 3rd, 1620, aged 4 months: Richard, Aug. 12, 1621; Mary, March 23, 1622-3. There were buried at Bradford, Widow Brighouse, 9 March, 1607; Edward Brighouse, 7 Oct., 1607; Mary, his widow, 17 April, 1609, and Elizabeth Brighouse, 10 June, 1610. Henry Brighouse built Bonegate House in 1635. His son married Susan, dau. of John Gill, of Lightcliffe, in 1658, and died in 1681, and was buried at the foot of the pulpit in Elland Church. His widow left her property to Henry, son of her brother, John GILL. This Henry married, in 1701, Mary ——, and their children were Daniel, Henry (who married Ursula, dau. of Wm. B. Cotes, Esq., J.P.,) and Ann, who married Edward LEDGARD, Esq., of the ancient Ledgards of Mirfield. She died in 1783, having inherited Bonegate, &c., from her brother Daniel, who died in 1762. Mrs. Ledgard's two eldest sons having died, the third son, Edward, inherited the property. He married Susannah, dau. of Mr. Wm. Armitage, of Woodhouse, Rastrick. He died in 1812, leaving two sons, Daniel (died 1830,) and William Edward, whose son, Mr. Wm. Ledgard, sold Bonegate nearly forty years ago. The arms as furnished by Mrs. Denison and Mr. Eyre Ledgard, p. 263, excepting, of course, the baronet's hand, have been used by the Ledgards of Mirfield, Bradford, and Brighouse. The arms of Brighouse are recorded as, Sable, on a fess between three lions rampant or, as many crescents of the first.

Brighouse is not dependent, fortunately, on a solitary staple trade, for it is difficult to class it with either the woollen or cotton towns. Wool, cotton, silk, worsted, carpets, dyeworks, card making, corn millers, tanning, currying, chemical works, print works, printers, maltsters, brewers, stone and brick merchants, wire workers, iron and brass founders, market and nursery gardeners, carriers, are topics on which the commercial history may be written. To take but one of the most modern of these, the brass founders. Thirty years ago, my friend, Mr. Robert BLAKEBOROUGH, by way of a hobby, experimented in brass founding. Now the names Blakeborough, Brighouse, are moulded on waterworks' fittings as far as Yokohama, along with Japanese hieroglyphics that the Brighouse moulder could not possibly read. For above a century the CARTERS of Giles House, &c., have been amongst the leading townsmen and manufacturers of Lightcliffe, and the late Mr. Daniel Carter spent a life-time for the town's benefit. He died in 1870, aged 62, his mother, Ellen, widow of Mr. John Carter, of Giles House, in 1864, aged 92. Jeremiah C., stuff maker, Lightcliffe, born at Greetland in 1712, married Elizth. Sykes in 1739. Their son Jeremiah, born at Lightcliffe in 1745, married Agnes Nyberg, a Swedish Moravian. We have a long account of the family, but must content ourselves with notes on two Lightcliffe natives.

The Rev. John Carter became B.A. in 1824, M.A. in 1827, D.D. in 1840. He was educated at St. John's College, Cambridge, became Curate of Aberford 1825-31, and was Master of Wakefield Grammar School, and Vicar of Saxton, near Tadcaster, many years. He died in 1878. The Rev. Edward N. Carter was educated at St. Bees', deacon 1825, priest 1826, Curate of Batley 1825, Vicar of Heckmondwike in 1842. He died suddenly Feb. 29, 1872, aged 71.

The story of the COOPERS of Brighouse and Rastrick for two centuries is so mixed up with Quakerism that it must be considered along with the history of the Friends. The CLAYS of Rastrick were also iden-

REV. JOHN CARTER, D.D.

tified with that Society formerly. For nearly a century they have been the chief commercial family in Rastrick, and our readers will be pleased to see the portrait of Joseph Travis Clay, Esq., who gave his life energies to philanthropic, educational, civil, and commercial pursuits. We had some difficulty in persuading his son, Mr. John W. Clay, F.S.A., J.P., that the public had a right to this memento. Mr. John Clay, a distinguished Friend, died in 1843, aged 69; his widow, Mrs. Elizabeth, in 1873, aged 97. There are other portraits we should have liked, and must get for a supplementary volume. Mr. Thos. Bradbury CHAMBERS, a worthy and notable native, who died in 1885, aged 60, and Mr. Alfred CAMM, of Well Holme, who died in Oct., 1843, aged 41, are amongst the number. Cheetham, Cliffe, Crowther and Crossley figure in the commercial history. The DRAKES, of Ashday Hall, and Fixby Knowl previously, were trained in the legal profession. They acquired estates in Brighouse which passed to Baron Pigot, who married the sole heiress. Mr. Thos. DEARNALLY was an institution in himself; a genealogist, saddler, cheap will-maker, eccentric Quaker,—no one was more generally known or respected, or more 'kensback.' Samuel DYER, now of London, was formerly an assistant teacher under Mr. Wm. Lundy at Prospect Place. In 1891, Mr. Dyer again identified himself with Brighouse by having printed

JOHN BAINES, ESQ.

by Mr. Hartley, the "Dialect of the West Riding," 143 pages. There are a few local references, but the most curious thing is the number of foreigners who subscribed for it. DYSON and DENHAM are familiar business firms for future record. The EMPSALLS have been a well-to-do family in Lightcliffe for three centuries, the most notable member at present being Mr. Councillor Thomas Thornton Empsall, of Bradford, a noted antiquary and bibliophile. His mother was one of the Rastrick Thorntons. His grandfather, Mr. Joshua Empsall, had three sons, Jere., Daniel and Joseph. Jere. and Daniel were known for miles round as eccentric, 'cute, racy bachelors. A portrait of the elder, by Mr. Lumb Stocks, is in existence.

MR. THOMAS DEARNALLY.

Mr. T. T. Empsall has rendered special service on the Bradford School Board and Corporation, especially in promoting the Free Library, which is a model one. He has been President of the Bradford Historical Society since its foundation in 1878. For a pedigree of the FIRTHS of Toothill, see *Yorkshire County Magazine*, 1891. Mary, widow of Thomas Firth, of Firth House, died in 1842, aged 77. Betsy (née Horsfall?) wife of another Thomas Firth, died in 1864, aged 74. She was an "Elder" amongst the Friends. Her husband, the celebrated Quaker, who refused to let Sir John Ramsden become owner of *all* Huddersfield unless he would cover the biggest floor of the warehouse Mr. F. owned there with sovereigns edgeways, whose beautifully white painted gates marked the extent of Toothill, whose kind smile was bestowed on the poorest child, and whose half-crowns judiciously distributed by himself on St. Thomas' day, though he cared nought about saints' days, was the last of the worthy family at Toothill. He died, without issue, on March 3rd, 1869, aged 79. Mr. Scorah, Bradford, a Hipperholme native, has kindly supplied the portrait. Another branch of the family built and resided at Firth House. Akin to the Firths, and also members of the Society of Friends, were the FRYERS, who resided at Toothill Grove. The old Toothill Hall stood where a farm house stands on the top of Toothill Bank.

A few interesting particulars will be found in "Recollections of a Beloved Sister," [Mary Ann Fryer, died 1873, aged 62, an Elder.] by her sister, Mrs. Harvey, Leeds; privately printed. I wish some friend would favour me with a copy. An outline pedigree appears in *Yorkshire County Magazine*. Joseph Fryer, an Elder, died in 1846, aged 65, his widow, Ann, in 1865, aged 79. Their son, Joseph Jowett Fryer, in 1846, aged 39. Old Rastrick folks were never tired of speaking about old Doctor Joseph Fryer. He was father of Joseph, (manufacturer), who was father of Mrs. Harvey, mentioned above, and grandfather of Mr. John Firth Fryer, B.A., York School, and of Mrs. Hanbury (née

MR. THOMAS FIRTH.

Pease), formerly of China, now residing in Italy. The old Doctor's third son was Simeon, an esteemed surgeon in Rastrick, whose third son, Mr. Alfred Fryer, born at Rastrick, has recently died in Cheshire. Alfred became head of the firm of Fryer, Benson and Forster, sugar refiners, Manchester and Antigua. He was always of an inventive turn. In 1865, he produced the "Concretor," by which the juice of the cane became solid, and loss in shipping was obviated. He joined the Nottingham firm of Engineers, Manlove & Co., and soon after

SAMUEL BAINES, ESQ.

established that of Fryer & Co., at Rouen, now conducted by his younger son, H. D. Fryer. In 1884, he retired from active business. His Refuse Destructor, for transforming refuse into cement or paving blocks, has been adopted in many large towns. He fitted up at Wilmslow, his residence, an astronomical observatory, and became intimate with Lockyer, Proctor, Balfour Stewart and other scientists. He was author of " Peculiarities of Vital Statistics of the Society of Friends," "Floating Lightships," "Influence of Forests on Rainfall," "Balance of Trade," "Cost of Living in various Countries," "The Silver Question," "Wilmslow Graves—a local history," and edited " American Investments " for the Jarvis Conklin Co., Kansas.

He frequently crossed the Atlantic on business. "The Great Loan Land " was issued for that Company. His Wilmslow home contains mementos of visits to Egypt, Palestine, the Indies, and the Far West. He died at Wilmslow, Dec. 13, 1892, and was buried in the Friends' Burial Ground, amid widespread tokens of sympathy and regret. The *Publisher's Circular* had a small portrait of him ; the one we give is from the "American Investments." His family consists of Alfred Cooper Fryer, Ph.D., M.A., Henry Dyson Fryer, Sarah Maria, wife of Rev. J. Collins Odgers, B.A., Mary Emily, wife of Rev. J. Stuart Reid, and Gertrude Anne Fryer, of Wilmslow.

Amongst our local authors space must be given to the Rev. F. G. FLEAY, of Hipperholme Grammar School, a noted Shakespearian scholar. He only held the office a short time, however. The Rev. W. E. LITTLEWOOD, his precursor, has published several educational works also since his removal from Hipperholme. The Rev. Benjamin FIRTH had been a schoolmaster at Scholes before 1805. He was the means of building Wyke Independent Chapel, and then added pastoral duties to scholastic ones. He rented the Victoria Mill, erected by James and Henry Noble in 1837, and in 1842 became owner thereof, but in 1849 Mr. Samuel Baines purchased it along with the Prince Albert and Canal Mills, built by Mr. Firth. Mr. Firth supplied some of the streets with gas from December, 1843. He was also a versatile educational writer as his school books shew, and to add to all, a controversialist with trenchant pen, as shewn by "Church *versus* Dissent, or Tory Spite and Virulence overshooting their mark, &c.," published by request. By B. Firth, Manor House Academy, Hartshead Moor. 2nd edition, 1835, 6d., 32 pages. S. Easton, Printer, New Road, Brighouse. So far as I remember, this is the first Brighouse printed pamphlet, though I have a trade circular printed by Easton, March, 1834, when A. and J. Atkin from Halifax inform the Inhabitants that they have taken the house lately occupied by Mrs. Empsall, opposite the Church Lane. The Rev. B. Firth's memoir appears in the Congregational Year Book, 1854.

If ever there was pleasure in having a medical gentleman attending one, it was when Robert FARRER, Esq., M.R.C.S., &c., was called in. He happily lives still at Scarborough, but the author has nearly forty years' pleasant reminiscences of Dr. Farrer's gentleness, skill, and urbanity. His sons follow the profession; but they cannot be more beloved by a whole town than their father has been. In his public capacity as Medical Officer, Local Board Member, &c., Dr. Farrer has gained the highest esteem.

The FIELDS of Sowerby and Shipley had an offshoot in Lightcliffe formerly, and the FOSTERS of Queensbury not only still own land in Hipperholme, but Major Jonas Foster, the third son of John Foster, Esq., of Hornby Castle, made Cliffe Hill his home, and was the main promoter in the erection of Lightcliffe New Church. Major Foster removed to Ludlow shortly before his death in Feb., 1880. The GOODAIRES of Rastrick, GIBSONS of Slead Hall, and General GUEST of Lidgate, can only be mentioned by name here. The GOODALLS have been closely identified with the commercial prosperity of Brighouse during the last hundred years.

In 1811, the Rev. Philip GARRETT, Wesleyan Minister, published at Manchester a 12mo. pamphlet of 28 pages entitled, "A Scourge to Calumny," arising out of the Brighouse Wesleyan Chapel dispute. William HATTON, of Lightcliffe, published "A Sketch of Methodism in Halifax and its vicinity, from its commencement in the year 1741 to the present period, 1824." Halifax. Thomas Walker, printer; 36 pages. I should like to see a copy. The Rev. Robert HARLEY, F.R.S.,

REV. ROBERT HARLEY, F.R.S.

VEN. ARCHDEACON BARBER.

F.R.A.S., M.A., for some years minister at Bridge End Congregational Chapel, has published several special sermons and mathematical works, to be referred to hereafter. The Rev. J. B. Lister, his successor, was author of a couple of volumes. Mr. Scholefield, one of the first ministers at Bridge End, was father of the Rev. Prof. Scholefield, of Cambridge, a voluminous author. Mr. Meldrum and Mr. Lowell, also of Bridge End, printed portly books in George III's days.

John HANSON, of Rastrick, the antiquary of three centuries ago, has been previously referred to. He married the heiress of a Rayner, of Liversedge, whose ancestor had married the heiress of de Liversedge. In the Bodleian Library is Mr. Hanson's collection for a History of Liversedge, now being incorporated into Mr. Peel's "Spen Valley." Mr. Hanson compiled a Pedigree of the Hansons, with arms emblazoned, on parchment. I have printed this in the *Yorkshire Genealogist* from one of the ancient parchment copies, but refrain from reprinting it here, as the Manor Rolls give the evidences of the same, and we hope to enlarge the pedigree shortly. Sir Reginald Hanson, Bart., LL.D., M.P., late Lord Mayor of London, Sir W. H. Hanson, of Melbourne, W. D. Hanson, Esq., J.P., Bideford, are representatives of branches of this ancient family, and the name is retained in the Ormerod family by marriage with

a descendant. The Misses HOWORTH of Bethel Street, were the fashionable dressmakers of 1800. Their brothers, William, of Ipswich, and Thomas, of Idle, became clergymen. An 8 page pamphlet was printed at Idle by John Vint, in 1830, 2nd edition, price 2d., entitled "An Elegy to the Memory of the Rev. Thomas Howorth, late minister at Idle, who departed this Life the 22nd day of April, 1830, by Benj. Greaves." Mr. Howorth became curate of Calverley in Feb. 1779, at £40 a year. He became curate of Idle Chapel soon afterwards, which he held till his death. He was the first person buried in the New Church that he was the chief means of erecting. His

REV. T. HOWORTH.

nephew, William Howorth, produced two volumes of poetry that deserve the highest encomium. "The Cry of the Poor" and "The Redeemer" are volumes that I sought for many years, and now highly appreciate. A tablet is erected to his memory in Brighouse Church. For more than a century the family resided in Red Beck valley, before removing to Brighouse. The portrait of the Poet is from a chalk drawing in the possession of his nephew, Mr. W. H. Howorth, Cleckheaton.

MR. WM. HOWORTH.

The publications of Oliver HEYWOOD, and the publications respecting him, would occupy several pages, so I beg to refer the reader to the five volumes I have printed respecting him.

Isaac HEATON, d. 1871, aged 84 nearly, was school-master at Bedford's School for half a century or more. He printed a pamphlet on the origin of the school, of which he was the last master.

One of the most notable families of schoolmasters and clergymen in these parts last century was the HUDSON'S, whose services were secured for Idle, Bingley, and Hipperholme. Perhaps Hipperholme Grammar School was never so popular as during Mr. Hudson's mastership. He was buried at Coley in March,

1835. In 1739, his grandfather, the Rev. Thomas Hudson, late master of Hipperholme school, buried a child at Coley, and the family had resided in Hipperholme a hundred years earlier still. The Rev. Richard Hudson was Master of Hipperholme School 53 years, Lecturer of Halifax 65 years, Incumbent of Bolsterstone, and Vicar of Cockerham. Yet with all his duties he reached the age of 86. He was B.A., Cambridge, in 1768, Eighth Wrangler, M.A. in 1771, when Master of Halifax Grammar School, removing to Hipperholme in 1782. Amongst the founders of Brighouse, in a double sense, must be recorded Mr.

REV. R. HUDSON.

JOSEPH TRAVIS CLAY, ESQ.

George Hepworth, architect and surveyor, who was pre-eminently the Builder of Brighouse. The family has been located at Yew Trees and Hove Edge for three centuries. Mr. George Hepworth was interred at Brighouse Church in 1875, aged 76 ; his wife, Elizabeth, in 1877, aged 67.

YEW TREES.

Mr. George Hepworth, the son and successor of the architect, has reared several noble piles, especially Woodvale Mills, built for Mr. Kershaw; but he has also gained a position as photographic artist as evinced by his charming book—"Brighouse, its Scenery and Anti-quities," 1885. The work consists of thirty platinotype photographs of buildings in Rastrick, Hartshead, Kirklees, Brighouse, Lightcliffe, Cromwellbottom, Shelf, and Coley, with a page of descriptive matter to each view. To Mr. Hepworth I am indebted for the excellent portrait of his father, and for views from which several blocks have been made.

A pedigree of the Hoyles, like that of the Hansons, would fill a fair-sized book. A notice of the descendants of Mr. Elkanah Hoyle, of Hipperholme, of whom several were eminent clergymen, appears in my *Yorkshire Genealogist,* vol. 2. A branch settled at Daisy Croft, one of whom erected the cottages at the Brighouse end of the old Bridge. At Lillands and New Road resided the Helms, leading men in the Rastrick staple trade. At Crow Trees, from 1870 to the time of his death in 1891, Mr. Samuel Hirst took up his residence. The old family of Hirst were regular visitors to Brighouse Tourns. Robert Hirst, of Greenhead, who died in 1625, appointed his cousin Edward Hanson, of Woodhouse, and Sir John Ramsden, executors. The history of the family for centuries is interwoven with the town of Huddersfield. Mr. Samuel Hirst, born in 1818, was the eldest son of

Samuel Hirst, of Huddersfield. The younger Samuel married, in 1839, his cousin Angeline, dau. of John Hirst, of Baltimore, U.S.A. Their two sons are John Abraham Hirst Hirst, Esq., J.P., &c., Retford, and Samuel Edgar Hirst, Esq., M.A. (of Cambridge), Inner Temple, Barrister-at-Law, of Crow Trees.

ARMORIAL BEARINGS.— The Hirst family have used the following for three, if not four, generations, although I do not think they are registered in the College of Arms.

Arms, Gu: on a Chevron Arg: engrailed, three annulets of the first.

Crest, an Arm counter embowed cutting an ostrich feather with a scimitar.

Motto, Deus mei fortitudo.

HIRST OF RASTRICK.

The late Mr. Samuel Hirst having married a co-heiress, he placed his wife's arms on an escutcheon of pretence in the centre of his own shield, and being a first cousin of the same family the arms are alike, except the label to distinguish the arms of the eldest son.

In 1725-9, Samuel Hirst, attorney-at-law, resided at Thornhill Briggs.

The Rev. Robert Harrison, master of Hipperholme Grammar School, and curate of Hartshead where he was buried July 13, 1761, resided in Lightcliffe 1747-61. Mr. John Harrison, attorney-at-law, of Slead Hall, was buried at Hartshead, Feb. 3, 1754-5. Elizabeth Marsden, grand-daughter of Thomas Harrison, Slead Hall, was buried at Hartshead April 20, 1755. Ann, wife of Mr. Thomas Harrison, Southowram, maltster, was also buried there in 1764. The Rev. Robert Harrison's children, so far as I have found entries, were *Swaile* and *Richardson*, bap. at Coley, 1749. Swaile was buried at Hartshead, Oct. 16, 1750. *Catherine*, daughter of the Rev. Robert H., was bap. at Coley in 1760.

T. T. EMPSALL, ESQ.

SLEAD SYKE MILL.

William HOLLAND, of Broad Oak, manufacturer of stuffs, removed from Hove Edge, where his son was born, to Slead Hall as a tenant, in 1785. The son, John, has rightly been styled the Crossley or the Salt of his day, in the religious, political and commercial worlds. He removed from Slead Hall to his own property Slead House, building the mill called Slead Syke Mill, and the Warehouse at Slead Syke. He was the pioneer in the worsted trade, and no merchant was better known or more highly respected at Halifax Piece Hall, or Bradford Market. In 1811, he introduced into Yorkshire the manufacture of moreens, which had been previously made at Norwich only. He was the moving spirit in the Congregational body of West Yorkshire, and the great supporter of Airedale College.

SLEAD SYKE MILL.

His wife, Elizabeth, daughter of Mr. Hodgson, of Halifax, was a most estimable lady, whose name is still fragrant in the district. He died in 1845, and was buried at Halifax, the funeral sermon being printed by request:

COMFORT for the Dying Christian. A Sermon occasioned by the Death of John Holland, Esq. of Slead House, near Halifax, preached in Bridge End Chapel, Rastrick, on Lord's Day, Oct. 12th, 1845; by Robert Bell. Published by request. Halifax, H. Martin; sold by G. S. Keir, Brighouse. 1845. 27 pp.

Of Mr. Holland's family, we may note that William, of New House, died in 1885, aged 79; Samuel died in 1847, John in

MR. JOHN HOLLAND.

1864, Joseph in 1887, aged 72, all s.p., but four daughters married, and had issue.

George HIGHAM, Esq., died Feb. 20, 1860, aged 59. He resided at Bonegate House many years. Mrs. Ann Higham died March 3, 1858, aged 56. Their eldest son, George Wm., died in 1853, aged 25; John, son, in March, 1859, aged 23; Thomas, son, in May, 1861, aged 27; James Rhodes, son, in July, 1863, aged 24; Sarah, their daughter, wife of Mr. Joshua Tolson, in Sep., 1859, aged 30. We are indebted to Mrs. Brooke, of the Rydings, for the excellent portrait of her father. The arms of the Higham family are given on page 273. Other familiar names in the development of Brighouse are Joseph HAMERTON, (died in 1840, aged 84), from whom Hamerton Yard is named, John HARGREAVES, (died in 1888, aged 79), Surgeon HOPKINSON, (died in 1830, aged 49), John HARTLEY, a famous Methodist

MRS. HOLLAND.

DR. FARRER.

local preacher, the HANSONS, veterinary surgeons here and at Norwood Green for a century, and the HOYLES of Daisy Croft, of whom James died in 1826, aged 49, and George in 1841, aged 74. No name is more familiar than that of JESSOP, a family that has been identified with the commercial progress of Brighouse for more than a century. They came from Kirkheaton district as shewn in the *History of Bridge End Chapel*, and in that and neighbouring parishes they were influential yeomen for some centuries. Richard Jessop, of Low Mill, left his impress on the trade and moral training of Brighouse in its juvenility. His son, of the same name, was a leading spirit in the local Sunday School Movement. Richard, the father, died in 1835, aged 78. Mr. Thomas Jessop, the Registrar of Births, &c., knew Brighouse from 'thread to needle,' and in connection with Messrs. Barber, solicitors, had much influence in legal matters. He died in 1879, aged 72. His son, Mr. Thos. Rd. Jessop, F.R.C.S., whose name as a Surgeon and a Specialist is a household word within a wide radius of Leeds, we are proud to claim amongst our eminent natives, and to his kinsman, Mr. Charles Jessop, our thanks are due for the portraits that adorn this all-too-brief notice of the family. Mr. C. Jessop has evidently been 'touched' with the antiquarian spirit, as shewn in the reprint of a lecture, 23 pages, on "Brighouse in the 18th and 19th Centuries," 1892. The story of the "Brighouse Press" may be briefly told. Following Mr. Easton, we had Messrs. Keir, Siddal, and Rushworth as printers and booksellers, and Joseph Turner as bookbinder. Halifax has had its newspapers, off and on, since 1759, when the "Union Journal, or Halifax Advertiser" was started.

On Jan. 1st, 1859, Mr. Jonas Yates, Siddal's successor, issued the first number of the "Brighouse and Rastrick Chronicle," a monthly newspaper that is now extremely scarce. It only existed three years or so. Mr. John Samuel Jowett, from Bradford, then in his father's name, commenced the "Brighouse News" on Feb. 17, 1866, first monthly, then weekly. On March 14, 1873, Mr. A. B. Bayes began a weekly paper called the "Brighouse and Elland Express," named since the expiration of the first year the "Brighouse and Rastrick Gazette." Our third weekly paper, the "Brighouse Echo," with an Elland edition also, dates from June 24th, 1887, and is very vigorously published and edited by Mr. John Hartley and Mr. J. Caldwell. For some years Mr. Hartley issued a dialect almanack annual. He was a printer under Mr. Yates when the "Chronicle" was started. From the Brighouse press, Mr. Cawthra Woodhead has passed to South Africa, where he edits a newspaper, &c.

John KING Lane has preserved to us the name of an eminent Quaker resident, who was one of the chief men in conducting town's business before Local Boards were instituted. His house, near Prospect Place and Mont Blanc, was demolished nearly forty years ago, and not yet rebuilt, though the cellaring was completed. John King died 7th of 4th month, 1853, aged 75, and his widow, Sarah, 8th of 1st month, 1854, aged 77.

s

Two hundred years ago, the name of John KERSHAW, gentleman, constantly appears in the West Riding Sessions' Rolls as juror, or as chief constable for the wapontake, and he served the public offices and directed the town's meetings of Hipperholme-cum-Brighouse for many years. His residence was Hoyle House, then a secluded better-class house. His only daughter and heiress, Mary, married Wm. Richardson, Esq., of High Fernley, of the notable and learned family at Bierley Hall, lately represented by Sir Mathew Wilson, M.P. By a singular coincidence the Kershaw estate at Hoyle House, &c., has recently been acquired by Richard Kershaw, Esq., of Crow Nest, whose father, Mr. Richard Kershaw, came from Wyke to Bonegate Lane, Brighouse, and commenced the business of market and nursery gardener. From former old buildings in Wyke, bearing the family initials, from old deeds we have seen, from Oliver Heywood's Diaries, and from church registers, we learn that the Kershaws of Wyke have had extensive possessions in that township. They have evidently branched out from a place called Kirkshaw, in Calderdale,—east and west, as the early pages of this book and old Rochdale deeds prove.

KERSHAW ARMS.

The Wyke Kershaws have buried their dead, amongst other places, at Lightcliffe, where a gravestone records the interment of Richard Kershaw, of Wike, in 1727, aged 60; Joshua in 1728, aged 29; Timothy in 1733, aged 60. The family have borne for coat-armour, Argent, three crosses crosslet sable, on a chief azure three bezants or, the centre one charged with a cross gules. Crest, the stump of an oak eradicated and sprouting fesseways proper, thereon a pheasant, in the beak a sprig of oak, proper. Motto, Qui Invidet Minor Est.

In a future volume we hope to preserve the portrait of so notable a worthy as Mr. Richard Kershaw, senior, not less on account of his prominence as founder of an important industry carried out on artistic, beneficent, and honourable lines, than as progenitor of a family who have carried the fame of Brighouse to many distant towns in artistic horticulture. Nearly all his sons have had engagements in planning parks, cemeteries, conservatories, &c. Having known the sons and grandchildren personally, it is gratifying

MR. ALFRED FRYER.

to note the marked heredity, physical, moral, and linguistic, so eminent in the grandsires. A nobility of character is the most prominent feature, and such, may be guessed, must be an essential in the gentleman who can rise to the ownership, and even improve upon the appearance of Crow Nest Park, and who can devise so palatial a factory as the renowned Woodvale Silk Mills. Sir Titus Salt's eye caught the slightest disfigurement at Saltaire, and would have it immediately removed. Mr. Kershaw's training and inclinations are similar to those of his worthy predecessor at Crow Nest, a mansion that demands several illustrations to do justice to its internal and external beauty. We give, by Mr. Kershaw's favour, two views of

CROW NEST, (North Front.)

the south aspect, but a hundred views are not so gratifying as an hour's sojourn amongst the profusion of hot-house and other plants that adorn the mansion and its grounds. The celebrated Mr. Carr was the architect, and the house dates back more than a hundred years. Yet, the height of the rooms is 16 feet, and the beautiful ashlar stone seems as perfect as ever. Probably the greatest wealth about Crow Nest lies in the valuable beds of stone, which Mr. Kershaw knows how to reach without disfiguring the surface.

He was the first to discover the finest beds on the Granny Hall estate, now being worked by Messrs. Farrer and others. Indeed, it seems that all he has put his hand to has prospered. Several tried to establish the Silk business in Brighouse since Mr. Robert Newton, but with only varying success and some failures, till Mr. Kershaw gave his attention to it, and the noble pile at Woodvale, where the town-denizens go as it were into the country to work, is a standing monument to his genius. The surrounding woods and shrubbery, the scrupulous cleanliness and punctuality, the architectural excellence under Mr. George Hepworth's superintendence, the vastness of the concern, several blocks of the square being hid from the photographic view, all testify to months of laborious planning. It goes without saying, that the care and taste displayed in the structure implies complete sanitary arrangements, drainage, light, ventilation for the seven hundred people engaged in this busy hive. Three blocks cannot be shewn by only one photograph, and one of these is five storeys high. Every modern improvement in the art of silk spinning is here used. The establishment covers over five acres, and forty thousand spindles are in operation. This vast concern commenced so recently as 1864 in Brighouse, but the present mills were opened in 1880. Mr. Kershaw's name has for years been identified also with Brighouse as Chairman of Local Board, &c.

Our pages shew that the LISTERS have been considerable property owners, and branches of them have resided in Hipperholme township. Their pedigree is distinctly proved to Mr. Richard Lister, of Halifax, who was living there in 1400, presumably son of Robert Lister, the litster or dyer, constable of Halifax in 1372, who seems to have been grandson of Bate the Lister, or dyer, of Halifax, about 1298. Bate, we know, had two sons, John and Richard, the latter an important townsman from 1329 to 1338. The Otes, Waterhouse, and Lister families have been the owners of Shibden Hall for four centuries. Miss Kettle, in her story of "The Mistress of Langdale Hall," has added a glamour to the interest centred on this ancient timber mansion. The Miss Lister of last generation forms the central figure of the story. Our special interest in the family, for these pages, is because various old deeds at Shibden Hall record the history of Lightcliffe homesteads, and the owner, John Lister, Esq., M.A., County Councillor for Hipperholme, is a gentleman whose antiquarian labours and favours have, for a quarter of a century, been appreciated by the writer. The LANGLEYS, of Hipperholme, were about the most important family there last century. They bore for arms, Argent, a cockatrice, azure. Their mansion is one of the finest we have remaining, with its internal oak gallery, ceilings, &c. It has been sub-divided into tenements this century, and many notable families have resided there, including the Shaws, Scorahs, and some Grammar School Assistant Masters. Close by lived Mr. William LANCASTER, solicitor, Bradford, a native of Brighouse, born 1816, buried in Brighouse Cemetery in 1883. John Lancaster, of Brighouse, died in 1818, aged 76. The LEDGARDS have been previously mentioned as representatives of the Brighouses of Brighouse. Edward L., of Bonegate, died in

T. T. ORMEROD, ESQ.

1812, aged 66 ; his wife, Susannah, in 1818, aged 62 ; Wm. Edward, in 1827, aged 51 ; Elizabeth, his widow, in 1845, aged 66.

DR. WM. LUNDY.

William LUNDY demands notice as a prosperous schoolmaster at the Rastrick Common British School. He was a native of Malton, and left Borough Road College, London, in 1837, for Rastrick. In 1853, he established a high-class boarding and day school at Prospect Place, Brighouse, having obtained the foreign titles of M.A. and Ph.D. He also joined the College of Preceptors. Square hats worn by the pupils added to the grandeur in rustic eyes, and Dr. Lundy's establishment became widely known and popular. He had some good assistant masters too. He printed a few school books, on " Phrenotypics," " Palestine," " Le Lecteur Francais," &c. His labours were cut short by excessive study in 1860, aged 44. Mrs. Sarah Lundy, his widow, spent her widowhood in temperance and philanthropic labours in Huddersfield, and was buried at Bridge End Chapel in 1886, aged 71. The Doctor's brother, Joseph, ex-schoolmaster, became Mayor of Windsor.

Edward Jackson LOWE, an esteemed curate at Brighouse published a small religious dialogue whilst there. Lightcliffe Church was noted far and wide for the musical excellence of its services. I have " A Collection of Hymns and Occasional Pieces for the use of the Congregation of Lightcliffe Chapel," 3rd edition, Halifax, printed by Jacobs, 1819, 74 pages. The settlement of the Moravians in Lightcliffe, and the fostering hand of Wm. Priestley, Esq., afterwards of Thorp Arch, whose fine library is preserved in Halifax Church, tended much to make Lightcliffe and the district renowned for vocal and instrumental music. Luke Settle, George Lister, Ephraim Noble, and others, were eminent teachers and psalm-tune composers.

The LEPPINGTONS, of Lane Head, were known in the early Victorian years as manufacturers at Leppington Mill, Brookfoot. The Macaulays, of Slead Hall, were noted for a long ancestry, mostly surgeons since Aulay McAulay, of Huddersfield, 1727. Dr. Macaulay, of Halifax, keeps up the name and profession. MORTON, MELLOR, MITCHELL, MARSDEN, MILNES, MORRELL, are well-known local names of Brighouse tradespeople. "Marsden Mayoralty; with sketch of the Life of Henry Rowland Marsden, Mayor of Leeds," 181 pages, 1875, is interesting to us as his father was pricked or lotted for a soldier at Rastrick in 1811, and served in the 90th foot. John MOORE, Hipperholme, was the author of "A Terrier or Field Book, the number and measurement of every close in Halifax Township, with names of the owners, &c., so that the labourer with plough, scythe or sickle, will find the measurement of every close." Halifax, Dec. 1797, pp. iv, 27; printed by Jacobs. Map and List of Subscribers. 104 poles make a day-work. The Rev. Mr. Morrison, of Halifax, was one of the most eminent of Mr. Birch's curates at Brighouse, and during his residence there, published several popular sermons. Besides the NORCLIFFES and the NORTHENDS so often mentioned, now represented by the Rev. C. B. Norcliffe who inherited Sir Norcliffe Norcliffe's estates at Langton, and the Hon. W. D. Northend, Salem, Mass., whose ancestors were of the East Riding branch, the NICHOLLS of last century and the NOBLES of this require to be mentioned.

REV. SAMUEL OGDEN.

GEORGE HIGHAM, ESQ.

The history of the Brighouse postal arrangements is the biography of the John Noble who trudged many miles daily with letters before and after penny postage was devised. John Noble died in Oct., 1869, aged 65 ; Joseph Noble, silk spinner, in 1878, aged 66.

We must claim the Rev. Samuel OGDEN, D.D., curate of Coley, afterwards of Elland, which place he left in 1762 for Cambridge, where he died in 1778. His Sermons, with Life, were issued in two volumes, 2nd edition, 1780. The long and interesting life story of Mr. Richard OASTLER, of Fixby, steward of the Thornhill estates, must

MR. RICHARD OASTLER, (Factory King.)

also be as briefly referred to. A list of his controversial tracts would fill a page. His life has been written in a pamphlet by Hobson, of Leeds, in 1838, and in Croft's History of the Factory Movement. His works on the "Halifax Tithes," the "Fleet Papers" written by him in the Fleet prison, are only some of the productions of his trenchant pen. The meeting called to commence a fund to liberate him from prison, and one to commence the memorial fund were held in Brighouse. The statue at Bradford resulted from the last-named meeting.

The ORMERODS are a very old Lancashire family. Richard, son of Samuel and Mary Ormerod, of Clough fold, in that county, and John Ormerod, settled in Brighouse. Richard was buried in Rastrick

Churchyard in 1813, aged 20, and John in 1853, aged 77. Susan, wife of the latter, died in 1815, aged 38. Their two sons, Hanson, of the Hollies, who died in 1890, aged 83, and Thomas Theodore were amongst the most conspicuous natives of modern Brighouse. They were identified with the civil development of Brighouse from 1846 when the township became governed by Commissioners, with its educational advancement from Sep. 22, 1846, when the informal meeting for establishing the Mechanics' Institute was held in Mr. Robert Newton's warehouse, Victoria Mills, and with the political organisations from earlier years. Mr. Hanson Ormerod's specialty was as President of the Liberal Association, but few local institutions failed to receive his support. Whilst he was universally esteemed, it may be justly stated that his brother was as universally loved. Were I not a life teetotaller, I might be suspected of partiality in writing thus of a wine and spirit merchant, but my remarks are understated rather than exaggerated. It is Professor Ruskin who remarks that " Every noble life leaves the fibre of it for ever interwoven in the work of the world." Few, perhaps, realize how this is the case with many silent, quiet workers for good, who are most missed when death has silenced for ever the kindly voice, and checked the ever ready, generous help.

One of these quiet, Christian lives, (whose influence still lives in, and beyond the centre of its life-work,) was that of the late Thomas Theodore Ormerod. He was born at Brighouse in the year 1809, and died in the place in which and for which he had worked and lived, Sep. 18, 1879. He carried on (in conjunction with his brother) his father's trade, that of a wine merchant. He was connected with many of the progressive, movements of this century. In politics he was a staunch Liberal and in religion a Nonconformist, although confirmed in the Church of England. For many years he was the President, and always a liberal supporter of the Mechanics' Institution, which he, together with the Rev. Joseph Birch, Mr. Baines, Mr. F. Barber, and others, helped to establish. He also took a warm interest in establishing a local Penny Savings' Bank. He was one of the most generous contributors to the Halifax Tradesmen's Benevolent Institute, and he was also well known as a friend and supporter of the Crossley Orphan Home. During the exciting times of the Corn Laws Agitation, he took a warm and active interest in seeking their abolition. For more than twenty years he was the Hon. Treasurer to the Local Authorities, and on the formation of a Local Board in 1867 he was presented with a valuable piece of plate, on which was the following inscription : " Presented by the Local Board, on behalf of the Ratepayers of Brighouse, to Thomas Theodore Ormerod, Esq., as a token of their appreciation of his services as treasurer under the Brighouse Improvement Act, the duties of which office he faithfully and gratuitously discharged for twenty years."

As a Sunday School worker in connection with Bridge-end Congregational Chapel he was wonderfully successful, and held the post of Superintendent for about 40 years. In 1856, the teachers and scholars of the Sunday School presented a pair of globes to him; on the terres-

WOODVALE SILK MILLS.

trial globe a silver plate bore the following inscription : "Presented to Thomas Theodore Ormerod by the teachers and scholars of the Bridge-end Sabbath School, as an expression of their high approval of his talents and worth as a superintendent of the school for the past twenty-six years. Brighouse, January 23rd, 1856." The presentation was made by the Rev. Robert Harley, F.R.S. In 1869, an illuminated framed address was presented to Mr. Ormerod by the teachers of Bridge-end Sunday School, the address being signed by all the teachers, and the presentation made by the Rev. J. B. Lister. In 1882, three years after Mr. Ormerod's death, a portrait of him was presented to the Sunday School bearing the following inscription : "T. T. Ormerod, Esq., forty years superintendent of the Sunday School, and nearly forty years deacon of the Church : April 15th, 1882." The Missionary and Bible Societies were warmly supported by him, and all sects spoke of him as being not only tolerant, but generous towards them. Strangers of all creeds and politicians generally found a welcome at Mr. Ormerod's house, and the Liberal Candidates at election times were frequently entertained by him. A Conservative Member of Parliament would meet with a hearty welcome when coming to preside at some meeting or lecture of general interest, and it has happened to the amusement of all parties that the Conservative Member would be a guest one month, to be speedily followed by the Liberal Candidate or Member when the excitement of a General Election set in. The late Lord Frederick Cavendish was amongst the last political guests entertained by Mr. Ormerod, and Principal Fairbairn's first visit after settling for a time in Yorkshire was to Mr. Ormerod's house. Mr. Ormerod's kindness to the poor was proverbial, and to within three weeks of his death, when sadly enfeebled by illness, he was in the habit of calling himself to enquire for, or relieve those who were in trouble or need. His private life was without reproach, and in all good works he found a ready helpmeet in his wife.

Although a strict Sabbatarian, Sunday, with Mr. Ormerod, was never a gloomy day ; but as one of his daughters wrote, "a day made bright and happy by his, and my mother's influence." Two sayings he always impressed on his children and scholars' minds, "Be good, and you will be happy;" and "A merciful man is merciful to his beast." Many a time we have heard him explain to hired drivers the advisability of going gently up hills, and he presented sundry coins to donkey drivers if their animals were carefully tended.

He loved music dearly, and for many years raised the hymns in the Sunday School with no aid from tuning fork or instrument ; himself taking tenor or high baritone as the case might be. It was always his custom to have sacred music after supper, especially on Sundays ; and the solo he perhaps most enjoyed singing was "But Thou did'st not leave" from the "Messiah," and in many of the choruses from the "Messiah" and Mozart's "12th Mass," he heartily joined. It was a pleasure to him to the last to play the grand old hymn tunes out of "Holdsworth's Psalmody" on the piano. His death was, like his life, peaceful and quiet. For some years his health had been failing, and one by one his public duties and offices had to be relinquished. He passed away on the 18th of September, 1879, in the brilliant sunshine of an early autumn morning.

Another axiom of Mr. Ormerod's may be mentioned here, as in these days "old-fashioned notions" are apt to be disregarded. "Give away a tenth of everything you possess." By this rule he regulated his expenditure, and from its observance considered much of his after prosperity due. Any notice of Mr. Ormerod's life would be incomplete without these slight allusions to his private character and home life. In common with the thousands of Sunday Scholars who received beneficent training at his hands, I unhesitatingly place this memorial. His son, Mr. Thomas Ormerod, has high poetic and literary qualifications, but no collection of his fugitive pieces has yet been issued. His connection with Yorkshire Mechanics' Institutes, Chambers of Commerce, Liberal Clubs, &c., will not readily be forgotten. The daughters of Mr. T. T. Ormerod are not unknown as writers and musical composers. Mr. Theodore Ormerod succeeds his father and grandfather in the business established much more than eighty years ago.

A notable curate under Mr. Birch, at Brighouse, was the Rev. John PHILLIPS. He had printed at Bath, in 1846, but bearing the name of E. S. Keir, Brighouse, bookseller, a 12 page pamphlet on "Marriages," a sermon preached in Brighouse Church, Feb. 8, 1846, by John Phillips, M.A., assistant curate. We learn from "The Righteous Man: a sermon at Brighouse Church, January 4, 1852, on the death of the Rev. John Phillips, M.A., Pemb. Coll., Oxford, formerly curate of Brighouse, by Joseph Birch, M.A., Pemb. Coll., Oxford," printed for private circulation only, by E. S. Keir, 1852, 16 pages, that Mr. Phillips was born in Jan. 1813, educated in Gloucestershire, Curate of Egglingham, Laithkirk and Brighouse successively, died at Bidford, Warwick, 21 Dec., 1851, and was buried at Blockley, Worcester. Mr. H. J. Barber has lately given me a pamphlet of 16 pages printed by Whitley and

Booth, Halifax, in 1892, entitled "Reminiscences of the Rev. John Phillips," by the Rev. G. Sowden, M.A., Vicar of Hebden Bridge, and Rural Dean of Halifax. It is a welcome addition to our local bibliography, doubly so because the author is a native.

The late Rev. Sutcliffe Sowden, B.A., friend of the Brontës, and the Rev. George Sowden, now of Hebden Bridge, brothers, belonged to the family located at Thornhill Briggs and Sutcliffe

SUTCLIFFE WOODBOTTOM.

Wood. Rev. Sutcliffe Sowden, B.A., was of Magdalen College, Cambridge; ordained priest in 1841; accidentally drowned in the Calder, and was succeeded in the incumbency of Heptonstall by the above-named brother. Their father, Samuel, lived to a great age, and was

THOMAS JESSOP, ESQ.

blind some years. He married Martha, daughter of Mr. Wm. Sutcliffe, who settled at Woodbottom in 1780, having previously been huntsman for Mr. Thompson, of Chapel-le-Brier.

Samuel was son of John Sowden, of Thornhill Briggs, a leading Methodist, who died March 21, 1829, aged 91 years, leaving six out of ten children then living, 45 grandchildren, and 53 great-grandchildren of whom 23 were married. He died in the house where he was born, and never lived a month in any other. The Sowdens left Woodbottom in 1865. On a window in Dewsbury Town Hall may be seen *inter alia* the arms of PEEBLES. A notice of the notorious 'Devil of Dewsbury,' son of John Peebles, curate of Lightcliffe, with copy of the arms, belongs rather to the ecclesiastical history. The history of the PRIESTLEY family, (Surtees Society), by Jonathan Priestley, of Winteredge, Oliver Heywood's friend, must be included in local bibliography. William Priestley, Esq., just referred to as a musician, was born in Oct., 1779, and resided at Lightcliffe many years. He was the son of John Priestley and Elizabeth his wife, second daughter of Wm. Walker, Esq., J.P., D.L., Crow Nest. Wm. Priestley was educated at Hipperholme Grammar School. He was eminent as an amateur musician, antiquary and literary gentleman. He married Eliza, daughter of Dr. Paley, Carlisle. He died in 1860, at Thorp Arch. Joseph PARKINSON, farmer, Pond, had reached 90 years at his death in 1867. Several of his sons, farmers, lived over 70 years. · Lieutenant Henry PITT, R.M., born 1796, died 1874, was a well-known resident at Slead Syke Mill and Lane Head. George Fredk. Augustus PARRY, son of a private schoolmaster at Brighouse, died in 1890, aged 63. He was the eccentric bellman of his day, rather more than half-witted. Wm. PEARSON, of Hoyle House, the farmer and country pig-killer, was a splendid type of the West Riding race ; robust, oval face, full rounded visage, aquiline nose, florid complexion, grey eyes, brown hair, deliberate in speech, slow in movement, snappish in retort, appetite like a hunter, digestion like an ostrich. Would there were more such !

Dr. Pollard* and Dr. Pritchett are well-known Rastrick names. The pedigree of the former we have not seen, but that of Pritchett appears in *Miscell. Genealogica*, 1892. The Yorkshire branch starts with James Pigott Pritchett, Architect, of York, born in 1789, died at York in 1868. He was one of the sons of the Rev. Chas. P. Pritchett, and several of his brothers were clergymen. He married (1) Peggy Maria, dau. Robert Terry, Esq., at Beckenham in Kent. She died in 1827 at York, leaving issue (*a*) Rev. Richard Charles Pritchett, born at York, 1814, died at Bristol, 1881 : (*b*) Chas. Pigott Pritchett, born at York, 1818, died at Hastings, 1891 ; (*c*) Maria Margaret, born at York, 1817 ; married John Middleton, Esq., whose son, John Henry Middleton, M.A., D.C.L., F.S.A., &c., Cambridge, was born at York in 1846. J. P. P. married (2) Caroline, dau. John Benson, Esq., Thorne, co. York, by Anne Atkinson his wife. She died at York in 1879, aged 76, leaving issue (*d*) James Pigott Pritchett, Architect, Darlington, born at York in 1830. His Congregational Churches are specially renowned.

* His son, A. T. Pollard, Esq., M.A., is Head Master of the City of London School.

He married Ellen Mary, eldest dau. Richard D'Ewes, Esq., of Knaresborough, and has numerous issue, mostly residing in New Zealand; (e) John Benson Pritchett, Surgeon, Huddersfield, born at York, 1831, died at Huddersfield in 1884. He married Annie, third daughter of Richard D'Ewes, Esq. Numerous family. (f) Henry Pritchett, Surgeon, Rastrick, born at York in 1832, married Maria, dau. Thos. Plint, Esq., of Leeds; issue, two sons and a daughter, all born at Rastrick.

The PINDERS are an old Brighouse family connected with the iron industry.

The outline of the first RICHARDSONS is as much as we can give to that family. Nicholas, of Bierley, was father of Richard, born in 1576, the father of Richard, born 1604. They had estates at Bierley, Woodhall in Calverley, Hipperholme, &c. Six of the latter Richardsons must be named.

(1) William, (father of Wm. born 1666, died 1716, who married Mary, d. of John Kershaw, of Hoyle House, merchant, and of Dr. Richard Richardson.)

(2) Richard married Susanna Field. (3) John.

(4) George, of Woodhall, b. 1644, d. 1696, married Sarah, dau. of Richard Langley, of Priestley Green, gent. She was buried at Bradford in 1709, and their grandson, George, the last male heir, was buried at St. Clement Danes, London, in 1748.

(5) Samuel, rector of Barnham.

(6) Joseph, rector of Dunsfold, married Elizabeth Peebles, Dewsbury.

The Brighouse RADCLIFFES commence with Abraham, born at Meltham in 1696. He married Betty, dau. Joshua Holmes, of Smith House, gent., heir of her brother John. Wm. R., the eldest son, was a merchant at Brighouse; born, 1733, buried, like his father, at Lightcliffe in 1778. Charles, the fifth child, was born at Brighouse, July 31, bap. at Rastrick Aug. 29, 1739. He died at Smith House in 1817, buried at Lightcliffe. He married Charlotte, dau. Chas. Radcliffe, of York, who was cousin of Abraham, of Brighouse. She was cousin to the first Sir Joseph (Pickford) Radcliffe, and was buried at Lightcliffe in 1797. Wm. Towne Radcliffe their son, an imbecile, b. 1789, d. 1862.

The RAYNERS, of Rastrick, have not yet traced their ancestry, but there is little doubt they are of the ancient stock, once influential in Clifton and Liversedge. The family or person that introduces a new industry into a district must be regarded amongst the local benefactors. When Mr. W. ROBINSON opened the calico print works, there was much curiosity evinced in the district, and since then the business has gradually developed under the guidance of his successor and son-in-law, Mr. F. LAXTON, as will be seen when the statistical chapter appears. Mr. Laxton's services on the Local Board have been appreciated by all, and he has recently been re-elected the chairman. His additional labours pending the Incorporation question must have been specially exacting, but his business tact has enabled him to wield them cheerfully. Presumably he will be Provisional Mayor on the arrival of the Charter.

DR. JESSOP.

In past times, more than modern ones probably, Yorkshire people have been of a provident disposition. Hove Edge, Brighouse, Rastrick, &c. had each sick and funeral societies in George III's. days. I have a tract of 16 pages, with 24 pages of Act for Encouragement of Friendly Societies, printed by Jacobs, at Halifax, 1817, giving the "Rules and Agreements to be observed by Members of the Union Society, established at the House of Mr. Jonas Broughton, Star Inn, Rastrick, July 7, 1794; with alterations, Oct. 4, 1817." This was Thomas Burgess' copy, who joined in July, 1810. Meetings were held quarterly; maximum age at entrance, 36; non-benefits first 18 months, then 5s. weekly; 6s. after three years' membership; 7s. after 7 years. Half-pay if sickness lasted more than 6 months. Ten bearers had to attend the funeral of a member. Easter Monday was the annual feast day. The Society box had five different locks for safety. I have Rules of an earlier association at Rastrick, whose members were landowners and farmers mostly. This was for the Prosecution of trespassers, thieves, &c. Co-operative principles are not new to our inhabitants evidently.

Bishop SPANGEN-BERG, the Moravian Author and Missionary, was head of the settlement when at Smith House. Rev. Joseph SWAINE, B.D., of Farnley, in 1788, Vicar of Beeston, 1804, second master of Leeds Grammar School, a Leeds benefactor, who died in 1831, aged 77, was a poor lad at Hoyle House. The Swaines were descended from the Anglian Sweyns.

Gawbutt Hall and Till Carr were the birthplace and residence of the late Mr. Lumb Stocks, R.A. Just before his death, I obtained from him his portrait and a list of his artistic

MR. LUMB STOCKS.

MR. LUMB STOCKS.

productions, chiefly in line-drawing, which will be found in *Yorks. County Magazine*. In 1839, he married Ellen, eldest daughter of Mr. Wm. Fryer, of Rastrick. He died April 28, 1892, aged 80, and was buried in Highgate Cemetery, London. He became A.R.A. in 1853, and R.A. in 1872. Sir F. Leighton, at the Academy Meeting, said "How much the calling lost in him it need not be said. How sterling and gentle a man had ceased to live in him his many friends best knew." In bibliography, Mr. F. SMITH, Tops Grove, Rastrick, compiler of Bradford, Halifax and Wakefield Directories, must be mentioned for his "Directory of Dewsbury and Batley, with Birstall, Cleckheaton, Heckmondwike, Mirfield, &c." 140 pages, 1878. The ancient SUNDERLANDS of High Sunderland and Coley, as a

GRANNY HALL

county family, will require special space. Their relatives, the Saltonstalls, of America, have had a separate volume devoted to their genealogy. Other branches should be noted,—as, the present family at Coley who migrated from Elland, and a race of farmers who have resided at Rookes, Lightcliffe, and Granny Hall, a place high in my esteem as my birth-place. Rufus Sunderland, of Rookes, removed to

MRS. SUNDERLAND.

Granny Hall farm. His son John, of Barnsley, died in 1876, aged 68. Another son, Henry, married Susan Sykes, of Spring Gardens, a foot-path then crossing the three fields from one house to the other. A wide road, with villa residences near, have driven elsewhere the feathery inhabitants that harboured in the hedgerows. Mr. James Sykes, of Spring Gardens, died in May, 1846, aged 64. Hannah, his widow, in 1855, aged 70. Their daughter, Susan, was born April 30, 1819, and the Sykes family, like many more local ones, had strong musical tastes. She was taught by J. Denham and Luke Settle, followed by the training of Dan Sugden, of Halifax. At 15, she made her debût at Deighton. On June 7, 1838, she married Mr. Henry Sunderland. She soon became renowned as the Yorkshire Queen of Song. She had a rich, powerful soprano voice, with wonderful flexibility and depth of feeling. Professionals and novices were captivated and entranced. Her rendition of sacred song was marvellously sublime, especially "I know that my Redeemer liveth." In 1842 she appeared

MRS. SUNDERLAND.

in London, and was personally complimented by the Prince Consort and the Duke of Cambridge. She took the leading part in the "Messiah" in London, Nov. 2, 1849, Dec. 22, 1851; in the "Creation," Dec. 31, 1855; and in "Elijah," Jan. 30, 1856, and the "Messiah," Dec. 10, 1858. The highest critics ransacked their vocabularies for expressive superlative adjectives. At organ openings and festivals in the provinces as well as the metropolis, in Scotland and Ireland, as well as in England, her services were sought and rendered. A special festival in her honour was held at Huddersfield. The Queen was so delighted with her singing, at the opening of the Leeds Town Hall, that she sent a command for her to sing at Buckingham Palace, when she was personally complimented. In the midst of her popularity she retired into private life, her farewell concerts being highly successful. Mrs. Sunderland never lost her good graces, and she is to-day as ever the kindly neighbour and respected friend by rich and poor. A presentation was made to her at a musical festival, June 2 and 3, 1864, at Huddersfield, where she had regularly assisted the Parish and St. Paul's choirs. A concert was promoted in honour of her Golden Wedding, in the Brighouse Town Hall, June 7, 1888, when an illuminated address, enclosed in a silver casket, bearing the letters S. S. and the white rose of York, and signed by Mr. T. Ormerod as chairman

F. LAXTON, ESQ.

of a committee, was presented to her. The "Mrs. Sunderland Musical Competition" was established, at her suggestion, with the funds raised at her golden wedding celebration. The competition takes place annually in Huddersfield, and is open to Yorkshire natives, or residents of five years recent standing, the maximum age being 25. Two vocal and one instrumental prizes are awarded yearly, and though the value is about five guineas each, they are highly coveted. Her son, Mr. Charles Sykes Sunderland,* solicitor, died in 1889, aged 45. Her daughter, Agnes, wife of Mr. Joseph Wheatley, died in 1864.

The SHAWS, of Rastrick, were also noted musicians, vocal and instrumental. They were amongst the founders of Pratt's Brass Band, the great Christmas attraction of former times, along with its rival the Waterloo Band. Choral Societies, Halifax Sunday School Jubilees, great Oratorios, were the delight of Mathias Shaw, of Rastrick, who was recently gathered to his fathers. The Shaws, of Hipperholme, were a well-known family. The Rev. Frank Shaw, son of Henry, of Girlington, was laid in Lightcliffe churchyard in 1890, aged only 25. Hardly another family has made so much impression on various Brighouse industries, or taken so active a part in civil affairs, as the SUGDENS. Mr. Thomas Sugden, the founder of the corn-mills, stands pre-eminently out amongst leading Yorkshire business men. Perseverance Mill was erected in 1832, and additions were constantly being made. Brighouse Old Mill, rebuilt and enlarged, was added to the immense concern when Mr. Thos. Richard Sutcliffe, who died in 1864, aged 63, retired, and to these Mr. Brooke's corn mill was added. The turn-out of waggons, each drawn by four powerful horses, was worthy of observation.

Mr. Thomas Sugden died in November, 1876, aged 78. His son, Mr. David Goldthorpe Sugden, a most capable business man, and a musician withal, died in 1871, aged 51. Another son, Mr. William, of Slead House, previously of Rastrick, died in 1884, aged 54. Mr. Henry Sugden, another son, is the one who has taken most hold in public and philanthropic matters, and his neighbours of every political shade give him deserved respect. Sunday School and Temperance work receive his attention as scrupulously as the calls of Local Board and Politics. He is a County Alderman, and Justice of Peace.

The SHARPS, of Hove Edge, are numbered amongst our oldest existing families. John Sharp was the great supporter of Methodism there and at Brighouse a hundred years ago. David Sharp was the township's road surveyor, &c. He died in 1878, aged 86. From Ripponden came Mr. Henry STOTT and Mr. Jonathan Stott, cousins, whose names will henceforth be remembered as founders of the cotton mills in Brighouse. The former died in 1879, aged 64, leaving several sons to carry on the business. The latter died in 1871, aged 58. His son, Mr. Jas. Maude Stott died in 1875, aged 30. Ann SMITH, spinster, of Hove Edge, and her brother, Joshua Smith, alias Lee, (d. 1877, aged 82,) were descendants of General Guest's mother.

---

* His grandfather was Jonas, not Rufus, p. 303.

T

SIR TITUS SALT'S BIRTHPLACE.

SIR TITUS SALT, BART.

The fame of Sir Titus SALT, Baronet, ex-M.P. for Bradford, is world-wide. He was born at Morley in 1803. His father, Mr. Daniel Salt, removed to Bradford when the future baronet was an infant, and he laboured with his father in the staple trade till 21. By 1850 he had become a rich man, and might have retired into indolence. He meditated on a large project instead, and it is asserted that he offered to purchase a slice of the valley from Brighouse Gas Works to Alegar Well. He fixed upon Airedale, near Shipley, however, and planned out the town of Saltaire, named after himself and the river, a place deservedly renowned throughout the world. Its conception, construction, and history take more of the romance than the money-grubbing notion. Mr. Titus became a tenant of Crow Nest for some years, under Mr. Sutherland Walker, but the owner requiring possession, he had to remove to Methley. However, at Mr. Sutherland Walker's sale, he became the purchaser of Crow Nest, and came to reside there again.

W. ROBINSON, ESQ.

Of his monuments at Saltaire we need not write, but Lightcliffe Congregational Church owes its existence to him as a substitute for the old Bramley Lane Chapel. Great and good men like Dr. Moffatt and Dr. Livingstone were welcome visitors to Crow Nest. His life story has often been told in magazines, and books like Balgarnie's "Life of Sir Titus Salt;" Holroyd's "Saltaire and its Founder;" Holroyd's "Life of Sir Titus Salt," 1871, 24 pages; "In Memoriam,— the late Sir Titus Salt, a Study for Young Men," by Rev. B. Wood, Bradford, 11 pages; &c. A statue to his memory has been reared

SIR TITUS SALT, BART.

near Bradford Town Hall, which was unveiled by the late Duke of Devonshire in 1874. Great alterations about the conservatories but not the house, were made by him at Crow Nest Park when he became owner. Saltaire was opened on his fiftieth birthday. Great banquets to his thousands of workpeople took place at Crow Nest on Sep. 20, 1856, Sep. 20, 1873 (his 70th birthday,) &c. He died at Crow Nest, Dec. 29, 1876. He had given away a quarter of a million to

SALTAIRE CONGREGATIONAL CHURCH.

SALT ARMS.

benevolent institutions in thirty years, besides his special erections. His body was conveyed to the mausoleum at Saltaire Congregational Church, the funeral procession being witnessed by 100,000 people probably. Lady Salt's remains have recently been interred there too.

"Joseph TERRY, member of the Mechanics' Institute, Brighouse," published his "Cottage Poems" in 1847, consisting of 22 short pieces, on Temperance, local scenery, &c., 32 pages, printed by John Siddal. Terry was book-keeper at a corn-mill, and worked energetically for the Christian Brethren Sunday School on Rastrick Common, the Temperance Society, and Mechanics' Institute. He was a Chartist also. He removed to Birstall Co-operative mill. His portrait appears in "Poems, by Joseph Terry," Dewsbury, 1874, pp. xv., 160. Mr. J. J. Lane, now residing at Brighouse, has also issued several Temperance and Poetic pamphlets. Under the commercial history, besides those named as pioneers in the stone-trade, must be named the Cliffes, Robinsons, Farrers, Bentleys, Thwaites. Mr. B. H. Thwaite, C.E., A.M.I.C.E., F.C.S., of London and Liverpool, is son of Mr. Benjamin Thwaite, quarry owner, who was killed in a quarry near Brighouse Wood in 1855. The THORNTONS, of Rastrick, are of an old sturdy yeomanry, combining, as was usual, manufacturing with farming, and taking their share in public duties on Local, School, and Burial Boards. Mr. John TAYLOR has probably been the most industrious and trustworthy

THOMAS SUGDEN, ESQ.

Poor Law Guardian and honorary servant Rastrick has had in modern times. The TURNERS, of course, are ubiquitous; they are found in various businesses, one has introduced fellmongering, another an iron-foundry, a third, confectionery and public baking, with offshoots to Bradford, Halifax, &c., another, house-painting, but was even wider known as a vocalist. Mr. W. Marshall Turner, Mr. O. Sladdin and his sons, Mr. Keighley, &c., are only a few more local musicians to add to previous names.

UPPER GREEN, Lightcliffe.

Messrs. WOOD, of Wilkin Royd Mills, wire manufacturers, have a reputation that has reached several distant countries. Their appropriate trade-mark, "The Old Oak Tree," bespeaks in any market the highest quality of goods. The wire trade came to us from Clifton, where cardmaking was carried on before 1681, for in that year "Samuell Brooke, of Clifton, cardmaker, was bound to appear at Quarter Sessions, Wakefield, Jan. 1681, by Wm. Farrar, J.P., for buying severall quantities of fforaigne yron wyre for making of wooll bands, ymported from pts beyond ye seas, contrary to ye statute."

Thornhill Briggs passed from the Thorpes, Listers, and Bedfords to Newsteads. In 1792, Messrs. Cartledge, of Elland, bought part of Newsteads estate and built thereon the mill, since owned by Messrs. Michael WALLER and Sons, a firm that has a large establishment here since the old mill was destroyed by fire in 1858. If space had allowed, a list of the conflagrations around Brighouse would have appeared in this volume. It must be reserved for another work, but our thanks are none the less due to Mr. Hopkinson, who supplied it at our request. A long and interesting pedigree of the WADDINGTONS, of Lightcliffe, is not quite completed. Notices of old tradesmen by the score, such as Messrs. Richard Wheatley, Wm. Navey, Benjn. Tiffany; and more recent commercial firms, as Messrs. Wilson, Smith, &c., Rastrick, are necessarily left over at present.

Wm. Howorth, Brighouse, (p. 284,) published "The Cry of the Poor, a Poem." London, 1837; pp. iv., 68; and "The Redeemer, a Poem." London, 1840; pp. 306. Extracts from the former:—

> The bustling mother plied her busy wheel,
> And only paused to spread each frugal meal,
> Or nicely sand the floor; or range, with pride,
> Her crockery in the 'delf case' side by side;
> Or rub the oaken chest till she might trace
> Reflected on its polished sides her face;
> Or trim the myrtle and geranium red,
> That gaily o'er the narrow windows spread;
> Or called, reminded by its grunting cry,
> To feed the hog that fattened in the sty;
> Or roused to whirl the good-man's worn out hat
> To scare the chickens from the garden plat.   .   .   .
> In nice prim cap, blue apron, kerchief fair,
> His partner sate in her well-cushioned chair,
> With feigned sternness in her look, the while
> Lurked on her lip a kind good-humoured smile,
> Teaching the girls to sew, and darn, and knit,
> That they might be for thrifty housewives fit;
> And when those great accomplishments were gained,
> To work the sampler only then remained,—
> That they, with honour crowned, the school might leave,—
> Its subject sure—"The Serpent tempting Eve;"
> Full in the front the fatal apple there
> With all the hues of Joseph's coat did glare;
> There too was Eve, for uncouth rhymes below,
> To those who doubted did the fact avow,
> And none could miss the Tempter to behold,
> With scarlet eyes, blue body, tail of gold;
> Then last, the needle's triumph to complete,
> And give to Fame, as surely was most meet,
> The skilful sempstress, letters small and great,
> With strange queer things for figures, did relate
> Her name and age; thenceforth in jet-black frame
> Extended out, th' achievement grand did claim,
> Chief ornament, the cottage walls to grace,
> Above King Charles's rules—its rightful place—
> To be at once the wonder and the praise
> Of gossips born and rear'd in less learned days.

HENRY SUGDEN, ESQ., J.P., G.A.

List of Subscribers.

(An asterisk denotes large paper copies of which only 100 are printed.)

Armytage, G. J., F.S.A., Clifton
Armitage, J. W., Lane Head
Aspinall, J., Clifton Common
Aspinall, J., Ravensthorpe
Atkinson, J., Springfield, Rastrick*
Ayrton, C., Weobley
Andrews, W., Hull
Ayrton, John, Brighouse
Armytage, Lady, Kirklees
Axon, Ernest, Manchester
Aspinall, Mrs. T., Brighouse
Aspinall, W., Brighouse
Aked, Miss, Brighouse
Aspinall, Johnson, Elland
Asquith, Ben, Brighouse
Aspinall, Dyson, Marsden
Anderton, H. F., Bradford *
Aspinall, Joseph, Sleadsyke

Bayes, A. B., Brighouse (4)
Baldwin, W., Halifax*
Bulmer, Mrs., Leeds
Brighouse Mechanics' Institute
Bradford Free Library *
Bottomley, C. W., Brighouse
Butterworth, T., Brighouse*
Brayshaw, H., Liversedge
Broadbent, T., Brighouse
Broadley, W., Brighouse
Bottomley, J. C., Brighouse, and *
Beaumont, J., Brighouse
Brook, W. R., Brighouse (2)
Barber, H. J., Brighouse*
Blakeborough, R., Brighouse
Blakeborough, W., Brighouse, and *
Batty, J. T., Montreal
Baildon, W. P., F.S.A., London
Benson, Capt., Burley *
Blackburn, H., Lindley
Bilton, Miss, Bradford (3)
Bond, Dr., Rastrick
Broadbent, H., Rastrick
Broadbent, J. A., Rastrick
Blackburn, C., Brighouse
Bottomley, J., Bradford
Balme, E. B. Wheatley, J.P., Mirfield
Brintley, Miss, Clifton
Brown, Dr., Brighouse
Barnett, T., Brighouse
Bell, J. M., M.R.C.V.S., Brighouse
Burton, E., Brighouse
Blackburn, Secker, Brighouse
Bilbrough, W. R., Beech Grove, Leeds

Beevers, A., Clifton
Beard, G., Brighouse
Black, J., Brighouse
Boothroyd, W., Brighouse
Brooke, Mrs., Brighouse (2 and *)
Byrne, Miss, Bracken House, Brighouse
Blackburn, T., Brighouse
Brook, Mrs., Brighouse
Brooke, E. C., Brighouse
Broughton, Goldthorpe, Brighouse
Bright, Daniel, Rastrick
Bolton, A., Brighouse
Bottomley, James, Brighouse*
Booth, R. J., Rastrick
Bradford Library and Literary Society
Bottomley, Tom, Brighouse
Brook, Wm., Rastrick
Beaumont, Charles, Rastrick
Brook, Joah, Brighouse
Bottomley, H., Brighouse
Baldwin, J., Brighouse
Bedford, Samuel, Brighouse
Barraclough, W.T., Holloway, Derbyshire
Brook, J. W. W., Halifax
Barclay, Mrs., Liverpool
Broughton, Harry, Liverpool
Byrne, Mrs. S. H., London
Bradford Historical Society *
Barraclough, T., London
Bentley, J. H., Castle Hill
Beanland, Rev. A., Victoria. B. C.
Bottomley, Geo., Brighouse*
Bottomley, Mrs. J., Brighouse
Bottomley, Miss E., Brighouse
Barber, Ven. Archdeacon, Chester
Brayshaw, Mark, West Bowling
Barber, Mrs., Shanklin, Isle of Wight
Broadbent, R, Stalybridge*
Bracegirdle, J., Brighouse
Bywater, Wm., 5, Hanover Square, W.

Cardwell, S., Brighouse
Carter, Rev. J. H., M.A., Weaste
Clayton, T., Brighouse
Collins, Mrs. Gent, Bailiffe Bridge
Carter, W. F., B.A., Birmingham (2)
Cordingley, John R., Bradford
Childe, H. S., Wakefield
Cookson, E., Ipswich
Camidge, W., York
Caldwell, T., Brighouse
Caldwell, J., Brighouse
Curtis, Mrs., Tuxford

Crossland, C., Halifax
Collyer, Rev. Dr., New York
Cheetham Hospital, Manchester
Crowther J., Brighouse
Carter, Wm., Brighouse
Chambers, W. J., Brighouse*
Crossley, John, Rastrick
Charlesworth, J., Wakefield
Cooke, Arthur, Brighouse
Caine, Rev. Cæsar, F.R.G.S., London
Carter, Dr., Rastrick*
Clay, A. T., Rastrick*
Cheetham, F. A., Rastrick
Cardwell, Mrs., Rastrick Common
Cliffe, Wm., Longwood
Cliffe, S., Elland Road, Brighouse
Carter, J. B., Norwood Green
Carter, Edwd , Birmingham
Cooke, Edwd., Barnsley
Crowther, William, Brighouse*
Clay, J. W., J.P., F.S.A.,*
Chambers, J. E. F., Alfreton*
Crossley, Tom, Oldham
Crossley, E. W., Dean house, Triangle
Clay, John, Rastrick
Cardwell, F., Brighouse
Crowther, Savile, brighouse
Cocksedge, John, Brighouse
Chadwick, S.J., F.S.A,, Dewsbury
Crowther, Job, Brighouse

Dyson, Mrs., Bridge End*
Dyson, G., Marsden, and *
Dyson, A., Grays, Essex, and *
Denham, T., Brighouse
Denison, S., Leeds
Dawson, W., Marsh
Denison, R. W., Bradford
Dale, Mrs., Bradford
His Grace Duke of Devonshire, K.G.*
Davis, J. W., F.S.A., F.G.S., Halifax
Dickons, J. N., Bradford
Drake, Isaac, Brighouse
Dennison, Mrs. John, Alverstoke*
Denham, Joseph, Brighouse
Dawson, Mrs., Rastrick
Dixon, Mrs., Rastrick
Dyson, Miss, Rastrick

Eland, John, London
Ellis, J., Lane Head
Embleton, J. W., Methley
Empsall, T. T., Bradford
Edwards, Dr., Brighouse
Elliott, W. H., Great Horton
Empsall, Sam, Brighouse*
Eastwood, Hy., Brighouse

Fell, T., Bradford
Farrar, G. A. Brighouse

Farrar, Dr., Scarborough, and *
Farrar, J., Oulton
Farrah, John, Harrogate*
Fawthrop, J., Bradford
Federer, C. A., Bradford
Fryer, S., Rastrick
Fawcett, E., Bradford
Foljambe, C. G. S., (now Baron), Ollerton
Foster, John, J.P., Queensbury
Freeman, Thomas, Rastrick
Firth, Jas. R., Rastrick
Fowler, Chas., Brighouse
Firth, Mrs. Rastrick
Freeman, Walter, Knaresbro'*
Firth, A. F., Lightcliffe
Firth, George, Rastrick
Furniss, George, Brighouse*
Farrer, Albt., Bridge end, Rastrick
Fryer, Miss, Brighouse
Fryer, Miss, G. A., Wilmslow
Fryer, Dr. A. C., Clifton, Bristol
Fryer, J. F., B.A., York
Foster, Col. W. H., Hornby Castle
Farrer, Robt., Surgeon, Brighouse*
Fryer, Miss E., Rastrick
Fox, J., bookseller, Brighouse, and *
Fielding, A., Brighouse

Greenwood, W., Brighouse
Garside, D. B., Todmorden
Gardner, Miss, Dishforth
Galloway, F. C., Bowling, and *
Guest, W. H., Manchester
Garfitt, S., Brighouse
Galbraith, Rev. A., Brighouse
Gledhill, A., Rastrick
Goodall, J. T., Brighouse*
Grandage, Harry, Rastrick
Georgeson, J. H., Brighouse
Goodyear, J. H., Brighouse
Gibson, Miss E., Clifton
Greenwood, H., Bailiffe Bridge
Garside, Fred, Rastrick
Goodaire, Mrs. Joseph, Rastrick

Halifax Public Library
Halford, E. R., Bradford
Howard, Dr. J. J., London
Hallowell, A., Rastrick
Hirst, S. E , M.A., Rastrick
Hirst, J. A. H., J.P., Retford
Hepworth, G., Brighouse
Hartley, J. B., Rastrick
Hall, H., Lightcliffe
Horsfall, G. H., Montreal
Horsfall, W., Montreal
Hoyle, S. P., Glamorgan
Hardy, S., Bradford
Hanson, W. D., J.P., Bideford (4 and*)
Hartley, John, Brighouse *

Haigh, James, Stainland
Hanson, Sir Regd., Bart., M.P., London
Hainsworth, L., Bradford*
Hovenden, R., F.S.A., Croydon
Houghton, Lord, Fryston Hall
Hopkinson, John, Brighouse
Hinchcliffe, O., Brighouse
Hoyle, Geo. H., Brighouse
Healey, George, Brighouse
Helliwell, John, Brighouse
Holt, C. E., Bailiffe Bridge
Hirst, Joseph, Clifton
Haigh, Miss Hannah, Rastrick
Hutchinson, W. A., Rastrick
Heron, C., Rastrick
Heron, Miss, Rastrick
Hall. Mr., Liversedge
Healey, William, Rastrick
Hoyle, Wm., Brighouse
Helm, C. H., Brighouse, and*
Hall, Mrs., Lightcliffe
Horsfall, T. W., Heckmondwike
Hopkinson, J., F.L.S., F.G.S., St. Albans
Hanbury, Mrs. Thos., Ventimiglia, Italy
Hartley, Miss S. A., Rastrick
Hartley, D., Brighouse
Haigh, Mrs. Ann, Rastrick
Halliwell, A. E., Brighouse
Halliwell, A., Brighouse
Helliwell, Miss, Rastrick
Hirst, Herbert, Brighouse
Hanson, H. W., Brussells Rd., New Wandsworth
Healy, Rev. W., P.P., Johnstown, Kilkenny
Horsfall, Jacob, Sleadsyke

Irvine, James, Chelsea
Illingworth, Thomas, Bradford
Irving, Rev. R. G., Rastrick

Jagger, W., Bramley Lane
Jowett, J. S., Brighouse
Jessop, C., Brighouse, and *
Jackson, John, Southport Hydro
Jowett, E. A., Brighouse (2)
Jackson, Wm., Rastrick
Jessop, Sam, Nelson
Jessop, Dr., Leeds

Kershaw, R., Crow Nest Park*
Kershaw, H., Douglas
Killingbeck, J., Kidderminster
Keighley, T., Brighouse
Kilner, G., Brighouse
Keir, S., Rastrick
Kershaw, Charles, Slead Syke
Kershaw, Dr. H., Pudsey
Kershaw, Albert, Brighouse

Kaye, J., Rastrick
Kershaw, J. H., Bingley
Kershaw, T., Bleak House, Cullingworth
Kershaw, J. A., Slead Syke
Kenworthy, Miss, Rastrick

Leeds Public Library
Leighton, F. B., Brighouse
Lockwood, F., Q.C., M.P., London
Lawson, Jos., Brighouse
Lancaster, G., Brighouse
Laxton, F., Home Lea, Brighouse*
Ledgard, Miss
Ludgate, Timms, Brighouse
Lucas, Rev.F.W., HipperholmeGram.Sch.
Lancaster, Samuel, Brighouse
Lancaster, Seth, Bradford
Leppington, W., Northowram*
Lee, J. H. Absalom, Bempton
Ledgard, Eyre, Algeria*
Ledgard, Armitage, Roundhay
Lumb, Benjamin, Rastrick
Ludgate, John, London
Lumb, Miss, Rastrick
Lister, Wm., Wakefield
Lister, John, M A., Shibden
Leach, A. H., Brighouse

M'Cormick, Rev. F., Whitehaven
Morton, J. W., Birds Royd
Marsden, J. W., Leeds*
Marillier, Eland H. J., Cotham
Morrell, W., Brighouse
Mayall, J., J.P., Mossley*
Murgatroyd, Mrs. J., Bailiffe Bridge
Marsden, R., Brighouse
Maw, G. W., Bedford
Magrath, Rev. Dr., Queen's, Oxford
Mitchell, G., Brighouse
Morrison, W., J.P., Malham
Margerison, S., Calverley*
Milne, Milne S., Calverley
Manchester Free Library
Milnes, Tommy, Brighouse
Maude, J. H., Brighouse
Marshall, M., Brighouse
Mellor, Samuel, Brighouse
Marsden, Mrs. Hannah, Brighouse
Mitchell, Samuel, Brighouse
Milnes, J., Cromwell Bottom
Marsden, Joe, Brighouse
Miller, Fred, Rastrick
Morrell, James, Gooder Lane, Rastrick
Marsden, Robt., Police St., Brighouse
Mortimer, Edward, Halifax
Milner, Mrs., Barnsley
Maile, Mrs., Dedham
Morrell, Allon, Brighouse
Morton, W. K., Horncastle

Norcliffe, Rev. C. B., M.A., Langton
Naylor, Joseph, Brighouse
Newhouse, W. H., Brighouse
North, Tom, Brighouse
Naylor, B , Rastrick
Nettleton, H., Brighouse (2)
Northend, Hon. W. D., Salem, Mass.

Oldham Free Library
Oldfield, S., Brighouse
Ormerod, Theodore, Brighouse*
Lord Bishop of Oxford*
Ogden, J. M., Sunderland (deceased)
Ormerod, Thomas, London
Oliver, J., Rastrick*
Ormerod, G. F., Rastrick *
Ormerod, Miss, Chagford**
Oldfield, Geo., Bradford
Ogden, J. H., Halifax

Paul, Kegan, Trench & Co., London
Pritchett, Mrs. M., Bristol
Pickles, W., Norwood Green
Pearson, Rev. S., Lightcliffe
Pinchin, F., Rastrick
Powell, D., Brighouse
Pilling, W., Brighouse
Patchett, J., Bradford
Poole, R., Bradford
Price, C., M.A., Westward Ho!
Powell, Sir F. S., Bart., M.P., Bradford
Pitt Rivers, Gen., Salisbury
Pearson, J. H., Brighouse
Pilling, John, Brighouse*
Parkinson, James, Brighouse *
Pollard, W. H., Brighouse (2)
Pilling, W., Rastrick
Peel, F., Heckmondwike
Parker, Major, Jersey
Pollard, A. T., M.A., London, W.,*
Pawson, A. H., Farnley, Leeds
Pinder, J., Brighouse*
Parker, Thos., Manchester

Robinson, F. A., Brighouse
Ronksley, J. G., Sheffield
Rayner, J., Manchester *
Randall, J., Sheffield
Rushforth, T. H., Ealing
Radcliffe, F., Elland
Rayner, F., Brighouse
Royds, C. M., J.P., Rochdale
Richardson, W. R., M.A., Shortlands
Radcliffe, Sir D., Birkenhead
Robinson, Frank, Rastrick
Roberts, John, Brighouse
Robinson, J. W., Brighouse
Robinson, J. A., Brighouse
Robinson, Albin, Brighouse

Rogerson, R. F., Brighouse
Robinson R. F., Rastrick
Rogerson, Rev. G., Brighouse
Roberts, J. S., Rastrick
Roth, H. Ling, Lightcliffe
Rawnsley, Mrs. A., Upper Lane,Brighouse
Ramsden, R., Thornhill, Clifton
Rhodes, W. Venables, Cleckheaton

Southport Free Library
Skinner, G., Lightcliffe
Schippers, F. G., Brighouse
Sykes, John, Brighouse Fields
Swift, G. J., Rastrick
Sugden, Henry, J.P., C.A., Brighouse*
South Kensington Art Department*
Squire, G., Ampthill
Sunderland, Joseph, Coley*
Salt, Edward, J.P., Shipley
Sykes, Dr., Doncaster
Stuart, Dr. J. A. E. Heckmondwike
Stowell, C., Bradford, and*
Shaw, Henry, Girlington (2)
S., J. W., Harrogate
Sykes, A. F., Bradford
Stancliffe J., Brighouse
Stockdale, A., Huddersfield
Smith, Col. R., Lincoln
Scruton, J., Bradford
Speight, H., Bingley
Sunderland, J. W., New Zealand
Stocks, Mrs. Lumb, London
Sugden, James, Clifton
Shaw, Miss R., Brighouse
Stott, A., Brighouse
Stott, Mrs. J. M., Rastrick (2)
Sykes, Mrs. C., Brighouse
Stedman, Rev. R. P., Brighouse
Stott, Henry S., Brighouse
Shaw, James, Hove Edge
Stenton, W. P., Brighouse
Sykes, J. G., Rastrick
Shaw, Giles, F.R.H.S., Oldham
Sladdin, O., Brighouse
Sutcliffe, Jno. Edward, Elland
Sutcliffe Benj., Clifton
Sugden, D. G., Brighouse*
Sowden, G. S., Brighouse
Shaw, Samuel T., Brighouse
Shaw, Joseph, Brighouse
Sykes, W., Brighouse
Smith, W., Lands House, Rastrick
Schofield, John, Bradford
Stocks, Herbt. W., London
Swallow, George, Rastrick
Scaife, Mrs. A., Rastrick
Smith, George, Brighouse
Sutcliffe, J. T., Leeds
Sladdin, W. H., Brighouse

Sharp, W. H., Brighouse
Shaw, W. M., Rastrick
Sunderland, Mr., Brighouse
Shaw, Henry, Rastrick
Sowden, Rev. G , Hebden Bridge
Sunderland, Mrs., Brighouse

Turner, John W., Brighouse
Thornton, John, Rastrick *
Thwaite, B. H., C. E., Brockley
Taylor, Rev. R. V., B.A., Melbecks
Tomlinson, G. W., F.S.A., Huddersfield
Taylor, W., Lightcliffe
Thornton, Wm., Brighouse
Thornton, G., Rastrick
Thornton, Jno. B., Brighouse
Turner, H. J., Brighouse
Taylor, John, Rastrick
Thornton, Ben, Brighouse
Thornton, Robert, Rastrick *
Turner, Jonathan, Brighouse
Thornton, Abm., Rastrick
Thorpe-Wood, H. W., Middleton-on-
    Wolds
Thairlwall, F. J., London
Tacey, Dr., Bradford
Thackray, W., Bradford
Tolson, Legh, Dalton
Thornton, Wm., Rastrick
Thornton, Mrs., Rastrick
Tinkler, Rev. John, M.A., Caunton,
    Newark
Thornton, Ernest, Rastrick
Thompson, J. B., Bristol
Turner, Ernest R. Horsfall *
Turner, Annie Horsfall *

Walker, John, Coley Mill
Whiteley, J., Queensbury
Ward, J. Whiteley, J.P., Halifax
Wood, Josiah, Hipperholme
Whiteley, J., Slead Syke
Whiteley, T., Brighouse
Wood, H., Hove Edge
Wilkinson, Johnson, Huddersfield
Wright, Sam. Bradford
Wood, W. Willis, Ald , Bradford
Woodhead, Cawthra, Natal

Walker, John, Brighouse
Wood, Matthew, Brighouse, and *
Waller, Miss, Bradford Road, Brighouse
Waller, Miss Lonisa, Brighouse*
Waller, Miss, Oakroyd, Brighouse
Waller, C., Grassmead, Brighouse
Waller, H. H., Rookeries, Brighouse
Woodhouse, John C., Wath-on-Dearne
Wilson, Col., Leeds
Woodd, Basil T., J.P., Knaresbro'
Wurtzburg, J. H., Leeds*
Woodhead, W. B., C.E., Bradford *
Woods, Sir Albert, Garter, Coll. of Arms
Wood, Mrs. S., Brighouse
Williams, E. W., Brighouse
Waddington, Mrs. H., Brighouse
Wheatley, Joseph, Brighouse
Whiteley, Robt., Brighouse
Wyatt, T., Brighouse
Waddington, Mrs. J., Rastrick *
Watson, J. H., Brighouse
Watson, George, Brighouse
Walker, H., Clifton
Woodend, Robt., Rastrick
Waddington, Joseph, Brighouse
Westwood, Arthur, Brighouse
Waller, Dan, Brighouse
Womersley, Wm., Brighouse
Woodhead, Jos., J.P., Huddersfield
Winn, A. T., Aldboro', Suffolk
Waddington, John, C.E., London
Wilson, Joe, Rastrick *
Whiteley, Fred, Rastrick
Wood, John, Grassmead, Brighouse
Wilson, Mrs., Dewsbury
Whiteley, Rev. A. H., Bradford
Wilson, J. G., Rastrick *
Watson, S., Clifton
Walton, John, Camm Street, Brighouse
Waiker, A. F., Meltham
Worsnop, W. H., Elland
Wilson, Mrs., Dewsbury
Wilson, C. Macro. Bolsterstone
Wright, N. W., Bradford

York Minster Library *
Yates, Geo. H., Melbourne
Young, M., Brighouse

INDEX OF SURNAMES AND PLACES.

(Place-names, if spelt like recorded surnames, are in *italics*.
The same name may occur several times on a page. The various methods
of spelling are not indicated here.)

U

Milne, 101, 113, 114, 116
Milner, Molendinar de
  Brighouse, 40, 42, 48 to
  62, 65, 67 to 84, 87, 90,
  93 to 105, 109, 115, 121,
  141, 153, 159, 208, 211
  to 213, 216, 222, 253
Milnes, 293
Milyas, 96
Mire, 56
Mirfield, 9, 36, 58, 71, 79,
  88, 91, 104, 105, 110,
  129, 169, 196, 200, 221,
  245, 254, 255, 277
Mitchell, Michell, 41, 42,
  97, 144, 147, 151, 153,
  155, 160, 166, 174, 178,
  181, 211, 218, 223, 230,
  234, 244, 245, 247, 248,
  253, 254, 293
Mixenden, 162
Modd, see Modson
Modeste, 47, 61, 80
Modson, (Maudson, Mold-
  son,) 68, 74, 113, 117,
  172, 218
Molot, 89
Monkbretton, 99
Moody, 119
Moore, 246, 294
Moorhouse, 188
Moravians, 251
More, 103, 106, 108 to 113
Moregateroide, 129, 142,
  235
Moreroids, 180
Morley, 9, 29, 38, 53, 95,
  221, 245, 246, 306
Morrell, 293
Morris, 277
Morrison, 294
Mortimer, 82, 273
Morton, 98, 100, 101, 103,
  253, 272, 293
Mounger, 200
Mowbray, 259
Musgrave, 161
Myers, 217
Mynsmith, 87
Mytholm, Mitholm, 152,
  153, 161, 162, 167, 170,
  177, 181, 183, 185, 230,
  246
Nalleson, Nelleson, Nele-
  daughter, 46, 52, 75, 81,
  82, 93, 99, 114, 123, 127
Navey, 310
Naylor, 56, 133, 134, 160,
  187, 202, 218, 259

Nelson, 181, 182
Nether Bradley, 166, 169
Nether Brear, Lower
  Brear, 167
Nether Edge, Elland
  Lower Edge, 219
Nether Mill, Brighouse
  Lower-mill
Nether Woodhouse, see
  Woodhouse
Nettleton, 49, 56, 57, 58,
  63, 118, 175
Neville, 69, 131, 145
Nevison, 239
Nevooman, 91
Newall, 81, 121, 123
Newark, 230
Newby, 247
New England, 181
Newhall, 142, 196
Newhey, 113
Newhouse (Hudd.) 154
Nowhouse (Lighte.) 253
Newlands, 119, 120, 139,
  144
Newstead, 259, 309
Newton, 291, 296
New Zealand, 185
Nicholls, 42, 43, 74, 75, 79,
  138, 146, 158, 168, 176,
  177, 179, 215, 218, 258,
  259, 273, 294
Nicholson, 236
Nidderdale, 273
Noble, 257, 281, 293 to 295
Nodder, 42
Noget, 78
Norcliffe, 41 to 43, 46, 54,
  57, 59, 73, 86, 88, 90,
  117, 122, 136, 137, 161,
  165 to 170, 173 to 176,
  178, 180, 210, 220, 229,
  244, 264, 294
Normans, 33
North, 179, 255
North Bierley, see Bierley,
  23, 153, 175, 187, 233
North Bridge, Halifax, 49,
  161
North Crosland, 228
North-edge, 123, 134, 159,
  169, 172, 180, 181, 188
Northend, 43, 44, 47, 49,
  54, 57, 60, 62, 64 to 66,
  70, 71, 73, 82, 93, 95,
  103, 105, 118, 121, 123
  to 129, 131 to 138, 141
  to 143, 145 to 148, 151
  153, 156, 158 to 174,

176, 178, 181, 186 to
  188, 210, 213, 216 to
  220, 222, 223, 228, 230,
  245, 294
Northeves, 100
Northland, N. land, Nor-
  land, 65 to 67, 169, 178,
  194, 225
Northloyne, 125, 126
Northmarsh, 134
Northourum, Ourum, 9,
  30, 33, 35, 38, 44, and
  every page to 200
Northtoft, 105
Northwood, 49, 51, 52, 56
Northwolley, 153
Norton, 135
Norwood green, 33, 43,
  158, 174, 175, 177, 181,
  183, 185, 187, 216, 229,
  230, 233, 246, 247, 259,
  289
Nostel, 73
Notyngham, 118, 142, 144,
  194
Nowell, 178, 179
Nunbrook, 152
Nunmonkton, 171, 180
Nunnery, 253
Nutter, 42, 147

Oastler, 295
Ogden, 8, 259, 294, 295
Oglethorp, 146, 151 to 153,
  170, 209
Okel, 182, 183
Okenbauk, 54
Okenshaw, 120, 169, 229
Okes, Okesgreen, 60, 61,
  65 to 67, 73 to 75, 84,
  100, 110, 113, 161, 177
Old-earth, 22, 134, 219
Oldfield, 131, 135, 141,
  143, 146, 151, 159, 162,
  165, 166, 231, 256
Oldford, 148, 154
Oldroyd, Holroyd House,
  60, 158, 168, 174, 178,
  179, 186, 224
Ollerton, see Allerton
Ormerod, 84, 283, 295 to
  298, 304
Osborne, 37, 45
Osburnrode, 114, 162, 167,
  170, 180, 186
Osgrabie, 232
Ossett, 66, 87, 101, 127,
  130, 143, 152, 250, 255
Otes, Oates, 42, 43, 53, 90,